A Virginia Yankee in the Civil War

A Virginia Yankee in the Civil War

The Diaries of David Hunter Strother

Edited with an Introduction

by

Cecil D. Eby, Jr.

Chapel Hill

THE UNIVERSITY OF NORTH CAROLINA PRESS

PRINTED BY THE SEEMAN PRINTERY, DURHAM, N. C.

To P. and C.

Acknowledgments

My greatest obligation is to Mr. David Hunter Strother for permitting me to make a copy of his grandfather's diaries and for assisting me in many other ways during the past six years. It was especially gratifying to receive the diaries themselves, rather than photostats or microfilm. Further, it is by his permission that these diaries are here published.

Civil War historians need no introduction to Mr. Boyd B. Stutler, who generously put aside his own research in order to read and to comment upon this manuscript. Without his encouragement and assistance my transition from American literature to history would have been much more difficult, if not impossible.

Both Dr. Bell Wiley and Mr. Alfred Mongin read my transcript of Strother's diaries, and both contributed to my conviction that the manuscript ought to be published. I wish to thank them for their instructive comments upon the diaries, particularly in pointing out how Strother's account of the war differed from other accounts written by participants.

Small portions of the present book first appeared in *Civil War History* and *The Iron Worker* during 1960. I think their editors, Mr. James I. Robertson and Mr. Marcus C. Elcan, Jr., for their interest in the Strother diaries.

Contents

Introduction   xi

   I. Up the Valley with Banks   3

  II. Down the Valley with Banks   34

 III. With Pope at Cedar Mountain   59

 IV. Chaos at Second Bull Run   83

   V. With McClellan at Antietam   101

 VI. All Quiet Along the Potomac   118

 VII. With Banks in Louisiana   132

VIII. The Campaign on the Teche   160

 IX. Behind the Lines at Gettysburg   181

   X. In the Department of West Virginia   198

 XI. With Sigel at New Market   215

 XII. The Hunter Raid   234

XIII. The Colonel Leaves the Army   276

Index   289

Introduction

In the English-speaking world perhaps the two subjects most written about have been William Shakespeare and the American Civil War. Both have been buried under so many tons of newsprint that it often becomes difficult to see the forest for the footnotes. Of the latter subject it is relatively safe to say that no other four-year period in our history has lured so many willing victims in the guise of diarists, chroniclers, antiquarians, and historians. On the eve of the Civil War Centennial we find all the participants in that war resting in peace, but present-day combatants still abound. Confederate money *has* been saved; the South has risen again; and the Greenback has come up, too. Despite Cassandra-like warnings from many publishers, who yearly predict the demise of the Civil War book, in wave after wave the blue and gray jackets come on. Lee's army has invaded Maryland thousands of times, at least in print. The former trickle of books about the Civil War now threatens to become a deluge. Somewhat to his dismay, the veteran Civil War enthusiast reflects that there are now so many books about his specialty that he cannot hope to read them all during a single lifetime.

Fortunately, one may be consoled with the knowledge that among the thousands of eyewitness narratives of the war only a very small number have attained or will ever attain anything resembling classic stature. The great majority are of barely passing interest, to be used by the historian rarely—by the nonspecialist not at all. The poorer recollections of the war fall usually into one of two headings: those too narrow and those too broad. "Narrow" works are those in which the participant fails to project his experiences into any meaningful area larger than himself. Too often the writer observed only those details of the war immediately in front of him. On the other hand, "broad" accounts are those in which the writer informs us about the grand maneuvers without giving us the immediacy of war itself. More often than not this writer was a commanding officer with little interest in the minutiae of battle.

Only rarely does one find a book written by a combatant who conveys the reality of the etched detail and who is able to place this detail on the broad canvas of a total war engaging a whole nation. Such a writer was Henry Kyd Douglas, whose masterpiece of dramatic action, *I Rode with Stonewall*, towers above most of its fellows like the personality of the mighty Stonewall himself. The narrative which follows, the military journals of David Hunter Strother, is another work of distinguished merit.

While it would be academic to make a prolonged comparison of these two narratives, it is nevertheless instructive to place them side by side. Douglas, of course, had the advantage of hindsight—he wrote his book many years after the war had been fought and a historical perspective had been formed. Strother wrote his in the field, before confusion had yielded to certainty. Douglas had the good fortune to support the more glamorous "lost cause" and to draw upon the inexhaustible lore surrounding such exciting personalities as Jackson, Stuart, and Early. Strother fought upon the side which won the war but which usually lost the battles. Further, he served under a succession of Federal commanders more often notorious for their faults than famous for their virtues. If such men as Franz Sigel and David Hunter ever become national heroes, they will require latter-day Münchhausens as their biographers.

Yet Strother's narrative contains something which Douglas' does not—a sense of contemporaneity. Since he was writing for his own future reference rather than for publication, he was able to chronicle many things which would have been unsuitable for a nineteenth-century publisher. His method was to record whatever struck his fancy at the moment and before the thunder had died from his ears. In sum, his is an "unheroic" narrative which, while it may perpetrate smaller errors of fact, nevertheless carries with it the ring of truth. Realism may be less exciting than romance, but time has a trick of making it more enduring and endurable. On the battlefield there is little time for retrospection and romance, and Strother wrote about the war as it was, not as it ought to have been.

Even after a hundred years it is not especially difficult to find out what happened in the Civil War; a more troublesome problem is to find out what people really thought and felt about it. The diary of

David Strother reflects the moods of the age, from the impatient over-confidence of 1861 to the dull despair of 1864. Moreover, it is valuable as well for its revelation of Strother's unique personality. There is a touch of Pepys in his habit of jotting on the same page beside grand events his own observations of a trivial nature. So the Gothicized horrors of the author among the dead at Kernstown are followed by an account of a fine supper and a pleasant evening at the general's quarters. It is amusing to find Strother's speculations concerning the whereabouts of Jackson's army on one page, and on the next his fear that the young Virginia girls might not find the Yankee soldiers as attractive as the Rebels. Sometimes he enjoys a sarcastic sally, as when he describes Pope and McDowell, in the process of being thrashed by Lee at Second Bull Run, sitting under a tree "waiting for the enemy to retreat." Or, again, during the demoralization following that battle when he buys a Washington newspaper to read "some accounts of our brilliant victories."

War could not subdue the playful streak in the man who had been a leading writer of humorous articles for *Harper's Monthly*. We enjoy his account of the Prussian aide-de-camp who, after eight months in the army, has acquired only a schoolgirl's ability to swear in English. A characteristic scene is the improvised, all-male cotillion among the staff officers before Cedar Mountain. Cavorting in a darkened tent, Strother starts to take an obscure bystander in his arms, discovers it is General Banks, whereupon the officers roar at his embarrassment. War is not all tinsel and thunder. Sometimes it provides a stage for masculine vanity. When a Virginia woman asks the Federal captain if he is *General* Strother, he replies that he is and rides quickly on.

Strokes like these give his narrative a comic dimension most often missing from other Civil War journals. In the long run, the most memorable accounts of the war will be those that convey, first of all, a sense of the author's own involvement with it, not just accuracy of historical fact. After all, for those who demand minute accuracy alone there are the *Official Records* (with over a hundred volumes to choose from). But few will read an encyclopedia for amusement as well as for information. We probably care less about the number of batteries at Antietam than we do about something more important —what was it really like? Strother tells us.

The superiority of Strother's journal to so many others can be attributed, in part, to his previous experience as a writer and artist.

During the 1850's he had been a free-lance contributor of sketches and essays to *Harper's New Monthly Magazine* (some say he was the best-paid contributor to that periodical). He had been trained to select those striking details that alone can transform reportage into literature. Strother knew that if he survived the war he would attempt to re-create for the public his own role in "that damnable, double-tongued war that lured the best youth to their graves with promises now broken," to use Moncure Conway's phrase. Into his notebooks he jotted down his daily activities, anecdotes, bits of apocrypha, and camp gossip, with little regard for total relevance or careful structure. Through them there emerges an unusually complete picture of a man and a nation at war.

Readers of *Harper's* were partially rewarded for his pains, since *Personal Recollections of the War* appeared serially from 1866 to 1868. The *Recollections* consisted of eleven articles—all of them illustrated by Strother's own wood drawings, a number of which are reproduced in this volume—treating the war from its outbreak through Antietam. Presumably Strother planned to continue the series—a note in the back of one of the diaries estimates that twenty-four articles will bring him a total of $10,800, "with copyright secured on the volume if published." The estimate was overly optimistic. The Brothers Harper, finding that their public was tiring of the war, broke off the series, and Strother's recollections were therefore never completed. Nearly a hundred years later, the original diaries are here published for the first time.

THE TEXT

The Civil War diaries of David Hunter Strother consist of twelve manuscript volumes and include a record of his daily activities from July 11, 1861, to October 15, 1864, at which time he retired from the army. One volume (number ten of the set) has been lost, but fortunately it covers a period of comparative inactivity in the Department of West Virginia between November, 1863, and January, 1864. In addition to the volumes just mentioned, there also exists an incomplete diary catalogued in the Handley Library at Winchester, Virginia; this contains miscellaneous notes from April, 1860, to June, 1861. As a matter of historical record, Strother's habit of journalizing continued after the war. A daily account of his activities may be found in some twenty other diaries which were kept until just five days before his death on March 8, 1888.

The present text omits altogether the period from July, 1861, to

February, 1862, since during this time Strother saw very little of the war at first-hand. He had joined Patterson's army at Martinsburg as a civilian topographer, had withdrawn from Virginia with the Federal Army to winter quarters near Poolesville, Maryland, and then, early in 1862, had been promised a captaincy by General David Birney. But when the spring campaigns began, Strother was induced by General Nathaniel Banks to join his staff for service in the Valley of Virginia. It is at this point that this text begins.

To have published Strother's manuscripts without omissions would have required four volumes. Cutting the manuscript has, in the editor's judgment, been absolutely necessary. I hope that nothing has been omitted which would be of major interest to scholars of the Civil War; certainly no uncomfortable revelations have been cut. The following is a partial list of the sorts of materials left out: predictions of things never to come, summaries of personal letters and telegrams, back-country movements of troops not engaging the enemy, digressions on family and neighbors, reconstructions of dreams, irrelevant conversations, and the like. The frequent ellipsis marks indicate those places where I am sparing the reader, not tantalizing him. Perhaps local historians and genealogists would profit from a complete edition of Strother's diaries. These, I fear, must wait for the Bicentennial.

Strother's punctuation (often nonexistent) and spelling (quite erratic) have been corrected. Paragraphs have been created, since there are none—or very few—in the manuscripts. The editor is, of course, not responsible for the veracity of Strother's observations or reports received at second-hand. His claims, for example, that General Meagher was drunk at Antietam and that President Lincoln feared Mary Todd was a Confederate spy require more than a few grains of salt. But to have eliminated such savory bits of camp gossip as these would have been unthinkable.

Footnotes intrude to identify significant personalities and principal events, but these are minimal in order to keep the bulk and cost of the book within reasonable bounds. (That kind of Civil War book consisting of more footnotes than text employs a technique of documentation too scrupulous for a work of this size). Identification of many minor figures occurs through the use of brackets in the text.

Preceding each chapter is a brief introduction to the larger events which follow. While this may prove useful for readers not especially familiar with the chronology and history of the Civil War, it is not intended as a substitute for *Battles and Leaders* or sound histories. Specialists will require no urging on my part to skip over these prefatory remarks in order to follow Strother's own narrative. No war diary has ever been written which is sufficiently detailed to conduct an uninitiated reader over a battlefield tour. But with maps and other paraphernalia, it is relatively simple to follow Strother's specific movements during all the campaigns he describes.

Those who are interested in David Strother as man or as writer may find two books—both published by the University of North Carolina Press—rewarding. *The Old South Illustrated* (1959) is a collection of his best writings and sketches of the ante-bellum South. My biography, *"Porte Crayon": The Life of David Hunter Strother* (1960), discusses his career as an artist, writer, and soldier.

RHETORIC VS. REALISM

Since *Personal Recollections of the War* was based upon the earlier diaries, it is interesting to place both accounts side by side in order to measure the differences. The *Recollections* is a nineteenth-century narrative: it is self-conscious, rhetorical, and often prolix. Digressions and purple patches frequently interrupt the narration of events. The diaries, on the other hand, are written in a direct and often colloquial style which is more modern than Victorian. Further, Strother was more willing, in the diaries, to include scenes decidedly hostile to the heroic conception of war: accounts of hospitals and the dying, of Federal looting and destruction, of moments in which decision and courage faltered. Many passages are reminiscent of John W. De Forest and Stephen Crane. Strother was at times aware of the unusual beauty of battle—the rare blossoms of shells bursting high in the air, night skirmishing suggesting fireflies on a summer evening, and the "blood, carnage, and death among the sweet shrubbery and roses," as he expressed it.

When Strother returned to his diaries after the war in order to prepare the *Recollections*, he revised them to conform to the rhetorical standards of his age. These standards required a writer to discriminate nicely in his choice of diction and to soften unseemly details. Battlefields must be recollected in tranquillity and seen through the astigmatic lens of peace. It was not the duty or the privilege of a writer to revive dirt, squalor, and cadavers with the exactitude of a Brady photograph. This is not to say that writers of the Civil War were dishonest. When they erred in their writing it was with a conviction that some things were better left unsaid. Details might be "colored" somewhat to conform to the requisites of public taste. It is interesting to compare Strother's original account of a detail of war with his revision:

Diaries (1862)	Recollections (1867)
Lying down upon a long box I was told by a guard that there was a dead man in that box. I replied that my lying there would not disturb his rest. So I stretched out to sleep, but presently a man came with a hammer and nails to close the lid, so I got away and sought a place in the tavern.	Seeing a long pine box there I stretched myself upon it. A sentinel stepped up and informed me that the box contained the body of a colonel. Looking through an opening I saw the ghastly features of the dead officer. I felt no loathing, but rather a sentiment of friendly respect—a glow of pride in our brotherhood; so I told the sentinel we would not disturb each other, and returned to my sleep.

The differences are striking. We see at once that in Strother's published version the dead man has been promoted to a dead colonel, somehow visible through an opening nowhere mentioned in the diaries. Further, in the original account Strother is ingloriously chased away from the coffin by one of the burial squad, but in the published version he has time to reflect—with a patriotic flourish—upon their "brotherhood" before returning to his sleep. In making these changes, Strother relied upon a formula which neutralized the honest, dry realism of the diaries. He could not have guessed that the *Harper's* gain would be our loss or that another century would prefer the simplicity of his diaries.

Sometimes Strother took small liberties with characterization, as the following vignettes of two Union generals show:

Diaries (1862)	Recollections (1867)
Hooker is a fine-looking man, tall, florid, and beardless. . . . Heintzelman is a knotty, hard-looking old customer with a grizzled beard and a shambling one-sided gait.	Hooker is a fine-looking soldier, tall, florid, and beardless, altogether very English in appearance. . . . Heintzelman [is] a grim, grizzled veteran, who looks as if he had mettle in him.

Since in the 1860's the Englishman was the glass of fashion, Strother no doubt felt he was doing Hooker a favor by denaturalizing him. Much more questionable was the disappearance of the colloquial vein in describing Heintzelman. "Knotty," "old customer," and "one-sided gait" are replaced by noncommittal words like "grim" and "mettle."

An indefinite number of examples could be used to show the changes which occurred in the diaries, but one more must suffice. Nowhere is the gap between realism and rhetoric better seen than in Strother's wholly retrospective applause of the glory of dying for one's country:

Diaries (1862)	Recollections (1867)
There is an order prohibiting private letters to be promulgated today. General Lee is said to be in command in front of us with the whole power of the Southern Army. Thus we are enveloped in a dark storm of war for a season and all communication with our wives and families cut off. This is better than ignoble idleness, and if final success crowns our arms, the glory will be all the greater to those who now suffer.	An order has been promulgated prohibiting all intercourse with the outside world by letter or otherwise. The whole power of the rebellion is said to be concentrated in our front, and the war envelops us like a dark storm-cloud, cutting us off for a time from all communications with family and friends, or even the encouraging sympathy of our loyal countrymen. I must confess I enjoy the dramatic grandeur of the situation. It is better thus to suffer, and even to die, than live ignobly, to witness perhaps the triumph of iniquity and the ruin of my country. But if final success crowns our efforts, dying or living, the glory of these dark days will be a heritage forever.

This is not, of course, to show that Strother's published *Recollections* are untrustworthy. Generally, they correspond closely to the earlier diaries in matters of significant fact. But there was ample room for romantic coloration and for recasting impressions of the war for the benefit of posterity. One wonders how many other narratives of the war underwent comparable alterations between the immediate experience and the transcribed record. It is not unlikely that public taste made rhetoric of them all—or at least of more than we now suspect.

Certainly few would quarrel with the assertion that Strother's notebooks are superior to his *Recollections* at almost all points.

The Man

David Hunter Strother was born in 1816 at Martinsburg in the
Valley of Virginia. His father, John Strother, a former lieutenant in
the regular army during the War of 1812 and later a colonel of the 67th
Virginia Militia, was a clerk of the circuit court and a leading Fed-
eralist-Whig of Berkeley County. After attending the local academy,
the younger Strother enrolled at the Pennsylvania Academy of Fine
Arts, but soon withdrew.

Having failed to obtain appointment to West Point in 1832, he
attended Jefferson College (Canonsburg, Pennsylvania) for a year, but
left without receiving a degree. After desultory attempts at the study
of law and medicine, Strother became an art student under Samuel
F. B. Morse in New York from 1836 to 1838. When his professor left
for Europe, Strother departed for the Ohio Valley, where he painted
portraits to support his travels.

From 1840 to 1843 Strother was in Europe, studying art in Paris,
Florence, and Rome. After his return home, he became a comparatively well-known illustrator of books during the winters, and in sum-
mers he assisted his father in the management of Strother's Hotel in
Berkeley Springs, Virginia's most venerable spa. In 1849 he married
Ann Doyne Wolff, a Martinsburg girl; their daughter Emily was born
the following year.

After having exhibited some sketches at the National Academy of
Design in 1853, Strother was invited by the Harper brothers to write
an account of an Allegheny fishing trip to accompany his sporting
sketches. Under his pen name "Porte Crayon," his first article, "The
Virginian Canaan," appeared in *Harper's New Monthly Magazine* in
December, 1853. This was followed by others, including four travel
series: *Virginia Illustrated* (published in book-form in 1857 and re-
issued in 1871), *North Carolina Illustrated*, *A Winter in the South*,
and *A Summer in New England*. Through his journeys north and
south Strother developed a strong awareness of the necessity for Union.
As the breach widened in the 1850's, he clearly saw that the South
must either give in or go under.

During the John Brown affair—which he covered as a correspondent
for *Harper's Weekly*—he deplored abolitionism as roundly as he supported the Union. When the war became an accomplished fact,

Strother planned to remain strictly neutral. His first wife having died in 1859, he married Mary Eliot Hunter of Charles Town in 1861 and withdrew to Berkeley Springs. But neutrality was impossible for him. In July, 1861, he joined the Federal Army at Martinsburg as a civilian topographer. Except for skirmishes with Johnston's army, Strother saw no military engagements until the following year.

Although promised a commission as captain of volunteers in the Army of the Potomac by General David Birney, Strother was assigned to the staff of General Nathaniel Banks in time for the disastrous Valley of Virginia Campaign in 1862. When John Pope arrived in Washington to take command of the Army of Virginia, Strother was called for service as the general's topographical expert. As a lieutenant colonel of the 3rd (West) Virginia Cavalry, he campaigned with Pope at Cedar Mountain and Second Bull Run. After Pope had been removed, Strother joined McClellan's staff in time for South Mountain and Antietam. Then when McClellan was, in his turn, replaced by Burnside, Strother joined Banks's expedition to Louisiana and took part in the first demonstration against Port Hudson and the Teche Campaign.

Returning to Washington in the late spring of 1863, he remained unassigned during the Gettysburg Campaign. At its close he was, however, promoted to the colonelcy of his regiment (which he never actually commanded in the field) and joined the staff of General Benjamin F. Kelley during the winter of 1863-64. During the Valley Campaign of 1864 Strother served as a staff officer under General Franz Sigel at New Market and as chief of staff under General David Hunter during the Lynchburg Raid. After Hunter was replaced by Sheridan, he resigned from the army.

After the war he was commissioned brigadier general by brevet and became for a time adjutant general of Virginia during Governor Francis H. Pierpont's administration. But in 1866 he returned from public affairs to his home in Berkeley Springs, where he assisted in managing the hotel and resumed his writing. *Personal Recollections of the War* was followed in the 1870's by *The Mountains*, the earliest "local-color" writing about West Virginia. He was saved from poverty in 1879 by his appointment as consul general of Mexico, a post he held until 1885. After the expiration of his consulship, Strother returned to West Virginia, living in Berkeley Springs and Charles Town until his death in the latter town on March 8, 1888.

Cecil D. Eby, Jr., Lexington, Virginia
February 20, 1961

A Virginia Yankee in the Civil War

"It will one day be considered a great privilege to have lived in these days, to have played a part in the greatest war that has shaken the earth for many a year, to have been acquainted with the actors, leaders, and localities of so famous a drama—the crushing out of the last traces of feudalism in the United States."—from Strother's diary

I

Up the Valley with Banks

Returning to Alexandria in late February of 1862, after a leave of absence to visit Berkeley Springs, Strother stopped at Frederick to pay his respects to General Banks, the commander of the Army of the Shenandoah. Banks, in need of officers familiar with the topography of the Valley of Virginia, requested Strother to serve on his staff. Strother, believing that he would be of greater service in the Valley than in eastern Virginia, applied to General Birney for permission to remain with Banks. The projected movements of the Union armies—McClellan against Manassas, Banks against Winchester, and Fremont against Staunton—would bring to a close, Strother thought, the war in Virginia.

Banks's army, under the personal supervision of McClellan, crossed the Potomac at Harpers Ferry and invaded Virginia. Through the use of a Negro spy, Strother discovered that Winchester would be evacuated by the Confederate army. After costly delays Banks occupied that city on March 12. Union reconnoissance concluded that Jackson would retire from the Valley without a fight. Therefore, while Banks was withdrawing part of his force east of the Blue Ridge, he was unprepared for the sudden assault by Jackson upon Shields at Kernstown on March 23. Even though the Union army successfully repulsed Jackson's attack, Banks fortified Strasburg for future emergencies, and in April pushed up the Valley in search of Jackson. By the end of the month Federal cavalry had scoured the country beyond Harrisonburg without discovering the Confederates.

In May, through anxiety in Washington that Banks's column had overextended itself, the Union army was required to retreat on Strasburg. No one foresaw the brilliant trap that Jackson was preparing for it; no one—certainly not Captain Strother—would have conceived it possible that by the end of May the Army of the Shenandoah would become a shattered mob seeking safety beyond the Potomac.

FEBRUARY 27, THURSDAY.—Clear and cold. Met General Banks[1] on the street on horseback who told me that McClellan was at Harpers Ferry and wished to see me. I mounted and rode by Jefferson, Petersville, and Knoxville to Sandy Hook. The road was alternate sections of stone and mud and in very bad condition. Sought the General's headquarters in a large green passenger car which stood upon the track. On entering saw Captain Beckwith[2] talking with a small man whom I did not recognize. He immediately addressed me, "Ah, Mr. Strother, I was just this moment talking about you and wishing for you." Beckwith named "General McClellan." From his late sickness he was so much thinner than when I last saw him at Edwards Ferry that I did not recognize him at first glance. He and Beckwith were looking over some maps of the counties from the Potomac to Winchester. I soon understood from his questions what he was after and was enabled to furnish him all the information he sought.

In the same car sat a dozen officers of his staff, among them the French princes, the Prince de Joinville[3] and his nephews—Louis Philip, Compte de Paris, and Robert [Duc de Chartres]. The uncle was a tall man, slender and bent, with a very unbecoming fur cap and an air by no means distinguished. The boys were in uniform as captains and were as much like young Americans as possible. They were the last persons in the presence I should have taken for French princes. There was a young Prussian noble there, Baron [Paul von] Radowitz, who had an air both handsome and distinguished.

Leaving here I met Colonel Clark[4] and accompanied him over the pontoon bridge to Harpers Ferry. The appearance of ruin by war and fire was awful. Charred ruins were all that remain of the splendid public works, arsenals, workshops and railroads, stores, hotels, and dwelling houses all mingled in one common destruction. . . .

1. Nathaniel P. Banks (1816-94) had been a speaker of the House of Representatives and governor of Massachusetts, 1858-60. During the war he commanded the Department of the Shenandoah in 1862 and the Department of the Gulf in 1863-64. After the war he returned to Congress.

2. Edward G. Beckwith (1818-81), USMA '42, was Commissariat for Banks in the Valley and Louisiana campaigns. A career officer, Beckwith was assigned to the claims branch of the Quartermaster Corps after the war.

3. The Prince de Joinville and his nephews were volunteer aides attached to McClellan's staff. From his experience, the Prince de Joinville wrote the controversial book, *The Army of the Potomac: Its Organization, Its Commander, and Its Campaigns* (1862).

4. John S. Clark was an aide-de-camp during the Valley Campaign and provost marshal under Banks in Louisiana. It was he who discovered Jackson's flanking move-

FEBRUARY 28, FRIDAY.—Clear and cold. . . . At General Sedgwick's quarters[5] I found the staff of General McClellan and the whole staff of the division. We presently started in the direction of Charles Town. The sun was high, the movement of our brilliant cavalcade was exhilarating. The view of these lovely scenes, the homesteads of friends I had loved, of spots endeared to youth and manhood by pleasant memories touched me deeply. To the land from which I had been exiled for seven months I was returning in armed triumph. It was glorious. At Halltown I joined General McClellan, and thus conversing on the chances of the war and the state of the country we rode into Charles Town. . . . At my mother-in-law's, Riddle stood on the porch to greet us.[6] We passed on by, three regiments of infantry paraded to salute, colors flying and bands playing. At the farther end of town some artillery was planted. This guarded the old Winchester dirt road and Smithfield pike. The commander in chief viewed the Berryville pike and determined to place some pieces there. At this point I left the staff at General Banks' request and returned to Charles Town. . . .

I saw Mr. Dutton[7] flying along the street and hailed him. He greeted me and said he was going to see about the occupation of his church. I went with him and found Colonel [Thomas H.] Ruger's Wisconsin men in occupation and taking up the carpets. The preacher was for getting out the pulpit furniture, Bibles, and candelabras. Presently looking toward the organ he saw a platoon of rugged-looking fellows around the organ and fumbling with the music books of the choir. He looked in agony at the prospective destruction and desecration. A moment after, the books were all open and fifty accordant voices rose in a thrilling anthem that filled the church with solemn music. The alarmed clergyman paused a moment. His face became calm and solemn. He turned to the officer in command: "You need not move the furniture from the pulpit, Sir. It will be safe, I feel assured. . . ."

ment prior to the Battle of Groveton, but his report was interpreted by Pope as a movement of the Confederate army into the Valley of Virginia.

5. John Sedgwick (1813-64), USMA '37, was here undergoing his first campaign of the war. He was soon transferred to the Peninsula, where he commanded a division and fought in most of the major battles in the East until his death at Spotsylvania, where he led the Sixth Corps.

6. Horace Riddle, Strother's brother-in-law, remained one of the few loyal Unionists in Jefferson County. After the war he became a Baltimore businessman. Mrs. David Hunter was the mother of Mary Eliot Hunter, whom Strother married in 1861.

7. The Reverend W. B. Dutton was the Presbyterian minister at Charles Town from 1849 to 1874.

Rode back to Harpers Ferry and reported to General Banks what I had seen and heard. News seemed to indicate the evacuation of Winchester without a fight.[8] He seemed much interested and proposed a ride over the river to communicate the same to General McClellan. The level ground from the bridge to Weverton and even to Knoxville was one compact mass of wagon mules and rail cars. Mountains of forage and boxed supplies lay beside the track, and campfires blazed wildly on the groups of teamsters huddled under the shelter of every projecting rock. With danger and difficulty we wormed our way among this crowd for a mile and a half and ascertained that General McClellan was gone to Washington. Recrossing the pontoon, the lights and campfires made a superb scene. The troops on the Heights had set the mountain woods on fire and the light shone grandly over the height. . . .

MARCH 1, SATURDAY.—I rose early but not early enough for some soldiers of the Rhode Island battery who came in for a drink of water and stole my new woolen gloves. I visited Captain Abert's quarters,[9] got a cup of coffee, and promised to breakfast there but was sent for by General Banks and dispatched to Charles Town on special business. At Mrs. Hunter's I sent for *An Agent*,[10] transacted my business, and then visited Tom Moore's family. I was here affectionately received by Mrs. Moore, who nevertheless reproached me for joining the Federalists. I parried the argument, took leave, and left with the kindliest feelings on both sides. . . .

I had numerous petitions by letter and personal application to relieve persons from difficulties they had got into with the soldiers. I interfered in every case and succeeded in giving much relief and apparent satisfaction. The amount of pig and chicken stealing was very considerable and all the way from the Ferry I saw soldiers with slaughtered sheep and hogs, carrying their whole or quarters upon their bayonets. There was also a good deal of fence burning but besides the seizing of food and fire there was no mischief done, no wanton acts of destruction. The sight of this beautiful valley, its rural wealth and improvements, seemed to have softened the hearts of officers and men.

8. Strother's information about the abandonment of Winchester proved correct, but the town was not occupied until March 12.

9. James W. Abert, USMA '42, taught Strother the art of map making during the fall and winter of 1861-62. Abert resigned from the army in 1864 and in later years became a professor of English literature at Missouri State University.

10. According to *Personal Recollections of the War*, this agent was a Negro slave of Charles Town.

MARCH 2, SUNDAY.—. . . The women of this county all seem fully assured that we will presently be driven back. I never saw such deep-seated infatuation. The men take more practical views and generally seem to have given the thing up. Some of them are still fearful as to ultimate results. I have been struck with the seedy, old-fashioned appearance of the whole people here. They look as if they had just come out of the Ark. . . .

In the afternoon I went to the headquarters of General Banks and found him perplexed at hearing nothing from Winchester. I reiterated to him my firm belief that there were not more than five thousand men there and that no resistance was intended. He did not seem satisfied and as I started to walk down street he proposed to go with me. As we passed down from the porch I saw someone in charge of a file of men with fixed bayonets. In the darkness I did not recognize the prisoner, but as he called my name in an undertone I perceived it was my messenger returned from Winchester. I mentioned the matter to the General and we immediately retired with the man to his private chamber. The examination corroborated my former knowledge fully and was highly satisfactory to the commander. We went to bed with a sense of relief.

MARCH 3, MONDAY.—Wet and rainy. On the way to headquarters I met the secret messenger and re-examined him, then made a diagram and notes of the information which I showed to Generals Banks and Hamilton.[11] On the strength of it an advance will be speedily ordered. . . . I also had the opportunity of quitting myself on another score. Fred Briscoe, Quartermaster in the Confederate Army, having heard me denounced and menaced after the Patterson Campaign, privately sent me a warning by a confidential servant to keep out of the way. The message was kindly intended and this morning, hearing his estate mentioned as one to be swept, I interfered and saved it.

MARCH 5, WEDNESDAY.—. . . At headquarters I met General Shields[12] on his way to take command of [Frederick W.] Lander's division. He looked older than when I saw him last and greeted me very

11. Charles S. Hamilton (1822-91), USMA '43, manufactured flour in Wisconsin until the war began. He served under Banks in the Valley and early in 1863 commanded the Sixteenth Corps in the West, but soon afterward he resigned from the army and returned to Wisconsin.

12. James Shields (1806-79) was born in Ireland but settled in Illinois, from which he was elected to the United States Senate. When war began, Shields abandoned his mining ventures in Mexico and as a brigadier general of volunteers met Jackson twice, at Kernstown and at Port Republic. In 1863 he resigned from the army and returned to San Francisco.

cordially. We then sat down and examined a plan I had drawn of the defenses and surroundings of Winchester. He gave his ideas of the probabilities of the campaign which indicated that Winchester might be reinforced from Manassas by way of Berry's Ferry or Strasburg. The ideas showed good appreciation of strategy but not sufficient acquaintance with the Rebel means of defense and power to reinforce. This remains to be proved, however. . . .

MARCH 6, THURSDAY.—Variable. The troops moving. . . . Visited Nat Craighill and on ringing the bell a little daughter five or six years old answered. I was troubled lest she should be frightened, but to my surprise she saluted me by name and smiled. When Mr. Craighill came in I showed him a neat volume, *The Army Officer's Companion*, observing that he probably knew the author. This was no other than his own son, Lieutenant W. P. Craighill, now a professor at the United States Academy at West Point.[13] On taking the book Craighill turned to the title page and reading the name he changed color and shook with emotion. With a tremulous voice he said, "Yes, I do know that name," and handed the book to his wife. She looked at it a moment, then burst into tears. Recovering herself for a space she said, "I hope William has not taken up arms." I told her I did not think he had, but was as I thought still at West Point. The father resumed the book, saying to me in an undertone, "He has three brothers in the other army. You must excuse the mother's weakness."

While she retired to the shadowed corner of the room to weep her fill, Craighill turned over the neatly printed pages with a loving and proud curiosity. I continued to tell him of the high esteem in which his son's character and talents were held by all the United States officers who knew him, until I could see how weak are the most bitter political prejudices against the stronger instincts of natural affection. The father's pride was dominant over everything else. As I rose to leave he asked me to leave the book with him for a short time. I told him I had brought it as a present for him.

From here I rode out to Joe Crane's, the scene of my happiest term

13. William P. Craighill, USMA '53, taught engineering at West Point from 1859 to 1863 and served as a fortifications engineer at Baltimore and elsewhere during the remainder of the war. Since his brothers were fighting in the Confederate Army, Craighill did not wish to take up arms against the South. He compiled *The Army Officer's Pocket Companion* in 1861, and translated various French military texts into English.

of boyhood and youth.[14] The barn, the white cottage dwelling, the Negro cabins all unchanged as when I played there thirty-five years ago. Entering the yard I saw two soldiers there, and a brood of Negrolings ran out to stare at me. Then Joe Crane himself came out and met me with a greeting as manly and cordial as if the eight months of bitter civil war had not been.

A mounted picket of the Van Alen cavalry came riding in with his eyes stretched and reported that he had been shot at from the house of one Wright. The ball passed by his ears and he afterward saw the man sneaking through the bushes with a gun, trying to get another shot at him. The officer of the guard was indignant and was about to sack and burn the house. Fortunately a neighbor witnessed the transaction and explained it. A foot soldier, prowling around seeking whatever he might devour, shot at a sheep, missed it, and the ball whistled by the trooper. This caused him to change position and, the prowler seeing him, he sneaked off through the bushes. So the house was not burnt.

The difficulty we have to contend with is chiefly that the army and the people are strangers to each other. The inhabitants believed that the army was a horde of Cossacks and vandals, whose mission was to subjugate the land, to burn, pillage, and destroy. Hence they are received with distrust and terror, and their slightest disorders magnified by the imagination into monsters and menacing crimes. The soldiery, on the other hand, thought they were entering a country so embittered and infuriated that every man they met was a concealed enemy and an assassin, and every woman a spitfire. Mutual acquaintance and an interchange of courtesies will soothe and even obliterate these prejudices, and soon a better understanding will be established. The land will be tranquilized and the great majority of the people will return to their duty and loyalty, better subjects than ever before. . . .

MARCH 7, FRIDAY.—. . . A stampede was got up last night by some of [Colonel P. M. B.] Maulsby's pickets. A squad of Michigan cavalry was sent to relieve them near Kabletown. The cavalry arrived after dark, were fired into, and one man and three horses shot. They returned the fire and both parties took to their heels. The Marylanders hid in stable lofts and fence corners. Sutlers and teamsters ran over the

14. Joe Crane, a resident of Jefferson County, was Strother's first cousin and his oldest living friend. After Crane had been imprisoned for killing a Union trooper in self-defense, Strother's intervention saved him from execution.

country and even to headquarters with the report that the Maryland regiment had been cut to pieces and captured. The cavalry had their story also and the combined report in the morning was that the Maryland First regiment and a squadron of cavalry had been destroyed. This choice morsel was swallowed and enjoyed by the Secessionists for an hour or two, but turned to emptiness by the return of the Massachusetts Second which had been sent out in the night to visit the scene of the reported trouble.

The Dutch caterer for the staff mess went into the country to buy some poultry and having selected his chickens offered in payment a United States Treasury bill. The proprietor, being strongly Southern in feeling, pushed the money back contemptuously, saying, "I don't want any of your damned Union trash." "Vel," replied the cool caterer, "I do vant dese secesh chickens, zo I dake 'em," and repocketing his money and lifting his fowls, he departed. . . .

MARCH 8, SATURDAY.—Fair and mild. . . . An excitement was produced in town by the arrival of a wagon load of Negro women and children with bag and baggage as if bound for a free country. They were stopped in front of the provost marshal's office for a long time and were the theme of much speculation for the citizens and soldiers. I understand they were forwarded to Harpers Ferry. Numbers of men have flocked into town more or less every day since our occupation. They were arrested and put into the jail. As the number increased, it was asked what was to be done with them. The quartermaster from Harpers Ferry had just desired a detail of men to load and unload army stores. It was suggested to send the Negroes there to do the work and so decided. Each day since, as they have gathered in, they have been marched in squads to Harpers Ferry and having disposed of the stores are still occupied in the repairing of the railroad. This all fairly in accordance with the professed intentions of the Government. The sending forward of the women and children, however, looks ominous and may bear a dark interpretation. Let us hear it explained. For my own part I would be glad to see the whole system wiped out, but the government cannot do it without sacrificing both principle and promises and without involving itself in endless and insupportable troubles. . . .

MARCH 10, MONDAY.—. . . Young Alexander, who had been passed through the lines at Riddle's interposition and on his sister's representation as an invalid in the last stages of consumption, came in apparently in good health and rampant with secession pertness. He went so far that he was arrested and sent to Washington. . . . News came of the sinking of the *Cumberland* and *Congress* frigates near Old Point by the iron-plated Confederate steamer, *Merrimac*. Whatever comfort Secessionists might have taken from the news, we gave it a passing objurgation and forgot it. It has struck me as singular the tenacious credulity with which Secessionists cling to every straw which seems to afford hope to their desperate cause. There is nothing too absurd for them to accept on the one side or too plain for them to reject on the other. I have never seen the human mind so enslaved by desire. They meet together in little knots to discuss flank movements and the grand strategy of falling back on somewhere. If a loyal man approaches them they are silent or disperse. Day by day the silliest and most improbable stories of Confederate victories are circulated. They count every troop and cannon that passes and underrate the force as much as possible. It is droll and at the same time sad and humiliating.

The reconnoissance occupied Berryville and advanced toward Winchester without finding the enemy stronger than a few horse pickets. Army trains, regiments, and artillery began to move toward Berryville. I packed for a move but on going to headquarters found there was no order issued yet for the General Staff. . . . After I had retired to bed, I was informed that a messenger had summoned me to headquarters immediately. I hurried up and found an examination going on of three Negroes. They were verdant but intelligent youths, in cornfield clothes, and had their wool plaited in barbaric twists. They were Fayette Washington's Negroes and reported that their master was carrying them into the town to sell them South when they lagged behind and escaped. This sounded to me very much like a fabrication, and although the General and Colonel Clark seemed to put some value on the military news they brought, I did not. . . . One stated that Jackson had sent ten thousand men to Strasburg, probably ten hundred —it was all the same to the Negro. I gave the General my views and retired.

MARCH 11, TUESDAY.—Prepared for a move and went to headquarters to ask permission to join the advance. Received it and rode with Colonel Clark. We sang, quoted poetry, and admired the country, passed trains, regiments, and batteries lumbering up the whole road. Got into Berryville and lunched on tongue and biscuit in the house of Treadwell Smith, the house where Major [R. Morris] Copeland says he heard me so bitterly abused. . . .

General Banks aside informed me that Manassas was occupied by McClellan and asked my views in regard to a movement on Winchester. I told him I thought it probable we should find nothing there and that it would in all probability be evacuated tonight. He desired a flank movement to cut them off by Millwood and Whitepost and seemed annoyed that the whole force should be suffered to escape. He engaged me to press the matter on General Sedgwick and others. I opened it to General Sedgwick, but, receiving no encouragement, desisted. . . .

MARCH 12, WEDNESDAY.—Fair. . . . An officer came in and reported that Generals Hamilton and Williams were in Winchester.[15] Seeing Colonel [Thornton F.] Brodhead mounted I proposed we should ride into the town. He consented and with his staff and escort we started. The day was fair and warm. Crossing the Opequon at Woods Mill, we saw a group of men, women, and children waving handkerchiefs and welcoming us with every demonstration of delight. I rode up and spoke to them, expressing my pleasure at the welcome. I told them my name, which they were well acquainted with and the man remarked, "Well, Sir, they have been longing to get you. Take care of yourself." As we pursued our way, many other groups and individuals welcomed us and shouted for the Union. The streets as we passed in were alive with soldiers and Negroes with a few white citizens. Our cavalcade passed Taylor's Hotel and took the street leading to the Romney road. Our intention was to visit and occupy Senator Mason's house.[16] When we came in sight of it, the National flag was seen floating from the portico. We then turned to a house apparently vacant and formerly belonging to the Widow Lee. Colonel Brodhead rang the bell and an old Negro answered. The house was the residence of Mrs. Ann Powell. The old servant, Simon Richards, and wife Nancy, recognized me and welcomed me warmly. We took possession and ordered coffee. The house was half furnished and just as the family had left it to visit their friends in Richmond. . . .

15. Alpheus S. Williams (1810-78), a Detroit lawyer, commanded a division under Banks. It was Williams who reported the famous "lost order" of Lee to McClellan at Frederick and gave his commander a detailed plan of Lee's movements. After Mansfield's death at Antietam, Williams took command of the Twelfth Corps. Assigned to Sherman's command, he led the Twentieth Corps on its march to the sea. After the war Williams was minister to El Salvador and congressman from Michigan.

16. James M. Mason (1798-1871) had been senator from Virginia, 1847-61. His capture aboard the Trent, while he was en route to England on a diplomatic mission for the Confederacy, nearly embroiled the United States in a war with Great Britain. Released, Mason lived in England throughout the war and did not return to Virginia until after the Proclamation of Amnesty. His home, "Selma," was burned in 1864.

Visited General Shields. The General was lying down reading. He welcomed us warmly and related some interesting anecdotes about Jeff Davis. He says Davis has some verbose talents, some capacity to write and speak clearly, but is a man of limited views and utterly wanting in magnanimity. He says when the bill to confer lieutenant generalcy on General Scott was discussed in Committee, he (Shields) sustained it and carried it through. Davis was so angry that he threatened, "If that bill was proposed in the Senate he would expose General Scott." Shields became excited and replied, "If Davis did any thing of that sort, he would most assuredly expose him." Shields went on with some harsh language, but the quarrel was stopped by some mutual friends. Shields says he hopes the Confederates will give us at least one good hard battle. He thinks the honor of the American name demands it.

MARCH 13, THURSDAY.—Cloudy. . . . General Banks has arrived and has his headquarters at Seevar's house. On the street I was addressed by a lady whom I did not know. She inquired if she could get a letter to her son in Richmond via Fortress Monroe. I told her it was probable she could and promised to forward it for her. We then talked of the events of the war. I told her Manassas was in possession of McClellan. She looked incredulous and asked, "Is that true, Sir?" I told her the news was official. I thought she would have fallen on the steps. "Good God!" she exclaimed. "Then Jackson is cut off." I said it was quite probable. We talked a little longer but I perceived she was confused and distrait, so I took leave.

I rode out upon all the heights overlooking the town of Winchester and inspected the fortifications about which we have speculated so much. I was profoundly grieved and mortified to see such wretched exhibitions of engineering from my own people. I cannot imagine how Joe Johnston and Jackson, who are educated military men, could have permitted such absurd exhibitions unless we suppose they never intended to defend the place and merely worked the troops at these ditches to amuse them with the idea of a defence. The platforms and truck carriages for the guns remained, but nothing of military value. Most of the works were parapets of earth about two feet high and three or four feet thick, some of them topped with small stones. The fort at Knavetown was a very inferior earth work, the parapets revetted with rails, boards, paling fence and some sandbags. Flour barrel gabions and a board fence formed the lines on either side of the Martinsburg pike. There were traverses of earth, stockade tambours for flanking musketry and all the imitations of field fortifications got up like the efforts of ignorant boys. It was humiliating. I could have sat down and cried. Returning to town I saw the wretched shanties in which the troops had lived surrounded by dead horses and everything indicates squalor, poverty, and folly. . . .

MARCH 14, FRIDAY.—I started via Berryville to make a reconnoissance of Castleman's Ferry. Out of town I met John Wall, who told me of the arrest of Union citizens by Jackson on leaving there. He says it was the most humiliating sight he has seen since the opening of the war. Grey-haired and prominent citizens marched like felons through the streets, tramping through mud and rain between files of soldiers. He says that act has done more to kill Secession sentiment here than anything else. He says retaliation would be impolitic, especially as there is no proper material upon whom to retaliate.

On the way I passed the toll gate on the Opequon bluff where two women had solicited my protection on my journey up. They stood in the door and I asked them if they had been disturbed. They replied no, except by one soldier who had been rude and used improper language. She said she showed him the paper I left and that had shut him up. She then asked my name. I told her Strother. "Oh, this is General Strother of Martinsburg?" I told her yes and rode on. . . .

Arrived at Berryville I found Adam alone at the Topographical Quarters. With him was a Negro named Bob, late a servant in the Southern army. Bob was sharp and a great wag. He says Jackson had the boats on the Potomac to cross his brigade more effectually to destroy the canal dams. The destruction of the canal seemed to be a great desire with them. They attempted it with all their force and strategy but were continually foiled by the massive strength of the works and the superior fire of the Federal guards. He seemed to think Jackson's brigade had very little idea of fighting at all. They took positions, outraged Union citizens, and as soon as the Federal troops approached they packed and fled. This, he says, has been the history of their movements throughout. On the retreat from Bath he says they lost at least a hundred horses. When a wagon stuck, the load was taken out and burnt. When one upset, it was burnt with its cargo. The troops froze because Jackson prohibited fires for fear the enemy would see them. Bob says it was well we lost the battle of Bull's Run. It opened our Old Uncle Sam's eyes, made him see things clear. At the same time it made the South stark mad.

Their self-confidence and credulity knew no bounds. They really believed their own extraordinary boastings, that they could whip the Yankees, five to one. Bob has made up his mind that they won't fight anywhere.

Captain Abert arrived from his reconnoissance of Castleman's Ferry. The width was calculated at 550 feet, the average depth 6 feet. . . . We got in after dark and reported at headquarters. I told the General of my wish to join the lower army at Manassas. He said he would prefer that I should remain with the troops of the division and go over with them across Loudoun. He desired me to assist Captain Abert in building the bridge at Castleman's Ferry. I promised to do so.

MARCH 15, SATURDAY.—Raining. General Banks, Captain Abert, and myself got on the cars for Harpers Ferry. The trip was dull and very slow. At Summit Point I saw my friend old Paul Smith. At the sight of me he shouted. I invited him in to see General Banks and presented him as one of the three men who had voted the Union ticket in Clarke County. He shook hands with the General and then fell to embracing me, swearing he would have lost his estate rather than to have missed this meeting. Having got over the extravagance of his joy he asked where the General was. The presentation had to be made over again. Arrived at Charles Town I got out and the others went on, the General to Washington, Captain Abert to get material at Harpers Ferry for his bridge. . . .

MARCH 16, SUNDAY.—Fair and cool. . . . Since the fall of Winchester our Secessionists here are becoming much modified and Unionists are speaking out. Much credit is awarded to Riddle and myself for saving the county and citizens from the wrath of the Federal Army. Some troops and trains have passed en route for Harpers Ferry. . . .

MARCH 17, MONDAY.— . . . After dinner, started in the cars for Winchester. . . . Went to General Williams' office and found a number of officers in high feather drinking punch. Williams is now temporarily in command of the division. It is reported that General Banks will return here tomorrow or next day. Vague, however. Coming up in the cars I saw two prisoners of [Turner] Ashby's men. When they were taken and confined in the guardhouse, the elder soldier said, "Lord, what a good sleep I'll have here tonight. I won't have to watch the Yankees."

MARCH 18, TUESDAY.—. . . Colonel Brodhead got me a sabre from the quartermaster and about two o'clock we took the road. A few miles brought us to Shields' column, horse, foot, and artillery, ten thousand men and five batteries, a very formidable turnout. After passing the greater part of the troops we overtook the General and staff. He was marching very slowly so as to allow Colonel [John S.] Mason, who led the flanking movement, time to get behind. Ashby was reported to be at Middletown. When within a few miles of this place, as we stood upon a height locating the points of the surrounding country, Mason's adjutant rode up informing us that his force had got into Middletown and that Ashby was in sight between them and Strasburg.

I felt disgusted at this information, because I knew that a gull would stand as good a chance to catch a fox, as our force to catch Ashby. As we approached the town a grand column of smoke was seen rising toward Strasburg. This we were informed was the turnpike bridge over Cedar Creek. As our advance reached the bluffs overlooking this creek, Ashby opened upon them with three pieces of cannon. I immediately rode forward to reconnoiter his position and saw the cannon supported by a body of cavalry and a battalion of infantry. Our skirmishers stood or lay in groups among the cedar bushes, exchanging shots now and then with the Confederate sharpshooters. On the brow of the hill was a battery of Parrott guns entirely idle, why I do not know. The shot and shell whistled over us smartly for half an hour, doing but little damage, however, as but one man was wounded on our side. General Shields got up about sunset and made some dispositions to cross the creek above and below. A company of cavalry was ordered to cross the ford just below the bridge, but the officer hesitated to do so because the light of the burning timbers exposed him to the fire of the enemy's riflemen. There seemed to be very little spirit shown on our side, either by horse, foot, or artillery. In the meantime it became quite dark and the troops were ordered to bivouac on the ground while Colonel Brodhead and myself returned to Middletown to find a bed.

MARCH 19, WEDNESDAY.—The Colonel rose about one o'clock this morning and rode back to Winchester, desiring me to send for him should any chance of a battle appear. When I got up, Michael, the Colonel's orderly, reported that he with the two other men and the light carriage had been left to my orders. He also insisted that I should be better mounted and said the Colonel had given him leave to steal a good horse for me, which he would do at the first opportunity. While I was at breakfast, Michael came in and informed me that he had stolen a horse and would immediately put my saddle on it. A few minutes after, however, the owner came in to complain and I had the animal returned to him, much to Michael's disgust. While our horses were being saddled, several of the citizens came to the tavern complaining of spoliation, chiefly in the article of beehives, honey being one of the great weaknesses of the Yankee soldier.

Crossing Cedar Creek the General expressed his annoyance that he should have been stopped by such a trifling obstacle, it being fordable everywhere, even for the infantry. On reaching Strasburg we again heard Ashby's cannon but he had opened at such a distance that his shells fell short a mile at least. Some very tardy maneuvers on our part were executed to place twenty pieces in position within range of the enemy. By the time the artillery and supporting infantry found their places, the enemy was retiring. A splendid volley covered the country before us with bursting shells, but I cannot flatter myself that they did any damage to the Rebels. A regiment of the Michigan cavalry, pushed forward to harass the enemy's rear, got the benefit of our fire and thereby lost four horses. They retired precipitately or they would have been destroyed by our own artillery. Fortunately no men were lost.

We pushed on for about five miles beyond Strasburg on the Woodstock road, columns of smoke rising as we advanced, from the bridges fired by the retreating Rebels. Near Bush Creek bridge Ashby's guns opened again, but as usual at a ridiculous distance. At this point we wheeled about and returned to Strasburg, the men growling at what appeared a retrograde step. The reconnoissance had been pushed as far as was intended, and General Shields fell back to get up his supplies and await further orders. He is certainly a man of pluck and enterprise and suits me better than anyone I have yet seen in the field. I must say, too, that Ashby has played his part handsomely in disputing our advance, displaying a great deal of personal boldness and military tact in checking so large a column as ours with his small force.

MARCH 20, THURSDAY.—Cold, rain, and wind. Paid a gouging bill at the Virginia Hotel. Left for Winchester and passed several regiments of Shields' division en route for the same place. At Newtown an old man came out and asked me to stop and come near to him as he was deaf. I did so and he began inquiring about the results of the battle. I told him there had been no battle that I knew of. He was astonished and said his neighbors had told him that wagon loads of dead had passed through the town. He had two grandsons in the Confederate Army. He was a Pennsylvanian and a Union man and told doleful stories of the abuses put upon them by the Southern troops. Their horses, teams, grain, fodder, Negroes, and white men were carried off without remorse. Every man that dared open his mouth to remonstrate or talk Union was threatened with death or captivity. The people generally had a cowed and stupid look. . . .

Called on General Banks and heard that a great excitement was raging in political circles in Washington. It was ascertained that the fortifications and show of force at Manassas and Centerville were sham. Partisans were furiously bent on extinguishing McClellan and resolutions were being prepared to that purpose. It seems probable that all military power of the Confederacy has been sent westward and southward. I doubt if there will be any adequate force to attempt resistance to a march on Richmond. General Banks is evidently a McClellan man and opposed to fanatical faction. O for a Buonaparte!

MARCH 21.—Cloudy. Called on General Banks and got permission from him to visit Charles Town to see my wife whom I hoped to find there. He granted it with usual complaisance and at the same time his manner induced me to think he would rather not spare me. As I could see no special reason why I should not go, I took leave and started. . . . I rode to Charles Town and on approaching my mother-in-law's house saw my daughter on the porch looking tall and beautiful. This day was the twelfth anniversary of her birth.[17] My wife was presently at the door to meet me.

MARCH 22, SATURDAY.—Cloudy. . . . It will take some time for the habitual dread of this Rebellion tyranny to wear away. People seem to be so cowed by it that they cannot feel assured of their liberation. It is really painful to see one's friends in such a condition, but it will doubtless wear off in time. This fear is no doubt at the bottom of much of the seeming sullenness and coldness of the people toward the United States troops. . . .

MARCH 23, SUNDAY.—Cloudy. In the afternoon walked with my wife on the turnpike. Returning we met the Henderson girls in their carriage. They passed without saluting us. Nothing can exceed the infatuated insolence of these miserable people. But the cup of sorrow and humiliation which they have prepared for themselves and which they must drain to the dregs is not yet fully tasted. Heard news that

17. Emily Strother was his daughter by his first marriage to Ann Doyne Wolff.

a fight was going on at Winchester, that General Shields was wounded, and that the battle was still raging.[18] This information I must confess disturbed me a good deal, although I did not give it full credence. Returning home I went to bed and soon after, Riddle knocked at our chamber door. I rose hastily, put on my pantaloons, and went into the hall where he told me with some agitation of manner that there certainly had been a battle near Winchester and we had suffered a great loss. I went to bed again and to sleep soundly.

MARCH 24, MONDAY.—. . . As I rode out of town I met Andrew Kennedy, who told me that the country was full of Henderson's cavalry and advised me pressingly not to ride alone, saying there was a special danger for me as being an object of hatred to the Rebels. I gave the subject a few minutes' consideration and then determined to go on, taking the precaution, however, to keep my right hand ungloved and my pistol holster unbuttoned. . . . In Berryville I found Captain Abert. There had been a battle at Winchester. Shields was certainly wounded and all General Banks' division was on the march from Snicker's Ferry to Winchester.

After dinner I started to Winchester overtaking en route Gordon's brigade. As soon as I could, I visited the field of yesterday's battle. It was two or three miles beyond the town on a ridge partially wooded and partially cultivated and some distance from the Valley pike. The fences were torn down and the ground marked with artillery wheels where the Federal troops had first taken position. A dead horse or two were visible and the body of a soldier with the top of his head blown off lay protected by a rail pen. Crossing a field and a wood I came upon an open ridge where marks of artillery wheels and another body of a United States soldier lay. Near here a picket guard lay by a fire and beside them upon a rail trestle lay fifteen dead Federalists. In a thicket and rock break about two or three hundred yards distant the Confederate dead lay. Entering the break I observed the bushes and trees cut to pieces with musketry in a manner terrible to witness. Here within a very small space lay forty bodies of the Confederates. The bodies lay among the bushes and trees just as they fell, and were without exception shot through the head with musket balls. The sun had set and the dull red light from the west fell upon the upturned faces of the dead, giving a lurid dimness to the scene that highlighted its ghastly effect.

18. The Battle of Kernstown between Jackson and Shields was under way. Wounded during the battle, Shields turned his force over to Colonel Nathan Kimball, his brigade commander.

From this thicket extending some distance along the line of a stone fence lay more bodies thickly strewed among the rocks, vines, and undergrowth. I searched through this bloody field with a sort of horrid curiosity, examining each gully and rock heap to find some still more hideous form of death than I had yet seen. There was enough to gratify one's taste for horrors, and in my seeking I failed to recognize any face with which I was acquainted. All the arms and equipments were taken away and the pockets rifled and generally all the buttons clipped off as objects of curiosity for the soldiers. It had now become dark and I turned to ride back to Winchester. . . . I got a good supper and passed the night at Gordon's quarters.[19]

MARCH 25, TUESDAY.—Last night I visited the courthouse where a number of wounded of both armies lay. In the courtyard were two pieces of cannon, twelve-pounders, taken from the enemy. In the vestibule lay thirteen dead bodies of United States soldiers and the courtroom was filled to its capacity with wounded, all of a serious character. A Confederate captain, Yancey Jones, was lying there with both eyes scooped out and the bridge of his nose carried away by a bullet. He was sometimes delirious and roared about forming his company and charging. An Ohio volunteer lay on his back, the brains oozing from a shot in the head, uttering at breathing intervals a sharp stertorous cry. He had been lying thus for thirty-six hours. A few stifled groans were heard occasionally, but as a general thing the men were quiet. There was another storeroom opposite Taylor's Hotel where we saw a number of wounded, all Federalists.

This morning I visited the Union Hotel where I saw two rooms filled with wounded and seven dead. In the room where the dead bodies were, lay a Confederate soldier wounded in the head. He seemed also delirious and was rolling a piece of lint in his hands and rubbing the floor with it. He also pulled the bloody bandages from his head and the soldier nurse told us that he occasionally got up and ran about so violently that he was obliged to bring him out from among the other wounded. In the next room was a fairhaired man whose fixed eyes and stertorous breathing showed him to be in the agonies of death. Some here were lightly wounded in the limbs and one with a broken thigh showed me the wound and begged I would have it attended to. George Washington of Jefferson County was

19. George H. Gordon (1823-86), USMA '46, served with Banks in the Valley and at Cedar Mountain. After Antietam he was assigned to Florida. Mustered out of the army in 1865, Gordon practiced law in Boston.

upstairs said to be mortally wounded. At the door I met a lady [asking] for permission to visit him. . . .

On the day of the battle General Banks was in Harpers Ferry on the way to Washington and I was in Charles Town with my family. The staff was on the field and did good service. The strategy of movement was said to have been feebly managed, but the men fought well and, as soon as permitted, made short work of it. The fire of musketry was the most tremendous on record. The thickets in which the enemy stood were literally mowed down by it. It was a fair, open fight, decided by pluck and discipline, and the Rebels with the self-styled Stonewall brigade were soundly thrashed. We had some advantage in numbers. They had advantage in position and a leader in whom they had implicit confidence. Our troops had no leader but were commanded by a senior colonel. The superior fire and courage of the infantry won the battle for the Government. "Thus endeth the first lesson for this valley."

From the commencement of the attack on Saturday evening until Sunday evening the women of Winchester were insolently triumphant. They confidently expected to see the United States troops driven out and as the dead and wounded were brought in during the day, these Rebel dames and maids were on the streets and at the windows radiant with anticipated triumph, insulting the soldiers on duty in the town and the families of officers who were there visiting their husbands. As the evening closed, the scene changed. Ambulances came in carrying their own wounded by scores, and escorts with long trains of Rebel prisoners marched through the streets. The she-braggarts disappeared from the streets, doors were closed, and lights put out. Anon, veiled mourners besieged the doors of the hospitals and guardhouses, begging permission to see a friend or husband among the wounded or prisoners. The cup of humiliation and sorrow is now at the lips of this insolent and inhuman race. Let them drain it to the dregs. . . .

Arrived at Strasburg I stopped at the Virginia House and found part of General Banks' staff there. Dr. [James] King stayed with Mrs. Phil Dandridge in Winchester and says the young ladies were particularly savage on me. One of them had a pistol I believe wherewith she desired to shoot me. [Major Delevan D.] Perkins also told me of some direful anger of the fair sex against me. King called on Mrs. Dr. Hugh McGuire to give her some papers and surgical engravings saved from the college.[20] She met him with great bitterness,

20. Presumably this is the wife of Dr. Hunter McGuire, Jackson's medical director.

telling him he was the first Yankee that had ever darkened her door. He stood in the rain and explained his mission. She seemed mollified but took no interest in the subject, saying they were totally ruined and she scarcely cared to save the pictures. She wanted to know, however, if her husband, who was a fugitive, could return in safety. Dr. King bluntly told her he was a dunce for leaving, as nobody would have troubled him or even have known of his existence.

MARCH 28, FRIDAY.—Bright and warm. . . . After tea General Banks paid Colonel Brodhead and myself a social visit. He talked more freely than ever I heard him. I have never heard anyone whose views agree more exactly with my own. He says both sections have been governed by extremists who have carried their points because of the moral cowardice of the people, or rather the mass of office-seekers who represent the people. He thinks, as I have always thought, that the Kansas-Nebraska Bill and the repealing of the Missouri Compromise line was the fatal act that opened the Civil War. He says that all parties disapproved of it, but that political cowardice, which was the leading characteristic of our past government, induced men to support it who foresaw its dangerous tendencies.

Speaking of Virginia, he characterized our late public men as a very inferior set, both in manners and intellect, whiskey-drinking being the common ground on which they all met. I have myself considered the Old Virginia people as a decadent race. They have certainly gone down in manners, morals, and mental capacity. There seems to be nothing left of their traditional greatness but a senseless pride and a certain mixture of dignity and suavity of manner, the intelligence of a once great and magnanimous people. It was high time that war had come to wipe out this effete race and give this splendid country to a more active and progressive generation. That this will be the final result of the war, I do not doubt.

MARCH 29, SATURDAY.—Cloudy. General complaint of sickness from the bad water in this vicinity. It commenced raining. The General came in and informed me that he thought of attacking Jackson, who lay behind Woodstock. I advised him to do so, by all means. He called in a second time to ascertain how much cavalry Colonel Brodhead could muster. The answer was 750 men. The General said he had telegraphed for a regiment of Vermont cavalry now lying at Poolesville, Maryland. He seemed preoccupied and undecided. He said it seemed that the Rebels were falling back on their whole line behind the Rappahannock and the Rapidan. . . .

I am told the staff officers have sent a paper to General Shields, stating their disbelief in Captain [R. C.] Shriber's story of his single combat with a Virginia trooper. The Captain showed a hole in his hat from a pistol ball, which he says was fired by a trooper whom he slew by a thrust of the sword. Shriber's two orderlies were killed and consequently there were no witnesses to the combat. The staff do not credit the story, and someone asking why Captain Shriber had wounded his hat instead of some other garment, the Prussian Captain [William] Scheffler replied, "Because it was the most cheapest part of his clothes."

MARCH 30, SUNDAY.—Raining and everything covered with a coating of sleet. General Banks mentioned that he had received a dispatch from General Fremont at Wheeling stating that he had taken command there. Fremont will have command of about thirty thousand men and will operate on our right. I suggested a march from western Virginia via Lewisburg, through Lexington to Salem, seizing the Virginia and Tennessee Railroad, threatening Lynchburg: we marching directly up the Valley, co-operating with McClellan in his movements forward. . . .

MARCH 31, MONDAY.—Still cloudy. . . . The army are short of rations. The General wishes to move on Woodstock tomorrow. The regular army, Beckwith and Perkins, opposed the move. The volunteers were in favor of it, and I spoke decidedly in favor of it. We will be but twelve miles farther from supplies there than we are here. By adding a little energy to our commissary department at Harpers Ferry and by drawing on the country around us, we may keep the troops from starvation. And the move is called for from the Eastern

WRITING HOME

division, who are ahead of us and advancing. The General asked my opinion as to where the enemy would meet us. I said if at all it will be Ashby's force at the Narrow Passage behind Woodstock and Jackson's whole force at Rude's Hill, two miles behind Mount Jackson. This last point I think will be the battle ground, if they stand at all.

APRIL 1, TUESDAY.—Fair. The troops were in motion early and about ten o'clock the staff got off. As we approached Woodstock, cannon were heard in front and the shells whistled over our heads. These were Ashby's guns planted on the opposite side of the town on some rising ground. A section of Parrott guns speedily cleared them out and our advance entered the town. The place has a more cheerful aspect than Strasburg and seemed teeming with women and children who were all out to see us. We did not stop but pushed on through toward the Narrow Passage, two miles and a half distant. Beyond Narrow Passage Ashby's guns again opened and our battery was again put in position to clear them out. The staff took position near the battery and we could see the enemy's cavalry escaping over the hills. . . .

Crossing Narrow Passage Creek we saw the turnpike bridge had been saved from total destruction and our columns of infantry passed over. As we reached the ridge beyond, a magnificent view was developed in front. From behind the woods about a mile ahead rose two columns of smoke. There was a free Negro cabin by the roadside, the occupants of which informed us that these burnings were the railway and turnpike bridge at Edinburg. An old bedridden mulatto talked away very freely and in a state of great excitement. She said if any lurking around should see them talking with us, they would run the risk of being shot as soon as we were out of the way, and that upon the slightest disobedience or restiveness, free Negroes were shot down like dogs. She wished us success, etc. . . . In the town of Edinburg we found the troops going into quarters, and the General's staff returning. With it we took rooms at the hotel in Woodstock. The beds had been occupied by the Confederates the night before and dirty enough they were.

APRIL 2, WEDNESDAY.—Cloudy. Made an office of the courthouse in Woodstock. General Banks looked about the building with much interest and observed that these quaint old buildings had turned out many strong men. In the adjutant general's office two prisoners were examined. One a Baltimorean, Lieutenant Duff of Ashby's cavalry, says he was carrying dispatches from Ashby to Baylor, stopped at a country house to get his canteen filled and to see the girls. While there, one of the children ran in and reported that a number of Federal cavalry were around the house. He looked out and saw they had round hats and blue coats, whereupon he burned his written dispatch, threw away his pistols, and ran to get his horse loose. The bridle being tied to a hard knot, he was detained until the troopers came upon him and took him. The prisoner also told me that Tad Thrasher was killed at the battle of Winchester. He fell with two wounds. There is some poetry in this. He is the man who arrested my father and stole my guns. This account is settled. The prisoner seemed to be plucky and full of warlike spirit. He seemed to be more anxious that his pluck should be fully recognized than any other thing. The other prisoner was an impressed country youth who seemed glad to be out of it on easy terms and said the majority of his comrades were of the same mind. He told frankly what he knew, which was next to nothing. . . .

APRIL 3, THURSDAY.—Clear and warm. . . . We rode to Edinburg after dinner and stopped by the way at General Williams' quarters in a farm house. With his chief of artillery he was examining some ground broken up and covered by fragments of shell thrown by our artillery on the day of the advance. From hence we rode all together to the battery on the hill commanding Edinburg and vicinity. We there saw a percussion shell thrown by the enemy and not exploded. The stopper containing the cap was of brass, finely manufactured and pronounced to be English, and I have no doubt it was. . . .

We had a long consultation about the topography of the country and proposed movements. The provisions have arrived, forage has been procured, and our forward movement made directly in face of the advice of the regular officers has proved a success. In the skirmish on the 1st instant, Ashby placed his guns on the turnpike and immediately south of Woodstock. One of his shells grazed the front of a wooden house, leaving its trace on the weatherboarding for ten or twelve feet. Another passed through the gable of the jail, perforating both stone walls. A third struck the steeple of the courthouse, tearing off the shingles. This reckless firing through a village filled with women and children seems to me entirely unjustifiable when we consider that he was maintaining no position and fired with no other object than the spiteful hope of injuring someone of our advance. . . .

APRIL 4, FRIDAY.—Clear and warm. . . . Rode to Edinburg with the staff and went upon the hills where the batteries were stationed. Saw a number of Ashby's men come out from the woods and commence firing. The distance was too great for effect, however. General Banks asked me to make a sketch of the ground for the purpose of placing pickets. I stayed behind and riding from one hilltop to another got what I could of the topography and made a very rough sketch. Entering the town I called at the Lutheran parsonage to get admission to the steeple of the church. I then mounted the steeple and took my observations, not without apprehension that I might become the mark of Confederate sharpshooters who lined the woods and fences on the other side of Stony Creek. I returned to the parsonage and while conversing a brisk cannonade was opened between one of our batteries and Ashby's. I suppose it was nothing, but the minister seemed much distressed and said the sound of the guns always made him sick and sometimes put him to bed. His family were smiling and cheerful but all seemed anxious to get to Shepherdstown, Virginia, to escape the war. . . .

APRIL 5, SATURDAY.—Raining. . . . A militiaman deserter came in and gave us some fresh information. He says Jackson's principal force lies between Rude's Hill and New Market without heavy guns or baggage and is ready for flight. The force is much disorganized, drinking whiskey furiously, scattered along the whole road to Harrisonburg and Staunton. He saw some of their baggage marked Waynesboro, a station on the Gordonsville Railroad at the western foot of the Blue Ridge. This indicates precisely the move I have looked for all along.

Was informed that Colonel [Jonas P.] Holliday of the Vermont cavalry had committed suicide, the cause said to be disgust with the bad discipline of his regiment. Colonel Holliday was a regular officer of New York, a tall man with a huge beard and of a melancholy mien, talking rarely and in monosyllables. I was introduced to him three days ago and remarked his sad and speechless demeanor. He ordered his regiment to march and remaining behind lit his pipe and blew his brains out.

On re-examining the shell marks on the buildings in this town it is apparent that the mischief was done by our own batteries. I fear we have a very inefficient artillery. . . . Today while walking out heard a deep-toned report like that of a distant gun very large, and about a mile off saw a column of white smoke leap up, curling over at the top until it took the shape of a huge mushroom. A succession of sharper reports followed like the explosion of a bunch of Chinese crackers, but louder. This afterwards ascertained was the accidental blowing up of a caisson filled with ten-pounder shells. Strange to say, neither driver nor horses were hurt, but the horses ran away for half a mile before they could be stopped.

APRIL 6, SUNDAY.—Bright and mild. Called at headquarters and talked with the General about the forward movement on Mt. Jackson. He has just heard from Fremont that the Confederate troops at Monterey and Cheat Mountain were falling back probably to effect a junction with Jackson at Staunton. . . . A sergeant brought in two deserters from Ashby's Cavalry. They were brothers, youths from Baltimore who had volunteered eight months ago. They were tired of the service and said many others were in the same condition and would desert when they got an opportunity. They said Jackson was at Mt. Jackson removing the stores. Their wagons were few and it would take them a long time to get them all away. They confirm the report of panic and disorganization and say there is talk of resisting at Staunton and the militia are engaged in fortifying there. A smart forward movement would probably enable us to capture some stores and material. The boys say at Edinburg the wagons were on the opposite side of Stony Creek and on our arrival they threw away many of their stores, but finding we did not cross, returned and gathered them up. I shall urge an immediate forward movement. Saw General Banks and expressed my views. He seemed to agree with them and said the forward movement should be made as soon as possible. . . .

APRIL 7, MONDAY.—Cloudy and mild. At headquarters saw a man who stated that in the Blue Ridge of Rockingham County were Union Virginians and refugees from conscription to the amount of a thousand men determined to resist the Confederate authorities and determined to fight to the end. . . . A snow storm beginning.

APRIL 10, THURSDAY.—Cloudy. Indications of clearing off. Snow several inches deep. This will keep the streams up and stop campaigning for a week or ten days. The mountains and forests covered with magnificent frost-work presented a grand spectacle. At headquarters this evening news was received from McClellan at Yorktown. He says Johnston is in front of him in person with large force, supported by very strong fortifications. His tone is not confident, complaining that part of his force has been detached. This is McDowell's army corps held in front of Washington. I don't like the tone of his message, however. He says he will do the best he can. Perhaps this is only the modesty of a man fully aware of the great hazards of war and awed (as the bravest well may be) by the greatness of the impending struggle for the possession of Richmond.

APRIL 11, FRIDAY.—Bright with frost. . . . Shields thinks that Lee is in front of McClellan. Lee has been appointed commander in chief of the Southern forces, which indicates that confidence in Davis is lost. Lee was the favorite officer of General Scott while in the U. S. Army. Davis was furiously jealous of Scott and consequently of anyone whom he patronized. Lee entered the service of Virginia when she made her first revolutionary movement, but when she was annexed to the Southern Confederacy, it was supposed he would resign. He did not do so, however, but has continued to serve in comparative obscurity. This was doubtless because of the ill-feeling between himself and President Davis. His promotion to chief command shows that the reverse of the Southern arms has ruined Davis's influence and it promises that a great battle will be fought in Virginia. If this battle is decisively lost, it will finish the Rebellion and the old Virginia oligarchy will perish with it.

APRIL 13, SUNDAY.—Cloudy and damp. Received an invitation to attend divine service with the staff of General Shields. Rode out with General Banks and staff to the campground near Edinburg and there found the brigade drawn up in hollow square around a cart where sat two preachers and an officer looking like a gallows scene precisely, wanting the gibbet. At our approach the band played a hymn tune and the congregation sang. Dismounting, we took our stand within the circle, when the preacher arose and without any preliminary words commenced his sermon. The text was "Would ye be made whole." He was a good-looking man and his discourse was addressed to the soldiery rather than the staff. His language was common and often ungrammatical, but his ideas were clear and manly. He had a subject, which was the power and beauty of self-control. The day before had been pay day and the usual amount of drunkenness and insubordination accompanied it. A prayer and thanksgiving for the Union victories in Tennessee followed the sermon. Then the old doxology was sung by the full congregation. During the ceremony General Banks in his regimentals stood a little forward in front of the preacher. Immediately beside him stood a boy about twelve years old, ragged and snub-nosed, in the most independent and critical attitude, devouring the General with his eyes, measuring him from top to toe, probably guessing how long it would take him to grow into a major general. The scene was American. . . .

APRIL 17, THURSDAY.—Bright. The captain of the bodyguard rode up and informed me that our staff had gone this morning at five o'clock. I got breakfast and rode forward at a trot. The columns of smoke in our front showed the Rebels were alert and at their usual work, bridge-burning. At Mt. Jackson were the charred and smoking ruins of the railroad cars and stock. This being the terminus of the railroad line from Manassas, it was doubtless intended as a permanent base of operations. The bridge over the stream at the farther end of the village was also burnt but the ford was easy. This bridge with the turn of the road I remembered perfectly and it recalled poetically to my mind how my life had been connected with this Valley. In it I was born. The first of my boyish exploits which gave me boyish notoriety was my pedestrian tour up this valley with my companion Ranson.[21] Twenty years after, I made the tour with three ladies and servant, which journey produced the Porte Crayon Papers. And now nine years after, I ride in the panoply of war—alone, alone—in the midst of the armed hosts. Today the Valley justifies all my praises of its beauty. The balmy spring air, the broad green meadows, the rocky crest of Peaked Mountain, and the fading range of blue hills invest the scene with marvelous beauty. The General seemed enraptured with it and never ceased to remark it, even amidst the excitement of the pursuit. The bridge over the Shenandoah beyond Mt. Jackson was saved by the activity of our cavalry. It was fired but put out before any damage was done. The troopers carried water in their nose bags to put it out. The lieutenant and two men engaged in burning it were taken prisoners.

I rode over the bridge and saw the enemy on Rude's Hill about a mile distant, about fifty men with three pieces of cannon. After waiting here for some time we were informed that the flanking force was opposite New Market and then our movements commenced. A battery took position on a flanking hill and after exchanging a few shots the Rebels left. Our infantry, ten regiments, two regiments of cavalry, and some artillery passed the bridge and deployed in battle array. Two regiments deployed as skirmishers. The rest of the in-

21. This is an allusion to a trip on foot up the Valley of Virginia in 1835, made by Strother and his friend James Ranson. The second trip of 1853, which Strother made in the company of three young women, formed the basis for his best-known travel narrative, *Virginia Illustrated* (1857). Because of these excursions, Strother was regarded as an authority on Valley topography during the war.

fantry advanced slowly on Rude's Hill. Although this movement was all sham, it was with its surroundings the finest exhibition of the war. The staff then rode forward to Rude's Hill. The view from thence, looking back, was beautiful in the extreme. Examined the Rebel bivouacs and saw the usual debris, empty barrels, broken cooking utensils, canteens, and old clothes, but nothing that could in any way be either useful or ornamental. They seem to be miserably provided— such bread I never saw. We got into New Market at dusk, miserably jaded. Some Rebel cavalry still hung about our advance, but a couple of shells from [Captain Clermont L.] Best's battery dispersed them. Jackson with his force had passed through here at ten o'clock double-quick, Ashby's force about three o'clock, all but the fifty men whom we saw in front of us. Our flanking column was still unheard from, but about ten o'clock Captain Norvell of the Michigan Cavalry reported they were at the river one mile distant and could not cross. This I expected. . . . Our quarters are at the house of Dr. Rice near New Market.

APRIL 18, FRIDAY.—Bright and balmy. . . . The General introduced me to a boy who had escaped from Pocahontas County to avoid the militia draft. He says that the country people generally are averse to the impressment and thinks they will presently rise against the authorities. . . . Colonel Clark says he saw a secession boy seven years old dressed in soldier's clothes drilling a squad of U. S. soldiers. I heard another boasting that the women agreed the Northerners were better looking than their own men. This indicates results some day. Anniversary of the capture of Harpers Ferry.

APRIL 19, SATURDAY.—Warm and clouding. . . . A Confederate prisoner was brought in, a good-looking man dressed in a blue overcoat, one of Ashby's lieutenants. I lay upon the sofa and regarded him with indifference, waiting to hear Major Copeland examine him. Presently he said he was from Martinsburg. This stimulated my curiosity and the major said, "You probably know Captain Strother." The prisoner turned quickly and joyfully held out his hand—Dick Staub! Dick romanced as usual upon all subjects upon which he was questioned. However, he verified the statement of one of our scouts which was thought too marvelous to be accepted before. A man named Taggart, pretending to desert, escaped to Staub, who was on picket duty. He was taken to Ashby and from him to Jackson, both of whom he deluded, telling them his whole company wished to desert. His McClellan saddle was much coveted and several officers tried it on their horses and rode around to try its seat. He was permitted to return to our camp, promising to bring his whole company over, saddles and all. According to Staub he Yankeed them all but himself. Some deserters tell us that Jackson is returning toward Gordonsville by a turnpike road from Harrisonburg. This suggests new features in the campaign and must be looked to. . . .

APRIL 20, SUNDAY.—Raining. . . . A number of refugees and deserters from the militia have come in, nine in one gang. It is confirmed that Jackson has gone over the ridge to Gordonsville and is reported that Staunton is occupied by Federal troops.[22] This is premature, but doubtless Fremont's advance is near there. . . .

APRIL 22, TUESDAY.—Variable clouds and sunshine. Woke up by a severe attack of cholera morbus, brought on by indigestion. Was down and suffering all day. Dr. King kindly attended me.

APRIL 24, THURSDAY.—A snow storm. Rose feeling better and ate some breakfast. The scene is curious, bright green fields, peach and plum trees in full blossom covered with snow. The signal men have discovered Jackson's camp on the valley slope of the Blue Ridge, on the road leading to Stanardsville. Our cavalry have scoured the country nine miles beyond Harrisonburg.

APRIL 26, SATURDAY.—Cloudy and damp. The streams are swelled everywhere, our repaired and rebuilt bridges washed away. The panic at Staunton is said to have been great on Milroy's appearance at Buffalo Gap. Private families with their valuables, flying off in all directions. County records sent off. The county records of Berkeley, Jefferson, and Clarke are said to have been deposited in Luray, Page County. Jackson still lies on the slopes of the ridge. I advise an attack on him. The General is anxious to do so. . . .

APRIL 30, WEDNESDAY.—Cloudy. This day closes the month and closes this book, the second volume of notes of my military adventures and here I make my last will and testament. I desire that after my just debts are paid that all my property go to my daughter Emily. I desire that my daughter will remain with my wife Mary Hunter until she is grown and as long as it shall be agreeable and convenient for them to remain together. I request my wife to permit no posthumous publication of papers or letters that I may leave behind me. This prohibition I wish to be considered absolute, in regard to all writings. Any paintings or sketches left may be used for publication or otherwise as may be most profitable. I sign myself

David H. Strother

22. Both rumors were untrue.

Was ordered with Captain Scheffler to visit the outposts in the Luray Valley. We rode over the mountain to Columbia Bridge where we found Colonel [Robert S.] Foster of the 13th Indiana encamped with his regiment, supported by a section of artillery and a squadron of cavalry. We rode over to the village of Alma and then returned to the signal station. We concluded to report on this observation that there was no danger of an attack and no necessity to strengthen the position. . . . Returning homeward we met the 1st Virginia Regiment going over to reinforce the outpost at the bridge. It commenced raining as we descended the mountain and I got to quarters feeling chilly and sick. Had a violent attack of cholera morbus. . . .

MAY 2, FRIDAY.—Still cloudy. Fremont is approaching from the west, McDowell and Abercrombie are perfecting their communication in the east. A grand move for concentration on the flank at Yorktown will soon be made and then look out for chips. The General tells the following good story. At a ball given by Colonel Maulsby in Frederick last winter there was a great deal of drunkenness and disorder. As the General was about to retire, his servant Frank came to him in a great rage (Frank is a Santo Domingo Frenchman, black as soot). He complained that an officer had struck him and in confirmation showed his swelled head and abraded cheek. The General sympathized and advised him to put grease on it. "Damn it!" screamed Frank. "It is not grease I want, it is satisfaction."

MAY 6, TUESDAY.—Bright and cool. Still sick and suffering. . . . Papers containing particular accounts of the evacuation of Yorktown arrived. The General read the tidings. McClellan started in hot pursuit. This indicates a caving in and the loss of Richmond speedily. What next? In the meantime we are falling back on Strasburg by order from Washington. Wherefore, God only knows, for I cannot think that those who gave the order know why they gave it. I have never been so low in faith and hopelessness as I am today in thinking over the conduct of the war and the management of public affairs. That the Rebellion will be crushed I do not doubt. It will be crushed by the mere weight and impetus of the forces now in movement against it. . . .

MAY 9, FRIDAY.—Bright and warm. We received news of the retreat of the Rebels beyond the James. Afterward a telegram from McClellan which seemed to show that the retreat had not taken place. I have from the beginning of the war maintained that the Rebels would leave Virginia and probably the field without a decisive battle.

Lately I have thought they intended to fight one battle and, losing that, to disperse. Now it seems they will not fight even that one.

MAY 10, SATURDAY.—Bright and cool. I think I am gaining in health. There is a hope that our retreat on Strasburg will not be insisted on and that our column may yet be saved that disgrace. All the news from Richmond goes to show that the enemy is caving in everywhere. Yet we are retreating. General Hatch made a reconnoissance to three miles beyond Harrisonburg without any signs of the enemy.[23] Yesterday four of the cavalry went out to get milk. Stopping at a house about a mile and a half from town they asked for milk, and some women told them they could get some at the next house ahead. They went on and as they passed the barn a short distance from the women, twenty Rebels came out and fired on them, killing one man outright and mortally wounding another. The four women were arrested and it was proposed to burn the house and barn.

Several days ago two companies of our cavalry riding toward Harrisonburg met a squadron of the enemy which they charged, sword in hand. Their charge was gallantly met by the enemy, who was presently routed, losing ten men killed, eight prisoners, and some wounded. We lost two killed. This is the first instance of a collision with the sabre and the result shows what I have always believed, that Ashby's men could not meet our cavalry in the charge. The company that tried it was the original command from Fauquier County.

23. John P. Hatch (1822-1901), USMA '45, commanded a cavalry brigade under Banks and an infantry brigade under Pope. Disabled at South Mountain, Hatch did not serve in the field again. At the end of the war he supervised the district of Charleston and later served as an obscure officer of the army until his retirement.

II

Down the Valley with Banks

MAY 12, 1862—JUNE 13, 1862

Having defeated Milroy's force approaching from the west at Mc-Dowell, Jackson followed Banks down the Valley to New Market. Then, moving his army across Massanutten Mountain into the Luray Valley, he fell upon the Union garrison at Front Royal on May 23. Fearful of being cut off, Banks withdrew toward Winchester but not before part of his army had been attacked en route near Newtown. The Union stampede, checked briefly at Winchester, began, and it did not end until the troops had crossed the Potomac at Williamsport. The news of Banks's defeat caused consternation at Washington. Shields was ordered to march up the Luray Valley and Fremont to cross North Mountain in order to box in Jackson. But after a feint at Harpers Ferry, Jackson withdrew up the Valley of Virginia and defeated Fremont and Shields on successive days near Port Republic on June 8 and 9. While the Union troops were being regrouped and re-inforced, the Confederates were on their way by rail to the Richmond front. The brilliant Valley Campaign of 1862 was over, but the North believed it had just begun.

Strother's journal is an accurate register of the Valley Campaign as it was seen and felt by one of its victims. The bewilderment, anxiety, and finally the disgust are chronicled carefully. Strother's account owes nothing to retrospect. Ironically, it had been Captain Strother who had minimized the Confederate striking arm and who had urged Banks to advance during the previous three months. With dismay he noted in his journal: "We ought to have cleaned out the Valley in three weeks after we entered it." The cleansing would take two more years.

MAY 12, MONDAY.—Bright and mild. . . . We packed up and started on the road to Woodstock. I rode in the carriage with the

General in the capacity of an invalid. We passed the marching army with its spoils of horses, dogs, niggers, and cattle. It reminds me of the advent of a party of mad sailors into some heathen village. The people look on in silence and fear at the doings of these mighty iconoclasts who fear neither God nor Ashby, who think Mason a fool, and who despise the power of Jackson. They seize upon a sheep or a nigger as if he were a sheep. They laugh at Southern rights and sacred soil. They are jolly with all and make love to the girls, and they bid fair to impress these as they do the niggers and sheep. . . .

Arrived at Woodstock to dinner which we took at our old quarters in the courthouse. . . .

MAY 13, TUESDAY.—Bright and warm. Started in the carriage with the General for Strasburg. . . . We saw a Negro family with bundles following the army, and this started a discourse as to the probable fate of Virginia. This state must be ruined utterly and partially depopulated, and its resuscitation must be owing to a new population emigrating from the North. The people that I have seen since the army came in seem to be besotted and incapable of grasping the new order of things which must inevitably follow this war. Perhaps when the danger is over and peace established they may revive a little, but my belief is they will not live to any practical appreciation of the change and hence a new people must possess the land.

Found headquarters fixed at a fine brick house a short distance from Strasburg northward on the pike. Here we found Captain [Charles H. T.] Collis and his Zouaves, who resumed their role of bodyguard. They appeared in new breeches of extraordinary redness. Commenced raining.

MAY 14, WEDNESDAY.—Warm rain. Have suffered all day with dullness and discouragement arising doubtless from physical exhaustion. The wet weather and the fact of our retreat to this place seem to have cowed and irritated everybody. I made a serious mistake in not going to Yorktown when I might have done so creditably and without impropriety. Under my present circumstances I could not fairly ask permission again to go.

MAY 15, THURSDAY.—Cloudy and cool. . . . General Banks has received a letter from General Birney through the Department asking for my return to Birney's staff. . . . I fear the Department of the Shenandoah is no longer to be the theatre of glorious deeds. The neighborhood of Richmond is now the great center of interest, and I ought to be there. Let the fates direct my course. . . .

IN THE RAIN

MAY 18, SUNDAY.—Bright and warm. . . . This war has developed a number of military ideas that will make their impression on the act of war all over Christendom. The huge artillery in use has shown the futility of stone and brick fortifications, while iron-plated gun boats and ships must sink all wooden navies into nothing. New ideas also have been developed in the equipment and locomotion of armies. How could any man have been so small in his views, as to exchange his birthright in such a nation for the pitiful pride of nativity in such a state as Virginia or South Carolina? I wonder how those men of intelligence who deliberately made a choice a year ago (of the Confederacy) feel now in view of the ignominious failure of the local cause and the magnificent vindication of the national power. . . .

At headquarters found the General and Colonel Clark looking over the map and discussing the position of the troops before our retreat from New Market. The mistakes and confusion on this line are attributed to McDowell's cowardice or jealousy. It has been through his representation that the authorities in Washington have been alarmed in regard to an advance on that city by the Confederates. He has kept forty thousand men idle near Fredericksburg, thwarting McClellan's plans, weakening and discouraging the Government and its defenders. His conduct has been most contemptible and explains Bull Run.

MAY 19, MONDAY.—Bright and warm. . . . Started in the cars for Front Royal. The country looks tender and beautiful in its spring clothing. Arriving there we walked to the hotel. On entering the sitting room I saw to my astonishment a pair of oil paintings, the products of my youth. A young lady came out and spoke to me. It was James E. Stewart's daughter; her father kept the hotel we were in. This revealed the history of the pictures, which I painted about the year 1837 in Martinsburg. Stewart rented my father's house and lived in it. Finding the pictures stored away in a lumber room he asked the privilege of hanging them up. I gave them to him absolutely. Since that time he has wandered to and fro upon the earth and lately for some years has lived as a clerk in Washington. Dismissed from there, perhaps on account of his Southern proclivities, he has retired to this little secluded village to make a living keeping tavern. Stewart was a playmate and schoolmate of my earliest youth and we were also at college together. He was not at home but was supposed to be in Richmond.

Miss Belle Boyd also presented herself, looking well and deporting herself in a very ladylike manner.[1] I daresay she has been much slandered by reports. She sported a bunch of buttons despoiled from General Shields and our officers and seemed ready to increase her trophies. The surroundings and polished conversation have softened me strangely, and I feel as if I would be glad to resign. We returned to Strasburg in the train about dusk.

MAY 21, WEDNESDAY.—Rained in the night and still cloudy. An old man seized the General by the buttonhole. "General, my wife has been planting a garden, some inghins and lettuce, and the soldiers have broke the fence down and took everything." The General said he was sorry and if it were not too late he would have it protected. "Well, I wish you would. The things ain't growed yet, but if they stay here and when they come up, there won't be a thing left."

There are some military plans brewing which I hope will change our position here. Brigadier General Greene[2] reported for duty. . . .

MAY 22, THURSDAY.—Bright and warm. The report is that Jackson

1. Belle Boyd (1843-1900), a famous Confederate spy, was the daughter of Ben Boyd, one of Strother's Martinsburg friends. It was probably on this occasion that she overheard the council of war through a hole in the floor and carried the substance of it to her Confederate friends. Arrested several times during the war, Belle made her way to England, where she went on the stage. Later she returned to America as an actress and lecturer.

2. George S. Greene (1801-99), USMA '23, saw his first action at Cedar Mountain. At Antietam he commanded a division of Mansfield's Twelfth Corps, and at Gettysburg his defense of Culp's Hill on the second day prevented a Confederate flanking movement. After the war he resumed his career as engineer and at the time of his death was the oldest living graduate of West Point.

is at New Market.[3] If true we are liable to attack at any moment. . . . Six prisoners were sent here and I was commissioned to examine them. The first was a boy eighteen years old (looked fifteen) with a bad black eye and leg hurt. His horse had been shot and fell with him, severely bruising him and he was thus taken. He seemed frightened and when called in commenced crying. The other prisoners were twenty-two and twenty years of age, one twenty-nine, all of Shenandoah County, simple country fellows who had entered the service through delusion or impressment and seemed glad to be safe out of it, as soon as they were assured there was no harm intended them. One had been an infantry soldier in the Battle of Winchester (33rd Virginia) and was shot through the chin. He was living at home and asked in great trepidation whether he was to be killed or not. Being assured that he was to be permitted to live, he was overjoyed and wished to take the Oath of Allegiance. These men said Ashby was at New Market and thought Jackson was at Stribling Springs. . . .

MAY 23, FRIDAY.—Clear and warm. . . . Heard that the Rebels had attacked Front Royal and burnt the bridges and destroyed the railroad. Nothing clear. A Negro came in and stated he had left the scene of action at five o'clock and that Kenley[4] was falling back fighting. He had burnt the bridge himself. Later a dispatch was handed General Banks, who read it and then retired to his room, asking General Crawford to consult with him.[5] There was some commotion and a general sending of orders to pack up. Presently the General got another dispatch, which being obscurely written with pencil was handed to me to decipher. It was from Passage Creek and read as follows, substantially:

> Second bridge east of Strasburg
> May 23, 7 o'clock, P.M.

General Banks—

I was attacked this afternoon about four o'clock by three or four hundred cavalry and some infantry, who dashed upon me and at-

3. Jackson was preparing an attack from New Market, but by way of the Luray Valley and Front Royal.

4. John R. Kenley, a Baltimore lawyer, commanded the 1st Maryland Regiment. Wounded and captured at Front Royal, he was exchanged in August, appointed brigadier general of volunteers, and placed in charge of Baltimore troops outside the fortifications.

5. Samuel W. Crawford (1829-92) had been a surgeon in the army before commanding a battery at Fort Sumter. Appointed a brigadier general in April, 1862, Crawford lost half of his brigade at Cedar Mountain. After Mansfield's death at Antietam he took command of a division and served throughout most of the campaign from Gettysburg to Appomattox.

tempted to burn the bridge. I defended it successfully and saved it with a loss of several killed and quite a number wounded. The enemy were close by and will probably renew the attack in the morning. I would like to be reinforced.

Hubbard
Captain, Commanding Post

The General then showed me the first he had received. It was from Winchester from a captain of the 1st Maryland Cavalry, saying that Kenley's regiment and force was destroyed. Kenley was dead, all his field officers and surgeons captured, and Jackson was marching on Winchester with twenty thousand men. He had seen ten thousand men across the river.

I told the General that this fellow was some coward who had ingloriously fled the field and covered his ignominy by monstrous lying. He telegraphed the officer in command at Winchester to question the person more carefully. The same statement was persisted in by telegram. The repetition, to my surprise, gained audience, and the order for movement was hastened. In the meantime another telegram from Winchester told the story of a second refugee, a major of cavalry, [Philip P.] Vought of the New York 5th, who made a cooler statement. He said his command had been taken, killed, and dispersed and that he had remained concealed in the bushes. He saw the Rebel force fall back on Front Royal, five or six thousand strong he supposed. He also overheard some scouts say they were only going to scour the country and then fall back to town. Vought left the concealment at eleven o'clock at night and got to Winchester. This story seemed truthful and reassured us as to the movement. General Banks went to bed and I sat up the remainder of the night. Telegraphed the Secretary of War the amount of the last telegram from Winchester.

MAY 24, SATURDAY.—Clouds and rain. . . . A strong reconnoissance of horse, foot, and artillery was ordered to advance to Cedarville and the fords opposite Front Royal. If this duty had been executed, we should have immediately known our position, but the troops sent, through timidity, utterly failed in their duty. They went down the road, heard a carbine fired, and retreated reporting that the enemy were in large force. The retrograde movement was commanded by starting all the trains toward Winchester. The troops followed and with them the staff. At Cedar Creek bridge we were met by a wagon master at full speed and apparently terrified. The General questioned him and he informed us the head of the train was attacked and the enemy in force was formed across our road. Just ahead several field officers rode by confirming the tidings. This was a shock. I had to that moment been tenaciously incredulous of an enemy in our rear. This seemed proof positive; in fact, I saw a body of troops indicated as the enemy and waited to hear the opening cannon.

We rode forward at dead silence, each heart manning itself for the death struggle. We met wagons and mounted teamsters rushing furiously back while the main line of wagons stood in the road stopped and many of them deserted by their drivers. Still no firing was heard. I rode close to the General summing up our position. I had till this time stoutly denied the possibility of an enemy in our rear. I was mortified at the utter failure of my judgment. I saw little way for any of us but an honorable death, for with Ewell in our front, Jackson must of course be close in our rear. The desperate attempt to cut our way through was all that was left for us. . . . I saw the General's countenance betokening this resolution. He said gravely, but kindly, "It seems we were mistaken in our calculation." It seemed this sentence conveyed a rebuke for my positive incredulity. I merely bowed and replied, "It seems so."

Approaching Middletown, five miles from Strasburg, the master teamster rode by cursing furiously at his underlings for stampeding the trains, threatening and ordering the fugitives back to their places. As soon as I heard this, I took heart and resumed my first opinion. It seems the head of our train was attacked at Newtown by about thirty Rebel horse. A number of sick on foot and in ambulances were captured and one sick man killed outright. An escort of our cavalry pursued them and captured one of their men. The prisoner was a youth from Bedford County and from his conversation I perceived he was well educated. In fact, he had left school to join the company. He said there were but parts of three companies of horse on our flank. We had started out of Strasburg with the intention of taking position at Middletown, but the march was still continued. I had strongly advised General Banks not to sacrifice anything at Strasburg. He said we would not, but at the same time precautionary orders were given to burn our stores there in case we retired still farther. With this information and the fact still potent that our communication with Winchester was open by road and telegraphy, the retrograde movement was continued. Captain Abert of the Topographical Engineers with Collis' Zouaves was left at Cedar Creek bridge to burn it when the last of our troops passed over.

At Newtown there was a demonstration on our right flank by some seventy-five or a hundred cavalry, to repel which a battery and a brigade of infantry were ordered out. We also heard a considerable firing of artillery in our rear. The enemy (Ashby probably) had attacked it near Middletown with horse and artillery. They cut off about fifty wagons, and captured the infantry escort and also the Zouaves D'Afrique, Collis and all. Thus ends the bodyguard for the present, and Collis' pretty little Jewish wife will tear her ebony hair for a while. Abert got off. Our baggage line was interspersed with wagons loaded with Negro families fleeing with the army. From the greybeard sire to the apish pickaninny at the breast, they streamed along, in wagons, on horseback, and on foot.

After leaving Newtown I left the staff and rode forward to Winchester, feeling so exhausted that I must have rest and food at all hazards. Since an early and hasty breakfast I had only tasted a bit of bread and butter with some Bolognian sausage from the General's snack. I overtook Colonel Brodhead and we rode together into town. He laughingly said the people of Winchester had prepared dinner for Jackson. I got a room at the hotel. I found to my surprise only the 10th Maine in Winchester instead of the five or six thousand men we expected. Went to bed immediately and slept the soundest and sweetest sleep I ever remember to have enjoyed.

MAY 25, SUNDAY.—Bright and pleasant. I rose late, dressed myself in a leisurely way, and went out for breakfast. I found the house in some confusion and nearly deserted. It was seven by the hotel clock. I asked the landlord if breakfast was ready, he said apologetically that all his Negroes had left, but they were trying to get something ready. I inquired if anything was going on. He said there was cannonading outside of town, but he knew no particulars. I supposed it was Ashby's battery and determined to go out and see as soon as I could get my breakfast. In the meantime I walked out to the stable to see how my horse had been treated. To my surprise I found the stable nearly deserted and my mare standing in her stall, saddled, bridled, and equipped. Several officers were at table, generally quartermasters and surgeons. I got a cup of coffee and a roll. A soldier came in and said to one of them, "They have driven our men off the hill." I took another roll and cup of coffee, paid my bill, when I saw a number of soldiers straggling rapidly by toward the Martinsburg pike. As I wondered at this, Lieutenant Horton, adjutant of the 2nd Massachusetts, rode by at a gallop. As he passed, he shouted, "Mount and ride. You have not a minute to spare. They are in the town." The rattle of small arms in close proximity reinforced his recommendation.

I mounted and as I rode, pistol shots were fired from windows and enclosures at myself and some straggling footmen that were passing. I saw the smoke and flame rolling up from our burning stores and saw our troops in full rout sweeping up the main street. There was a rapid crackling of small arms, chiefly pistol shots, all along the street. I saw at least twenty shots from houses and yards. Doubtless there were many more. As I drew up my horse within ten steps of a hydrant where several soldiers stopped to drink, I saw the flash of a piece from a gateway and one of the men fell over in the gutter apparently mortally wounded. I turned about and down the street saw another man falling, supported by his comrades. At the same time I saw Ruger's regiment (3rd Wisconsin) marching in organized column. I joined him and learned that we had formed in battle array on the other side of town, but after some maneuvers and some firing, we were outflanked and retired from the field, with the impression that we were greatly outnumbered.

As we passed out of Winchester on the Martinsburg road, I saw our straggling columns pouring out by every avenue with stragglers, horse and foot, covering the fields. When I got about two hundred yards down the road, the enemy rose the ridge on the northern end of Winchester and poured in a sharp fire of musketry into our confused rear. This quickened the movements. Accouterments and knapsacks began to be strewed along the route. Presently cannon boomed and the shot whistled and the shells hurtled over our heads. This seemed likely for a time to renew the scenes of Bull Run. At every report, the living mass started and quickened its motion as if shocked by electricity. Overcoats and knapsacks strewed the fields. I did not see many arms thrown away, however. Most of the regiments also kept their organization, but awfully diminished by losses and stragglers. One fellow rode by me with a groove ploughed in his horse's rump by a shell, a ghastly wound, but the animal traveled surprisingly.

Two or three miles out I joined the staff. I saw General Crawford first, who with a drawn sword was endeavoring to stop the fugitive stragglers. Seeing a dismounted trooper leading a sorely wounded horse, I got his sabre and assisted Crawford. General Banks then ordered some guns in position and with the rest of the staff gave his personal exertions to rally the retreat. By these means a considerable column was formed of loose infantry and several squads of cavalry organized. The sound of our own guns opening on the enemy's cavalry was very near disorganizing the men we had rallied, but at the junction of the dirt road from Charles Town we met two squads of Maryland cavalry who rushed forward with hearty cheers responded to by our men with the welcome cry of reinforcements. Although but these two squads appeared, the effect was good and the retreat was conducted better. Hatch's cavalry and the artillery kept the enemy more cautious in his pursuit and things began to assume a more hopeful appearance.

In the meantime the scenes along the road were pitiable and ludicrous. Droves of Negroes increasing at every step thickened the column. An enormously obese Negress and a mulatto woman dragging a heavy baby were weeping and gesticulating, "O Lord, they will kill us. They will kill us." Farther on was a grotesque fellow on a mule with a Negro wench behind him. Here half a dozen light wagons loaded with plunder and sprawling with babies were shoved out of the road to make room for a battery. Every black face wore an agonized and anxious expression. They said that Jackson had sworn to kill them all if he ever came back to this valley, which they seemed to believe religiously. Yet their masters tried to impress them with the belief that the Union troops would kill them if they got them. This latter story they did not accept at all and hence the retreat of the army. All that could move at all took up their bundles and walked, doubtless despoiling their masters as they left of everything they could lay their hands on. As the cannonade in our rear would increase, their bundles and stuffed pillow cases strewed the wayside. Broken wagons and dead horses now occasionally stopped the trains and were dragged aside. . . .

At Bunker Hill some talk was made of halting, but it was not attempted. I here saw a light wagon full of Negro women and children thrust off the causeway into the mill dam in imminent danger of turning over. I looked for the catastrophe every moment, but left without witnessing it. I suppose they got out. From this place until Martinsburg there was no disturbance of our retreat. During the day I saw a number of wounded with bloody gills and bandaged limbs riding on mules and horses of the abandoned teams. . . . As we neared Martinsburg I went forward with Captain Scheffler to find a position for making a stand. I chose the Big Spring. Scheffler thought the position too confined and one that could be turned. Nearing the town I again selected the rise at the southern end of town. Faulkner's house and enclosures made a strong point covering the Old Charles Town road while three parallel stone fences and a ridge for cannon covered the Winchester turnpike. Scheffler also thought this too limited and we passed on into the town. The streets were crowded with people all gazing with white lips. I heard my name called several times but I rode rapidly on to show Scheffler the position beyond the town commanding everything.

In the public square the officers of the provost guard came out. There was no news from Harpers Ferry. The telegraph operator had run off and carried his machinery. The cars had all been run back to Harpers Ferry. Not a breath of information could be gathered from that point, inducing the belief that the enemy had cut off the wires and the road. This was the greatest oversight in those conducting reinforcements. A word of information advising us that Harpers Ferry was intact would have decided us to remain at Martinsburg. As it was, this absolute isolation was ruinous and I ordered the trains to keep steadily toward Williamsport. We got into Martinsburg about 1:30 P.M. I rode over the position, which was a grand one, but had little hope that it would be taken advantage of. In the meantime the cannon opened and a brisk fire was kept up between our batteries. Returning to the public square I found the staff and General Banks at Staub's Hotel. . . .

Riding to the depot I saw Miss Lizzie Campbell with some other women at the depot ready to serve out the stores to the soldiers and people before the enemy came in. It was determined to use them in that way rather than destroy the buildings. Joined the staff and rode toward Williamsport. The cannon had been booming at intervals during our whole stay but now ceased. . . . It was now near six o'clock. I with General Gordon and Dr. King rode forward to Williamsport to secure food and night's lodging so much needed. The evening air was cool and delightful. The road was filled with straggling infantry dragging themselves along with difficulty, now and then dropping off into the fields and fence corners utterly exhausted. Gordon's brigade still kept the route but totally disorganized. Although nearing the terminus of a thirty-six mile march, many of them still marched strong and free. . . . An order came to General Gordon to halt his brigade and take position at Hainesville, the scene of Jackson's skirmish with Patterson's advance. He laughed at the futility of trying to execute the order. His men from mere exhaustion could not have stood up in line for five minutes. This was about sundown. Later our way was lighted by wagons and stores overthrown and burning. At Falling Waters a dozen or so were blazing together. The soldiers fell by dozens by the roadside and slept on the earth. They were scarcely distinguishable from stumps and stones in the twilight. I saw a woman leading a child about five years old and asked her how far that child had walked today. She replied, "Thirteen miles."

At length we arrived at the brow of a hill opposite Williamsport. Here were a hundred blazing campfires illuminating the wreck of Banks' army. A ferry of one scow run by a wire rope was all the means of crossing and this was engaged in getting over the sick and wounded. . . . The ford was swelled and only passable for high, strong horses. The entrance was blocked up by swamped wagons, which had stuck in the road and deep water while men were trying to extricate the braying and drowning mules. Seeing no better chance for a night's lodging, I dashed in and presently the water was sweeping over my horse's back. Keeping my eye upon a fire on the opposite bank, I pushed on. Several times my faithful mare was brought to a swim and once made a bad stumble so that her head went under. About midway I was pleased to see a dragoon following me and my animal being light I fell back and kept her under the lee of his more powerful animal to shield her as much as possible from the force of the current which threatened to sweep us away. In this way I got across wet to the middle and thus rode into town. I found things less crowded than I expected and by dint of perseverance managed to have my horse put away. The first man I saw here was Colonel Clark who had just got in from Washington and told me that Fremont and McDowell would forthwith throw forty thousand men on the enemy's rear at Front Royal and Harrisonburg. This was a good soporific. Getting off my wet clothes I got to bed and thus for me ended the eventful 25th of May, 1862.

MAY 26, MONDAY.—Bright and warm. On the street was a motley crowd of officer and privates, Negroes and hangers-on, refugees white and black all buzzing and felicitating each other and narrating their hairbreadth escapes. Many an unknown hand grasped mine with warm congratulation of my escape—privates and niggers alike. . . . The whole grass-covered surface of the bluff between Williamsport and the canal was covered with men asleep in the sun. At the point of the bank a signal party was operating and below on the shore troops were landing rapidly by means of pontoon boats, five in number, used as ferryboats. On the Virginia shore still remained many wagons and troops in bivouac. Two batteries were planted on the bluffs, protecting the stream and the baggage on the other side. The Virginia brink was lined with Negroes with their heaps of plunder. Many horses and wagons were stolen by soldiers wishing to take advantage of the retreat to get to their homes northward. Many more doubtless would have kept running if exhausted nature had not forbid. I met a Zouave who told me ten of their company had escaped.

Seeing Colonel Clark mounted and ready to start for Harpers Ferry I joined him, engaging Captain Scheffler to make my apologies to General Banks who was then over the river. Clark and myself rode to Sharpsburg by the river road. Thence we rode to Harpers Ferry by the usual route, night overtaking us at the five-mile schoolhouse. . . . Where the road reaches the river we found the pickets and from thence to the railroad bridge we passed a whole brigade sleeping on the rocks so thickly strewn and packed that our horses could scarcely find room to pass. At the ferry we found no one and Colonel Clark undertaking to pass the boat over, I held the horses while he and the orderly pulled the rope. Disembarked and repaired to headquarters on Shenandoah Street. We found here General Hamilton in citizen's dress sent up as military adviser, General Saxton,[6] and Colonel Miles.[7] Having briefly narrated our adventures, we found sleeping quarters. Mine was on a sofa in the entry at Hamilton's quarters. I slept indifferently well notwithstanding the orderlies were coming in at every hour of the night, and I could hear the monstrous lies they were reporting—an advance in force and imminent attack by the enemy.

MAY 27, TUESDAY.—Fair. As we passed through Sharpsburg yesterday we saw a number of men, stragglers from Banks' column escaped to Maryland. Some of the them had been arrested by the citizens in Shepherdstown and their arms taken from them. This being known, the Sharpsburgers went down with a piece of cannon and threatened

6. Rufus Saxton, USMA '49, had an undistinguished career during the Civil War. Earlier he had served with McClellan in West Virginia. After Harpers Ferry, he was sent to the Department of the South as a military governor. Saxton retired from the army in 1888.

7. Dixon S. Miles, USMA '24, had commanded a reserve unit at Bull Run. Charged with the defense of Harpers Ferry in March, 1862, he surrendered the garrison to Jackson on September 16 and died the same day of wounds.

to bombard the town unless the prisoners were released and their arms restored. It was speedily done.

We understand there are from five to seven hundred of the retreating soldiers arrived here. This will reduce the loss of Banks considerably. Clark told me that in his interview with the cabinet, they at first thought lightly of his fears in regard to Banks. Then as he enforced his views, they considered them more seriously and at length from the telegrams from the General himself they agreed to move up reinforcements. The news of the attack on Kenley came. Then came the panic and Fremont and McDowell were both ordered to reinforce en masse. . . .

MAY 28, WEDNESDAY.—Threatened rain. Went forward with a reconnoissance toward Charles Town. We saw nothing until we arrived at the hill near the Charles Town toll gate where a sharp fire of musketry was opened on our advance by some Rebel pickets stationed on the road at the fair ground. Ashby was there as usual, circus-riding up and down. We brought up our battery and opened with shells. I asked the Captain to fire low to save the town. Half a dozen shots cleared them out. In the meantime, flanking parties of cavalry were sent around the town. Having cleaned out the pickets, the artillery opened on our own troops. Three or four tumbled off their horses, which caused great excitement among the fools at the supposed loss of the enemy. I stopped the firing and urged the Colonel to advance his infantry now that the enemy were gone. Instead of this, he ordered three cheers for Captain Loder. The whole command responded. Somebody then called three cheers for somebody else and so they went on cheering like fools at a public meeting.

Riding forward, I got the cavalry to advance, which they did in good style, notwithstanding some straggling shots against them. When I got to Mrs. Hunter's house, I stopped and stood guard over it. The troops went firing down every cross street as they rushed to the other end of town. Some stopped and, breaking open the town hall, set fire to it. As it began to burn fiercely, I endeavored to get some soldiers and then some citizens to put it out. The soldiers did nothing and the citizens who showed willingness to act were deterred through fear of the soldiers. I appealed to the colonel of infantry just marching by and then to the major commanding the rear guard, but they flatly refused or evaded my request. The flames rose fiercely and threatened to destroy the village. Seeing a young officer with a squad of men halted in front of Redmonds, I inquired his name and corps.

He said he was Captain Healy of the 8th New York Cavalry. I asked him to put himself and squad under my command. He cheerfully did so. I put him to guard the streets and then invited the citizens to get out their engines, and to prevent the further progress of the fire. Negroes, women, and all turned in, and in an hour or two the hall was burned down but all the adjacent buildings safe.

Passing to the lower part of the town I saw the colonel of the regiment ordering the opening of a store. I inquired as to its propriety. He said he had been ordered to search for Confederate arms and stores. This was a lie. Seeing his men carrying out tobacco I asked him if those were Confederate stores. He looked abashed and called to the men to stop taking the tobacco, but they paid no attention to him whatever. I left in disgust. Returning to the house I got a milk toddy, my dinner, and a cup of coffee. While we dined, cannon began to roar at the other end of town and scattered horsemen galloped to the rear. Presently a whole squadron rushed by as if the devil was after them. I also noticed the infantry double-quicking it up the street in a body. I rode down far enough to see the smoke of Ashby's cannon crowning the high ground on the old Winchester road. Everything looked like a disgraceful stampede. For the first two miles the road was strewed with plunder gotten by the rascals during their three-hour sojourn in the village.

Several miles from town I saw a countryman riding down the road guarded by a file of cavalry. I recognized my friend and cousin, Joe Crane. He was riding a work horse without saddle. His clothes were spotted with blood and his hand bloody and maimed. His face was livid but firm. He said a trooper had come to his house and was taking his horses before his eyes. He remonstrated and resisted. The man sabred him and Joe shot him dead. I grasped his hand, promised my best service, and advised him to report immediately with his guard to headquarters. He rode on and left me sad and appalled. Joe was my father's favorite nephew and his best friend. He must be saved. . . .

Getting back to Smallwood's hill the whole army of ten or fifteen thousand men was in commotion and forming line of battle. The reconnoissance instead of forcing Ashby to show his strength ran away at the first shot, each exceeding the other in lies to cover his cowardice. I met General Hamilton and possessed him of Joe Crane's case and afterwards the history of the reconnoissance. He laughed and returned to town incredulous of the approaching battle.

Saw a Yankee woman at headquarters who had just arrived from Winchester. She had a pass from the Confederate authority there and appears to have conversed freely with their leading military men. She says the people of Winchester expected Jackson confidently for some days before he came and were making preparations for him. She says that several days before our retreat she saw a horseman clad in grey clothes, the homespun dress of a farmer, ride into Winchester. His military air was unmistakable, however, notwithstanding his disguise. She saw him approached by several citizens and earnest words were exchanged, such as "in great force"—"will be here in a few days" —etc. She did not know to whom he alluded at the time but guesses now. She was out to see the battle of Sunday morning and saw our troops retreating. The Confederates following poured in at every street like a flood of dirty water. They were grey, ragged, and

CONFEDERATE STRAGGLERS

unwashed, clad in all fashions, but hats, beards, and persons all of one uniform dust color. With hideous yells and war whoops this mass of twelve thousand men poured through the streets, rushing to stores and houses, demanding food and drink, others greeting friends and acquaintances. Stories of burning the hospitals and maltreatment of the sick she does not verify. . . .

She says General [Isaac R.] Trimble and others conversed with her freely and told her they were now going to carry war into the North, break through our lines, arouse Maryland, and occupy Philadelphia.[8] They gave her a pass without difficulty and exacted no promise of silence. The number of men in their column was estimated at from eighteen to thirty thousand. She says they took but few prisoners from us and most of these were the sick and hangers-on about our army, of which we had a great number, more than should have been permitted. These with some nurses and camp women were herded in the courthouse yard to make a show for the people.

MAY 29, THURSDAY.—Fair and warm. In the evening saw a deserter from a Louisiana regiment named Clarke, who says he was pressed into service. He says that the Confederate force yesterday was encamped two miles beyond Charles Town and that they advanced today, one brigade with a battery crossing at Key's Ferry to occupy Loudoun Heights. Ewell's force was in front of us at Halltown and Jackson was going toward Shepherdstown, their object being to cross into Maryland, flank, and if possible capture us. Today a cloud of dust rose from the turnpike at Charles Town and approaching, continued to rise as far as Halltown and even this side. There was also a line of dust cloud apparently on the Shepherdstown road clear across the horizon and another line towards the Shenandoah. These clouds indicated the movements of large bodies of men, although at the time I thought they might be caused by movements of Ashby's Cavalry. While we stood watching, the regiments were drawn up in line of battle behind the crest of the hill and the chaplains were praying and encouraging them. I had no faith in the enemy being in force, and therefore the scene seemed ridiculous rather than solemn. Returning to town the prisoner was called and after examining him for some time I became convinced that his story was true and expressed that opinion to General Saxton. A council of war was held, wherein reliability of this information was discussed. The result was that the information was accepted

8. Trimble's remark about Jackson's invasion of the North was undoubtedly a ruse to deceive the Union commanders and to permit Jackson to carry off the stores captured at Winchester.

and during the night all our stores, baggage, and part of our troops retired to the Maryland side. I slept in an open entry and had a poor night of it, scouts tramping in and out and doors slamming all night. At two o'clock I rose and with some difficulty found my servant and horse, had him saddled, and mounted ready for any emergency.

MAY 30, FRIDAY.—Fair. The crossing of the river was a slow process. A rope ferry with one boat and a single-track trestled railroad bridge were the only passage. A retreat under any pressure by these insufficient lines and by raw troops would have been disastrous in the extreme. As it was, the crowd and danger were considerable. Mounted men led their horses over and several leaped forty feet into the river. The horses were taken from wagons and artillery, and the wheeled vehicles pushed and drawn over by hand. One falling upon an overthrown locomotive engine which lay in the stream was instantly killed, while strange to say several others swam out and were saved. I then remembered the ford made by the engineers of Patterson's army and went to the point where I found some troopers already trying it. It was deep and tortuous but quite practicable for horses, so I returned to town relieved in regard to the means of personal retreat in case of necessity. . . .

I being without a position or orders here had attached myself to Hamilton's staff. He going to Baltimore, I was again a waif in the crowd. Colonel Miles seeing me said I should cross over to see the battery of Dahlgren guns, and having nothing else to do, I took his advice. My horse, otherwise restive and scary, was led over like a willing lass, as wisely careful as if she appreciated the necessity of it. Mounting the Maryland Heights I saw our battery of nine-inch Dahlgrens and ship's howitzers commanding the whole area of Harpers Ferry and also the Shenandoah mountain. It was manned by a detachment of the naval brigade. I felt little apprehension of any successful attack from these points. . . .

After dinner the rain ceased and the cannonading beyond Harpers Ferry became more rapid. At the top of the ridge overhanging the town and crowned by the Superintendent's house I found our troops in force and engaged in throwing up intrenchments. Trees and hedges were cut down and some eight or ten guns were in position. Smallwood's on Old Furnace Ridge seemed deserted except by a troop of cavalry and some loose infantry engaged in gathering up our camp equipage and tents left standing from the previous day. This looked ominous and riding forward to the ridge I met a lieutenant who asked me if I was going to draw the enemy's fire. He said they had driven us from the ridge and were in force on the opposing ridge towards Halltown and about fifteen hundred yards distant. I now perceived that the fire had ceased and that all our men were behind the hill under cover. Riding to the top I found some stragglers covered by bushes obscuring the enemy. As soon as I appeared on the crest, they commenced loading their guns and ranging them. I saw their artillery on either side of the turnpike road and several hundred infantry lying along a fence in the edge of the wood which crowned the hill. Presently their guns opened. Half a dozen shots were fired before they got my range, but the shells began to burst over my head in close proximity and hurtled to the right and left of me, landing on the slopes of the Potomac bluffs beyond Bolivar. They used six guns and their practice was good. Satisfied with this reconnoissance, I returned to the Ferry and saw a number of men on Loudoun Heights standing on the block houses. . . .

I saw Colonel Miles, who told me the enemy had showed twelve guns in front. With these accumulated facts pressing upon me I now began for the first time seriously to entertain the opinion that the enemy might be in earnest about invading Maryland. They must certainly have been fully posted in regard to the movements of McDowell and Fremont, yet there seemed undoubted evidence that they were in full force before Harpers Ferry and boldly pushing upon our retiring lines. The report of their crossing at Key's Ferry was also verified by their occupation of Loudoun Heights. I must confess that I was profoundly troubled by this aspect of affairs. The more so as I knew how incompetent our raw and undisciplined troops were to prevent the execution of their purpose. It was certainly a wild and desperate venture on the enemy's part, but it was like Jackson. . . .

At headquarters I observed a well-dressed regiment in the street and then General Saxton very much excited walked to headquarters, followed by half a dozen officers. On the steps he turned to the colonel and lieutenant colonel of the regiment (New York 71st). "Your men," said he, "are poltroons and cowards. They have refused to take the oath of allegiance in face of the enemy, and I don't want them about me." The officers attempted to explain with faces expressing mingled anger and mortification. He would listen to nothing, however, and I left the disagreeable scene. At Sandy Hook I retired early that I might arise strong to meet the events of the next day.

MAY 31, SATURDAY.—Fair and variable. . . . I started to ride over to the Ferry, but found the bridge occupied with railroad trains. The boat was on the other side with a wagon on board and stationary. Two men had just been dragged out of the river, drowned in attempting to ford, so that the chances for getting over seemed few. Found a company of cavalry, New York 5th under Major [George H.] Gardner, on its way to Antietam Furnace. I determined to accept their escort and to return to General Banks. . . . Arrived in Williamsport in the afternoon and at headquarters found them very easy about the enemy. An account of things at Harpers Ferry and fears of the invasion of Maryland stampeded the General and a dispatch was immediately sent to Washington advising them of the condition of things.

I was delighted to meet Captain Abert and to know he was not captured as supposed, but got back through Bath and Hancock with the Zouaves and New York Cavalry. He was left with the Zouaves to burn the bridge at Cedar Creek and was entirely cut off from the main body by the enemy's attack at Middletown. In attempting to regain their line of march, the Zouaves met a regiment of Rebels and checked them with several volleys, behaving with admirable coolness. Retiring they fell back upon a battery of Federal artillery and a battalion of cavalry also cut off. This detachment made its way by backroads to within a short distance of Winchester, the battery rejoining the main body. The others were not so fortunate, but got out on the Bloomery road, passing through Pughtown. Next day he passed through Bath and saw all my friends there. The party got to Williamsport safe, with thirty-four wagons and General Hatch's staff baggage, supposed to be lost. But two of the Zouaves were killed. The old teamster whose likeness I have drawn, when closely pressed, overthrew his wagon, killed his mules, and was himself killed. He was a Frenchman of Crimean notoriety.

After tea I went to headquarters and presently a man was brought in by the patrol, who proved to be one of our spies just from Martinsburg and Winchester. He says they occupied Martinsburg with eight regiments of infantry and committed many outrages, seizing every eatable they could find. Ashby is reported to have said, "We have got ourselves in a bad box," and everything went to show they were in desperate circumstances as they thought themselves hemmed in and surrounded. In a moment the nature of the enemy's movement on Harpers Ferry flashed upon me. They were aware of their position and making a demonstration there to enable them to cross the Shenan-

TEAMSTERS

doah at Key's and Snicker's Ferry and escape southward east of the
Blue Ridge. The whole matter seemed palpable and cleared my mind
of much perplexity. I expressed my views to the General and now
urged the advance upon Martinsburg.

JUNE 1, SUNDAY.—Rainy and variable. . . . The news from Harpers
Ferry is as I expected. The enemy has retired. A letter from Ed
Pendleton assures me that the Secessionists of Martinsburg have behaved with great propriety during the late Confederate occupation and
that Jackson forbade arrests to be made, promptly releasing such as
had been arrested. . . . The latest news is that Jackson has retreated to
Winchester. If this is true it seems likely he will escape, as he would
scarcely have risked himself there if he had not some assistance.

JUNE 2, MONDAY.—Fair and warm. . . . Our retreat from Strasburg
has certainly been an extraordinary affair. Six thousand men overloaded with baggage and impeded by a thousand sick and several
thousand fugitives have retired in the face of twenty thousand men
with comparatively little loss themselves and inflicting a very serious

loss upon the enemy. They brought off all their artillery and all their important baggage and have lost not over six or eight hundred men.... Returning to camp we find Major [Wilder] Dwight and Dr. [Lincoln R.] Stone, returned from Winchester where they were prisoners. Dwight was captured in the streets while assisting some wounded and Stone remained with the sick and wounded. They say our prisoners and wounded were treated with the greatest courtesy. There is not a Confederate soldier on this side of that town.... When Captain Abert was wandering near Winchester, a lady from a country house ran out and earnestly warned him not to go forward toward the Martinsburg road. That road, she said, is in possession of our troops. The Captain thanked her and asked to whom he was indebted for this service. She said her name was Lovett and added, "I have lost my husband in the Southern army, and I would not wish any other woman to suffer as I have."

JUNE 3, TUESDAY.—Fair and warm. Rode over the river to Martinsburg. Found the troops in possession, behaving very badly. They were robbing and insulting everyone, searching houses and breaking into stores.... When our troops left here on May 25th, a number of women with tears and grief lowered the U. S. flag and gave it to a trusty messenger to carry after our army to Maryland that it might not be desecrated. The Confederate troops who came here were chiefly Ashby's men, although most of the young men from here enlisted in other corps came to see their friends. They took everything they could lay their hands upon in the way of clothing and food, especially salt, sugar, and coffee, but in other respects did not misbehave. The younger ones talked wildly about going into Maryland, but there seems to have been no special intention of that sort among the leaders. Their coming to Martinsburg was in all probability not in their original plan.... General Banks and staff came into town about five o'clock in the afternoon, the troops had a dress parade, and things assumed a more cheerful aspect....

JUNE 4, WEDNESDAY.—Raining hard.... The move was ordered for Winchester. All along the road the remnants of the flight were scattered. The streets of the town looked forlorn in the extreme. From what I can learn here, Jackson is gone beyond pursuit. Thus culminates this disgraceful affair, the most disgraceful to the Federal armies that has occurred during the whole war. I am utterly humiliated to have been mixed up in it. Fremont came around by Moorefield and Wardensville (instead of crossing to Woodstock) and fell upon Jackson's rear. He is pursuing him with some energy, but without much hope of overtaking his more alert and active enemy.

At supper I sat beside an insignificant, boyish-looking man in citizen dress. Seeing Colonel [Othneil] De Forest opposite, I opened conversation. The little fellow at my elbow was struck with something I said, and with a marked German accent began questioning me closely. His questions showed military knowledge and rare astuteness, so that I guessed who it was. Presently he invited me to come to his room and introduced himself—Major General Sigel.[9] I went up with him and pointed out localities on the map and gave him some other information about the country. . . .

JUNE 5, THURSDAY.—Cloudy and drizzling. . . . Was stopped by a man named Meredith, late of Baltimore, who was very joyful to see me and being drunk and having been in Italy, kissed and embraced me. As he was a clean, well-dressed fellow I did not resent it. Met some reporters of newspapers who seemed sneaking, disagreeable fellows, except Barnard, who is gentlemanly and agreeable. He promised to write a letter on the subject of the lies circulated about Rebel atrocities. It will do good. Some arrests have been made today of persons accused of shooting soldiers in the streets on May 25th. A boy and a Methodist minister are the parties. . . .

JUNE 7, SATURDAY.—Bright and warm. Went to see the Paymaster and found that he was not willing to pay me, unless I had a certificate from the General that I was a regularly commissioned officer. As the General knew less of the subject than I did, this seemed absurd. I therefore determined to go to Washington and settle the matter definitely. The General gave me leave for ten days. . . . Rode to Charles Town, a thunder storm menacing. On the porch saw my wife and daughter and had a joyful meeting. The rain came down immediately after I entered the house, where I spent one of the happiest evenings of my life. . . .

JUNE 9, MONDAY.—Clear and warm. . . . My wife, daughter, and myself went to Harpers Ferry in the carriage. Got my ladies aboard a small boat and was ferried across the river, still high and rapid. Arrived in Baltimore without remarkable incident. The elegant rooms at the Eutaw House looked especially cheerful. Listened to a grand

9. Franz Sigel (1824-1902), a German immigrant to the United States, was successful in the western campaigns of 1861. Under Pope he commanded a division in the Bull Run Campaign. He later led the Twelfth Corps. His failure at New Market in 1864 terminated his command in the field.

serenade given to General Wool, who had just arrived to take command of the city.

JUNE 10, TUESDAY.—Clouds and rain. . . . Started at five o'clock for Washington in the train. Arrived in due time and took lodgings at Brown's Hotel.

JUNE 11, WEDNESDAY.—Fair and cooler. Newspapers report that Fremont had a collision with Jackson near Harrisonburg, losing eight hundred men and that General Ashby was killed on the other side. Went to the War Department and ascertained the condition of my affairs. Got my commission made out dated March 22nd. This leaves me to lose one month's pay, which pay the officer says should be made up to me by paying me at the rate of $125 per month, the same I was receiving in the topographical corps. I was questioned as to continuance with Birney and agreed to give up my position there for the chance of getting a better one from Pierpont,[10] who is at Willard's. . . . Walked to Willard's to see him and found him in his room surrounded by his constituents, he lying on the bed with his coat off. I was very politely received. We talked over the campaign in the Valley and then over my own affairs. He engaged to meet me tomorrow that we might go to the Secretary of War where he hoped to procure me the appointment of major. . . . Pierpont is a sound, direct thinking man. He desires the abolition of slavery in Virginia and would divide the state to accomplish that object for Western Virginia. He sees the necessity of authorized severity in dealing with the Rebels after the war and fully agrees with me upon that point: that unless the party who made the rebellion is crushed by confiscating and disenfranchising its leaders, the war will have been fought in vain.

JUNE 12, THURSDAY.—Fair. . . . Pierpont, on examining into his regiments, found a vacant lieutenant colonelcy of cavalry and wrote to the adjutant general of Virginia to send me the commission therefore. He assured me that I need give myself no further trouble about it. The newspapers say that Shields has been licked by Jackson and they say so little about it that I fear it may be something more serious than at first reported. . . .

JUNE 13, FRIDAY.—Fair and warm. . . . I went to the war office and

10. Francis H. Pierpont (1814-99) had been active in Western Virginia politics before the war. When Virginia seceded, he was elected provisional governor of loyal Virginia. After Richmond fell in 1865, Pierpont moved his government there, taking Strother along as adjutant general of Virginia. In 1868 he was replaced and returned to his legal practice in West Virginia.

presently was invited to a private conference with the Secretary [Edwin Stanton]. I expressed the opinion that our infantry was our chief dependence and that artillery was comparatively useless in the Valley. We had erred there in trusting too much to it. The Secretary heard with attention and said he was pleased to find my views accorded with his. He said Banks had called for five batteries and Shields for several, an inordinate proportion, and he would not send them all they wanted. I suggested the idea of concentrating the troops under one leader. He replied thoughtfully—"Then Fremont will be in command." I did not reply except to say that one head was better than many. The Secretary said he had known me long and agreeably through my writing and if I was as accomplished a soldier as I was an artist and writer, the country had much to thank me for. In describing our retreat from Strasburg I took occasion to mention General Banks' personal bearing as courageous and cool. He asked if General Banks had not good assistant commanders. I named Williams, Gordon, and Hatch. He said the retreat was admirably conducted and was the military feat of the war, but I don't think he cared to give the credit to Banks. This probably because Banks's political friends have attacked him unsparingly.

On entering the office I met General Meigs.[11] He talked with me a long time about the relations of the departments with our army in the Valley. He says the commanders there have had full latitude to use all the resources which had been accorded to them. They seemed to think they could not blow their noses without orders. They fell back on the Government for everything and did nothing for themselves. Then they blamed their ill success on the Government. . . . I return to my original opinions in regard to the conduct of the campaign. We ought to have cleaned out the Valley in three weeks after we entered it. . . .

[Strother returned to Winchester on June 17.]

11. Montgomery C. Meigs (1816-92), USMA '36, had supervised the construction of the Capitol dome before the war. From May, 1861, until the end of the war he was Quartermaster General of the army.

III

With Pope at Cedar Mountain

June 18, 1862—August 15, 1862

Although Jackson's army had long since moved east of the Blue Ridge, the Army of the Shenandoah marched warily up the Valley to the Strasburg fortifications. June passed with little activity save concentration, and Strother summarized affairs when he wrote, "The Government sends generals and artillery when we want men." On the Peninsula, McClellan held his own against a force half his size.

Meanwhile, changes were afoot. On June 26 General Pope, a recent arrival from the West, assumed command of the Army of Virginia, consisting of McDowell's, Banks's and Sigel's corps—Fremont having resigned. On the following day Captain Strother was called to Washington to assist the new commander in the preparation of maps for the approaching campaign. Pope's strategy was to advance upon Gordonsville and Charlottesville, to protect Washington, and to threaten Richmond from the north. Planning a concentration near Culpeper, Pope took the field at the end of July, after a costly delay. Since McClellan was withdrawing the Army of the Potomac from the Peninsula, Lee detached Jackson to contest the advance of Pope's army.

On August 9 Jackson fell upon Banks at Cedar Mountain and defeated him before the rest of the Union army arrived on the field. Sigel had been lost in the woods; Banks attacked when he should have retreated. General Pope and staff—including David Strother, who had received his commission as lieutenant colonel a short time before—arrived on the field about sunset and unwittingly occupied a position that was fired upon by both armies. On the next day the Northern and Southern armies faced each other, neither of them taking the offensive.

June 18, Wednesday.—Warm and variable. . . . General Hatch seeking quarters went to Mrs. Logan's house. She declined to let him have rooms, saying there were none to be spared. He persisted, and she said if he came to the house, she would have to leave. He said she was free to leave and he should locate himself. He asked what rooms could be assigned to him. Mrs. Logan said there were four vacant rooms in the attic. Hatch was indignant and selected three of the first floor rooms, parlors, etc. Mrs. Logan, seeing this determination, seized a light stand with an ornamental flower basket upon it and undertook to carry it away. Hatch ordered her to return it, saying she should remove no article of furniture from those rooms until she had apologized for offering the attic. . . .

They insist here that Ashby is dead, although the people will not believe it. What better end for a gallant and chivalrous gentleman. He was a man limited in mental powers but of grave and generous nature. He believed he fought in a just cause and, having made a fine reputation, died gallantly in the midst of his renown. Better that than to have lived to be conquered, impoverished, disenfranchised, and exiled perhaps. I lament Ashby like Deloraine did Richard of Musgrave:

> I'd give the lands of Deloraine
> Stout Musgrave were alive again.

I have never blamed Ashby for the arrest of my father. He did not order it and doubtless would have disapproved of it. McDonald is the great offender in that matter, and if the Lord spares him, he will have to account to me therefore. . . .[1]

June 19, Thursday.—Fair and pleasant. . . . Walked toward the depot to see the burnt storehouses. About twenty buildings were burnt, those facing the Union Hotel, now hospital. General Banks has returned from Washington. He wears a Puritan hat, which becomes him as it is accordant with his face and makes a strong characteristic picture. Perkins talks rather despondingly in regard to our military position. This tone he must have got from the General or from Washington. I do not like it much, but I do not see that a

1. At the beginning of the war John Strother, a Unionist of Morgan County, had been arrested and tried for treason to the state of Virginia. He was released, but his incarceration may have hastened his death, which occurred in January, 1861. His son believed that Colonel Angus McDonald, a former friend of his father, was responsible for John Strother's imprisonment. The death of Colonel McDonald in 1865, following his capture by Hunter's army, was attributed to David Strother, who was at that time Hunter's chief of staff.

reinforcement of twelve thousand men should alarm us, who have equal if not superior force. Went with Major Perkins to visit General Hatch. He says the young lady seems quite resigned and is glad, since the rooms had to be taken, that he took them. . . .

JUNE 20, FRIDAY.—Fair and cool. . . . We dined and took the road for Strasburg. The people of Winchester, seeing the movement intended, were in high state of excitement, some supposing it meant a retrograde. Many Negroes questioned me about it, and I gave them the consolation of knowing we were going to Strasburg. As the staff wagons started down the cross street, several groups of citizens appeared to be watching intently to see whether they turned northward or southward. When the train took the Strasburg road, there was an amount of whispering and violent gesticulation among them evidencing surprise and disgust. Three miles on my route the General overtook me in his mule carriage and asked me to ride with him. I gave my horse to a clerk and got into the carriage.

Approaching Middletown we saw two sentinels at the gate of a country house, and on inquiring we ascertained it was the headquarters of General Sigel. The General stopped and we went in. While the two generals talked together they were joined by a third, Major General Fremont—a middle-sized, middle-aged man with a weatherbeaten face and a grizzled beard, shot and thin.[2] He looked like a man who had seen hardship. I was introduced and observed the Path-Finder narrowly. His countenance was alert and his eye quick, his manner modest and gentlemanly. In due time the conference broke up, and we rode on to our encampment a little way beyond Middletown.

From the conference I learn that Shields will probably be retained at Front Royal, thus giving us predominance in the Valley. In that case we need fear no attack but will probably take the offensive. In putting together all our information before and after the raid of Jackson, we are unable to assign any rational motive for his conduct at Harpers Ferry. Why did he lie before Harpers Ferry for four days when he must have known of the preparations to cut off his retreat? What the devil was he after?

2. John C. Fremont (1813-90) had been placed in charge of the Department of the West early in the war. Largely through his radicalism, he was removed and placed in command of the Union troops in Western Virginia, with orders to co-operate with the force in the Valley of Virginia. Outgeneraled by Jackson and affronted when John Pope was appointed his superior, Fremont resigned from the army, relinquishing his command to Sigel.

JUNE 21, SATURDAY.—Fair and cool. The time is approaching for another battle. Shields is to withdraw from Front Royal today. Our combined force will then be left at less than twenty thousand men. Reinforcements will be sent in from all quarters as rapidly as possible to fill up the numbers but our army will be composed of odds and ends partially disorganized. The New York 8th Cavalry is semi-mutinous and will be sent back to Baltimore to be reorganized. They have refused to serve as light artillery. . . .

At the Winchester depot I heard the surgeon of the Bucktail rifles telling the particulars of the death of Ashby. During the skirmish he came forward to order his men to cease firing and to charge the Federal troops. His horse, pierced by a ball, fell with him and as Ashby rose, he also fell, shot through the chest by a rifleman. The rifleman himself was instantly killed, and the doctor exhibited the bullet taken from his body. . . .

JUNE 25, WEDNESDAY.—Clear and cold after a blustering night. The early morning between sunrise and breakfast is the time in which I most enjoy physical existence. The lie-a-bed habits of our staff astonish me, as they lose the best part of the day for action and business.

We now have in this department three major generals and ten brigadiers and about twenty thousand fighting men with, all told, about 120 pieces of artillery. The Government sends generals and artillery when we want men. There seems to be a bad feeling among the troops—discouragement and a sense of inferiority which will tell unfavorably if they get into action. . . . Crawford reports a reconnoissance through Milford on the Luray road and thence across the ridge to Washington and Sperryville meeting no enemy. News indicates that Jackson is moving toward New Creek. . . .

JUNE 27, FRIDAY.—Fair and warm. The news that Ewell is marching on New Creek is not much credited here. In fact, the idea that the enemy have so large a force in our front seems improbable, as the former army of twenty thousand was nearly perished for want of subsistence, and how could it be increased without depots and transportation, two things in which we know they are deficient? Visited Fremont's artillery camp and examined a twenty-gun battery of steel breech-loading guns, one and one-half-inch caliber, a sort of light mountain artillery. If they work well they might be made very formidable, but these seem to be too complicated in their loading arrangements, liable to get out of order, and are not well spoken of by artillery officers. They have not yet proved in battle.

After tea I rode with the General and Copeland to Fremont's headquarters in the Hite house, an old English manorial dwelling characteristically picturesque. The Major Generals talked privately together, no doubt upon the subject of General Pope's appointment to supreme command in all Virginia outside McClellan's district, thus superseding at one sweep Fremont, McDowell, Banks, and Sigel. Major [Leonidas] Haskell, commander of the Fremont bodyguard, talked with Copeland on the force, seeming highly indignant at this move. I did not enter into the conversation at all. The conference ended and we rode back to Sigel's quarters and stopped there, where the General had a private conference with Sigel. The aides and adjutants of his staff were still more openly indignant than at Fremont's quarters, although it was known that Pope's appointment did not change his position in the least. Both Fremont and Banks ranked Pope, but Sigel is junior to them all, so he had nothing to complain of. The result of it all is, as I was told by Copeland, that Fremont has asked to be relieved of his command and has been relieved. Copeland urged General Banks to do the same, but the General says nothing and will keep his own counsel. Unless there is more in the case than I know of, he will not resign or withdraw. This would be the great part and, from what I know of General Banks, he will play it. . . .

The General asked me if I knew Pope. I told him I did not. He said Pope had telegraphed him to send [Captain Samuel B.] Holabird and Beckwith to meet him, also Captain *Streeter*. As there is no one of that name in the division, the General thought he might mean myself and telegraphed asking if it was not Captain Strother he wanted. No answer as yet.

JUNE 28, SATURDAY.—Fair and hot. Before breakfast, General Fremont with a large retinue rode over to visit us as he was passing. Our General had just risen and came out to meet him. Fremont had on his usual uniform and a white slouched hat. His manner was graceful, dignified, and prepossessed. They had a short conversation; then he mounted and rode away to Martinsburg on his way to New York. At breakfast the General received a telegram which he handed to me. It contained the verification of the supposition that the former telegram calling for Captain Streeter meant Strother. Upon this I got ready to go to Washington. . . .

Entered Winchester and got a lunch at Taylor's Hotel. The Negro waiter said of Colonel Ashby that he was a general favorite and a true gentleman, sober and considerate. There were few like him in the Southern army. The officers were generally hard drinkers and rowdy in their habits. The Negro observed, "You know, we can tell who are gentleman."

Dr. McCormick, a Union man like his brother-in-law Judge Parker, was in a terrible stew about the policy toward Negroes. He declared the army was systematically employed in running them off, and the war had degenerated into an abolition raid. I told him that the abolitionizing of the Border States was an inevitable incident of the war but not its intention. Although a strong party had endeavored to make it the object of the war, I did not see that it had got the upper hand of the conservatism yet and I still had faith that it would not. At 5:30 in the afternoon I started for Charles Town in the train. Talked with an officer of Fremont's Corps who was at the Battle of Cross Keys. He said their left wing was severely handled, but their center under Milroy was victorious and pressing the enemy back, while the right wing was intact, not having fired a shot. To their surprise and disgust, Fremont ordered them to withdraw. Another said Fremont's army stood for a day and a half drawn up in order of battle on a road parallel to the Strasburg pike and about five miles back of it, when Jackson was passing by on his retreat. Having got all his prisoners and wagons safely across Cedar Creek, Jackson massed his force in position and rested for a day and a half. When he moved, Fremont attacked him with artillery, and Jackson went on when he was ready.

JUNE 30, MONDAY.—Arrived in Washington about nine and took breakfast at Willard's. Went to the War Department and reported to General Pope.[3] He is a stout man of medium height, prepossessing manners and appearance. He is young and alert, not unlike Stone. He received me politely but was so pressed by business that he could not talk with me and desired me to meet him at 8:30 at Willard's. . . . At the time appointed I visited the General's room and found [Doug?] Wallach there. The General was questioning him, and he gave pretty correct answers as far as regarded the county of Culpeper and adjoining counties, but in describing a crossroad or mountain gap he always mentioned the name of the man who lived there and gave his genealogy. This so worried Pope that he turned to me and, finding

3. John Pope (1822-92), USMA '42, was promoted to major general of volunteers after his force captured Island No. 10. After the Battle of Corinth, Pope was called to the East to command the Army of Virginia, which was to assault Richmond from the north. When defeated at Second Bull Run, Pope was sent to the inactive Department of the Northwest. He retired from the army in 1886.

my answers more to the point, he continued to question me. At the end of the conversation General McDowell came in, limping from a recent fall from his horse.[4] His manner is not strong but his conversation was clear and concise, showing a good understanding of the subject in hand. He advised Pope against taking any thirty-pounder Parrotts with him, saying the twenty-pounder answered all the purpose and was more easily transported. . . . He soon left and the conversation on Virginia topography was resumed. He at length said he must have me with him, to which I readily consented. One question Pope asked and reiterated. Why did we not advance and occupy Charlottesville and thus cover the Valley? To this I made no answer except by shrugging my shoulders. He said there must certainly be some reason for not doing what seemed at first glance to be so plain to any military man. His plan is announced to be to concentrate the whole force of Northern and Western Virginia and to take position at Charlottesville. He will probably have eighty thousand men and will from thence menace Richmond and Lynchburg and the canal and railroad lines along the James, at the same time protect the Valley and Western Virginia. It was the plan discussed in our camp and urged by me from the first. In fact, I supposed on entering the Valley that that position was our fixed object. Why it was not carried out was because we had politicians directing our Departments instead of soldiers. I did not say this to General Pope, however.

JULY 1, THURSDAY.—Fair and warm. . . . Met General Banks at Willard's and walked up the Avenue with him. He attracted some attention. He professed himself pleased with Pope and has evidently determined to acquiesce in my appointment. After tea I visited Pope's room where several officers were collected. The General's conversation was lively and desultory. He reads character and talks like a keen, cool man of the world, kindly withal. He says Fremont is not a bad man nor dishonest. He is simply foolish. He has not the sense of a boy sixteen years old. In money matters and in responsible places he is the victim of sharpers. Fremont's countenance indicates as much. He has also sized Sigel. Pope is a much cleverer man than I

4. Irvin McDowell (1818-85), USMA '38, was until 1861 largely a headquarters officer. Through Winfield Scott's influence, he won the respect of the administration and did not entirely lose it by his failure at First Bull Run. In March, 1862, he was assigned the First Corps of the Army of the Potomac with orders to defend Washington. After Pope arrived to command the Army of Virginia, McDowell was given the Third Corps. For his failure to assist Pope properly at Second Bull Run, McDowell was released from command, although later he was exonerated. After retiring from the army, he lived in San Francisco, where he became Park Commissioner.

at first took him for. . . . A Major [James F.] Meline, with whom I was conversing, engaged me to mess with him. He says there will be four officers in the mess and a camp chest is to be bought at $50.

JULY 2, WEDNESDAY.—Warm rain. The affair at Richmond is certainly a serious check to us and exhibits weakness. We are today more besieged than besiegers. There has been a fresh call for three hundred thousand men. . . . I have been studying the geography of Virginia to kill time. How singularly and how frequently has the aimless knowledge gathered up in my earlier days been turned to my advantage. Studies that I pursued from pure idleness have turned up trumps and I find myself holding a full hand. . . .

JULY 4, FRIDAY.—Warm and cloudy. Was disturbed all night by crackers and discharges of firearms. The Eternal Fourth still survives. I had hoped the war would have been virtually settled by this time, but we are further from it than ever. . . . Repaired to General Pope's headquarters and had some conversation with him on the subject of the campaign. He thinks a position at Sperryville would command the Valley by threatening communications in case the enemy passed over into the Valley by the Virginia Central. I think he is right, although at the time I recommended Charlottesville or Gordonsville. We would be more advanced at these places and more exposed. . . . With Beckwith I discussed our generals and our cause. Both of our great commanders have apparently been outwitted and deceived by the enemy. Halleck has been eluded by Beauregard, McClellan overwhelmed and forced back by the Richmond concentrated power. Our troops are lying all over a vast territory disconnected and useless, while they mysteriously and quickly concentrate on important points and overwhelm us. They are the better soldiers, but we will beat them in the end. As we get more serious in the work and cast aside politicians and fanaticisms, we will beat them gloriously. The great mind which is to rule is not yet come to light. The Napoleon of this revolution is not yet in command. . . .

Met General Prince and accompanied him to his quarters.[5] He has served in Florida and California and showed me some sketches in his notebook. His brother the Major came in and we discoursed on military movements in general. All agreed that army baggage was properly named by the Romans *impedimentum* and that an individual was the better with the least amount possible. This was Thoreau's idea in

5. Henry Prince, USMA '35, commanded a brigade under Augur at Cedar Mountain, where he was captured by the Confederates. After the war he was a paymaster until his retirement in 1879.

his view of the journey through life in *Walden*. Thoreau died lately.

At night Harry Wise[6] came in and we went together to General Pope's room. Hunter and the Negro question were discussed. It was thought by all parties that the war had necessarily given the death blow to slavery. Wherever the Union armies move, the old system of master and slave falls. The disorganization that follows can never be cured. The Negro becomes free absolutely or worthless and dangerous property. Pope's ideas are clear and strong. He thinks they ought to be taken and used remorselessly whenever needed. The arming of them in organized regiments is only doubtful as a matter of policy. They will not make soldiers but as laborers they might be extensively used. Congress should let the matter alone. Let the commanders in the field use Negroes as circumstances require and never interfere to return them to slavery which they voluntarily renounce. Damn Congress.

JULY 5, SATURDAY.—Fair and pleasant. Yesterday several long trains of ambulances filled with wounded passed by the Hotel, all from the Peninsula. Several wounded subofficers came into the Hotel limping and supported by friends. They got their dinners and then lay upon the sofas in the saloons, surrounded by groups of listeners while they lionized.

One subject of conversation yesterday evening was the President. He is universally esteemed as a sincere, honest man, shrewd but modest, practical, earnest. He has a keen appreciation of the humorous, exhibited in his smutty fables, told after the manner of Aesop to illustrate points and characters. This Western coarseness, however, covers a deal of wisdom and determination. . . .

The army of the Valley moves today toward Sperryville. Yesterday a volunteer hero dined with us at the Hotel. He was escorted into the crowded dining hall with two attendants and a crutch, still wearing the bloody pantaloons, torn and powdergrimed, which he had worn on the field, swearing lustily and swaggering. . . .

As we passed the Capitol, Beckwith and myself commented on the superb and costly character of the building and the beggarly scoundrels who were sent there to regulate the country. The contrast is as great as is to be found in some of our palatial hotels and steamboats with the people who frequent them. With the gorgeous development of the

6. Henry Augustus Wise (1819-69) was an officer in the navy, serving in the Bureau of Ordnance. He had been a friend of Strother before the war and was the author of several books, the best known of which are *Los Gringos* (1849) and *Tales for the Marines* (1855).

Capitol buildings, the character of the representatives has degraded from year to year. . . .

JULY 6, SUNDAY.—Fair and warm. Rose early to breakfast and saw General Pope come in with a friend. I perceive he rises early, which is the reverse of the habit of General Banks and staff. Saw a major general's shoulder straps on the shoulders of a very small man with a boyish face and manner. This is Mitchel just from Tennessee.[7]. . . Met Mrs. Holabird in the hotel parlor. She was acquainted with the Craighills of Charles Town and says the old people hold no communication with their loyal son since he has refused to leave the service of the United States. The scene which followed the production of his publication had more significance than I supposed at the time. The heat is intense. . . .

I am told that Union sentiment is weakening in Virginia. I have heard it in many instances. For example, enter a butternut farmer—"I always was a Union man, but they come to my house and took every chicken my wife had, and I can't stand by any government that allows its soldiers to steal chickens." Next is a woman—"We were always Union at our house until our son Tommy was pressed into the Confederate Army. He didn't want to go, and he run away twice, but the last time they tied him and threatened to shoot him, so now we're all on that side." Number three is a lawyer—"It is useless to prate about sustaining a government which won't acknowledge the writ of *habeas corpus* and that arrests me for opinion's sake." But the Confederacy—"Oh, that's another matter; they're revolutionary. I always was a Union man and they arrested me. But I gave my parole and they have treated me very civilly ever since." Number four has large sums of Confederate money. Number five acknowledges to you in a whisper that he is afraid to express Union sentiments until he is assured the Federal government can protect him. And such are the ideas and such the conversation of a people who "cannot be conquered." I feel assured that when the Union Army shall have overthrown the Confederates in a decisive pitched battle that nine out of ten of these invincible people will become quiet citizens of the government that is able to hold them. They will be whipped out of their treason as easily as they were kicked and frightened into it, as soon as

7. Ormsby M. Mitchel (1809-62), USMA '29, had been a celebrated astronomer and lecturer before the war. His raid from Shelbyville, Tennessee, to Huntersville, Alabama, in April of 1862 was one of the most striking Union campaigns of that year. For a time Secretary Stanton considered him as candidate for command of the Army of Virginia, but in September he was assigned the Department of the South, where he died of yellow fever shortly afterward.

the National Government takes hold of them as remorselessly as their present masters have done.

JULY 19, SATURDAY.—Cool and cloudy. Finished tracing a map of Central Virginia. Read the President's appeal to the Border State members of Congress. I was shocked at its tone. It supposes that slavery is the cause of the war and proposes that slavery be abolished in the Border States because a certain party thinks so and will not support the war unless this cause is abolished. How false and feeble in theory. Party spirit is the cause of the war and prevents its termination. . . .

JULY 21, MONDAY.—Cloudy and hot. This is the first anniversary of the Battle of Bull Run. A year of war and things do not look better for our government. Had an interview with General Pope on the subject of the topography of Central Virginia. He desired me to get as much information on the subject as possible, also to ascertain if some men could be got for secret service in that quarter. . . . Today I saw Wallach, who introduced a man named George Smith, a late resident of Culpeper County. He gave me such valuable information in regard to the topography of the country below. I had two interviews with him, one in the morning and one at night in my own room. After he left I went to General Pope's room and saw there several persons, one of whom I think he addressed as Halleck. When these went away, Pope approached me and said, "Captain, the man you were talking with today, I am told, is a damned rascal. When you are done getting information from him, hand him over to the provost marshal." This astonished me, as I had judged from the man's speech and demeanor that he was honest. I think so yet, and hope General Pope may be mistaken.

JULY 22, TUESDAY.—Cloudy and cool. . . . Took a walk to the Capitol. On returning to Willard's after tea met Halleck in the hall.[8] He is a thoughtful, soldierly-looking man and his advent here is of hopeful significance. He will be, in fact, the chief of the army. The small fry of generals and politicians who have heretofore managed our military affairs to our ruin are superseded. McClellan has expressed his acquiescence and even a decided wish for it, as it will free him from the petty persecutions, criticisms, and thwartings. Penfield intro-

8. Henry W. Halleck (1815-72), USMA '39, succeeded Fremont in Missouri in 1861. His successes in the West brought him a call from Lincoln to serve as the President's military adviser in 1862. After Grant's ascension, Halleck was demoted from General in Chief to Chief of Staff.

duced me to General James of Rhode Island,[9] the inventor of a cannon projectile and a tall, fine-looking man.

JULY 24, THURSDAY.—Bright and warm. Spent the day at Colonel [John N.] Macomb's office studying topography. Except plans of the improvements on the rivers, I found little to add to information already obtained. Pope sent for me, asking for more information in regard to the country. He was crabbed because it was not forthcoming. The truth is, it is not to be had. . . .

JULY 25, FRIDAY.—Bright and hot. Spent the day at Colonel Macombs' office improving the map. General Pope called again for information and got but little. He is dissatisfied with the map and wants more. I went down to the Department to get his orders executed but found every person gone and the halls empty. Determined to do it myself and made some purchases of paper and glue to finish the map.

JULY 26, SATURDAY.—Bright and hot. . . . General Pope sent for me while at tea. He wanted to know the locality of certain places. I told him promptly. He seemed in an irascible mood and got into a wrangle with [Colonel George D.] Ruggles, who held his own in the argument, however. Ruggles is to give an order assigning my position with commutation for quarters. We will probably go to the field on Monday.

JULY 29, TUESDAY.—Bright and warm. Reported to General Pope ready to start. The enemy, he told me, had drawn in their outposts and were fortifying at Gordonsville and Charlottesville. Hatch has been relieved of his command for failing to go to Gordonsville and Charlottesville at the time he was ordered to advance there. It was a great failure on our part not to have destroyed the road and depots at those points. The General is much disgusted at the failure. Was ordered by General Pope to telegraph McDowell and speed his coming. I did so by the American Telegraph at Willard's. Paid nothing. Started in carriages for the railroad depot on Seventh Street and Maryland Avenue. The people on the street were very curious to see General Pope and were staring at a great rate and asking questions.

We passed on to Alexandria and with but a moment's delay through to the Orange and Alexandria road. The country on the route to Manassas Junction looked very forlorn and desolate. There were no fences and no cultivation. Many remnants of houses had been gutted,

9. Charles T. James (1805-62), a self-taught textile engineer from Rhode Island, had made a fortune in New England before the war. After serving a term in the Senate, James turned to the development of rifled cannon, and in October of 1862 he was killed by one of his own experiments.

burnt, or defaced. Some few were occupied by Negroes. At Bull Run, the first stream we crossed, are some small bluffs covered with wood, but the stream and features of the country are on a much smaller scale than I expected. Thence to the Junction the country is an open plain, spotted with camps and villages of pole and mud shanties, formerly built by the Confederate troops. At one camp stood a formidable-looking cannon, a burnt log mounted on cart wheels with a grotesque stuffed artillerist leaning on the piece. I have never been so utterly surprised as I was by the appearance of the country around Manassas Junction. The account of it has been that it was a rugged, broken, unapproachable stronghold with commanding ridges and deep ravines, impenetrable woods and all commanded by and raked by formidable field works. . . .

At the Junction are a number of storehouse buildings, Negro eating shanties, where pies are manufactured. From here to Warrenton Junction the road runs in a direct line through a country gently undulating and partly wooded with small timber, poor soil, without cultivation or inhabitants. The Warrenton stem leads immediately into a more fertile and populated region with bolder features, hills and forests increasing until the town of Warrenton, embowered in trees. The General was conducted to his quarters in a large seminary on the outskirts of town. It belonged to a Dr. Bacon from the North and was established by him as a female school. Major Meline found quarters for our mess in the house of a Mr. Stillman, a lawyer. Our host was resigned, social, and complaisant. He had a family, a wife and six children, and said he was ruined by the war, but seemed reasonably cheerful about it. I walked about the village and saw a dress parade by the New York 9th. The town is a queerly planned and straggling place with many prettily ornamented cottage residences and a fine hotel, the Warren Green. The people were out and mixing freely with the soldiers. . . .

JULY 30, WEDNESDAY.—Bright and warm. Breakfast on corn bread and an egg. Joe's first attempt at coffee not a success. Joe is a Virginian, a native of these regions, and professes to have been a servant of General Longstreet. He knows the country between this place and Richmond and is to talk with me on that subject this afternoon. He seems, however, to have more desire to give us his military views than anything else. He says we ought to advance in three columns, and this is his great idea of military strategy. His knowledge of the country does not amount to much. He has no knowledge of maps. I got some points from him, however. He says we should cut the Southside Railroad and approach Richmond from the west. . . .

JULY 31, THURSDAY.—Warm and cloudy. Was aroused by the drums of a brigade marching southward. Formerly the movement of troops excited me grandly. This morning I felt pained and saddened at the sight of the thinned regiments. I am less hopeful of results now. . . . We rode through the town to a handsome house on the Sulphur Springs turnpike, and there General McDowell and staff joined us. Thus reinforced, our cavalcade headed by the two Major Generals started off upon the Sperryville turnpike. . . . We crossed Hedgeman's River on a temporary bridge at Waterloo, the head of slack water navigation of the Rappahannock. About three-quarters of a mile after, we rode into a beautiful green field surrounded by forest. The tents were here pitched in three lines. While I sat in front of a friend's tent, General McDowell approached and claimed acquaintance. Sitting down, we had a pleasant half of an hour chiefly about trouting, of which he is very fond. His manners are very kind and he talks agreeably. . . .

AUGUST 1, FRIDAY.—Fair and warm. . . . Our ride today was dusty and hot in the extreme. The country as we approached the Blue Ridge became more rolling and picturesque. The hills increased to mountains and the cultivation in the valleys was on a better scale than in the region below. . . . One mile from little Washington we found General Banks' headquarters in the edge of a wood, romantically situated. Had a pleasant interview with General Banks where we discussed the evacuation of Richmond. The General has information upon which he relies that this evacuation is accomplished. The circumstances he mentions may indicate it but do not prove it. . . . General Pope called for me and inquired the locality of Madison Mills. I don't know of it and the cook Joe says it is the same as Liberty Mills. The General seems disposed to be querulous and unreasonable on the subject of this minor topography. However, we will work it out no doubt. . . .

AUGUST 2, SATURDAY.—. . . In the course of the last three or four days I have had some conversation with Mr. Smalley, reporter for the New York *Tribune,* who introduced himself on the march.[10] He seems to be a worthy, modest gentleman with whom pleasant inter-

10. George W. Smalley was used by Hooker at Antietam for carrying messages to divisional commanders. After the battle he rode thirty miles by horseback, caught a train for New York, and wrote a five-column story for his newspaper. By seven o'clock the following morning he delivered his copy to the *Tribune* in person.

course could be had, and I will endeavor to get over the prejudice against his vocation and connection. I was astonished to find that Scheffler had been in this army for eight months and has not learned to swear. His servant having misbehaved, Scheffler ordered him to the guardhouse and addressed him thus, "You rascal damned. Go immediately, you bad fellow damned." General Prince says he never saw Pope in such a jaded and irascible condition as he is now. His whole deportment is different entirely from when I first met him.

I was sent for this morning by General Pope, who wanted to know some localities and gave me some dispatches in which several places were mentioned not down on the maps. I found them all out. . . . Pope thinks the Confederates had not more than seventy thousand men engaged in the battles below Richmond. This I think quite likely. General [John] Buford went this morning with six thousand cavalry to perpetrate some raid upon their lines and the next few days will be anxious ones for the commander.

AUGUST 3, SUNDAY.—Fair and hot. . . . I was sent for immediately after breakfast by the General to locate Mechanicsburg. When he made the inquiry, he said sharply, "Not Mechanicsburg near Richmond." I answered quietly, "No, but the village in Louisa County, fifteen miles from the Courthouse, toward Gordonsville." He then looked at the map and was satisfied, but he made no acknowledgment for the promptness with which his question was answered. . . . Received yesterday evening by mail the sheet of the Virginia map with another photograph of Central Virginia sent from Mecklin of the Topographical Bureau. . . . Colonel [T. C. H.] Smith and myself discussed Pope. Pope has always thought that the great key of the Rebellion lay in East Tennessee and that region should have been occupied in the beginning of the war. He believes in aggressive war continually, large bodies of cavalry offending the enemy lines far in advance, with his main body strongly posted to support the advances, in case they are pressed, that they may retire securely on the infantry in position. He is an indefatigable worker and a military genius, so says Colonel Smith. . . .

Went to Brown's tent where I met Scheffler and the other German aide-de-camp who speaks Italian also, Orndorff. The party was lively and I got to dancing a cotillion with imaginary partners. In my gyrations, bowing and skipping, I approached a figure in the twilight and was about to turn him for a partner. It was General Banks, and a great laugh followed at my expense. . . .

AUGUST 4, MONDAY.—Fair and hot. . . I find there is a good deal of material for pleasant social intercourse on our staff. Walked out on the hills to philosophize in the moonlight. Drum and bugle were sounding retreat through the semicircle of camps. The thousand glimmering lights upon the hillsides shone through the soft mist like the lights of a great city. These went out one by one and I returned to quarters. Missing my way I wandered for half an hour through a cavalry camp within the radius of two hundred yards. Then went back to General Banks' quarters and took a new start and got home.

AUGUST 7, THURSDAY.—Fair and hot. Was aroused at four o'clock and for two hours the camp was a busy scene of hasty cooking, packing trunks, striking tents, and loading up wagons. We went ahead a mile and a half to the town of Washington, an inconsiderable village of 350 inhabitants. When the staff came through I joined it and rode on through heat and dust to Sperryville, a village even smaller than Washington. On a hill above town we stopped at the headquarters of General Sigel in a country house of plain architecture shaded by three majestic oaks. I was presently sent for to bring in my map and went into a room where Sigel and Pope with a number of other officers sat talking. The map was produced and I helped myself to some cherry bounce on the table. Presently General Carl Schurz came in, a pale, wide-foreheaded, red-mustached, spectacled, effeminate-looking German.[11] He had sharp, hazel eyes, was thin and tall, the very pattern of a visionary, itching philanthropist and philosopher such as disturb society everywhere with their restless conceits and babblings. . . .

We rode on to the encampment of General Banks' division on the rolling hills near the Hazel River. The scene was most beautiful. The stream was alive with bathers, joyous and noisy. Blue peaks rising to the eastward and the grand outline of the Blue Ridge to the west. We crossed the river by a covered wooden bridge forty feet across, then riding three hundred yards farther arrived at our encampment. . . .

AUGUST 8, FRIDAY.—Fair and hot. Rose early and got off by seven o'clock. We were out of the mountains. The country was milder in its features, more level and open, no shade to break the midday sun, which was almost intolerable. Pope is a bright, dashing man, self-confident and clearheaded. He has a good memory and has been a topographical engineer. I observe that he is wonderfully quick

11. Carl Schurz (1829-1906) retired as Minister to Spain in 1861 to accept a division in the army of Fremont, later Sigel's. Although untried as an officer, he covered the retreat at Bull Run. After the war Schurz was a cabinet officer under Hayes and a noted reformer.

to seize all information on this subject. He remembers it all if once told and wants new details. Whether his mind grasps general subjects with capacity and clearness I have not had an opportunity to judge. He is irascible and impulsive in his judgments of men, but in his pleasant moods, jolly, humorous, and clever in conversation.

Arrived at Culpeper Court House, I remembered the places well from a former visit in 1853 under very different circumstances. We rode out to McDowell's headquarters, at the house of Doug Wallach about three-quarters of a mile from town. Presently Pope ordered me to ride out and find where Colonel [Speed] Butler had located headquarters. I mounted and rode through the town and at the signal station on the other side met an acquaintance who inquired of General Pope's whereabouts and showed me a signal message for him stating that the enemy were advancing by Robertson's River and were skirmishing with our advance. I found our camp established a mile in front of Culpeper and the body of McDowell's troops, with nothing between us and the enemy but some cavalry and infantry pickets. . . .

Fugitive cavalry came in by ones, twos, and then by companies, reporting the advance of the enemy in force. An order then came for us to strike tents and retire behind the town. Joe meanwhile brought in the dinner, a pair of stewed chickens, corn bread, and coffee, and a bottle of Catawba wine. As soon as swallowed, Major Meline and myself mounted and rode for General Pope at McDowell's headquarters. Some two hundred riffraff of cavalry with Negroes and led horses came pouring in from the front, looking miserably thin and jaded. This was dispiriting, but as we entered the village the sound of martial music met us, and up the street in gallant array came General Crawford at the head of his brigade. He saluted me heartily and said he had heard from Pierpont and that he understood I was appointed lieutenant colonel. I rode on to the rear. Meanwhile all the troops of the division marched southward after Crawford. Before I left Wallach's, Smith[12] came in and told me he had been to Louisa Courthouse and that there were no Confederates there and that an expedition might be filled out to cut Jackson off on that line. He also said Jackson had about thirty thousand men and did not intend to fight at Orange but desired to toll Pope across the Rapidan toward Gordonsville and would fight him there. I mentioned this to the General, who was pleased with the intelligence. He said he had already sent

12. This was the man who Pope insisted should be turned over to the provost marshal as a worthless and unreliable scoundrel.

out from Fredericksburg and that King had destroyed the railroad below Louisa, at Fredericks Hall. . . .

AUGUST 9, SATURDAY.—Fair and hot. Slept well with a half consciousness of hearing wagons moving all night. It was Banks' division passing through. Immense wagon trains were parked about us this morning but the troops had passed on. Was startled by artillery firing about five miles in front. The war, which for a space did fail, now trebly thundering swelled the gale, the distant cannonading becoming hotter and heavier. The thuds of the guns seemed also to approach us at Culpeper. About four o'clock in the afternoon the order was given to mount. Riding through the town the windows and porches were clouded with pale, anxious faces of women, children, and grandsires. As we approached the scene of action, the pounding of cannon became heavier, and rattling volleys of musketry mingled with the din. Regiments of Sigel's and McDowell's divisions were pouring forward and saluted us with cheers and music as we passed. Leading the 12th Massachusetts I remarked Colonel Tim Bryan cheering and waving his hat lustily. Nearer the field we saw numbers of men trailing wearily along on the back track towards Culpeper. Officers were sent immediately to stop them, but their bloody bandaged heads and limbs showed they were the wounded, sullenly retiring, many still having their arms. There were no cowed or stampeded men, as I had seen at most of the other battles. There was a temporary lull in the war as we got upon the ground about sunset. General Pope rode immediately to the front where he met General Banks. They and their staffs and escorts gathered on an eminence near a wood where it was supposed we had pickets. The roughly handled brigades and batteries of Banks' division were slowly retiring, and we occupied at that time the ground which the enemy had occupied in the morning.

As the fresh divisions arrived on the ground, they cheered the general-in-chief. An officer coming out with the colors of the 46th Pennsylvania, Colonel [Joseph F.] Knipe, said that the colors remained and only six men left to follow them. Although this was evidently a lie, the colors were cheered all along the line. The divisions were posted en masse to the right and left, while in the meantime the cheering had attracted the attention of the enemy, revealing the position of the commander-in-chief. The result was that by the time the moon was risen a shell screamed over our heads and burst just beyond. Then came another and another, then half a dozen at a time, hissing, screaming, and bursting over, scattering fragments of deadly missiles in nervous contiguity, some striking within ten feet of where I lay. When the shelling became serious, we retired from the brow of the field and holding our horses' bridles, lay and sat upon the ground looking up and about at the fiery track of the missiles fired against us. This game lasted half an hour. When it was over, I felt relieved and observed the party generally more excited and cheerful than during the operation.

Then we heard some trampling in the wood and presently a body of cavalry issued from the forest and passed along until their flank entirely covered our position. Turning suddenly, they yelled and poured in upon us a rapid and continuous volley from carbines and pistols. We mounted in hot haste, as the enemy were not more than fifty paces from us. In attempting to mount, General Banks was overthrown and his hip badly hurt by the horse of a dragoon, the rider of which was killed. By the time we had started across the field, the fire in our rear became more furious. The balls struck around us so rapidly that I thought it impossible for anyone to escape. Colonel Ruggles, the adjutant general, and Captain [William W.] Rowley of the Signal Corps lost their horses by shot. Major Meline streaked it afoot, his horse having escaped from his groom. General Pope stuck his head down and, striking spur, led off at full speed. I gave my mare the reins and, as we crossed a hollow, a regiment of our own infantry seeing a dark mass of cavalry advancing opened fire. Thus we had it front and rear and only our being in a hollow saved us. I swerved to the left to avoid the fire of the U. S. troops and with the body of the staff pushed on toward a fence. Seeing it was five rails high, I held up my mare to let the young fry of the staff try it. They rushed on without checking and some half dozen of them crashed together on the fence, broke it down, and tumbled one upon another. I thought men and horses would be killed by the crush, but all righted again unhurt, the only loss being of Captain [Edward] Haight's sword.

We rode on for two hundred yards to get safe out of the range of fire, then stopped to count noses. Several horses without riders galloped with us; among the missing were General Pope and Major Meline. As we knew Meline was afoot, we thought probably he had been captured, but hearing nothing of the General we began to be uneasy about him. In the search I presently found myself with a dozen officers in the center of a field bordering on the Culpeper road. While standing here the enemy opened with artillery on our front and right flank. The two U.S. batteries in front of us then opened in reply and, as we retired to avoid the cross fire of shells, one of our batteries on a hill behind opened a rapid fire on our front batteries. The full moon had been under a cloud during all the previous proceedings and now she shone in full glory. On three sides was blazing the artillery and the air filled with hissing and bursting missiles. Regiment after regiment was seen retiring; squads of horse ambulances and batteries of guns filled the Culpeper road.

I thought for a while that Pope was killed or taken and the game was up. I found myself alone on the road, Marshall having started off to stop the battery on the hill which was playing upon our own men. An officer here told me that General Pope had gone on the road toward Culpeper Court House. I doubted it and determined to wait in the road until I ascertained where the staff would retire. To my right was a house in a grove where the surgeons were dealing with several hundred wounded. In the meanwhile the batteries had been keeping up the most furious fire I ever heard. It was a steady roar, and the blazing of the guns, the bursting of shells, and the vast columns of white smoke obscuring the woods and piling up like snow mountains in the moonlight was a scene so dramatic and grand that it will not be soon forgotten. An officer rode by and informed us that the staff was in advance. Riding forward we found Generals Pope, Banks, McDowell, and Sigel sitting on a pile of fence rails under a tree. With the rein in my hand, I lay down behind some bushes and slept. From this sleep I was aroused by the enemy's musketry and the whistling of balls. The Generals had again been doing picket duty for the army. After this second stirring up, the staff retired to an open field behind the front lines and there remained until daylight. Here I found a sheaf or two of wheat, and lying down upon it with the bridle rein in my hand I slept and dozed for an hour or two while my mare amused herself eating my bed. The moon sailed grandly through the heavens, edging with silver some picturesque banks of clouds to the west. At each moment a shooting star would mark the blue firmament. The red planet Mars was in the ascendant. Tomorrow was Sunday, the great battle day. . . .

AUGUST 10, SUNDAY.—Fair and hot. Thus we waited until broad daylight when General Pope and company returned and we rode back a little way to Colvin's Tavern, where we took our frugal breakfast. Mine was two hard crackers and a cup of cold, black tea from the General's jug. About half past five we opened with half a dozen guns but there was no reply. Skirmishers were pushed forward and a faint rattling of musketry was heard which continued for several hours. Meanwhile it became evident that the enemy had retired from our front and information was brought that they were attempting to turn our right flank. General Pope sent me with a message to McDowell notifying him of the fact and requesting him to send out Colonel Boyd with the cavalry to ascertain the nature of the movement. I rode to McDowell's quarters and found the movement of cavalry already being executed. The house where he quartered was a fine brick mansion belonging to a Captain Nalle, late of the U. S. Navy. The house had been the home of plenty and refinement. It was now a hospital and the handsome shaded enclosure about it was covered with dead and wounded, while the interior was more like a butcher's shambles than a gentleman's dwelling. Beside the piano stood the amputating table. Rich carpets hurriedly bundled into corners were replaced by bloody blankets and sheets. The furniture not removed was dabbled with blood and cases of amputating instruments lay upon the tables and mantelpieces lately dedicated to elegant books and flowers. In the yard soaked stretchers and mattresses contained the worst cases of the wounded, some of whom died as they lay waiting for the surgeon. The lighter cases had a knapsack for a pillow and an armful of hay for a bed. Blood, carnage, and death among the sweet shrubbery and roses. Captain Nalle's wife and daughters were more than flower nurses, for when the wounded men were brought in they tore sheets and garments of linen for bandages and with womanly hearts lent assistance to the sufferers.

Returning hence to the wood I waited in some suspense for the renewal of the battle, but even the rattle of musketry had died away and it became evident that neither party intended to urge the fight this day. The enemy's flank movement was met by a corresponding disposition of our troops and he retired. It seemed as if he meant to retire altogether, although we had information that he had been reinforced during the night by Hill's division. Pope thought so and I perceive he is both sanguine and incredulous. . . .

As we got to Sigel's wood the rain fell so heavily that neither trees nor gum coats served to protect us against it. I met Generals Gordon and Crawford, who looked worn and sad. Gordon pointed to a group of three or four hundred men, saying there was what was left of his brigade. They both looked discouraged as did General Banks, but physical exhaustion may have had something to do with it. At Captain Nalle's house I found McDowell and Pope sitting on some boxes under an apple tree. A squad of soldiers carried a dead man by on a litter, others following with picks and spades. Looking on this spectacle, Pope remarked, "Well, there seems to be devilish little that is attractive about the life of a private soldier." McDowell answered, "You might say, General, very little that is attractive in any grade of a soldier's life." Five bodies were carried by us and buried under a tree, but after the first, no comment was made. . . .

AUGUST 11, MONDAY.—Fair and hot. . . . The enemy asked for a flag of truce to bury the dead which thence continued all day. They had left both their dead and wounded on the field, even the body of General [Charles S.] Winder where it fell. The corpses are hideously blackened and swelled, already putrefying. One poor fellow had built himself a shelter of green cornstalks, crawled into it, and died. Many wounded were brought in who report that the Rebel pickets had treated them kindly, had washed the gore from their faces, and given them water to drink. The stoic patience of the wounded is astonishing. Among the many hundred I have seen, I have rarely heard a groan or a complaint.

General Buford, chief of cavalry, got in today, having retired from Madison through Sperryville and thence to Culpeper. General King[13] arrived from Fredericksburg with two fine brigades. Officers under the truce met their acquaintances on the Rebel side. Major General Stuart of the Southern cavalry was there and talked with Marshall in a cheerful, friendly manner. Marshall says, however, that they are evidently very much down and the gayety was only superficial. We are now speculating on the chances of a battle tomorrow. . . .

AUGUST 12, TUESDAY.—Fair and hot. The enemy had not shelled the house as expected and had disappeared from our front. We had positive information that their rear guard passed beyond the Rapidan. They probably commenced their movement yesterday morning when the truce was demanded. Buford was immediately ordered forward with his cavalry. . . . I rode to look at the late battlefield. The whole country for three-quarters of a mile, wood and open ground, was strewed with broken belts, cartridge boxes, knapsacks, bayonet scabbards, bloody blankets, jackets, overcoats, hats, and shoes. The shoes were generally those discarded by the Rebels, who had exchanged with our dead and wounded. Trees from eight to twelve inches through

---

13. Rufus King (1814-76), USMA '33, had been engaged in the defenses of Washington in 1861 and 1862. Taking the field in the Bull Run Campaign, he led the division of McDowell's Corps that was attacked by Jackson at Groveton. Epilepsy forced his resignation from the army in 1863, when he was made minister to Rome.

were cut down by the shot. In one of the larger trees a twelve-inch ball was buried, which shows that a good-sized tree is some protection against artillery fire. . . .

AUGUST 15, FRIDAY.—Mild and rainy. Beckwith told me that General Banks wanted me to call over to see him. Going through the town I met Crawford at the head of his brigade marching out just where I met him on the day before the battle going to the front. The band played the anthem of the Pilgrim Fathers, which sounded greatly in the streets of the wasted town. I was much affected by the appearance of these troops. Many a familiar face I missed from among them, but their warlike array and stern countenances gave promise of future victory. The slaughter of Cedar Mountain had not cowed them. While at General Banks', an old gentleman came in who turned out to be the celebrated John S. Pendleton.[14] He stated that his estate was wasted to the point that he must starve with his family or be permitted to leave the country. He wanted to ask no favors but he must save his family from starving. When rising to take leave of General Banks, his native hospitality stuck out. He offered to send him anything in his power to render his condition more comfortable, but recollecting himself, he said, "Damn it, I got nothing to send anybody." It reminded me of my last interview with Joe Tidball in Winchester, who first invited me to tea—then said, "No, damn it, I've got no tea nor anything else." Poor Old Virginia. . . .

The official reports give our loss in the battle of Cedar Mountain in killed, wounded, and missing at about twenty-seven hundred men. There is no accurate estimate of the enemy's loss, but there is every reason to suppose two thousand at least. This makes Cedar Mountain one of the bloodiest engagements of the war, considering the numbers engaged and the time.

AUGUST 17, SUNDAY.—Fair and cool. We rode up Cedar Mountain to the house of the Reverend Mr. Slaughter, from whence there is a most beautiful view. This house has been completely gutted by the Rebels and a fine library utterly destroyed because they found therein some correspondence of Northern men on the subject of colonization. It was pitiable to see the fragments of fine old books in divers languages, blowing about the yard. Among others, I saw fragments of an illustrated Italian work of Il Vaticano. The furniture was equally destroyed. On Cedar Mountain I saw a company of our men digging

14. John S. Pendleton (1802-68), a famous Virginia Whig, had been chargé d'affaires in Chile and in Argentina before the war. After his retirement from diplomacy in 1854, he practiced law in Culpeper County.

up something that had been buried in search of a treasure. Digging away, they came to a dead horse in a state of putrefaction. This, instead of discouraging them, only raised their hopes afresh. The horse must have been buried to conceal the treasure. When I left them they could hear a hollow sound at every stroke of their mattocks. Doubtless their hopes proved as hollow as the sound. . . . I was introduced to Major General Reno, a short, stout man with a quick, soldierly look.[15] He is a man of the regular army.

15. Jesse L. Reno (1823-62), USMA '46, had served with Burnside in North Carolina. Appointed major general in July, 1862, Reno was killed leading the Ninth Corps at South Mountain in September.

IV

Chaos at Second Bull Run

August 18, 1862—September 5, 1862

By August 18 Pope knew that he faced Lee's whole army, and he withdrew across the Rappahannock to a position nearly impregnable to direct attack. Reconnoissance and artillery marked the progress of the campaign until August 22, when Stuart, after a broad sweep to the west, fell upon Pope's trains at Catlett's Station and discovered Pope's plan for defense. Discovering that Union reinforcements would eventually outnumber his own force, Lee worked his army north-westerly in a direction away from the route of reinforcement. He then sent Jackson on a circular march to the Union rear in order to attack Manassas Junction and sever Union communication with Washington.

The Confederate plan was a striking success. After taking Manassas Junction, Jackson went into hiding to await support by Longstreet's force marching behind over the same route. Pope, seeing an opportunity to crush Jackson before this support could arrive, withdrew from the Rappahannock line, but he succeeded only in wearing down his men by marches and countermarches in all directions. On August 28 Jackson came out of hiding and attacked King's division near Groveton. Now assured that he could crush Jackson, Pope launched his attack the next morning and seemed to be unaware that Longstreet held the Confederate right. On August 30 Lee began the counterattack that drove the Union army back into the fortifications at Centerville.

Of all his engagements in the war, those at Groveton and Second Bull Run were most confusing for Strother. Although serving as an aide-de-camp for Pope, it is clear that he understood only what came directly under his eye. His faith in Pope's capacity as a commander had been shattered, but Strother was not blind to the apparent jealousy among the McClellan-Porter clique that had contributed to Pope's failure.

AUGUST 18, MONDAY.—Fair and a cool night. . . . About dinner time a sudden summons was given to pack up and strike tents. The explanation was the enemy was in our front advancing with the whole army of Richmond.[1] We were to retreat beyond the Rappahannock. The wagons were loaded and sent off, but the staff remained until midnight about bivouac fires. Then we started and had a rough ride through the baggage-encumbered roads. Things looked confused and ugly, but Pope infused some of his unlicked energy into them and made everything move. Rode on to the Rappahannock Station and ford about eleven miles, the whole road a continuous line of wagons. Some were broken and overthrown and one was burnt. As the morning broke, I found myself unwell and at the ford.

AUGUST 19, TUESDAY.—Fair and warm. A mile beyond the ford I saw the end of the staff train still pushing on towards Warrenton Junction, so I tied my horse and laid myself under a tree. In the meantime trains and droves passed by in rapid succession. I lay here until two in the afternoon, then rode to Bealeton. General Pope handed me the commission sent by Pierpont. . . .

AUGUST 20, WEDNESDAY. Fair and warm. There is an order prohibiting private letters to be promulgated today. General Lee is said to be in command in front of us with the whole power of the Southern Army. Thus we are enveloped in a dark storm of war for a season and all communication with our wives and families cut off. This is better than ignoble idleness, and if final success crowns our arms, the glory will be all the greater to those who now suffer. Pierpont's letter with the commission requests me, if possible, to take command of the battalion of cavalry, but I think there is an order expressly prohibiting any officer now in active service from changing his position or leaving his post. . . . Rode on to the Rappahannock Station and found the army posted in order of battle. The artillery crowned all the eminences behind and between the infantry stood deployed in line supported by the regiments in mass. The scene was exciting. Generals Pope and McDowell sat dismounted upon a hill overlooking our position and the ground on the south side over which the enemy must advance. This field was open for a mile and a half, and on the edge of the woods bordering its extremity some horsemen of the enemy reconnoitered our position. We waited until after sunset and, no enemy appearing, we of the staff rode to our quarters. . . .

1. On August 16, Halleck wired Pope to withdraw beyond the Rappahannock. On the following day an order of Lee's march fell into Pope's hands, assuring him that the Confederates were in front of him in full force.

Today I saw the adjutant general of Major General Stuart of Confederate cavalry, captured by a scouting party. This party was very near capturing the General himself, who, hearing the firing, leaped from his bed and escaped half-clad and on a horse barebacked. His hat, coat, sash, and sword were captured. The adjutant was a Major Fitzhugh, tall, red-bearded, with a grey jacket gold embroidered on the sleeves and a gold star on the collar. He was guarded and on his way to Washington when I met him.

AUGUST 21, THURSDAY.—Cloudy and warm. . . . The enemy's batteries have opened and ours are replying. They were reconnoitering our position at the different fords with artillery. We fought back and the affair lasted all morning. . . . Mounted videttes covered the front of a wood to the front, but the affair was confined entirely to the artillery. . . . Colonel Clark came in with some important tidings of the enemy's movements. A large force is reported moving toward our right up the river. He says that forces of the enemy were across the river, and the collision between our infantry and theirs took place on this side. The signal men were waving fire signals from the top of the house, and everything went to show that the night and the approaching morning would bring forth great events.

SIGNAL-STATION, MONTGOMERY COUNTY

AUGUST 22, FRIDAY.—Rainy and warm. An officer came round at two o'clock this morning to arouse us, saying that the order was that we should breakfast before daylight and be off by dawn. The attack is expected to commence on our right, maintained by Sigel. At daylight we were mounted and the opening gun was heard, which was presently followed by a rapid and continuous fire from Beverly's Ford and some point farther up the river. We took position in a field beside the Warrenton road and then I was sent with a message to order up General Williams and his troops to our right by this road, but I found my message was anticipated. . . . A heavy thunder shower broke upon us. During the progress of the storm, Sigel's guns were heard roaring in unison with the artillery of Heaven so that we could not tell one from the other. He drove back the enemy and followed him across the river with three regiments. These, in turn, retired before superior forces and the fighting of the day closed without any decisive results.

AUGUST 23, SATURDAY.—Cloudy and warm. The artillery commenced early at Beverly's Ford and Rappahannock bridge, and it continued for several hours with great fury. We suspected in the pertinacity of the cannonade a feint to divert our attention from the flank movement on the right. Meanwhile the river had risen six feet during the night and we were forced to withdraw a brigade and batteries from their position on the south side of the railroad bridge, the bridge being menaced by the flood. The retreat was accomplished in safety, and the enemy's attempt to occupy the hills thus vacated was repulsed with loss to them. During this action General King, whose batteries had been hotly engaged at Beverly's Ford, came to quarters and presently fell down in an epileptic fit which disabled him for the day. . . . Colonel Butler, who had gone with our staff brigade train to Catlett's Station, returned with the report that the enemy had crossed in large force at Warrenton Springs, and a portion of their cavalry led by Fitzhugh Lee had fallen upon our baggage train there and destroyed a portion of it, capturing all the horses and several officers of the quartermaster department.[2] Meline's trunk was specified as lost and the Major General's wagon. The Excelsior mess chest has gone up, an early doom for so comfortable an institution. If the captors have nothing more to put in it than we had, I wish them joy. . . .

Meanwhile long columns of troops were steadily marching to the right of our line, and from the hills to the east the encampments disappeared one by one. So the firing at the lower ford lulled for a time, and it was evident some general movement was in progress. The

2. The raid on Pope's baggage train at Catlett's Station was led by Jeb Stuart, who had circled the Union lines to the far west in order to get in Pope's rear.

great rise of the river had prevented the necessity of guarding the fords, and Pope was concentrating to fall with his whole power upon Jackson's Corps, divided from the main army of the Confederates by the swollen stream.[3] I heard the order given to attack the enemy's column as soon as met. We soon were mounted and at four or five o'clock were at Fayetteville, halfway to Warrenton. Here we heard a cannonade in front of us. It was heavy and continued, and I was sent ahead to ascertain what it meant. I rode forward until I overtook General Sigel, who informed me that it was his advance led by Schenck, Milroy, and Stahel. I rode still farther and saw the smoke of the opposing batteries upon the bluffs of Great Run, three miles from the Warrenton Springs. We rode forward on the Warrenton road and the firing of artillery and musketry continued until a late hour. We sat by the roadside for an hour until it ceased and then in the darkness and through the fields sought a house wherein to pass the night. About ten o'clock we arrived at Mr. Shumater's, three miles from Warrenton, a country house occupied by an old man, his wife, and about a dozen daughters with an additional litter of grandchildren. The girls were pretty, gentle-mannered, and complained that they had been sadly robbed and insulted by soldiers. I went to sleep booted and spurred in a small outbuilding upon the floor in company with half a dozen other officers.

AUGUST 24, SUNDAY.—Cloudy and cool. . . . The old man's Negroes had run away, his sheep and pigs had been shot, and his dairy and hen roosts robbed, yet the family was kind and hospitable. The young ladies served us at table with a hospitable grace pertaining to Old Virginia and nowhere excelled in Christendom. . . . Entering Warrenton we rode through the town and took position on an eminence beyond looking toward the Sulphur Springs. Sigel had pushed the enemy and during the night Jackson had retreated to Waterloo bridge to recross there and rejoin the main body of the Confederates. Sigel is in hot pursuit in his rear and McDowell's column follows the main Waterloo road. About one o'clock we rode into town and took dinner. A good supper and a good bed did much to repair my fatigue of previous days.

AUGUST 25, MONDAY.—Clear and pleasant. Ascertained here that the raid upon our baggage train on Friday night was conducted by Major General Stuart with his whole command of cavalry and a battery of artillery. The troops passed through Warrenton, three or

3. The command belonged to Jubal Early, not to Jackson himself.

four thousand strong, well clothed and equipped and fairly mounted. The men were full of fire and health. Their attack upon the camp at Catlett's Station was made during the heavy thunder storm and was a complete surprise. The cavalry rode among the tents and their shock knocked some of the officers out of bed. Colonel [Robert E.] Clary, chief quartermaster, was drinking a glass of punch which was knocked out of his hand by the rush of the cavalry. Every man, white and black, high and low, fled on his own hook. Fortunately the enemy commenced plundering, breaking open and examining the contents of trunks, chests, desks, etc. They built themselves fires and by their light selected what they wanted most. The Bucktail Guards, amounting to about a hundred men, rallied from their panic and gathered in the darkness and poured in a volley upon the marauders, fatal to a dozen or more of them. This fire was so galling that they, ignorant of the force thus rallied and unable to return the fire with effect, retired from the ground. The officers of the expedition say they only remained three-quarters of an hour, while some of our officers who lay concealed in the bushes near at hand insist that they heard them breaking open boxes and plundering round all night. It is ascertained that a great deal of the pillaging was done by our own teamsters and camp followers after the Rebels had departed. This raid seems to have been undertaken to avenge the indignity put upon General Stuart some days ago by our cavalry.

After midday we started from town and rode to our camp pitched between Warrenton Junction and Catlett's. The first man I recognized was Joe the cook at a fire with his stew pan. In the yard stood a number of officers over their rifled boxes, chests, and desks. Ruggles, [John H.] Piat, Haight, and the general commanding had been among the principal victims, having lost everything. I next found John, who met me with smiling face. "My baggage, John?" "Everything safe, Sir." "The pony?" John rolled up his eyes, "Gone up, Sir, with the rest." The Excelsior mess chest was safe. We had a comfortable supper and I retired to bed early for a good night's rest. I had scarcely dozed when Colonel Clark came in big with news. He had observed from the mountain tops a vast force of all arms with a full train of over five hundred wagons moving around our right by way of Amissville, Gaines Cross Roads, and the Chester Gap Road. He supposed they were striking for Rectortown to get in our rear, and General Banks had sent him posthaste to deliver the news to General Pope.[4]

4. Clark's report of Jackson's flanking movement was interpreted by Pope as a general movement into the Valley of Virginia. Jackson was able to march through

This news was no soporific, but I was not a Major General, so I went to sleep after turning it over in my mind.

AUGUST 26, TUESDAY.—Bright and warm. . . . Clark's column of Confederates has probably gone into the Valley. The addition of McClellan's veterans to our force, now actually accomplished, gives confidence to all. The opening of the battle will no longer be a painful sound. Sigel has been pounding away continually with artillery to little or no purpose. As a Prussian, he relies entirely too much on that arm and is altogether excitable, helter-skelter, and unreliable as a military leader. He has, however, some hardheaded common sense men with him who will save him from disaster. Troops are still pouring in by the trains.

AUGUST 27, WEDNESDAY.—Fair and pleasant. Heard cannon to the northeast evidently on the line of our railroad communications with Washington. Pope sent me with a message to Major General Heintzelman, ordering him to send two brigades back on the line to silence the enemy's attack. Seeking for General Heintzelman's quarters I fell into General Hooker's. He was just mounting and said he was about to visit Heintzelman and would conduct me. We passed large bodies of troops moving toward Warrenton. Hooker is a fine-looking man, tall, florid, and beardless.[5] At Heintzelman's I delivered my message. The veteran said he and his troops had been hurried down here on the cars without horses, ambulances, baggage, or artillery. He said they ought to have been marched down with all their appliances and their very movement would have guarded the road; as it was, they were naked, with only their arms and their clothes. Still, he immediately put the brigades in motion. Heintzelman is a knotty, hard-looking old customer with a grizzled beard and shambling one-sided gait.[6] Evidently a man of energy and reliability, and esteemed a capital soldier.

Returned to headquarters. Eleven o'clock. We hear cannon again in the direction of Warrenton. Troops are moving en masse toward Manassas. At two o'clock the staff rode in the same direction. News

Thoroughfare Gap and to cut off Pope's communications with Washington by striking Manassas Junction.

5. Joseph Hooker (1814-79), USMA '37, had served on the Peninsula under McClellan. At Antietam he led the First Corps and, after Burnside's release, Hooker commanded the Army of the Potomac at Chancellorsville. After being transferred to the West, Hooker was snubbed by Sherman and resigned from the army.

6. Samuel P. Heintzelman (1805-80), USMA '26, commanded the Third Corps on the Peninsula until withdrawn to support Pope. Second Bull Run terminated his command in the field.

was brought that the bridges at Bristoe were burned by the enemy and farther on an officer rode up from Hooker, saying that the enemy were in force in his front across the railroad and that he was in want of ammunition. They were engaged and had been for some time. As we approached nearer the scene, the remains of the burnt bridges were seen over Kettle and Broad Runs and we met stragglers and wounded men by the wayside. . . . Arriving on a hill overlooking Broad Run a battery opened beyond a wood and the smoke rolled over the trees about a mile ahead of us. This was our own battery, Hooker with his division having crossed the run and occupied the woods beyond. I was ordered to ride to the front and tell General Hooker of General Pope's arrival. When I got into the wood in advance I met General Grover,[7] who said the enemy were in force formed in line across the railway. Their line seemed to be a mile long, and they showed a good deal of cavalry and one battery. General Hooker said he wanted more men. The enemy, he said, had opposed him with four brigades and had made a long and stubborn fight. He had entered the fight with six thousand men, but losses and straggling had reduced it to four thousand. His men were fatigued, out of ammunition—some had but four rounds in their boxes—and he wanted reinforcements. Hooker's manner was dignified and soldierly.

Returning to the staff, I saw seven Confederate prisoners. Talking with them I satisfied myself that Jackson with probably twenty-five thousand men was somewhere in front of us. The force actually engaged here was the division of Ewell, not over six thousand men and one battery. McDowell is in position on their flank with thirty or forty thousand men towards Thoroughfare Gap. Tomorrow there will be a grand denouement. . . . .

AUGUST 28, THURSDAY.—Cloudy and warm. Before dawn I heard the commander-in-chief shouting, "Come, get up. Wake up. Get breakfast and get ready." We were all soon upon our feet. The General sat smoking his cigar and listening for the opening sounds of the battle. At intervals he nipped into delinquents of all grades, white and black. Scouts came in who reported that the enemy were moving to the left. This will throw them on McDowell. Presently came the long-expected cannonade to the westward or northwestward. About midday the staff mounted and rode to Manassas

7. Cuvier Grover (1828-85), USMA '50, commanded the brigade in Hooker's division that made contact with Jackson's army after its march to Manassas Junction. In 1863 Grover commanded a division of the Nineteenth Corps in the Department of the Gulf.

Junction. As we approached the place we could see the smoke rolling up from the burning cars destroyed by the enemy last night. Just at this point I was sent back with a message to Fitz-John Porter and Heintzelman to order them forward to Manassas. I found Porter and delivered the message, then found Heintzelman and Hooker in the edge of a wood. Thence I rode back to the Junction by a road on the left of the railroad.

At the Junction I witnessed the widespread ruin made by the Confederates. Long trains of cars lately loaded with stores of all kinds were consumed as they stood on the track, smoking and smoldering, only the iron work remaining entire. The whole plain as far as the eye could reach was covered with boxes, barrels, military equipment, cooking utensils, bread, meat, and beans lying in the wildest confusion. The spoilers had evidently had a good time and feasted themselves while they destroyed. . . . At the Junction the village occupied by Negroes, sutlers, pie venders, and storekeepers was wasted, and droll exhibits of furniture, cookery, and wardrobes scattered around were everywhere visible. I rejoined the staff located under the shadow of one of the redoubts. From here we rode toward Centerville, hearing the enemy were in that direction. Pushing across Bull Run, the staff stopped on an eminence to look at a battle that was going on some three and a half miles to the left.[8] The fight commenced fiercely about sunset and continued until after dark. We could see the smoke rising above the trees, and as it grew darker the flash of the guns and bursting of the shells could be distinctly discerned. When it became dark we rode back to the south side of Bull Run and encamped in a low damp spot.

AUGUST 29, FRIDAY.—Clear and warm. At three o'clock I was aroused by Ruggles to carry a message to Fitz-John Porter[9] then lying at Bristoe. Kearny had entered Centerville the evening before and it was understood that McDowell had cut off the enemy's retreat. Porter was ordered to bring up his corps to Centerville as there would probably be a sanguinary battle this day. I trotted rapidly toward Bristoe Station, the road being alive with moving trains. The day began to dawn as I passed the Junction and by the time I reached Porter's quarters it was broad daylight. An orderly showed me to his tent,

8. The battle observed was Groveton, being fought then by King and Jackson.

9. Fitz-John Porter (1822-1901), USMA '45, commanded the Fifth Corps on the Peninsula. Sent to support Pope via Falmouth, Porter failed to attack Jackson's right on August 29 and was relieved of his command in November. Proved guilty of misconduct, he was cashiered from the army in January, 1863. In 1878 Porter succeeded in clearing himself and was reappointed to the army as a colonel of infantry.

where I found the handsome general lying on his cot covered with an elegant fancy blanket. I lit a candle for him and delivered my dispatch. He read it coolly while I looked at his watch, which marked 5:20 exactly. The orders were issued to move the troops immediately, and Porter sat down to write some dispatches while the rest of the staff and myself sat down to breakfast. While writing he looked up and asked how to spell "chaos." I told him and at the same time divined what he was thinking about. He told me he had had daily communications with Washington and said they made many inquiries there for Mr. Pope, having heard nothing of him. While at breakfast I heard the first gun of the day. During my ride back the guns kept booming from time to time, but slowly and with intervals.

Arrived at Centerville I found the staff at a house on an eminence. From this height we could see the battle which had now begun to thicken. The cannonading was waxing heavier and the smoke rolled heavily above the woods in several places showing extended lines and a hotly contested action. Columns of dust all converging toward the battle indicated the march of ours and the enemy's supporting columns. We could even speculate upon the advance of Longstreet through Thoroughfare Gap and his repulse by Ricketts, and then Ricketts falling back on the main body. The order was given to mount, and we all followed Pope on the Warrenton turnpike toward the battlefield. Many stragglers were toiling along the heated and dusty road toward the battle while others were asleep or skulking through the woods. Under every convenient shade were parties of "fricoteurs" cooking, picking chickens, washing corn, and making themselves comfortable in every way. These recreant hogs. Pope cursed and shamed them with little effect. When near the great field, I was ordered back to hurry up the ammunition trains.

Having expedited my ammunition order, I returned as rapidly as possible to the battlefield. The smoke was rising more than ever and the roar of the guns still more grand. I found Pope and staff under a pine tree on a commanding hill overlooking most of the field but the enemy shut out by an intervening hill occupied by our artillery, now in full blast. The scene was grand and terrible. The roar and crackle of musketry continued. The artillery men of thirty pieces in sight worked with a fierce activity. The infantry massed in line lay behind the hills, occasionally changing position to avoid the shells which fell near or among them. I saw two horses performing the most extraordinary gyrations, a shell having burst between them. They hopped and bowed, then tumbled one over the other and rolled, then rose again and repeating the same uncouth performance presently fell and lay there. I saw them afterward, both dead, one having lost his foreleg and the other his hindleg by the shell. I was sent on a hill to the front to order General Reno to put forward his division to clear a large wood from whence our artillery was annoyed by the enemy's sharpshooters. I delivered my message to Reno, who immediately formed and advanced his troops in beautiful style. From the wood a rapid and scattering fire was pumped upon us. Reno advanced to the wood, entered, and a furious fire of near an hour's duration ensued. The result was that we were driven out in the end with much loss and Reno himself came back to report. Shells then commenced flying over our heads so fast that the staff changed position.

Large bodies of troops were then seen moving out from a wood on our extreme left, and Sigel's troops in the center began to give way, leaving by twos, threes, tens, and dozens. I was sent to the left to ascertain whose troops were moving, and another aide was sent to arrest the retreat of Sigel's men.[10] I rode across country to reach my destination, apparently a mile and a half distant. I ascertained that they were the Pennsylvania reserve under General Reynolds. General Schenck, to whom my orders were addressed, lay concealed from the enemy to the right of these reserves. I delivered my message, which was not to show his men yet. The same order I gave to Reynolds. I then returned to the staff.

General Kearny came up, and Reno having failed to carry the woods in the center, Kearny was ordered to do so. He went in and a most furious fight followed, continual and rapid volleys of musketry for two hours without any intermission. Toward sunset Kearny came in and reported that he had carried the wood, that his loss had been awful, but that of the enemy had been three to one. The enemy had marched on him in lines ten deep, which had been mowed down by the steady fire of his infantry. After Reno's repulse and before Kearny went in, it was thought proper to shell the woods. Reno hesitated as he said it was full of the wounded of both armies. Nevertheless, as it was a point of great importance, thirty pieces were brought to bear upon it and it was shelled for half an hour. Then Kearny carried it with his divisions as stated. The staff and escort then rode forward under a fire of the enemy's artillery from the left. . . . We remained here under fire until after dark, when on our extreme left there oc-

10. Pope was obviously unaware that Longstreet had supported Jackson and that Sigel's position was untenable.

curred a very sharply contested and very beautiful combat of musketry. The woods and meadows sparkled as with lightning bugs in July. With this combat ended this bloody and hard-fought battle. . . .

I have written principally what came under my eye and have as yet no knowledge of the whole plan of the battle. When from Bristoe, Pope sent McDowell and Sigel forward to Gainesville and Thoroughfare Gap, he expected to catch Jackson with about twenty-five thousand men and cut off his retreat with forty thousand under those two generals. From Centerville he pushed Kearny on his rear and from Broad Run ordered Fitz-John Porter to march first on Centerville; then countermanding these orders, he turned his march from Manassas Junction toward Gainesville to strike Jackson on his flank. It was the prevailing opinion that he had Jackson trapped, and so secure were we in our ability to handle him that we already enjoyed the victory in advance. At the conclusion of Friday's fight, Pope was firmly of the opinion that Jackson was beaten and would get off in the night.

AUGUST 30, SATURDAY.—Fair and warm. Pope found the enemy still in front of him and was told that parties of cavalry and even batteries had been seen on our flanks. These reports he counted for nothing and sent me forward with orders to General Ricketts on our right to advance his corps and feel the enemy cautiously. I found General Ricketts in the edge of a wood looking rather dejected.[11] I delivered my message, when he told me that he had already felt the enemy with his division and had been repulsed with infantry en masse and had also been shelled. General Duryée, who led the attack, had been wounded in the hand and was present, much excited.[12] He swore that the enemy, instead of retreating, were in force and menacing. Ricketts more coolly assured me of the same thing and asked what information General Pope had to base his idea of the enemy's retreat upon. I could not tell him, and he then requested me to say to General Pope that he did not deem it prudent to advance under the circumstances, yet if he peremptorily ordered it, he would go in with the certainty of having his division used up. I rode off and reported his

11. James B. Ricketts (1817-87), USMA '39, commanded a battery at First Bull Run, where he was taken prisoner. After his exchange, he was made brigadier general of volunteers and commanded a division under McDowell at Cedar Mountain. At Second Bull Run he opposed Longstreet at Thoroughfare Gap and held part of the Federal right wing. Later in the war Ricketts fought in the Wilderness and at Petersburg.

12. Abram Duryée (1815-90) rose to command through the New York militia. At Antietam he was wounded three times, was furloughed, and resigned from the army early in 1863. Duryée was police commissioner and dockmaster in New York after the war.

answer to General Pope and asked if I should return to General Ricketts with further orders. He hesitated a moment and then replied testily, "No, damn it. Let him go." Pope was walking to and fro apart and smoking as usual, evidently solving some problem of contradictory evidence in his mind. His preconceived opinions and his wishes decided him. McDowell came in and they spent the morning under a tree waiting for the enemy to retreat.

About three in the afternoon there was a sudden order to horse, and the staff moved rapidly to the left to a ridge overlooking the ground to the left. The enemy's artillery occupied a ridge which covered the gorge of Young's Run on both sides of which our troops lay. Between us and this ridge the woods rung with volleying musketry from Porter's Corps, which had attacked the enemy in that direction. Porter, having entirely failed to get up the day previous and having done nothing in Friday's fight, his conduct was strongly commented upon, and in his interview with Pope this morning there was doubtless some bitter talk. With this opportunity to reinstate himself and the fine reputation of his troops, much was expected from his corps today, but the impression is that it acted but feebly and soon gave way.

The enemy's attack seemed to prevail, as his fire was heard clearly advancing on our extreme left and turning our position. With a glass I could see an aide-de-camp riding rapidly along the brow of the hill where the cannon were posted, stopping to give directions at each gun. I remarked to Pope that this looked like a desperate attempt to force a road to Warrenton for retreat. He seemed pleased with the idea and then exclaimed, "By God, they are taking off their artillery anyhow." Just then a number of regiments marched over the brow of the hill and rapidly descending to its foot formed line of battle in two lines. To the left of this movement I also discovered a battery of light artillery advancing with speed against the wood where Porter was engaged. As these regiments moved, I could see our shells falling among them but producing no confusion or hesitation in their advance. The musketry now opened fiercely on our left, and the hillside where Schenck commanded was covered with our flying troops. There was also a stampede on the center among Sigel's men and the fugitives filled the main road to Centerville. I was ordered to ride with all speed to General Heintzelman on our extreme right and bring over the two brigades of Ricketts. I found Heintzelman, who said that Ricketts could not move as he now occupied a most important position, but he said there was a whole division of Pennsylvania reserves disengaged. So I took the discretionary power of ordering them over at double quick. When I got back to the left things looked badly. Infantry, artillery, and cavalry were breaking and hurrying off the field. The Centerville road was crowded and the whole army seemed to promise another Bull Run stampede. Staff officers with swords were rallying the fugitives, and a line of steady cavalry with drawn sabres were endeavoring to stem the disgraceful tide. The enemy's fire was fiercely advancing on our left and the whole position was under a storm of fire. This was evidently the crisis of the battle and the campaign, and a disgraceful defeat seemed imminent.

The line of battle on the left was now forced back until it lay at right angles with our general position. The fury of the contest was unabated. Reno's steady legions were now massed on the left, the reserves were over, and the panic ceased. The enemy's advance seemed to be checked, but their attack still persisted. From the sounds that rent the air there seemed to be new missiles introduced into the fight. These were sections of railroad iron which hurtled through the air with a whirring, like an old-fashioned spinning wheel. They were fired by the Rebel artillery in default of better ammunition and were sufficiently effective when they struck. I saw them kill some horses and they fell among the staff with a thud, throwing dirt over us, but injuring no one. As we were just behind the infantry who were resisting the enemy's attack, we were frequently enveloped in a shower of musketry, the balls as they struck in front, between, and behind us knocking up a column of dust. Their singing, unless they came very near, was drowned in the roar of firearms. I saw a bullet strike the shoe of a horse standing next to mine. The horse stamped his foot a little, but was not hurt.

The sun set red and angry behind the battle cloud, and as it grew dark the fury of the contest abated but did not entirely cease. Our right and center had been ordered to fall back on a line with our left, which had been driven back. It was now quite dark with a quarter moon only to shed its dim light. . . . When I led General Sigel to Pope's position, he began to talk and suggested they should not leave the field. Pope curtly checked him and said that he had not sent for him to receive suggestions but to give him orders, as his mind was made up what to do. These were to fall back on Centerville with his whole force and to see that the movement was executed smoothly and in order. Reno was ordered to hold the position on the left where the enemy's attack had been checked until everything had retired and was safe, then to form the rear guard and retire on Centerville. Pope observed to the Generals about him, "Everything is now arranged. If I could be of any further service, I would remain, but as I cannot, we will ride back to Centerville." It was seven or eight miles distant to Centerville, but by that night's ride it seemed twenty. We at length arrived and after wandering around in the dark for an hour found headquarters in a house near the main road. . . .

In this campaign Pope was entirely deceived and outgeneraled. His own conceit and pride of opinion led him into these mistakes. On the field his conduct was cool, gallant, and prompt. When the facts of the case were forced upon him, he met them with soldierly coolness and energy, but he was in the general planning of the campaign unable to cope with his opponents. For myself, the mortification of failure and defeat was for the time forgotten, and I slept.

AUGUST 31, SUNDAY.—Raining. During the night my sleep was frequently broken by moving to and fro of officers and orderlies, Generals talking in loud, excited voices. A discussion took place between Pope and another officer in regard to McClellan. The officer maintained that McClellan's plans had been interfered with. Pope curtly and rudely declared it was not so; he had seen the written papers proving the contrary. He said McClellan had endeavored to screen his failures and lay the blame of his incapacity on the Government and he had positive proof of the facts. He said that it had been prearranged that McDowell's or some equivalent corps should remain in position between Washington and Richmond and that when McClellan marched on Yorktown he had gone with the predetermined idea of having a siege of something and although there were but ten thousand men at Yorktown, he squatted there to have the siege and permitted in the meantime all his power to oppose him. There was undoubtedly some force in these remarks. The officer defending McClellan still defended him but made no satisfactory reply to these charges.

In speaking of the force engaged in the two days' battles, Pope said he had but fifty-seven thousand men. Of these about seven thousand ran away, most of whom were gathered in Centerville by the guard there. Our dead and wounded were left on the field. Our loss in the battle by killed, wounded, and disorganization will probably exceed twenty thousand men. . . .

Generals Sumner[13] and Franklin[14] had got up with their divisions

13. Edwin V. Sumner (1797-1863) commanded the Second Corps on the Peninsula and at Antietam. After Fredericksburg he was relieved at his own request.

14. William B. Franklin (1823-1903), USMA '43, commanded a brigade of raw

and I saw them at headquarters. Centerville is itself an insignificant village, on a commanding ridge and powerfully defended with earth works. The country around was cleared of forests and rethickened by a year's growth of bushes. The position by nature is very strong and it was skillfully fortified with detached bastions and redoubts with lines of parapets connecting some points. On the sides and summits of these ridges lay our whole army and its recent reinforcements, numbering seventy thousand men. The scene was grand, yet sorrowful. The stern desolation of war marked everything. The living, wounded, and dead were mingled. The huts of former occupants and the bivouac fires of the present were all together. Dead animals swelled with corruption and the whitening bones of those long decayed lay beside each other. Fresh graves were beside the weed-grown sepulchres. But no man thought of these things. Each seemed intent on relieving the little human necessities of the now. Food and rest took precedence of all thought and sentiment.

I was called on to ride to Fairfax Court House with an order to all guards to permit sick and wounded to pass free to Washington. I thought the order a very unnecessary one, as I did not suppose any guard was silly enough to require it. Yet I was glad to have something which would take me away from headquarters. The road was covered with ambulances, wagons, and stragglers on horses and afoot. Among those were hundreds of government employees and citizens who had volunteered to come out to Centerville to nurse the wounded. There were fifty or a hundred city hacks seen among the muddy and begrimed vehicles of war that moved about the army. The citizens were sent back as likely to be more in the way than useful, although their effort was well intended. . . . I delivered my orders and went into the vestibule of the courthouse to sleep. Lying upon a long box I was told by a guard that there was a dead man in that box. I replied that my lying there would not disturb his rest. So I stretched out to sleep, but presently a man came with hammer and nails to close the lid, so I sought a place in the tavern. It was filled with wounded. Amputations and dressings were going on and the floors were clothed with blood. There were no groans or outcries, however. In a vacant pantry I found a board upon two barrels and upon this I slept for two hours. Then I rode back to Centerville.

recruits at First Bull Run, but by May of 1862 led the Sixth Corps. At Antietam his force arrived too late to be of use. Following a feud with Burnside, Franklin was sent to Louisiana as leader of the Nineteenth Corps. After the war he was a vice-president of Colts' Firearms.

A flag of truce has been sent by Pope, asking permission to take the wounded off the field and parties were over the lines already executing that duty. Officers were discussing the battle. In war I am an extremist. In war men should not maneuver but should fight. I like Pope's pluck in fighting. He expected support and should have had it. If the support had been at hand, the disasters of Saturday would have been a brilliant victory. Fitz-John Porter failed in his duty in not attacking the enemy on the flank as he moved from Gainesville to the field. He failed perhaps from ill will toward Pope. The question will be tried by the proper tribunal. The advance of Franklin and Sumner had not been as expeditious as was possible. It is said it was purposely delayed, by McClellan. Thus through the jealousy of commanders the great cause of nationality is jeopardized, if not lost.

From Centerville our headquarters was moved back two miles on the Fairfax road. A few tents were pitched and immediately occupied by the magnates and junior officers of the staff. I was left out, so with Devins stretched a blanket upon the tent ropes and made my lair on the wet ground, my feet sticking out into the rain.

SEPTEMBER 1, MONDAY.—Clear and warm. . . . The General and staff rode around all day from one general's quarters to another, planning and consulting. All the trains behind Bristoe with 150,000 rations had been destroyed and Banks had retired from Manassas Junction on Bull Run. We heard guns in that quarter occasionally and reports were brought of a move to throw a force on our right by the Little River turnpike. . . . The General gave the staff permission to go back to Fairfax Court House to pass the night in camp. . . .

SEPTEMBER 2, TUESDAY.—Cold and windy. . . . I was ordered out on the Alexandria road to search for and recall Sigel, but before going far I found he was not on that road at all. I therefore bought a newspaper and read some accounts of our brilliant victories. Heard the news that General Kearny had been killed last night and his body sent in by the enemy under a flag. Thus ends the one-armed hero of the war, a man of great valor and energy and a serious loss to us. About four o'clock we rode toward Alexandria. After riding several miles through a quiet and secluded region we came in view of camps on Munson's and Upton's hills. These were occupied by our troops and it was a cheering sight to see them. On the crest of these heights I first caught a glimpse of the Seminary steeple near Alexandria where I had stayed in Kearny's command last winter. The next crest showed me the dome of the Capitol at Washington, still unfinished. Behind,

I could hear the boom of the enemy's guns. Here another byplay took place but so lost in the grander gloom of the national drama that I scarcely noticed it. Near Fort Buffalo stood McClellan and suite, sitting stiff and soldierly on horseback as if waiting to pay his respects to our approaching column. Pope and McDowell passed by without noticing him. Presently their attention was directed to the fact that the General, late commander-in-chief, was present. They turned and rode toward him. As they advanced, he met them and they exchanged greetings. The bands played and the troops cheered for McClellan but were silent when the other general passed. . . .

SEPTEMBER 3, WEDNESDAY.—Fair and warm. . . . Dr. Johnson of the Michigan Cavalry just called in and tells me he is from the late battle-field. He found there the body of my kind friend Colonel Brodhead of the 1st Michigan Cavalry. He says he leaves on the field between two and three thousand of our wounded who are perishing with hunger. He comes to see General Pope about getting them off the field. . . . The camp is full of rumors today as to changes in the cabinet and army commanders. At Buford's we discoursed on the late battles. Buford made a cavalry charge on the left, checking the enemy's cavalry completely. It was in this charge that Brodhead and many other officers of the 1st Michigan were killed. Buford said Brodhead was wounded and surrendered, when he was shot by the excited men. Our men also shot several officers whom they had taken. Buford thinks the retreat should not have been ordered. I am inclined to think that if we had held the ground the victory would have been ours. . . .

SEPTEMBER 5, FRIDAY.—Fair and pleasant. . . . Got permission to visit the city with a letter recommending a leave of absence for several days. Ruggles rode in with me. He has suffered from the same brutish treatment by Pope that others complain of, and he threatens to resign. On that subject there is no diversity of opinion among Pope's officers. . . . There seems to be a furious and universal outcry against Pope. The regular army, it seems, are his most uncompromising enemies and chiefly carp at his personal character, which they say is bad. There is certainly little to attract in Pope's manners, but I am not so sure that the loss of the battle on Saturday is altogether chargeable to his mismanagement. Jealousy and feeble support on the part of the regulars, and the slow advance of Franklin and Sumner seemed to have assured the loss of a battle. The outcry against McDowell is absurd beyond belief. He is charged with cowardice, treachery, and a host of other crimes too preposterous to name. . . .

V

With McClellan at Antietam

September 6, 1862—September 24, 1862

After Pope's release from command of the Army of Virginia,
Strother was absorbed upon the staff of General McClellan, who took
the field in pursuit of Lee after the Confederate armies had invaded
Maryland. McClellan's staff was large, well oiled, and professional
looking. As the Army of the Potomac moved toward Frederick, it
seemed to radiate confidence.

On September 13 a lost Confederate dispatch, giving the full plan
of Lee's Maryland Campaign, was put into McClellan's hands. Aban-
doning his usual caution, the Union commander pushed through
Crampton's and Turner's gaps and compelled Lee to concentrate his
army at Sharpsburg. Franklin's Corps, delegated to relieve the sur-
rounded garrison at Harpers Ferry, was stopped in Pleasant Valley.
On September 15 Harpers Ferry fell to Jackson, who immediately
hurried his troops to the support of Lee. Meanwhile, McClellan
gathered his legions to crush Lee against the Potomac, but he had
waited one day too long.

On September 17 the Battle of Antietam began with unco-ordinated
Union attacks upon the Confederate left, center, and finally the right.
In each instance the assaults were neutralized. At the end of the day
the Confederate army had been cut to pieces but still held the field.
On September 18 McClellan inexplicably awaited an attack that never
came, and on the same night Lee began to withdraw to Virginia.
McClellan's grand opportunity to destroy Lee was gone, and, with it,
his career as a Union commander.

SEPTEMBER 6, SATURDAY.—Fair and pleasant. Went to Willard's and
saw Colonel B. S. Alexander of the Engineers, who informed me that
Pope was relieved of his command and would probably be sent

west. . . .[1] In the evening I met Major Meline and other officers of our staff, some of whom are going west with Pope. Saw Garrett of the B & O Railroad, who told me that five thousand men of the Rebel advance marched into Frederick this morning.[2] This move must be the ruin of the Rebellion, since to suppose they can conquer the United States is absurd. They must then perish by their own movement. This evening sixty pieces of cannon and about twenty thousand infantry passed up G Street moving on the Frederick road.

SEPTEMBER 7, SUNDAY.—Fair and warm. . . . General Pope, clad in neat citizen dress, left for the West accompanied by the majority of his staff. He gave them a general invitation to accompany him to the western command. I did not go even to pay my respects to him, although fallen as he was in public opinion I was strongly tempted to. I am now glad I did not for although prompted by a feeling of generosity toward a fallen man, it would have been a false exhibition of interest and very probably would have been received in a manner to increase my irritation against him. Let him return to his wallow in the swamps of the Mississippi. . . . Saw Major Slack and spoke to him about getting an appointment on the staff of McClellan. He said he thought he could serve me and promised to attend to it immediately.

SEPTEMBER 8, MONDAY.—Fair and warm. . . . McClellan has taken the field against the enemy and troops are still marching out toward Frederick. Saw Major Slack who tells me he has spoken to Colonel [Seth?] Williams of McClellan's staff, who says he will remember the request. . . . Colonel Clark told me in the evening at Willard's that General Banks was appointed to the command of the city of Washington and desired me to be assigned to staff duty with him. This seemed to promise some relief from the fatigues of camp life. About half past eleven I was aroused by a military telegram, an order to report in the morning to McClellan at Rockville. This was not repose but action. So I went to sleep again.

SEPTEMBER 9, TUESDAY.—Warm and cloudy. . . . I left the city at three o'clock. The road to Rockville was filled with trains and stragglers. It was hot and dusty and I arrived at the town about sunset. To the left of the town, half a mile toward Great Falls was the en-

1. Barton S. Alexander, an outstanding engineering officer, had been in charge of defensive fortifications during McClellan's evacuation from Harrison's Landing and had been rushed to Washington to assist in preparing the city for an attack from Lee.

2. John W. Garrett (1820-84), the president of the Baltimore and Ohio Railroad, was often blamed by Confederates for their inability to seize Washington, since his telegraphers usually picked up the advance of the enemy before the Union army.

campment of McClellan's headquarters on an open hill. The Commander greeted me cordially, recalling the last time we had met at Charles Town. He then formally asked me to become a member of his staff, to which I consented. After this, maps were produced and the General stated his plans to me. He had information which, he said, he could not reject—that the enemy lay behind Monocacy a hundred thousand strong.[3] He had forces at Poolesville, Barnestown, Goshen, and Mechanicsburg. The enemy had not turned toward Hagerstown nor toward Gettysburg, but had advanced to New Market on the Baltimore road and occupied Ridgeville on the B & O Railroad. He named about eighty thousand men which he had posted at the different points, and proposed to advance his whole line to Parr's Ridge, occupying Ridgeville, Damascus, Clarksville, and Barnesville. Sugarloaf Mountain was already occupied. I gave the General all the information I had about the Ridge, the towns, the fords and crossings of the Monocacy, and the country about Frederick back to Harpers Ferry. We then discoursed generally about army matters. He said his cavalry had entirely the prestige of Stuart's, having cowed it in many combats so that it would not stand at all. Our conversation was clear, unembarrassed, and agreeable. On parting the General pressed my hand warmly and expressed great satisfaction at the information I had given him, his gratification at having me upon his staff, etc. I replied that it was a position I had coveted from the beginning and hoped I would be useful. This kind, manly reception, so different from the manner of Pope, reveals the secret of McClellan's popularity with the officers and men. . . .

SEPTEMBER 10, WEDNESDAY.—I finished three copies of a map, designed for Burnside, Sumner, and Franklin. I cannot but feel that I am in a superior atmosphere to that which surrounded John Pope. I saw Rush's lancers pass at a distance with their red pennants and long lances; they had quite a "middle ages" appearance.[4] A paper enjoining upon all officers to endeavor to suppress pillage was handed to me and I signed it to prove service.

SEPTEMBER 11, THURSDAY.—. . . Saw a copy of the letter said to have been written by Colonel Brodhead just before his death, saying, "I die one of the victims of Pope's imbecility and McDowell's treachery." The letter is not unlike Brodhead. He says "from my dying couch." I understood he died upon the battlefield and Dr. Johnson, who re-

3. McClellan was, as usual, vastly overrating the size of Lee's army, which was about half that size.
4. The 6th Pennsylvania Volunteers, commanded by Colonel Richard Rush.

covered his body, made no mention of this letter. If it was really written by him, his friends were most imprudent in having it published. What does it prove? Except that it was the opinion of a highly excited and dying man not remarkable in life for the coolness and fairness of his views. Colonel Brodhead was a man to whom I was personally attached and whose moral and social qualities I respected. I was indebted to him while in the Valley for many kind and polite attentions. Yet I do not think the opinions of a dying man are worth as much as those of a living one.

We are all packed for starting, harnessed, and tents partly struck. It promises to be a rainy day. As far as I have observed, the tone of those surrounding General McClellan's person is eminently conservative. Personal grievances have perhaps biased my judgment, but my natural character leads me to prefer strong and active measures in war. . . . The great error of our Government in this war is that it has yielded too much to an extreme faction which tolerates no liberality of views. In its insulting fury it drives into the ranks of the Rebellion all who are weak, irresolute, and confused. Instead of dividing to conquer, they have united and concentrated a whole people against the Government. . . .

Franklin having been ordered to Sugarloaf Mountain, it was supposed our move of headquarters depended on his success. We moved about four o'clock across the fields to the Frederick road. McClellan's staff is quite numerous and of high rank. It is about fifty strong with two generals and a half a dozen or more colonels. There is more appearance of military etiquette and soldierly bearing about it than I have yet seen. . . . . On a little meadow near the Seneca our tents were pitched. I fell into conversation with an officer next to me. He talked of Berkeley Springs and mentioned many incidents of the past year familiar to me but which I did not think were generally known. He then asked of the geography of the country and the enemy's probable intentions. He took me to his tent and I discovered it was General Marcy, McClellan's father-in-law and chief of staff.[5] He here showed me telegrams from divers points to show that the enemy had no troops in front of Washington but was massed with his whole force on the Monocacy. Further that a movement en masse had been commenced toward Hagerstown and the points in front (east) of the Monocacy had been abandoned. The cavalry at New Market that

5. Randolph B. Marcy (1812-87), USMA '32, was the father of Mary Ellen Marcy, McClellan's wife. Marcy served as chief of staff for his son-in-law during the Peninsula and Maryland campaigns. After the war he became Inspector of the Army.

Burnside was ordered to attack had also yielded with little resistance. The retrograde movement on Hagerstown I said meant a retreat into the Valley of the Shenandoah by way of Williamsport.[6] This seemed to be the received opinion. . . .

SEPTEMBER 12, FRIDAY.—Cloudy and warm. Tents struck at eight o'clock and the staff took the road early. Talked further with General Marcy as we rode. The indications seemed to confirm our last night's judgment of the places of the enemy. General White[7] was at Martinsburg with several thousand men, Colonel Miles at Harpers Ferry with ten thousand. The enemy's movements might have the additional éclat of enveloping and destroying these corps. To prevent it, we must press him. . . .

A mile before reaching Urbana we halted in a lovely grove surrounded by grass fields like shaven lawns. Here camp was pitched. . . .

SEPTEMBER 13, SATURDAY.—Fair and pleasant. Started early and entered Frederick City at about ten o'clock. Here an ovation awaited us that touched the inmost soul. The whole city was fluttering with Union flags. From windows and balconies handkerchiefs were waving while faces beamed with joyful excitement filled every opening. The sidewalks were crowded with citizens of every age, sex, and color. No formal cheering, no regulated display, but a wild spontaneous outcry of joy. Old men rushed out and barred the passage of our cavalcade to grasp the hand of McClellan. Ladies brought out bouquets and flags to decorate his horse. Fathers held up their children for a kiss and a recognition.

Riding around several streets the General at length took the turnpike toward Baltimore and in the eastern suburb stopped to visit Burnside who was encamped there. A cavalry officer narrated some incidents of the occupation of the town the day previous. Both parties had cavalry and artillery and fought through the streets. Our troops charged and drove the enemy, but rallying he turned and drove us back upon our artillery. The gunner stood by his loaded piece with the cord taut in his hand and ready to pull. A stupid trooper rode against the cord and discharged the piece full into the faces of our column,

6. Jackson's movement back to Virginia was a maneuver against Harpers Ferry, not a retreat.

7. Julius White (1816-93), a Fremont supporter, was driven by Jackson from Martinsburg to Harpers Ferry, where he placed himself under the command of Colonel Miles and surrendered on September 15. Placed under arrest, White was exonerated. Resigning from the army in 1864, he resumed his business career in Illinois.

killing two and wounding a dozen. Our infantry finally drove the enemy out. . . .

Lee entered Maryland evidently indulging the hope that the state would use and welcome the Confederate army. The cold reception, the terror of the sentimental Secessionists, the fact that he lost five men by desertion where he got one recruit, must soon have disenchanted him and caused his retrograde movement, preparing for a return to Virginia by Williamsport. After provisioning and refitting the army to the extent the country affords, this will be his course, gobbling up Miles at Harpers Ferry and White at Martinsburg if possible. The enemy's troops behaved well towards the country and citizens—better than ours will do, I fear. . . . We encamped a short distance on the west of Frederick in a pleasant clover field. General Marcy informed me that great apprehensions were entertained in regard to Miles' safety and consulted me as to his probable position. I gave as my opinion that he would occupy Maryland Heights and defend it successfully if he had determination enough to do so.

SEPTEMBER 14, SUNDAY.—Pleasant. Some distant guns at intervals. Troops all moving westward over the Catoctin ridge and into the Middletown valley. We rode rapidly to Middletown and there the Commander stopped at Burnside's quarters in a field at the eastern end of town. I was sent for by the commander-in-chief who wished me to find a man true and reliable to go to Harpers Ferry to carry a message to Miles. I found an acquaintance and endeavored to make the arrangement. A Dr. Baer assisted me. About two o'clock news came that the enemy disputed the passage of the ridge in force. The staff mounted and rode forward, taking position between two batteries on a high spur from whence most of the localities were visible. [Jacob] Cox's brigade and [Orlando B.] Willcox already occupied the height on the left dominating the high road.[8] [Samuel D.] Sturgis was ordered forward to reinforce them and to attack and drive the enemy. His glittering columns could be seen for a mile, crawling up the winding road. Reno, who commanded this corps, then mounted and said he would see to it in person. Toward the crest of the ridge on the right of the turnpike the Rebels were seen pouring up in continuous column to the high wooded crest which formed the key of the position in that quarter and from which one of their batteries was playing upon Reno's Corps. On our side we could at the same time see

8. Strother was witnessing the assault upon the Confederate forces at Turner's Gap, the principal action in the Battle of South Mountain.

Hooker moving up toward the same crest and a bald summit behind it with a division of fifteen thousand men.

While these elements of the battle were massing and approaching each other on the right, a steady rattle of musketry with increased activity of the batteries showed that Reno, whose columns we had seen enter the wooded crest, was now fully engaged on the left. Meanwhile [John] Gibbon with a brigade and section of artillery marched on the National Road in the center. The musketry on the left was long continued and rapid, but at length got out of hearing over the ridge, showing that Reno had driven the enemy. The smoke from Hooker's musketry now rose on the right, and columns of the enemy's infantry were seen moving back. Notwithstanding the advance of our two heavy flanking columns, Gibbon's advance was arrested by a battery of the enemy commanding the turnpike and a sharp fire of infantry from the wooded slopes above the road. During this contest we could hear heavy thugs of cannon and musketry from Franklin's attack at the Burkittsville pass, three or four miles distant.[9]

As night fell, the fight on the turnpike with Gibbon became hotter and more interesting. The enemy's battery was gone, but Gibbon still worked his two guns and held the ground. We watched this contest till nine o'clock, then the staff rode off to a house on the road about a mile toward Middletown. . . . We had carried all our points and inflicted a great loss on the enemy, but our loss had been considerable. Reno, the gallant and dashing Reno, had fallen. Sturgis came in and in his rough way told us of it. He had pushed in with the advance and received a mortal wound in the body from a musket ball. As he was carried by on a stretcher he cried to Sturgis, "Sam, I'm dead." His voice was firm and manly. Sturgis says he ordered a section of artillery forward but found the way so encumbered by Rebel dead that he ordered forward a regiment to clear the way so that the bodies might not be crushed by the artillery wheels.

White, it was thought, had retired from Martinsburg and joined Miles at Harpers Ferry. Miles having withdrawn from Maryland Heights, our troops were concentrated on Bolivar Heights, while Jackson was moving via Williamsport and Martinsburg to intercept their retreat on Romney. This news Captain [Charles H.] Russel of the Maryland cavalry brought. The question tonight was whether the

9. Franklin was directed to cross South Mountain at Crampton's Gap and to open communication with Harpers Ferry; however, Harpers Ferry fell before Franklin pushed his force down Pleasant Valley.

enemy would retire during the night or reinforce and dispute the pass.

SEPTEMBER 15, MONDAY.—Fair. . . . The morning news has assured us of further success. Franklin has forced the pass at Burkittsville and gangs of Rebel prisoners are occasionally seen passing toward Fredcrick. Banks' Corps under Williams is up, and I saw my old acquaintances, Generals [Willis A.] Gorman, Gordon, and Crawford. The staff soon mounted and rode up the road on the left where Reno's Corps fought. At the summit we came upon their dead lying scattered through the woods and on the summit in a stone fence lane entering the road at right angles. The dead lay so thick that the lane was choked with them. Here Sturgis had them thrown aside to move his artillery forward. Their trappings were stripped off by the soldiers for mementoes of the battle. These dead were all killed with musketry and lay in all possible positions, some with countenances distorted, hands grasping leaves and sticks, others placid and one with a pleasant smile on his face. Squalid, filthy, and bloodstained as all these corpses were, there were some splendid specimens of manhood among them, tall, handsome, athletic fellows with well-turned features. . . .

At Boonsboro we stopped at a white house on the entrance to the town. I was sent with a message to Mansfield commanding Banks' division,[10] ordering them to turn down the Sharpsburg road, flanking Cedarville and entering Sharpsburg through Porterstown. Returning, I met Gordon, who was in high spirits and shouted, "Is not this glorious!" I thought so indeed but so frequently has misfortune followed on the heels of hope that I not yet dared to feel glorious. I reported to McClellan and then told him what I had heard from Booth, that the cavalry had (under Fitzhugh Lee) taken the pike to Hagerstown. "I know it," he said. "Pleasonton has followed and taken 250 prisoners." The masses of enemy infantry have moved to Sharpsburg. "There we are going to press them," he said quietly. Thus the alert and far-seeing Chieftain has already known and provided for everything. So we mounted and rode rapidly to Keedysville, halfway to Sharpsburg. The whole road was through masses of troops and our movement was escorted by one continuous cheering. Stopping on a hill half a mile beyond Keedysville, we drew up to reconnoiter the enemy who opened on us a rapid fire from two batteries. It did no damage that I could hear of. After dark General Marcy led the

10. Joseph K. Mansfield (1803-62), USMA '22, had been an engineer and expert on coastal defenses before the war. Commanding the Twelfth Corps at Antietam against the Confederate center, he was mortally wounded.

staff back to a hill near the village church where we lay down to sleep.

SEPTEMBER 16, TUESDAY.—Cloudy and warm. I was told that Miles had surrendered his whole force ignominiously at Harpers Ferry, ten thousand men. Did I not know that some damning misfortune was in store for us? The personnel of the staff remained nearly all day lying about the church with General Williams. I became restless and rode to the front. The cannonade had long ceased and all was quiet, but I saw enormous masses of infantry lying on the hills and met six batteries returning to take position on our right. When I got to Newcomer's brick house[11] where headquarters were, I found the General about to ride out. I joined him and we rode several miles to the right, crossing Antietam and flanking Sharpsburg in that direction. While we rode, a citizen joined us just from Harpers Ferry who reported that Colonel Miles had lost a leg at the fight there and had only surrendered about five thousand men. All the cavalry, about two thousand, had got away and passing by way of Williamsport had captured 112 of Longstreet's wagons, destroying 62 wagons of ammunition and sending 50 wagons of flour into Pennsylvania.[12]

The staff at length reached the position where Hooker was posted. Large bodies of troops were moving to the right and pushing forward through the woods cautiously, shelling in front of them wherever the enemy appeared in any number. Hooker recognized me and called to me and shook hands in a very friendly manner. Having put these troops in, we returned to Newcomer's. . . . I believe the enemy are not before us in force.

SEPTEMBER 17, WEDNESDAY.—Clouds and threatening rain. While at breakfast the cannon opened. The battle was evidently commencing. This was about 7:30 A.M. The fruits of Hooker's movement presently became apparent by the flight of Rebel troops from the wood on the right and the opening of musketry. Sumner's Corps was ordered up to fill a gap between Hooker and the center, and his columns could be seen moving beautifully into position. On the center General [Israel B.] Richardson and [Thomas F.] Meagher moved in handsomely and joined battle. The fire became tremendous. Our troops advanced, wavered, broke, and fled, then rallied and advanced again, leaving the earth strewed with blue jackets. Franklin advanced to reinforce

11. Headquarters was at the Pry House, not Newcomer's.

12. As would be expected, the rumor circulating through the Union army underestimated the loss at Harpers Ferry and overestimated the results of Colonel "Grimes" Davis' escape.

Sumner, while on the left Burnside with thirty-five thousand men made a flank movement to strike Sharpsburg by forcing a bridge over the Antietam one mile from the town.

Up to ten or eleven o'clock artillery fire raged along the whole line while musketry was heavy on the center and right. The right advanced, the center was checked but held its ground, Burnside made no progress at the bridge, which was fiercely defended. I went forward with a message to General Pleasonton[13] of the cavalry to advance two squadrons on the turnpike to reconnoiter Sharpsburg. Pleasonton answered gallantly, "I will do it, Sir," and ordered up the squadrons. Hooker was driving the enemy when I returned to the General, and our center was advancing. A Rebel regiment on the center which stood like a wall under heavy fire of musketry and artillery retired in order. McClellan was in high spirits. "It is the most beautiful field I ever saw," he exclaimed, "and the grandest battle! If we whip them today it will wipe out Bull Run forever." I answered, *"Fortuna favet fortibus."*

Fitz-John Porter's Corps fought under Burnside, while Porter himself remained with McClellan as counselor. They sat together during the morning in a redan of fence rails, Porter continually using the glass and reporting observations, McClellan smoking and sending orders. His manner was quiet, cool, and soldierly, his voice low-toned. I perceive he liked all about him to speak in low tones. The intense excitement under his manner was also very apparent. Presently news came that Hooker was wounded, that Mansfield was killed, and that Burnside's progress was unsatisfactory. He took the bridge and said he could hold it. A message was sent to him that if he could do no more, his command would be transferred to some other work.

Pleasonton had advanced two batteries on the center which were doing good work. Sumner was checked and a Rebel division poured from the disputed wood and advanced at full charge on his position across an open field. Their rush was at double-quick and was fearful to see. As they advanced they were hid from our view by a wood and the smoke of some burning buildings which the enemy had fired in the morning. The fire of Sumner was tremendous, and after some time of suspense the debris of the Rebel column was seen fleeing disorganized back across the open ground, followed by a storm of shells and balls.

13. Alfred Pleasonton (1824-67), USMA '44, commanded the cavalry at Antietam and afterward. He is credited with having saved Hooker from disaster at Chancellorsville in 1863. After the war Pleasonton became an internal revenue officer and later a railroad president.

A brigade of ours followed them cheering, but stopped in a sheltered hollow short of the wood from whence they kept up a skirmishing fire. The Irish brigade made a gallant rush on the center and forced the enemy back behind his batteries. [Captain William M.] Graham's battery then advanced most gallantly under a tremendous fire of at least forty guns and took position at short range, whence he opened on the enemy with effect. This position he held for some time, driving the enemy infantry still farther back. By one o'clock there was a general lull all along the line. Then came in news of more generals' fallen—Sedgwick wounded, Richardson wounded, [George L.] Hartsuff wounded, [Napoleon] Dana wounded. A feeble note from Sumner complaining that his command was cut to pieces and desiring reinforcements. All wore a serious air. From the signs of the day and the report of the prisoners it was evident the enemy was before us in full power, and the fact that he had risked a battle in his present position showed that he felt great confidence in his power.

From one to four the fight lulled almost entirely. General McClellan rode over with two or three aides to see Sumner. Meanwhile a number of civilians and countryfolk gathered on headquarters hill, gaping around to see the General commanding and quite as anxious to see his favorite horse, Daniel Webster. At four o'clock the battle reopened by our attack all along the lines. Our exhausted ammunition had been replenished and the troops breathed. We carried the wood on the right and Burnside made his grand effort. His advancing rush was in full view and magnificently done. He carried the height and took a battery, but the enemy had massed his infantry behind the crest and their ordnance overthrew the blow and decimated the regiments which had gained the summit. The crest was regained and held by the enemy, and our troops driven down the hill stood doggedly and held the halfway ground when night closed. During these late operations, the enemy fired a stockyard and a country mansion, where light glared over the bloody field long after the sun had set. The staff rode to reconnoiter the condition of things on the left. A few sullen guns still roared their hostile growls. Some scattering musketry still licked along the lines, but all presently sunk into quietude.

> And thousands sunk down on the ground overpowered,
> The weary to sleep and the wounded to die.

We rode back to our headquarters camp at Keedysville, where a good supper and a good night's rest closed the day of the great battle. The armies in round numbers were a hundred thousand men on each side. The Rebels chose their position and we attacked. McClellan and Lee met face to face in a grand pitched battle on a fair field. Neither side can make excuses or complain of disadvantages. As far as the day went, we beat them with great slaughter and heavy loss to ourselves. How decisive the results of the action, time can only show when the smoke and dust shall have been blown away. Toward evening the enemy sent troops to secure and hold the fords on the Potomac behind them. This looks like retreat.

SEPTEMBER 18, THURSDAY.—Clouds which lifted about nine o'clock. We have thirty-two thousand fresh men to put into battle today if it recommences. The enemy will not attack from all appearances. The orders given to our generals were to hold their positions but not to attack. To Burnside it was to withdraw the troops over the Antietam if he could do it safely. Four or five cannon shot of ours broke the stillness of the morning, but no response from the enemy. I think they will retreat by way of Harpers Ferry as a small rear guard can hold the road against our whole force. Saw General McClellan ride to the front and was called to accompany him. We rode to Sumner's post on the right where the General remained for some time in consultation. We then rode to the point of woods where there had been hard fighting. Generals Franklin, Smith, and Slocum with staff officers lay on some straw in the field behind the wood. Near them was the spot where General Mansfield fell, the trees scarred with bullets and broken with cannon shot. In every direction around men were digging graves and burying the dead. Ten or twelve bodies lay at the different pits and had already become offensive. In front of this wood was the bloody cornfield where lay two or three hundred festering bodies, nearly all of Rebels, the most hideous exhibition I had yet seen. Many were black as Negroes, heads and faces hideously swelled, covered with dust until they looked like clods. Killed during the charge and flight, their attitudes were wild and frightful. One hung upon a fence killed as he was climbing it. One lay with hands wildly clasped as if in prayer. From among these loathsome earth-soiled vestiges of humanity, the soldiers were still picking out some that had life left and carrying them in on stretchers to our surgeons. All the time some picket firing was going on from the wood on the Hagerstown turnpike near the white church.

With one good-looking young Rebel from South Carolina I

talked. He was shot through the thigh, bone unbroken. Our men were talking to him kindly and I told him he would soon get well. His voice was soft and subdued. The fire of battle had gone out in his soul. Another was sitting up on the stretcher and had taken a drink of water. He looked sleepy and nodded slightly. His face was bloody and his eyes swelled shut. A ball had entered the bridge of his nose and come out the back of his head. This cornfield had been fiercely disputed and had been several times traversed by infantry, horse, and artillery. The green corn was downtrodden and wilted. Where the regimental line was formed, they fell one at every ten yards about. Here was a long grave of ours made in a rain-washed gulley, certain to be washed out the first time it rained hard. I remarked on it to one of the men, who replied, "To be sure they will," and went on digging.

In the midst of all this carrion our troops sat cooking, eating, jabbering, and smoking; sleeping among the corpses so that but for the color of the skin it was difficult to distinguish the living from the dead. Getting back to camp I washed and refitted and a rain came on, laid the dust, and wonderfully refreshed the atmosphere. A man came from Governor Curtin[14] reporting that he had forty thousand men on the Pennsylvania line, but being state troops they refused to advance beyond. All the better they should not; they will be in the way. It is five o'clock and no attack yet by us. The enemy will undoubtedly get away. . . . Meagher was not killed as reported, but drunk, and fell from his horse.[15] It is reported that the Rebels were reinforced last night. I doubt it.

SEPTEMBER 19, FRIDAY.—Bright and pleasant. At breakfast I was not surprised to hear they had retreated. We are advancing but with too much caution to effect anything. Everybody looks pleased but I feel as if an indecisive victory was in our circumstances equivalent to a defeat. We rode into Sharpsburg, the General riding in an ambulance drawn by four grey horses. He has been unwell since the battle. The village was riddled with balls and shells. Scarcely a house but had been struck and one house was pierced six places. A shell had entered the window of one house and exploded in the parlor, but

14. Andrew G. Curtin, "The Soldier's Friend," was governor of Pennsylvania from 1860 to 1868.

15. Thomas F. Meagher (1823-67) was a leader of the Irish element of New York City and organizer of the Irish Brigade. After the decimation of his brigade, Meagher left the army. In later years he was the Territorial Governor of Montana, and in 1867 he drowned in the Missouri River, having fallen off a steamboat.

leaving a mantel mirror unbroken. A child was killed by one of our shells, but no other citizen was injured. In a kitchen were two dead Rebels who were cooking there when killed by a shell. I rode out from the village to see the field of battle on the Hagerstown turnpike. This was the field where our center and right advanced. In a lane hollowed out and affording some protection the dead lay in heaps. In some places they had been dragged together and corded up in heaps of ten or twenty. Elsewhere the men were already burying them. In front of this lane was a long double line of dead showing where they fell in line of battle. The line was a quarter of a mile in length and they were close enough to touch each other. In front of this again was another line along a fence row. They were at least a thousand Rebel dead on this field which joined and was part of that I looked at yesterday in front of Sumner. This advance had crushed Sumner and forced him back as we saw, but Franklin's supporting column got in just in time to receive them as they reached the edge of the wood. They were driven back in full flight. This exceeds all the slaughter I had yet seen. On the river side of the Hagerstown pike and in the wood behind the church there were many more bodies. On the field also were a steer and two sheep slain by the shot. . . .

I then rode out to examine the ground of Burnside's attack. It was hilly, rising from the Antietam bridge in terraces. Neither here nor at the bridge did I see any marks of a determined struggle and have concluded that the attack was feebly conducted. . . . We heard guns at intervals toward Shepherdstown and our troops poured through the village in that direction without cessation, but it soon came to be understood that the retreat had been successfully conducted and they were all safe, having abandoned only two field pieces. From the questions asked on the subject of local geography, I judge we may have some intention of marching on Harpers Ferry. . . . We captured yesterday an aide of General Stuart named Turner, a pleasant-mannered youth. I have met with no Rebel prisoner yet whose conversation amounted to anything.

SEPTEMBER 20, SATURDAY.—Cloudy and cool. . . . An old woman came up this morning examining all our tents for a tin bucket she had lost. She says a soldier borrowed it for General McClellan. Some waggish thief has doubtless visited her. . . . Approaching the river bluffs I saw Shepherdstown and many of our troops bivouacked behind the woods. McClellan reconnoitered from the height. Several batteries, including one thirty-two-pounder brass howitzer were play-

ing on the opposite heights. . . . An officer spoke with a prisoner of
the Rebels who says he captured the messenger who carried Pope's
orders to Sigel to attack at the late Bull Run fight. It is thus proved
that Sigel never got the order and he is consequently not guilty of
cowardice. . . .

SEPTEMBER 21, SUNDAY.—Morning fog and clear day. Yesterday
Colonel [A. V.] Colburn showed me an account of the Peninsular
battles written by the Prince de Joinville. One of the most clear-headed
and well-expressed papers I have ever read. I remained in camp all
day and wrote an account of the battle for General Marcy. In the
afternoon I was sent for to McClellan's tent where I found General
Pleasonton. He was about making an expedition to Romney and
Moorefield and desired to know something of the roads, all of which
I explained to him and then gave him my map of Virginia. Exhibit-
ing the map I had got up for Pope, the General was much pleased
with it and ordered a copy of it for himself. He has already ordered
the occupation of Harpers Ferry and Shepherdstown and told me that
in two days he would see me in Charles Town and three days in Win-'
chester. Went to the topographical quarters and made arrangements to
trace the map.

SEPTEMBER 22, MONDAY.—Fog, clear and warm day. Fitz-John
Porter reports that Lee's whole army is in front of him near Shepherdstown. He has the reputation of a stampeder. This report, however,
will change our program, I fear. From a reconnoissance by the General
to Burnside's position, my opinion of the fight there is fully sustained.
There are several fords for infantry below and above the bridge. They
could have been cleared out in half an hour and the whole force put
across the stream. The whole attack was criminally feeble and stupid.
We lost men and failed to do anything with a powerful force that
would have made our victory decisive. . . .

SEPTEMBER 23, TUESDAY.—Fair and warm. . . . General Burnside
came into the topographical office and from his conversation I understood that he did use the fords above and below the bridge. He said
he could not use them safely until the bridge was taken. [Samuel N.]
Benjamin's battery of twenty-pounder Parrotts did great execution.
It got out of ammunition and the Captain wished to withdraw his guns,
but Burnside would not permit it, but made him fire blank cartridges
to keep up the impression he had made upon the enemy. The fact of
this battery's being short of ammunition cost us great advantage in the
battle. In the evening heard Lincoln's proclamation freeing the

AN INTERIOR

Negroes of all states in the Rebellion on the first of January next. I fear that Father Abraham's paper wads won't do as much service as Benjamin's blank cartridges.

SEPTEMBER 24, WEDNESDAY.—Fair and warm. Pleasonton's expedition is deferred for the present on account of news that General Porter brings in—that the whole Rebel army lies in front of us. . . .

I spent the morning in topography and, feeling weary, idled during the evening. General Marcy told me he had used my description of the battle. He said it was rather modest and he had taken the liberty of strengthening several statements. I am already getting weary of inaction and wish we would move toward Virginia. . . .

Today was a light rain and a decided change in the weather from summer to autumn. The war is going against us heavily. The Revolution is raging at all points while the folly, weakness, and criminality of our heads is becoming more decidedly manifest. Abraham Lincoln has neither sense nor principle. McClellan is a capital soldier but has no capacity to take political lead. The people are strong and willing but "there is no king in Israel." The man of the day has not yet come.

This day closes this volume of notes. Sixty-three days ago I commenced it in Washington. Since that time I have made two important and bloody campaigns and have had more exciting interest to note than during all the rest of the war put together.

VI

All Quiet Along the Potomac

September 25, 1862—December 3, 1862

After Antietam the Union and Confederate armies, separated by the Potomac, stood in nearly the same positions as they had at the beginning of the war, fifteen months before. For Strother the prospect was dismal. Looking across the river to the steep cliffs of the Virginia embankment, he could see the spires of Shepherdstown. Somewhere in that enemy territory were his family, lost in the tangled march of the armies in the campaign that culminated at Antietam. His optimistic conviction that the rebellion would be quenched by the first victory of the Union forces was giving way to the realistic view that the war would last a long time. Inept bungling, chain of command, politics—these things had characterized the war as he had seen it fought by the Federal commanders. His journal begins to reflect the frustration of a man who knows the gigantic power of a country unable to use it effectively.

After McClellan, prodded by Lincoln, moved his army across the Potomac, Lee was gone. The campfires of pickets were the only signs of the army which had harvested the crops and had vanished. While gathering maps in Washington during early November, Strother learned that Burnside had superseded McClellan on November 7. Once again he was unattached until induced by Banks to embark with him upon a mysterious campaign in the Deep South, a venture which took him to New Orleans late in December.

This chapter treats a quiet interlude in the Civil War between active campaigns, and it shows something of the peculiar bitterness evolving between members of the same family split in their political loyalty.

SEPTEMBER 25, THURSDAY.—. . . Drew a map of Harpers Ferry and vicinity from memory for General McClellan which occupied me the greater part of the day. Another proclamation from Lincoln, suspending the writ of *habeas corpus*. These wild blows show that the revolution is progressing to its grand denouement. Violent and senseless proclamations to counterbalance great military successes on the other side indicate a giving way of strength and self-confidence. There was no necessity for them, and their appearance indicates cowardice in the government in addition to its other weaknesses. . . . Several ladies called to see the General but were disappointed as he is unwell and cannot see company. The balloon has been up several times today near the mouth of Antietam.

SEPTEMBER 26, FRIDAY.—I was told last night that Lee was at Snickersville which is an item to be considered. Worked at lettering my map and dropped a great blot upon it which vexed me excessively. Got an assistant in the lettering whose work is worse than the blot. . . . General Marcy tells me that the whole Rebel force is supposed to be between Falling Waters and Martinsburg. T. N. tells me the same.[1] Lee was not at Snickersville but on the Opequon. N. says the country about Hancock and Bath is all open.

SEPTEMBER 28, SUNDAY.—. . . By the papers I perceive that the President has issued a proclamation instituting a system of espionage, etc., the most contemptible that has ever disgraced any nation, and other orders the most futile and absurd that have ever been issued to assure a people of the incapacity of its rulers. I have seen the beginning and progress of this revolution, and every step taken in it seems to have been most wanton and unnecessary. I dare say cool and unimpassioned observers of all other revolutions in all ages have thought the same thing, and I, like all the other philosophers, must conclude that men, ideas, and forms of government have little or no influence over the destiny of nations. . . . We had divine service this evening at which many Generals were present, Fitz-John Porter, Cox, and Meade among others. Cox is a good-looking man and Meade is tall and wears specs.

SEPTEMBER 29, MONDAY.—. . . I have observed in this war that the fire of infantry is our main dependence in battle. There has been no bayonet charge from either side that amounted to anything. The opposing forces have never crossed bayonets to my knowledge. The only artillery taken has been such guns and batteries as were abandoned for want of horses to carry them off or deserted prematurely by their supports. The collisions of cavalry with the sabre have been rare and partial. The fire of the infantry then has been the main reliance, and

1. Thomas Nokes, a Union spy.

its fire has been terribly destructive. At short range (say two hundred yards) no troops can stand it more than a few minutes. At the attack on our right at Antietam, the Rebel division stood under it on even ground. It seemed as if whole regiments were mowed down where they stood. This division with the loss of half of its number of infantry broke and fled in confusion.

In all matters of soldierly discipline, in vigilance, alertness, fortitude, forced marching, secret maneuvering, strategy, and knowledge of our forces and plans the Rebel soldiers and generals have the advantage of us. . . . In fair, open fighting, we are their superiors, and in an equal pitched battle have beaten and will most generally beat them. There is in our favor the usual advantage that the army of a civilized power has over that of a semibarbaric people. Better organization, provision, and equipment, but less of energy, astuteness, and fortitude. . . . On most of the battlefields I have seen, our troops have shown more courage than the enemy. They have generally attacked, have marched on open ground under fire to dislodge enemies who fought under cover. The enemy's dead I have always found lying behind stone fences, in forests, and in dense thickets. Ours are generally found in the open field. At the Battle of Antietam for the first time I saw the Rebel troops standing in battle array in the open field and advancing in heavy masses across open ground to the attack. Their signal failure in this attack and their confused flight from all exposed positions prove my opinion to be justly founded. . . .

OCTOBER 1, WEDNESDAY.—. . . We hear guns all day and a courier informs us that Pleasonton is at Martinsburg shelling the Rebels out of that place. Another telegram brings news that Abraham Lincoln and suite will visit us tonight. Major [Granville O.] Haller went to work in haste and pitched three large tents and borrowed bedding enough to furnish the party with lodging. General Franklin to supper with us. He knew me at Berkeley Springs when he was a captain and I an artist. He is an easy, unpretending soldier, strong and manly. He says having forced Crampton's Pass on Sunday evening he moved over Monday morning and saw the enemy in great force across Pleasant Valley barring the way to Harpers Ferry. The force was too strong for him to attack. The firing at the Ferry had ceased for two hours and anon the whole Rebel line cheered repeatedly and then disappeared, doubtless having received the news of the surrender. Before leaving Washington, Mr. Seward spoke to McClellan expressing some fears about the troops at Harpers Ferry. McClellan thought they were in danger and with Mr. Seward went to see General Halleck, then Stanton, then the President. They were all from home. He then went to Halleck's house and found him in bed. Halleck treated the matter lightly, said it was a very good place to have a fight and next day McClellan was still further disturbed by thinking of the condition of the command there and went to the Cabinet council where he found all three of the persons he visited the day before. The position of things at Harpers Ferry was discussed and McClellan strongly advised a withdrawal of them towards Greencastle or Romney. Halleck thought as before that they were in no danger and it was a very good place to fight. The place was in Wool's command and General Mc-Clellan started on his Maryland Campaign without any authority there and is therefore not responsible for the disgraceful and unfortunate surrender. The President stayed at Harpers Ferry and will not be on here until tomorrow, so says the last news. His suite are military men and not Congressmen, thank Heaven. . . .

OCTOBER 2, THURSDAY.—The President comes today. General Pleasonton came in and gave some details of his reconnoissance to Martinsburg. He drove the enemy out and held the place for several hours. The county road bridges having been broken up and unfloored to impede the advance of the Union cavalry, the women of the town refitted them by replacing the planks. Over these Pleasonton entered. . . .

The President came in the afternoon and was received without ceremony. Afterwards rode out with McClellan and staff to see the battlefield. . . . After dark the President and suite came in from the battlefield and went to dinner. Two bands vied with each other in discoursing sweet music while the laughter at the President's hard jokes filled up the intervals until I went to sleep.

OCTOBER 3, FRIDAY.—Saw the President with an officer going to take a drink, I think. Then saw Lamon[2] who called me over to the great tent and presented me to his Excellency, who remembered me. I narrated the story that the women of Martinsburg had replanked the bridges for Pleasonton's advance. He seemed interested and pleased, and I took the occasion to vaunt the loyalty of Martinsburg. The President is a representative in all points of the tastes, manners, ideas, and capacities of the American people. He is American internally and externally, mind and person. He is neither great nor small, but a fair, average man of the race. He is the result of our system and that

2. Ward Lamon (1828-93), a former law partner of Lincoln in Danville, Illinois, had grown up in Berkeley County, Virginia. At this time he was Marshal of the District of Columbia and a counselor of the President.

system is entirely responsible for the manner in which he fulfills the duties of his office. If he fails, the system has failed conclusively and there will be an end of it. . . .

[After several uneventful days in camp, Strother moved with the rest of the staff to Weverton on October 8. On the following day he obtained a leave to visit Berkeley Springs and narrowly missed being picked up on the road by Confederate cavalry en route to Chambersburg. Most of his information about the raid, however, was gathered at second-hand. He returned to McClellan's camp on October 15.]

OCTOBER 16, THURSDAY.—At the breakfast table heard cannon. That doubtless is Hancock near Charles Town. I heard presently that General McClellan was going to ride, so I mounted and we all started for Harpers Ferry, six miles distant. Arriving there, we crossed the pontoon bridge and rode to Bolivar Heights. The whole hill was denuded of trees and covered with camps. On the summit we tarried, enjoying the fine prospect over Jefferson County and pointing out military positions. Riding toward Halltown we chose the ridge immediately at that place, right and left, for our pickets' outer line. Thence we proceeded rapidly to Charles Town. Hancock was in full possession and had his artillery planted commanding the roads beyond.

I had a joyful greeting from Riddle and wife and Mrs. Hunter. I found our General and staff in consultation on Dixon's Hill. He stayed there until evening and McClellan then started on his return to Maryland. I rode with them to the far end of town and then asked permission to remain and report to Hancock for duty next day. The General seemed pleased and told me to learn all I could. I got supper at Mrs. Hunter's and then set out in a heavy rain to seek Hancock's quarters at Andrew Hunter's.[3] I dismounted and all dripping entered the house, which was lighted up. In the library I saw several officers sitting around with Mrs. Andrew Hunter and Florence, who seemed to be entertaining them. When I entered the room, I gave a general salutation, "Good evening." Mrs. Hunter, on recognizing me, jumped up with an exclamation and calling her daughter fled the room uttering some incoherent words like "Good Lord—in my house. . . ." The officers looked astounded, but I sat down coolly and reported to Gen-

3. Andrew Hunter, Strother's uncle, was the prosecuting attorney during the John Brown trial at Charles Town in 1859. His house was burned in 1864 and Strother was mistakenly accused of ordering its destruction.

eral Hancock.[4] He thanked me and told me he would start at daylight. I then departed. . . .

OCTOBER 17, FRIDAY.—. . . The General rode out to look at the
positions about Charles Town. I asked if he needed me. He said not,
so I made preparations to depart. At the gate we met a Negro just
escaped from the enemy at the Berryville road. I got this fellow aside
and got some valuable information from him. He said the enemy had
not been reinforced since they left Maryland, except by conscripts. I
heard that Stuart had his headquarters at "The Bower"[5] and was
concentrating cavalry there. . . .

OCTOBER 24, FRIDAY.—Went to camp and delivered maps to the
topographical tent, a combined map of Berkeley, Jefferson, Loudoun,
Clarke, and Frederick, improved by myself and an improved tracing
of Buford's map of the Rapidan captured from Stuart. . . .

OCTOBER 25, SATURDAY.—Heard that Burnside's Corps was about
to cross the Potomac at Berlin. This will involve a movement of our
headquarters by Monday next. . . . Read in a life of Czar Nicolas.
People who say they would prefer the government of Russia to ours
speak inadvisedly. They do not know what they talk of. Our government has certainly gone on very well in peaceful times and not as ill
in war. Its mildness has been unexampled in the history of nations.
Whether it can stand its present trial remains to be seen. But whether
or not, it certainly has afforded to four or five generations the most
entire freedom in any human society. Whether the form of government very seriously affects the character and happiness of a people is a
debatable question. I do not think it does. . . .

OCTOBER 29, WEDNESDAY [in camp at Berlin, Maryland].—. . . Colonel Hall[6] of Fort Sumter memory came in. He led a regiment at
Antietam, and lost two thirds of his men. Says five men and officers
who held the colors were shot down. The enemy picked them off and
then rushed to capture the colors. The same game was played by his
men. The enemy's dead and wounded lay as if the command had been
given to regiments to lie down. When the fight lulled, many wounded

4. Winfield S. Hancock (1824-86), USMA '44, had served with McClellan on the
Peninsula and in Maryland. His enterprise at Chancellorsville gave him command of
the Second Corps. At Gettysburg he dissuaded Lee from concerted attack during the
first day and on July 3 repulsed the attack upon the Union center. In 1880 Hancock
was nominated by the Democratic Party for the presidency, but he lost to James
Garfield.
5. "The Bower," located a few miles from Leetown on the Opequon River, was
owned by Strother's cousins, the Dandridges.
6. Norman J. Hall (1837-67), USMA '59, served at Fort Sumter during its bombardment. After Dana had been wounded at Antietam, Hall took over his brigade.

crawled away seeking their comrades to carry them to the hospitals. As our troops advanced, the wounded put up their hands and held up their legs begging them not to tread on them. Passing over, Colonel Hall said to a wounded Mississippian, "You fought and stood well." "Yes," he replied, "and here we lie." These were Jackson's troops. Hall says the lines were at times within twenty paces of each other and stood firing at that distance. There was no collision with bayonets, however. He never saw one. At Antietam there were several charges after the flying enemy and vice versa, but no crossing of bayonets. . . .

OCTOBER 30, THURSDAY.—. . . The General's horse has been amusing himself wantonly kicking at all the other horses within his reach. I wonder if the horse knows that his rider is the Major General commanding. The General's orderlies and niggers are conscious of their dignity and the horse behaves as if he were also aware of his high fortune. This must be the favorite horse, Daniel Webster. . . .

OCTOBER 31, FRIDAY.—. . . Rode up to the signal station of Maryland Heights. The distance was hazy, still I had a good view of the position of the enemy's forces by the camp smokes which rose from behind the woods. The nearest was at Longmarsh Run, others near Millwood and Front Royal and near Snicker's and Berry's Ferry. Some train waggons and one or two tents were seen in connection with the nearest of these smokes. There was also a large smoke near Stephenson's Depot on the Winchester Railroad and another near Newtown as supposed. There was no indication of troops any nearer to the river, except some pickets occasionally seen at Duffields and Flowing Spring. The view was most charming. I dined with the signal men and promised them a better map. . . .

I arrived at camp about sunset. Here I reported what I had seen on the Heights. I then had some social conversation with the commanding general about some of my exploring tours in East Tennessee, etc. He thought the war would afford fine subjects for sketches and advised me to sketch more. . . . After I retired, the General came in to see Ruggles and received some account of Pope and his campaign. Ruggles gave a clear and accurate statement of matters showing understanding. On the night of Cedar Mountain, Ruggles was the sole staff officer who was with Pope when we escaped from the fire of A. P. Hill's advance. When Pope saw Ruggles come up, he exclaimed, "Where are the gentlemen of my staff?" Ruggles answered, "I do not know, Sir." Pope said, "Are you here alone?" Ruggles said, "I have seen no one else." Pope exclaimed, "This is horrible—," supposing them all to have been lost. As I first heard the anecdote it gave the impression that Pope's inquiry for the staff was made in an arrogant and offensive manner, and I am pleased to note this authentic and more creditable version of it. . . .

NOVEMBER 1, SATURDAY.—. . . Heard that our headquarters would move tomorrow to Wheatland, Virginia. At night a band came up to serenade the General, accompanied by a young officer, an Englishman. He was well-mannered and said his company was raised to fill a regiment to be called the British Volunteers, but the name was not liked and therefore the companies joined the New York 34th. We have Irish, German, Scotch, and French organizations, but the name of British volunteers would not be tolerated. So much for national prejudice.

NOVEMBER 2, SUNDAY.—. . . Struck camp early and started for Virginia. Rode to Lovettsville, two miles beyond, an insignificant village. While we stood talking there, some prisoners marched by and a young woman rushed out of the house shrieking and sobbing and threw her arms around the neck of one of the Secessionists and refused to leave him. He was her husband, and they went off together out of sight. From here we rode to Purcellville and to Snicker's Gap. The General rode at full gallop the whole route of twenty miles, stopping at the different villages for a short space to consult with the different commanders quartered therein. . . . The scene of the camp fires of the Corps on the plain was magnificent.

NOVEMBER 3, MONDAY.—. . . Rose early, as they were striking the tent over my head. Then went forward to Snicker's Gap. On the Gap it was windy and bitter cold. At Longmarsh Run I saw smoke of a Rebel camp, and another on the turnpike to Berryville between the river and the town. No other smoke was visible and only a few horsemen as videttes upon the road. . . .

NOVEMBER 4, TUESDAY.—. . . Rode with the others toward Upperville. The country was very open and beautiful to behold. Fine country houses dotted the landscape and all betokened an old and advanced rural civilization. We passed through Upperville in sight of Ashby's Gap. Everything was quiet, although large bodies of our troops were seen moving in parallel columns toward the South. Paris is a very forlorn village. From the summit of Ashby's Gap we had a view of the Valley to Winchester where I saw a camp at the south end of town and eight tents at Millwood. There were large camp fires apparently made for show. Our reconnoissance convinced me,

RECONNOISSANCE FROM ASHBY'S GAP

as I believe it did the others, that there was no force of the enemy in the Valley except a small one for demonstration.

Two men on horseback passed by us traveling from the river eastward. The General ordered me to overhaul them and ascertain who they were. I did so and the men showed passes to pass the lines. These showed me they were agents in the employ of the Secret Service. They assured me that Longstreet was at Culpeper Court House, that Hill had marched this morning toward Manassas Gap, and that the whole Southern army was south of us, the troops in the Valley being left only as a blind. This corroborated what a Negro had told me as I went up. The Secret Service reporter incidentally observed that Porter is the damndest stampeder in the army. He is now badly scared about the smoke in the Valley. This reminded me of Patterson's Campaign. . . .

NOVEMBER 6, THURSDAY.—. . . Captain [James C.] Duane came in and asked me if I would like to go to Washington. I accepted the proposition. The General desired me to go there to get all the maps that bore upon the country in front of us. I ordered my horse immediately, but delay in getting my written order detained me and I must wait until morning. . . .

NOVEMBER 7, FRIDAY.—Commenced snowing. . . . We drove to Salem, five miles. Fair road but narrow and hilly. Salem a little wooden town. At the depot we found cars and engines. The snow continued without intermission. The wind howled bitterly and the car was open and without fire. In spite of all my wrappings I was half frozen, the more chilled from the fact that I had not eaten a full meal for several days. To Alexandria where we arrived about midnight. Trotted into the frozen town, applied at one hotel but found no beds vacant. At the City Hotel there were beds, but nothing to eat. Not a mouthful to be obtained for love or money. A dollar to be paid for lodging. My companions were for resisting and going out to look further, but I advised acceptance of what the gods vouchsafed to us. So we went to bed supperless, four in an attic room, but a separate bed for each.

NOVEMBER 8, SATURDAY.—At nine we reached the landing and took the boat for Washington. Took a carriage for our lodgings, all in the vicinity of Willard's. A number of surveys were traced out and prepared to send immediately, others to be ready in a few days—of great importance to our movements. . . .

NOVEMBER 9, SUNDAY.—I heard that General McClellan had been superseded, Burnside taking the command. This news shocked and confused me greatly, and put the world at Willard's in a ferment. In the Hall I met Leutze the artist,[7] who did not recognize me. I recalled my self to his memory and went with him to his room and saw his sketch of the great painting for the Capitol, "Westward the Star of Empire Takes Its Course," a very grand conception, but my equanimity was so ruffled by the political news I had just heard that I was not impressed. Leutze, too, seemed excited and talked strongly against the action of the Government in the matter. . . .

At dinner I saw General Banks, who called to me and asked me to sit by him. He said he was about to be ordered south, perhaps to Texas, and asked me to accompany him.[8] I told him that in view of

7. Emanuel Leutze (1816-68), a German-born historical painter, is best known for his "Washington Crossing the Delaware." "Westward the Course of Empire Takes Its Way" may be found in the House of Representatives at Washington.

8. The Banks expedition was bound for New Orleans, not for Texas.

the retiring of McClellan, I would probably be at liberty and felt disposed to consider the proposition favorably with an engagement to visit him at ten o'clock. . . . Called to see General Banks according to engagement and found him with a secretary in his room. He told me he had spoken to Halleck and had his consent to my transfer to his staff if I wished it. I have not learned yet where he will take his command, and will not commit myself until I know where I am going. . . .

NOVEMBER 10, MONDAY.—. . . Saw General Banks and hear from him that he expects to be ready to move in a week, but he says I may have three weeks if I wish. I am doubtful about accepting any extension of time under the circumstances. . . . The result of the Harpers Ferry investigating committee in regard to the surrender is highly interesting and fully concurs with my own views entertained of the conduct and capacity of those engaged. I am not so sure that its implication of McClellan in the censure is just. But for the disgraceful and premature surrender of the place, McClellan would have been there in time. The report of the committee shows this. He had no right to suppose that the place would be thus prematurely surrendered. In questioning me on the subject I answered him that "a small force could hold Maryland Heights against a host—that as long as Maryland Heights was held by our troops, Harpers Ferry was safe—that it was fully understood by all those at Harpers Ferry that those Heights were the key of the position and that doubtless all their energies would be turned to holding them." Thus McClellan had every reason to believe that his movements were in time, and without the extraordinary incapacity and cowardice manifested in the management of the defense, he would have been in time. . . .

NOVEMBER 11, TUESDAY.—. . . Saw General Banks, who informed me that he would go to New York this afternoon and invited me to accompany him. I determined to do so. Wrote and mailed a letter to my wife acquainting her with my design to embark in General Banks' expedition. . . . Arrived at the cars in time. A crowd shouting and huzzaing about some cars in front of our train attracted our attention. It turned out to be an ovation to McClellan, who was with his staff and passing on his way to Trenton. He was standing on the platform of the train shaking hands with persons who were crowding around. The car in which he traveled was attached to our train and thus we traveled through Baltimore and Philadelphia, cheering and music greeting the deposed commander at every stopping place. . . .

NOVEMBER 12, WEDNESDAY.—Strolled out and visited the Harpers. Dr. Guernsey was delighted to see me and says the vacuum created in their magazine by my military life has never been filled. The old fogies were equally complimentary and the young men offered me every attention.[9] Mr. Fletcher Harper through Dr. Guernsey proposed that I should give them my portrait for their paper and having agreed to do so I accompanied the Doctor to Brady's, where two attempts to get a picture failed. The chief manager, an Englishman, was very complimentary, saying I was much read and well known in his country. Returned to the Astor House and went to dinner. General Banks and wife came in and sat near me. The Madame was gracious and said she was very glad I was with the General, for she was pleased when he had those around him that he liked. . . . It is nearly four years since I visited this city. Familiar sights and sounds are around me. We see or feel but little of the war on the surface here, but beneath our view it is no doubt felt. Old Harper thanked me for calling to see them in these warlike times. I recalled the story of the traveler, seeing in Rome an overthrown statue of Jupiter, who touched his hat to it, so I touched my hat to you. Mars is in the ascendant now, but afterwards literature may be recrowned and resume its sway. . . .

NOVEMBER 14, FRIDAY.—. . . Asked leave of absence of the General until the expedition starts, my address to be the Eutaw House, Baltimore. My opinion of McClellan is that he is the most capable man we have in military affairs. His head is clear and his knowledge complete. He wants force of character and is swayed by those around him. Fitz-John Porter with his elegant address and insinuating plausibility, technical power, and total want of judgment has been the evil genius, and has ruined him as he did Patterson. The people about McClellan, without taking into consideration their social and characteristic merits, were the most ungallant, good-for-nothing set of martinets that I have yet met with. I do not mean that they were inefficient in their special duties, but not a man among them was worth a damn as a military adviser—or had any show of fire or boldness. A self-indulgent and timorous policy seemed to pervade the whole surrounding and the General. His very mildness of manner, voice, and deportment show him unfitted by character to wield successfully a great power. . . .

NOVEMBER 25, TUESDAY [Baltimore].—. . . The feeling against Gen-

9. Alfred H. Guernsey was the editor of *Harper's New Monthly Magazine*, to which Strother had contributed before the war. The "old fogies" were the Harper brothers.

eral Wool[10] is very strong among the Union men of this city. The tone of a leader in the *American* is menacing against the Government if Wool is not removed. It does not occur to the loyal citizens of Baltimore that their loyalty does not entirely exempt them from law and responsibility to constituted authority. They would use the military authority for the gratification of their own private or party motives. With larger views and more sincere patriotism, Wool has refused to yield his authority to their schemes and hence he has become hateful to them. The "Will of the People," now that they have become accustomed to war, is beginning to show itself as of old.

NOVEMBER 26, WEDNESDAY.—Called to see John P. Kennedy[11] and had a long chat. Things seem to be in a tangle on the Rappahannock and look badly. He has news that the army is mutinous. . . . Kennedy first suggested to Seward the idea of occupying and dividing Texas and free-soiling it by settlement from Europe and the North. Texas has plenty of good cotton land and can supply the world. Free labor applied to cotton raising will succeed, if tried. This is then a field to make one's fortune, for we go as military colonists and will, if we please, become the leading men of the land. Driving out Rebels and Comanches will be an easy matter. . . .

NOVEMBER 28, FRIDAY.—. . . I was sitting in my room buoyant with happiness and, after expressing myself to that effect and considering the unusual elevation of my spirits, I felt assured that by some sudden blow it was immediately to end. I wondered what misfortune was to befall me. While I considered there was a tap on the door, "Ah, there it is." The telegrams were handed in. We were to sail on Monday. . . .

DECEMBER 2, TUESDAY [New York].—. . . I called to see General McClellan at the Fifth Avenue Hotel. He was not in and I left my card. Met General Marcy who looked so well that I did not recognize him at first. He seems to think it fortunate for his son-in-law that he was removed from command at the time when active campaigning must cease of necessity. McClellan was relieved in full movement and just as the bad weather set in, thus throwing the responsibility of inaction and delay on his successor. . . .

10. John E. Wool (1784-1869) was a veteran of the War of 1812 and the Mexican War. At the outbreak of the Civil War, Wool saved Fortress Monroe for the Union. In July, 1863, he retired from command of the Department of the East.

11. John P. Kennedy (1795-1870) was Strother's cousin and Maryland's best-known writer. In 1852 he served as Secretary of the Navy under Fillmore, and in 1860 employed his pen to keep the Border States within the Union.

DECEMBER 3, WEDNESDAY.—. . . Met William Kemble[12] at Astor's
and with him and Mrs. Kemble and a young lady went to the Fifth
Avenue Hotel to visit General McClellan. He was gone out to dine.
Our party then called on General Scott. A beautiful picture presented
itself on entering his room on the first floor. The veteran of three wars
sat enveloped in shawls under the chandelier and near a table in the
center of the room, his countenance full of dignity and benignity.
At the table three of his grandchildren were eating grapes under the
direction of the General. He received us with great courtesy and
recognized me when my name was mentioned and made kind inquiries
of my father. He spoke of his daughter Camelia and his grandson
Winfield who speaks French more fluently than he does his native
tongue. Why does the General consider it important that his grandson
should speak French better than English? He spoke of a dinner at
Mr. Blodgett's as a very superb affair, said he corrected the hostess's
pronunciation of *girl* and his comment brought on a conversation on
philology in which the lady showed much knowledge. This is one
of the General's weaknesses. . . . Walked a mile and a half to the foot
of Eleventh Street, East River, where I found the steamer, *North Star*.
I got a bunk and, covering myself with a dirty mattress of an upper
bunk, there being no other cover, I slept tolerably, dreaming of being
hunted by Confederates and making desperate defense from houses and
log cabins.

12. William Kemble was the son of Gouverneur Kemble, one of the Salamagundi
circle of Washington Irving's day. Strother's friendship with the Kembles dated from
the 1840's, when he was an artist and designer in New York.

VII

With Banks in Louisiana

December 4, 1862—March 15, 1863

Not until the expedition was at sea did Banks divulge their objectives—to relieve Butler at New Orleans, to open the Mississippi for transportation, and to reunionize Louisiana. General Butler's occupation of New Orleans had been so unguardedly corrupt that even Washington was alarmed. Banks, with Strother heading the Sequestration Committee, cleaned out the graft in the higher command, but was powerless to effect reform throughout the Department of the Gulf. Moreover, his efforts to win Louisiana for the Union were largely stifled by the mildness of his administration. While the planters liked Banks better than Butler, popularity had little to do with the political reconstruction of Louisiana.

Military operations proceeded slowly. While Baton Rouge was abandoned to a Union force under Grover, the expedition to Galveston resulted in the surrender of the Federal unit which was supposed to occupy the city. It was the navy, commanded by Farragut, which showed the greater vigor and enterprise. In March, Banks moved to the rear of Port Hudson and feebly engaged the garrison while Farragut's fleet ran the batteries and opened communications with Vicksburg.

It seemed to Strother that as Banks grew weaker, Farragut grew stronger, and the latter becomes the principal character of the present chapter. During his conferences with the crusty Admiral, Strother experienced rare moments of hope for the war in the West.

DECEMBER 4, THURSDAY.—. . . It seems from a general review of the campaigns that our armies are overfed and overbaggaged and move slowly in circumstance. It seems further that our West Point officers all seem to be drilled martinets, doing everything by acquired rules without adaptation to circumstances. Hence no victory has been improved on by either side. Our battles have been frequently well-contested and bloody without decisive results, no following up of retreats and destruction of armies. The man has not appeared yet who can wield the enthusiasm of the masses and lead them to victory by superhuman efforts and resolution. . . . After dark General Banks came aboard from a steam tug near the Battery. . . .

DECEMBER 6, SATURDAY.—. . . Saw a large propeller standing off and thought she was the *Alabama,* a Confederate pirate, so gave her sea room. She was probably one of our blockading fleet off Cape Hatteras. We saw the lighthouse beyond.

DECEMBER 8, MONDAY.—. . . The General came up in the afternoon and we discoursed on the subject of French intervention. We agreed that in the present condition of things it was not to be feared. Beckwith and I resuming our conversation, the subject of politics, came to the conclusion that our system of government must fail in the North as it has done in the South. There is, however, some hope for the United States if the intelligence and civilization of a people can save it from decadence politically. . . .

DECEMBER 10, WEDNESDAY.—. . . About 4 P.M. the vessel turned her prow due westward and still runs in that direction. It seems impossible to lead any other than a purely animal life at sea. Two days ago I first heard that our destination was New Orleans. I was at first disappointed but having made up my mind to it, am seeking all the consolations that may be drawn from the change in my calculations.

DECEMBER 13, SATURDAY.—. . . On rising found we were near land. Ship Island in sight, covered with pines at the eastern extremity, and a naked sand spit on the west with a lighthouse and a number of store houses. A dozen vessels were lying off the place on the leeward side. Many encampments were on the beach. Soldiers were seen wandering on the sands. . . . We have been eight and a half days making this point and without seeing land. The weather has been eminently fine, and the passage smooth and prosperous. At about 2:30 P.M. we started to sea again. . . .

DECEMBER 14, SUNDAY.—. . . I rose early to see the entrance to the famous river. I sat on a pile of tents on the upper deck and waited for daylight. The east at length began to redden and soon day followed. The milky appearance of the water and several shapeless mudbanks with a line of reedy growth indicated the entrance to the river. On our left just on entering is a lighthouse and a short distance up is a small collection of wooden houses built on either side of a little bayou like a nascent Venice nipped in the bud and falling to untimely decay. This is Pilot Town. For many miles the most melancholy scene presented itself; the widening shores are covered with dead trees, decaying stumps, and brown acres of reeds with other coarse swamp herbage. Huts were seen rising here and there thatched with palm leaves and framed with refuse of wrecked vessels. The few inhabitants visible were of indescribable color and race and seemed fit occupants of the dwellings. . . .

As we advanced farther the aspect of the dwellings improved; the inhabitants were in gay-colored dresses and all waved us a welcome with hats and handkerchiefs. The dwellings then began to appear surrounded by groves of orange trees in full bearing. It was splendid to behold, and the Northern troops who saw them for the first time raised shouts of joyful excitement. Next came Fort Jackson on the right bank and Fort St. Philip on the left. These formidable works taken lately by our fleet under Farragut were again in good repair and fully armed. . . . We next passed the Quarantine, the most cheerful-looking place by comparison we had yet seen. As we journeyed, the character of the improvements and natural features began to improve. The noble live oak rose in shadowy groves; the cypress forests were lofty and dense. Superb sugar plantations with their light and elegant great dwellings, villages of Negro cabins, steam refineries, etc., lined both shores. We were looking upon the glory of Louisiana. So the scene went on increasing in richness until we came in sight of the city. . . .

All the while I sat and discoursed with General Banks. He opened to me for the first time his views and plans of campaign. The great moral motive of the expedition was the reunionizing of Louisiana by getting up a counter current of popular feeling against Secession party. . . . The military point in view was the opening of the Mississippi to trade and travel by taking Vicksburg. To this end the General said we could concentrate a hundred thousand men. These with the gun boats under Farragut would be our military power. As the General overheard the bursts of admiration with which the lovely scene was hailed at each bend of the river, he smiled and observed, "Thus it is that we will possess and regenerate the country. Half of these fellows, who see this blooming land for the first time will never willingly return to their bleak and sterile homes in New England." On the supposition that Butler's rule was violent and high handed and that the people were suppressed rather than won over, our policy was foreshadowed as conciliatory. Kindness after the rod is the strong card. But knowing the character of the population I am not sure but Butler's policy is the safest. . . .

Arrived opposite the lower and old French part of the city about sunset. General Banks and staff embarked for shore and the St. Charles Hotel. Beckwith, myself, and several other staff officers remained on board the steamer. There was a fire in the city, but no noise.

DECEMBER 15, MONDAY.—. . . The appearance of the great levee of New Orleans was very different from what it was when I last saw it, February, 1858.[1] Most of the shipping visible were United States ships of war, some few trading vessels, steam tugs, and transports. The immense waste of the steamboat levees was naked and desolate instead of being covered as I had seen it with uncountable wealth of sugar, cotton, and the great staples of northwestern trade. The great mart of the southwestern world was a decaying desert. . . .

A bystander asked me for a Northern newspaper, introducing himself as the reporter of the *National Advocate*, a copy of which he gave me. I inquired about the condition of the city. He answered by an expressive wave of his hand, meaning, "Look around and you see it." I asked him how they like Butler's administration. He twisted his mouth and winked slyly. On being encouraged to speak out, he gave us to understand that Butler was regarded with great horror. A light then seemed to strike him and he got me aside and asked breathlessly and mysteriously, "Colonel, is Banks come to supersede him, indeed?" I did not know, but from my manner he inferred it and then cut a few subdued capers. . . .

Near the St. Charles things looked up a little. Companies of soldiers were marching to relieve guard on the levee and elsewhere. Here I was told that the cane cutting we saw on the coast was not done by the proprietors but was carried on by Northern speculators who hired the Negro labor and were working the crop on shores with Butler. Butler had been literally playing the part of a Persian satrap. . . .

At ten o'clock we took the carriages, and the General and staff went to pay their respects to General Butler.[2] We found him in his office.

1. Strother's travels to New Orleans before the war were incorporated in "A Winter in the South," a series that ran in *Harper's New Monthly Magazine* from 1857 to 1858.
2. Benjamin F. Butler (1818-93) had been a Congressman during the 1850's. At the beginning of the war he landed the 8th Massachusetts at Annapolis and relieved the Washington blockade. In May, 1862, Butler occupied New Orleans and quickly became a virtual dictator until relieved by Banks. While his abuse of the citizenry and his corrupt regime were tolerated by the Government, he overstepped himself when he seized Confederate funds from the French consulate and thereby called forth the wrath

The door was guarded by well-drilled and neat sentinels of infantry and by a guard of dismounted cavalry who received us ceremoniously. General Banks presented us on our entrance to General Butler. This latter is a remarkable-looking man. Stout in person, nervous and peculiar in manners, he has a large head and a striking profile not wanting in dignity and greatness. His manner is affable and his conversation bright and agreeable. Commodore Farragut was there and to him we were presented also.[3] He has a prominent nose, bald head, but there is nothing striking about his appearance. Butler's countenance is altogether indicative of more refinement than I expected to see. His drooping left eye gives his face a somewhat sinister expression and his eccentric nervous manner is somewhat disturbing, but altogether the impression he made on me was favorable and strong. There is something in him more than any man I have met with yet in similar position. He discoursed with us on the subject of the city and environs, pointed out the fortifications, advised Holabird not to encamp the troops but to put them in the cotton depots and other vacant buildings as more healthy and convenient. . . .

Walked to Canal Street, Rue Royal, Hotel St. Louis, to the Old Cathedral, Jackson Square, but little business remained and a few people. The place looked like a decayed city of the Old World and I returned home with a feeling of melancholy. . . .

DECEMBER 16, TUESDAY.—. . . We went in state to relieve General Butler. His office was filled with officers of his staff and field officers of his regiments. After the usual introductions, he formally delivered over the Department in a neat speech. General Banks replied with equal felicity. General Banks then retired when Butler ordered closed doors and read his farewell order. Several officers wept during the reading, and the General himself seemed much affected. . . .

DECEMBER 17, WEDNESDAY.—. . . Banks invited me to accompany him on board the flagship *Hartford* to visit Admiral Farragut. She carries twenty-six Dahlgren guns and has a crew of four hundred men. Everything on board was trigly neat and orderly. O, for a country where quarterdeck government is in the ascendant! We were hospitably shown about the ship and drank wine with the Commodore.

of foreign nations. He served out the war in Virginia and North Carolina, then after the war re-entered politics.

3. David G. Farragut (1801-78) was born in Tennessee but lived in Norfolk from 1828 to 1861. When Virginia seceded, he moved to the North and early in 1862 was made commander of the Gulf Blockading Squadron. His naval forces compelled the surrender of New Orleans in 1862 and Mobile in 1864.

He explained the position of Vicksburg and prophesied some more rough work presently. . . .

After dinner Colonel Beckwith and I walked to Jackson Square and enjoyed the tropical plants there. Some stonecutters were carving General Jackson's motto on the base of the equestrian statue of the old hero, "The Federal Union, it must and shall be preserved." This was in pursuance of General Butler's order. . . .

DECEMBER 18, THURSDAY.—. . . General Banks said we would advance on Port Hudson. That place taken, Vicksburg would no longer be tenable. He felt every assurance that our efforts to establish the counter-revolutionary current here would be successful. He was in high spirits. We went to get a cup of tea, and, finding the dining room closed, I slipped off to bed. The General afterwards sent up his servant to ask me to go out to get some oysters, but I was already abed and declined the invitation.

DECEMBER 19, FRIDAY.—. . . I sat and talked with Beckwith. General Grant is a thick-head but a fighting man. Rosecrans is a clear-headed soldier and equally a fighting man, the most promising soldier we have in the field. The story of McClellan's marriage was this. Mrs. Marcy, mother of Nelly Marcy, desired the match between Mc-Clellan and her daughter. The courtship was feebly pursued by Mc-Clellan until he was sent abroad to the Crimea with the military commission. During his absence, the Marcys stayed at Willard's and the young lady was attended to by several young officers. Among them the preferred one was A. P. Hill and to him Miss Marcy became engaged. This was much against the will of her parents, and when McClellan returned, he, ignorant of what had been going on in his absence, renewed his mild attentions. On discovering the condition of things, he called on Hill and, receiving assurance of the truth, he pleasantly and formally relinquished all claim to her, and after this magnanimous act retired from the field. The Mother, more pertinacious of her views, took the girl away from Washington and secluded her from her lover Hill, and the passion being a wishy-washy affair was presently forgotten by both parties. McClellan was whistled back and was married, having in the meantime resigned his commission in the army and accepted the lucrative position of superintendent of the Ohio Central Railroad.

This same passionless magnanimity has characterized his military administration. He had not the harshness to crush an incompetent and worthless officer to whom he was personally attached.

He failed to acquire absolute ascendancy over the weak and timid men at Washington when their fears, ignorance, and confusion would have naturally and gladly thrown all power into his hands, but he confined himself with quiet and scrupulous care to the reorganization of the army and thus by neglecting a political opportunity he permitted weak and unprincipled intriguers to get the complete upper hand of him, so that when his campaign began, he was shorn of that authority and power which was necessary to enable him to complete it successfully. . . .

DECEMBER 21, SUNDAY.—. . . The property agent appointed by Butler desires to keep his post. He thought all the property of Secessionists ought to be seized and sold. To the question—"Who are the Secessionists?" he replied, "All the people here are Secessionists. There are no loyal people." "Then who would you sell to? Would you go on to sell all the property?" Being pressed further, he agreed there was a difficulty and that in his opinion there were no loyal people except in Massachusetts, adding after some hesitation "and the other New England states." And these are the moles who are to administer government for the United States, a nation embracing all climates, all races, and all ideas. . . .

After dinner the Reverend Hedges called on me and narrated the circumstances of the quarrel between the church and General Butler, the closing of the churches, and the arrest and trial of several Episcopal clergy. The Southern church under the influence of the bishops held a convention and declared separation from the Church of the United States. This convention substituted the prayer for the President of the Confederate States for that for the President of the United States. The Southern clergy almost en masse accepted the order and read the prayer as changed. On his arrival, Butler ordered the omission of this prayer. This order was obeyed. Things went on thus for five months until General Shepley, military governor of the state, ordered the Reverend Dr. Fulton as follows:

New Orleans Sept. 29, 1862

Special Order No. 33

Revd. Dr. Fulton: The omission in the service of the Protestant Episcopal Church in New Orleans of the prayer for the President of the United States and others in authority will be considered as evidence of hostility to the government of the United States.

By order of

Brig. Genl. G. F. Shepley
Military Governor of Louisiana

To this order the six clergymen returned a response containing the joint protest against civil or military interference in matters belonging to church government and against "their omission of the said prayer being taken as evidence of disloyalty to the U. S. Government." They omitted the prayer because it was no longer a part of the liturgy of the church to which they belonged. Butler then closed all the churches, tried three of the clergymen, and condemned them to imprisonment in Fort Warren. They were sent off but I believe never imprisoned. The other three were tried and condemned and had their trunks packed to leave, but the arrival of General Banks relieved them of the execution of their sentence. This is the history given by Hedges, and I promised to ask General Banks to rescind the Order No. 33 so that they might administer the communion to their mournful flocks who were hungering and thirsting for the bread of life. I knew General Banks' opinions well enough to feel sure he would issue the order. . . .

DECEMBER 23, TUESDAY.—. . . Madame Shepherd, on hearing the news that the Negroes were not to be freed, declared that all the ladies in New Orleans would like to have a chance to show their contempt of General Butler and to kiss General Banks. . . . Spent the evening in General Banks' office. Admiral Farragut was there and talked a great deal. He wanted to take Mobile Bay for some time but the Government refused permission. He got the map and explained how he would do it. His plans were very clear and decided. Farragut is from Norfolk and said he thought ironclad ships and rifled guns would ruin the army and navy. Formerly wooden walls and smoothbore guns at short range were good enough and men went in and decided a battle. Now men considered it a sufficient apology for shirking a fight that they had not iron armor or rifled guns. I observed that the Duke of Wellington had come to the same conclusions before and had said that long-range firearms would ruin the British Army. The Admiral seemed much pleased to find his opinion seconded by the Duke. . . .

DECEMBER 24, WEDNESDAY.—The streets during the last few days were gay with the population of the city who have come out like gophers in the sunshine. The cannon from the flagship proclaim that Butler has departed, and I suppose New Orleans will breathe freer. . . . The General gave us the news received by telegraph of Burnside's failure at Fredericksburg. By the newspaper account it seems to have been a very stupid as well as feeble attack. This defeat, although involving nothing decisive, will furnish material for a great Rebel rejoicing and will I fear seriously dampen our prospects here. To weaken the enemy by conciliation we need a decided military success. This reverses the case. . . .

DECEMBER 25, THURSDAY.—. . . On the general subject of the Negro I am fully posted. I believe him capable of improvement by giving him responsibility under a firm and proper discipline. The defect of his enslaved condition is the absence of all responsibility, making him thriftless and childish. The discipline of slavery is his salvation. Continue this discipline and make him at the same time a free man so far as responsibility goes and he will improve within certain limits. This may be also said of the white man. . . . I was introduced to a couple of officers, a major of Texan cavalry and a Captain [Thomas M.] Buchanan, commanding a gunboat squadron on the Atchafalaya River. The naval officer urged an expedition against Opelousas, where Governor [Thomas O.] Moore had convened the legislature of the state. I promised to speak to the General about it and, finding an opportunity, did so. He seemed struck with the proposition and ready to adopt it. . . .

DECEMBER 26, FRIDAY.—Was called on by Thorpe,[4] city surveyor, and with him visited the various public works inaugurated by Major General Butler and superintended by Thorpe. These were first the rebuilding of the wooden levee in front of the city, partially decayed and partially destroyed by the burning of the cotton when the city was captured, regarding the eastern levee behind it and works strengthening the levee encroached upon by the current of the river. Second, the covering of the customhouse by a temporary roofing to preserve it from the weather. The customhouse has already cost three millions of dollars and is not yet under roof. This vast structure of stone, iron, and cement is going to decay in its present exposed condition and is for the most part useless. Under General Butler's orders, estimates for covering it were made by an expenditure of thirty thousand dollars. Mr. Thorpe is carrying on the work completing the roofing which will last fifteen years and will furnish much valuable house room to the Government for storage, public offices, or accommodation of troops. . . . Called in at the office and was assigned to the Sequestration Committee and hope that my connection with this business will be but temporary as the order indicates. . . . The expedition

4. Thomas B. Thorpe (1815-78) is best known for his essay, "The Big Bear of Arkansas," a classic of frontier humor.

to Opelousas was discussed and was opposed by the two naval officers. They think of nothing but taking Port Hudson. . . .

DECEMBER 27, SATURDAY.—. . . Went to the office on Lafayette Square where the Sequestration Committee organized. As we proceeded to transact business it was clear that the whole system had been one of enormous and unblushing fraud and rapine, in which United States Volunteer officers were engaged in company with speculators outside the army. . . .

DECEMBER 28, SUNDAY.—In company with Thorpe, a Mr. Ingraham, city drainer, and several newspaper reporters I took the Mexican Gulf Railway and started to visit the plantation of Dr. Knapp, twelve miles down the river. The country through which we passed had an air of neglect and quantities of cane were standing on the ground perishing for want of labor to secure it. Knapp was a Northern man who had lived here for a number of years, and, although a good fellow, had a loud and overbearing manner. From here we were invited to visit and dine with Major Walker whose plantation was a mile or two distant. We were received here by the Major, who was a polished gentleman evidently having seen much of the world. A former Virginian, Mr. Merrit, now sugar planter, was there and remarked to me that he had also a superb distilling apparatus, useless to him this season because of General Butler's order closing all distilleries. His friend Major Walker had been fortunate enough to obtain a permit from General Butler to distill rum, whereby he would make a hundred thousand dollars. He himself had applied for a similar permit, but the person making the application for him had been told by Colonel [Andrew J.] Butler, brother of the General, that they touched nothing but big figures now and that a permit would cost fifty thousand dollars. The planter did not care to risk so much and in consequence his distillery was stopped and his refuse thrown away. . . .

A Mr. Russell, Yankee civilian, sat next to me. He spoke of the condition of the Northern regiments which started out clean, trig, with habits of civilized neatness and good health. At present they were ragged, dirty, lousy, degraded in apparel and in habits. Their moral character had suffered similar degradation. He asked if it was owing to war or absence of female society. I attributed it to the latter cause, having seen communities in the West composed exclusively of men in times of peace equally degraded. California and Pike's Peak furnished many similar examples. I went even further to state that I believed the low spirits of our troops was owing to their yearning for female society, that the outrageous and unreasonable resentment expressed by them against the Southern women, who frowned and looked bitter at them, was the result of a yearning for the sunshine of woman's smile to which they had been used at home. I further instanced the splendid reception given to the Union troops by the women of Frederick and attributed the victories which followed to the inspiration of the smiles of the Maryland ladies as much as to their gallant leader McClellan. . . .

DECEMBER 29, MONDAY.—. . . Have had a day of driving business in settling horse cases. Three French women all told their stories at once. When a lull took place I put in something in the shape of a response, at which they all started again and like the Cousin Sally Dillard story repeated their complicated griefs.[5] When another lull ensued, I again put in and explained how General Banks could not interfere in individual cases but would issue a general order to protect their rights. They all began again and retold their everlasting stories. . . .

While at General Banks' headquarters three officers of the Negro regiments called with a petition that he would countermand the order sending them to the forts and would give them a chance to distinguish themselves in the field. They said they wished to be tried and to solve the problem of whether they could fight or not. They were so nearly white that they might have passed for Mexicans, neatly dressed and not bad-looking fellows. General gratification is expressed that these regiments are sent to the forts, as they were insolent and overbearing toward the white people of the country, yet I do not doubt but what they will in time make tolerable soldiers—never first-rate ones, however. . . .

JANUARY 3, SATURDAY.—. . . I went with the General to visit the *Hartford*. In the Admiral's cabin, Mobile was again discussed in a manner which induced me to believe that an attack was meditated in that direction. Drawings of the forts, Gaines and Morgan, were examined. I hope it will be tried. . . . The General received a telegram informing him that Galveston had been reoccupied by the enemy killing and capturing all our troops there and destroying two blockading vessels.[6] Four ironclads had come out and did the busi-

5. "Cousin Sally Dillard" was a famous story written by Hamilton C. Jones, a North Carolina humorist, about a garrulous but irrelevant witness.

6. A Union force from New Orleans took nominal possession of Galveston on December 24, but on January 1 a Confederate command under John B. Magruder defeated the Federal force, destroyed the *Westfield*, and captured the *Harriet Lane*.

ness. . . . At dinner the General seemed to give up our cause and charged the system of government with the failure. That is, his discourse led inevitably to that conclusion, although he would not accept the conclusion just in square terms. . . .

TOPOGRAPHICAL ENCAMPMENT, MAGRUDER'S

JANUARY 4, SUNDAY.—. . . Went aboard the *Hartford* again and found Admiral Farragut in the dumps about the Galveston affair. His professional pride seemed to be touched and he has ordered a court of inquiry into the affair. The official report of the officer commanding one of the vessels which escaped was read to us. It seems the United States vessels were lying in different places out of supporting distance and some of them aground. They were attacked before daylight by a ram and four steamboats which were barricaded to the upper decks with cotton bales and filled with riflemen. These came down upon the *Harriet Lane* and before she could use her guns, her decks were entirely swept by fire. Her captain, [J. M.] Wainwright, Lieutenant [Edward] Lea, and half her crew were killed outright. She was then boarded and captured. The flagship having got aground was blown up to prevent her falling into the hands of the enemy. Her commander, [W. B.] Renshaw, and several men were killed by the premature explosion of her magazine. The troops in the town of Galveston, 250 men, three companies of the 42nd Massachusetts, were killed or taken. The *Harriet Lane* is the swiftest vessel in our navy and unless retaken will be used to work us mischief.

Three strong boats are already gone to retake her if possible. This affair seems to indicate overconfidence on the part of the naval officers. It was certainly well done and well planned by the Confederates. . . . Drove around town with the General. The evening was fine and the balconies were alive with women and children. A number of the women showed their disgust of us by grimaces and gestures. I cannot imagine how any *man* could feel resentment against such silly and childish exhibitions. . . .

JANUARY 8, THURSDAY.—This is the anniversary of Jackson's victory over the British. The General seems to be low-spirited this morning and begins to accept the certainty of the fall of the Republic. I do not see myself what ground there is for hope. The confident tone of the Northern press is gone, and the Southern papers are filled with accounts of victories. Our armies seem to be affected by the feebleness and cowardice of the Government and so far from assailing and crushing the enemy are scarcely able to take care of themselves. . . . So the blind Polyphemus, after wasting his strength in gigantic but misdirected efforts to strike the enemy, will lie down and die. What is to come after his death, who can imagine?

The most charming pages of French literature are those describing the lives and characters of their distinguished people in state, war, and society. What a miserable collection would the lives and characteristics of our democratic people produce— ignorance, vulgarity, vanity, and brutality. . . .

JANUARY 9, FRIDAY.—. . . Rode out with the General. Reports are rife that he is to be Secretary of War. He laughs at them. He says such reports made his position in Washington disagreeable. In consequence he asked the President to send him to Texas. He was sent here to relieve both himself and the President of the embarrassment of having him pushed forward as Secretary of War.

JANUARY 10, SATURDAY.—. . . The General was very anxiously awaiting the mail, hoping to get letters from his family and some important political news. He received instead several stale newspapers and a quantity of Lincoln proclamations put up in the form of tracts, handbills, and little books two inches square. These came from a man in high position in Massachusetts and seem to be the ammunition chiefly relied on for carrying on the war. The honorable individual who sent them doubtless collected the money for their publication and kept five per cent for his trouble. "To such vile uses must we come at last, Horatio." I have never seen the General so handsomely aroused. His scorn and contempt were sublime.

JANUARY 11, SUNDAY.—. . . The American people is certainly a great people—morally, intellectually, materially. Its energies are immense, its virtues are brilliant, its capacities for power and greatness are unlimited. But it has no head, no superior class to lead and develop its power and give direction to its energies. It seems now as if ability and superiority had been so long hunted out of public life that it has ceased to exist among us. Can it be true that our system has really leveled the human mind to that degree of meanness which we see exhibited at the head of public affairs, or does capacity still lay perdu among that class which has so long been denied participation in government that it has forgotten its faculties and lost its ambition? Of one thing I am fully convinced, that with our present elective system it is hopeless to expect anything but meanness and incapacity in the public councils. But if that system were changed *now* the question is—whether its practice for a century has not withered up all capacity for honor and command. . . .

JANUARY 14, WEDNESDAY. . . . At dinner saw a caricature in *Harper's* which was very deep into the President. Columbia asks princely, "Where are my fifteen thousand sons murdered at Fredericksburg?" Lincoln replies, "That reminds me of a little joke. . . ." Stanton and Halleck stand by, while on the board of the War Theatre is "On to Richmond, played every night by a select company of star generals."

JANUARY 15, THURSDAY.—. . . There was a going and coming in the house all night. Orderlies riding to and fro, which signified some movement of troops and of events. The news at breakfast was that General Weitzel was pushing the enemy back and that Commander Buchanan was killed.[7] The officer was in command of the gunboat squadron on Berwick's Bay and was killed by a shot from a Rebel sharpshooter. . . .

JANUARY 16, FRIDAY.—It is clear that Butler enriched himself and officers by robbing the country within our lines and trading with the enemy. A citizen presented to General Banks a regularly authorized contract signed by the Rebel Secretary of War and expected to be signed by Butler. The citizen stated that he had negotiated the matter with Butler. The contract called for an exchange of one bale of cotton for sixteen sacks of salt. The citizen offered General Banks a hundred thousand dollars if he would enter into the contract. Other offers on a large scale have been made to Clark, showing by

7. This movement was made to protect the city from any attack from the South by Berwick's Bay.

the open and innocent manner that it has been customary to conduct business in that way. The General says he would not permit one to foreclose a mortgage or sell a man's estate for debt in the present circumstances. . . .

JANUARY 20, TUESDAY.—The General asked me this morning to accompany him to Baton Rouge. Weitzel[8] told us of some of the details of his late campaign. Buchanan exposed himself rashly. He advanced against the gunboat of the Confederates fearing that the troops would board her and deprive the navy of the credit. He was standing on the deck directly exposed to the fire of the Rebel sharpshooters. He knew where they were posted and had pointed the locality out to General Weitzel. Nevertheless, he was so eagerly bent on pushing his boat ahead of the skirmishers that he gave no heed to their fire. He was struck under the right temple, the ball coming out back of the opposite ear. His death was instantaneous. Commander Buchanan always insisted that his Uncle, Commodore [Franklin] Buchanan, now in the Confederate service at Mobile, was a good Union man and that but for the action of our Government would have been in the United States service today. Buchanan was one of those who resigned under a misapprehension and afterwards tried to recall his resignation, but he was treated with contumely and refused an opportunity to reconsider. Thus he was driven from the Northern service and has been one of the most able officers of the Confederacy. He commanded the *Merrimac* in her action with the National fleet at Hampton Roads. . . . Went aboard the *Brunswick* and started up the river. . . .

JANUARY 21, WEDNESDAY.—. . . Saw Baton Rouge through the fog. This lifted before we arrived at the landing. The asylum for the deaf, dumb, and blind is a very showy building, and the shell of the state capitol looked handsome. The levee was muddy and the town generally had a dirty and forlorn appearance. We went ashore and visited General Augur's quarters.[9] Here we got horses and rode

8. Godfrey Weitzel (1835-84), USMA '55, had worked on the fortifications of New Orleans before the war, and in 1862 he was appointed chief engineer for Butler's army. He served as a field officer under Banks until late in 1863, when he rejoined Butler on the James River. In 1864 Weitzel commanded the Seventeenth and later the Twenty-fifth Corps. It was his force which took possession of Richmond in April, 1865.

9. Christopher C. Augur (1821-98), USMA '43, was commandant at West Point when the war began. After service with Banks at Cedar Mountain, Augur was transferred to New Orleans and commanded the left wing of the army during the siege of Port Hudson. Late in 1863 he was given the Twenty-second Corps and served in the Department of Washington.

around the suburbs visiting the earthworks now being thrown up by Negroes. A portion of the town near the old U. S. barracks had been burnt when the place was attacked some time ago by Breckinridge. At the barracks, now an entrenched camp, we saw General Zachary Taylor's house. . . .

We went to visit the ram *Essex*. She is a curious marine monster and looks very formidable. She mounts ten guns ranging in caliber from an old thirty-two-pounder to a ten-inch Dahlgren. On her gun deck her sailors stood around her guns and saluted us with short Roman swords. They were armed in addition with revolvers, and altogether the scene was most grim and piratelike. . . .

General Banks spoke very despondingly of the state of public affairs, saying that he saw no hope of a fortunate or speedy conclusion of the war. Yet he agreed with me that there was no possibility of peace. I think the President's proclamation has settled that matter beyond a doubt. . . .

JANUARY 22, THURSDAY.—Walked two miles down the levee to the Crevasse. Several hundred Negroes were working under sergeants making a new levee. I asked one of them how he liked his freedom. He said, "Pretty well." He didn't have to work quite so hard as when on the plantation. . . . At two o'clock General Banks came on board and the order was given to fire up. The evening was fine and the river banks looked magnificent. We got to New Orleans about midnight and anchored in the stream. Retired to bed dreaming of the grand panorama of the coast and of my sweet friends at home.

JANUARY 28, WEDNESDAY.—. . . The General quoted from Napoleon, "The world belongs to the phlegmatic." Those who act in a twinkling are too fast and do mischief, their works cannot stand. There is some philosophy in this idea. My father acted on it and Banks is very much influenced by it. . . . I met Lachenmeyer. His business was to get permission to bring over some cotton from the other side of the lake, to accomplish which he must have a permit to take an equivalent in salt or provisions. I told him the order was positive that no provisions could be permitted to pass our line. He told me there was a thousand bales there and that if I would enter into the venture I would ensure me twenty-five thousand dollars. I declined the proposition civilly, not indignantly, for such traffic has been so much the practice of the Butler dynasty that it was very natural for the man to make the offer. People seem to have forgotten that money will not buy a man everything. If one sells an estate, a house, a horse, and afterward repents of his bargain, he may repurchase his property. But having once sold his honor he cannot buy it back. . . .

JANUARY 29, THURSDAY.—. . . At night Admiral Farragut and Commander [Thornton A.] Jenkins, both Virginians, came in and discoursed with Colonel Clark and myself on the subject of taking Mobile and a movement into Opelousas. The Admiral said if he knew they were fighting at Vicksburg, he would run the batteries at Port Hudson and go up to assist Porter. He also advised the same thing which I had suggested, passing above Port Hudson to the West and holding the communication between there and Vicksburg and attacking it from above. . . .

FEBRUARY 2, MONDAY.—. . . At the Sequestration Office I found business enough. Several planters called to see what arrangements could be made in regard to having their slaves returned. Some of these seemed quite willing to accept the General's proclamation; others seemed much outraged by it and thought it would ruin the country entirely. The proposition of giving the Negroes one hogshead in twenty was accepted by me, thus raising a fund to be distributed at the end of the season among the laborers according to their merits and capacities. This, with the feeding, clothing, and caring for the families, seems a fair offer on the part of the planters. On talking with the General afterward he answered fully and unreservedly that the planters should have their Negroes returned, that they should be returned from the camps, and wherever they were found. . . . The chief of secret service with McClellan is [Allen] Pinkerton, the celebrated detective, said to be a very skillful man in his business and a very bad man. This is the person with whom Lincoln took morning drinks and stood with to be photographed [at Antietam]. . . .

FEBRUARY 3, TUESDAY.—. . . Captain [W. Sturgis] Hooper, who has hitherto acted with us with great facility, I find is beginning to take views from the abolition standpoint. The Captain is absolutely and decidedly at variance with Beckwith and myself on the subject of the General's proclamation. After my conversation with General Banks last night I felt fully authorized to state to the planters (who accepted the contract proposed) that their servants would be returned to them and forced to work for their living. Hooper declines positively to accede to any such proposition and insists that our plan does not recognize in any way the slaves as party to the contract and that the General will fall if he attempts to carry out any such plan. He washes his hands of it and gives us as reason that public opinion in

Boston is to be considered, and that it is more important that public opinion there should be satisfied than that the planters here shall be saved from ruin. Hooper is clever, sincere, frank, yet it is hard for me to conceive of such subject servitude to a prevailing opinion. . . .

FEBRUARY 4, WEDNESDAY.—Wrote out my understanding of the proposition, in short as follows. The planter agrees to support the slave, and to give him of the crop one hogshead in twenty and one twentieth of any other staple. The authorities agree to return all slaves to their places and enforce obedience and industry. The General came in and read my proposition. He assented to it as he had done to verbal statements of the same character. Hooper then gave him his views. The General then came out explicitly saying he had no intention nor authority to force the slaves back to their masters. He depended solely upon moral suasion. He would advise them to go. It was now entirely clear to me that the proposition asking the planter to guarantee support and wages to his slaves who were to be held by moral suasion would fail. My effort to reconcile the Massachusetts idea of the Negro with the planter's practical knowledge of the same animal was a total failure. It was fair enough while we dealt in generalities, but now the practical statement of the subject developed the vast gulf between. The guarantee of the authorities to enforce return of the slaves without contemplating a resort to physical force is, to the planter, the play of Hamlet with the part of Hamlet left out. . . . Hooper read a paper he had prepared. He had introduced a clause requiring the assent of the slaves. This the General disapproved of absolutely. Hooper seemed to have no other ideas throughout than to guess how the thing would read to a Boston audience. The General seemed solely interested to accomplish a good result within the limits of his authority and willing to let it take its chance with the public. . . .

FEBRUARY 6, FRIDAY.—It seems there was a meeting of planters last night at the St. Charles, and Maillot had nearly succeeded in getting a unanimous vote accepting the proposition. Maillot came up to see me and arranged some amendments to our proposition, bringing it back nearly to the paper I had first written. This paper the General approved without criticism. It also gave great satisfaction to the planters. Maillot urged me to have them printed immediately that the plan might be put in execution without delay to the end that factious persons might not have time to get up a formidable opposition to the plan. The order was printed and the General on reading it said, "This is the greatest thing that has ever been done in this country."

He looks upon it as the first step in the transition from slave to free labor. . . .

FEBRUARY 8, SUNDAY.—. . . Holabird pitched into the West Point aristocracy. The engineers have generally showed incapacity for command. Yet they have been advanced into all the high places in the army. The pride of superior technical knowledge has banded that corps into an exclusive society in the army and there is a decided jealousy between them and the other branches. There being no head to the family, the children quarrel with each other. . . .

FEBRUARY 13, FRIDAY.—At breakfast a paragraph in the *Picayune* was read, stating that an attempt to assassinate General Banks had been made the evening previous by someone armed with an air gun. The General was very angry and ordered a note to be written threatening to suppress the paper. . . .

FEBRUARY 16, MONDAY.—Governor Shepley is from Maine. He spoke with admiration of Judge Beverley Tucker's book, *The Partisan Leader*,[10] as a prophetic work and generally remarked how much more far seeing were the Southern statesmen and Southern gentlemen than the Northern. General Banks agreed with him. The truth is that the Northern people were too busy getting rich to study statesmanship. The best minds and best men of the country were occupied with other matters than public affairs. The political men in power were either paltry thieves with no more capacity than to invent petty tricks to plunder the Public Treasury or fanatical ideologists more dangerously bent on turning the government into a machine for carrying out their silly and impracticable conceits. The Southern men in public life (making a fair allowance for bullies and blackguards, some of them the lowest and coarsest stamp) were men of power and sagacity, natural leaders of people. Ambitious and unprincipled, but still strong men. . . .

FEBRUARY 17, TUESDAY.—[William] Luce called in at the office to see me. He gave us some of his experiences in the Confederate prisons. He says my views of the condition of the Confederates were surprisingly accurate. He was every day surprised at the truth of my descriptions. He said their military display was hollow and that dissatisfaction was widespread. We had nothing to do but advance,

10. Nathaniel Beverley Tucker (1784-1851), the half-brother of John Randolph of Roanoke, was for twenty years a professor of law at William and Mary. An agrarian and aristocrat, Tucker poured forth works on Southern Rights. His novel, *The Partisan Leader* (1836) was presumably written to show how the election of Van Buren might precipitate the South into civil war. Strother knew Tucker personally, having visited him at Williamsburg in 1849.

and the Confederates could not imagine why we did not advance. The private soldiers were totally ignorant of the causes of the war and used to ask him frequently what it was about! Luce tells me that during his captivity in the Valley he heard many bitter threats against my life and felt glad that he was captured instead of myself. This is very characteristic of Luce. . . .

FEBRUARY 19, THURSDAY.—. . . Talked of the condition of public affairs and came to conclusions not very flattering. I prophesied that the war would last twenty-five years. . . . After dinner there was a council of war to discuss the expedition up the Atchafalaya to take Butte à la Rose and open communication with Grant. Augur advised a flank march around Port Hudson eastward to occupy Bayou Sara, and Emory[11] said he would prefer a direct assault on Port Hudson. Both these generals were evidently opposed to the Atchafalaya movement and suggested impossible and futile movements instead. I was very little pleased with the council and saw there what has ruined us from the beginning of the war, "The disposition to exaggerate the numbers of the enemy."

FEBRUARY 24, TUESDAY.—. . . Clark has got home from his expedition above Baton Rouge for the exchange of prisoners. He says the Rebels look very seedy and gaunt and that one of the privates offered a soldier fifty cents in silver for four crackers. He says there are not near so many men at Port Hudson as is reported and that we might easily take it by assault. . . . Generals Augur, Emory, and Weitzel dined with us. The conversation turned on the Mexican War. General Taylor was not considered a skillful tactician, but was a man of heroic courage and won his battles by fighting. That quality is what has not been exhibited in any high degree by either side in this war. Taylor they said in the beginning of the war had a great contempt for both cavalry and artillery. He believed in infantry alone. His experiences in Mexico changed and modified these prejudices. A typesetter is not an author, nor is a drill sergeant a general. And after all the man who is brave and will make his troops fight it out must win in the long run. . . .

FEBRUARY 25, WEDNESDAY.—. . . There has been great trouble between the whites and the Negro regiments. At Ship Island Colonel [Spencer H.] Stafford of the Negro regiment was in command of the island and had also four companies of whites. He ordered the white

11. William H. Emory (1811-87), USMA '31, campaigned on the Peninsula, in Louisiana, and in the Shenandoah Valley. He ended the war as commander of the Nineteenth Corps.

captains to do duty under a Negro officer of the day. They refused and were arrested. All the other officers refused in like manner and were put under arrest. The privates were then ordered to duty by the Colonel in person and likewise refused and were all sent to the guard-house. The difficulty was evaded by removing the white companies from the island. . . . In fact, these officers, white men, being in command of black regiments have attempted to enforce social equality upon the white troops. These resent the association and treat the Negroes with studied contempt. I saw an orderly order a Negro captain out of the hall with the same contempt that he would have shown to a mangy dog. The shoulder-knotted Ethiopian pulled his foretop and scraped his foot obsequiously and left without a word of remonstrance.

MARCH 1, SUNDAY.—Several vessels were stopped at Donaldsonville loaded with supplies and ammunition for the enemy. The Yankees are supplying the enemy through Matamoros, also the French in Mexico. . . . At the railroad depot at Carrolton I got upon the levee and rode homeward. In the camps was divine service in two places. I came upon a congregation of Negroes grouped around an old grey-haired preacher who was haranguing. They were in the midst of some brick shacks which had been fitted up as an encampment for contrabands. The scene was eminently picturesque. The venerable old preacher stood upon a platform on which was a table and a book. On either side of him sat three dignified darkies. Around on benches and on the ground were grouped plantation Negroes, men, women, and children, ragged, hooded, blanketed, and resembling a collection of savages, their positions eminently classic. When I entered, I was addressed by a white soldier who desired to know my name and purpose. I told him. He then apologized and said their orders were very strict. An officer named Rice had come there and enlisted some sixty of them and that was forbidden to do so. Meanwhile one of the assistants came down from the scaffold and supposing I was a preacher (as I wore a black military overcoat) invited me to mount the rostrum. I declined and told him to go on as if I was not there. The old man was all the while preaching away to the best of his ability, eliciting a few groans from his audience, but his remarks did not seem to stir his audience very deeply. There were some powerfully dramatic faces in that group. . . .

MARCH 4, WEDNESDAY.—. . . It is determined to make a demonstration by land [at Port Hudson] while the fleet runs past the batteries.

There seems to be no idea of a grand attack. Grover thinks the place will fall by starvation if the Red River is closed by a blockade. . . .

MARCH 5, THURSDAY.—. . . At tea Admiral Farragut and Captain Jenkins came in. The conversation took a social turn. The Admiral cried out against the manner and quality of the appointments in the increased navy. Says they are obtained by procurers at from fifty to one hundred dollars a place. Three of the officers who ran away from Galveston and arrived at this port were put under orders by the Admiral. They deserted and escaped to New York. He says he will have them shot for cowardice. He is opposed to monster guns, preferring a great number of small ones. A shower of balls is better than one ball or shell fired at long intervals. . . .

MARCH 7, SATURDAY.—. . . Aboard the *Hartford* we found the usual work of hoisting boats, etc., going on. The Admiral said we would be at Baton Rouge on Tuesday morning and would then keep right ahead to Port Hudson. The General's news about Price[12] being at Clinton with thirty thousand men to strike the flank of any movement on Port Hudson the Admiral did not believe. He said the enemy had fought us with lies and he had no doubt this was one of them. He was for going in anyhow to prove the truth of these reports. The Admiral was excited and the fire of his nature blazed out. A gallant sailor of the old school. . . . Got on board the *Empire Parish* where we found all our company ready to go up the river. It was quite a reunion of our staff officers, some of whom I had not seen for two months. . . .

MARCH 8, SUNDAY.—. . . Luce is aboard. Luce told his Negro boy that he must take good care of his trunk when he left the city. The boy replied, "This trunk must and shall be preserved," parodying Jackson's declaration in regard to the Federal Union. . . . Arrived at Baton Rouge about six P.M. General Banks and staff determined to remain all night on board the boat. Taking the horse and mules ashore by the bridge, several men were kicked overboard and several horses and mules fell in, but no serious accident. General [George L.] Andrews is our chief of staff, and I hope things will be arranged in a more military manner than heretofore. The story about Price with thirty thousand men is not confirmed. . . .

MARCH 9, MONDAY.—After breakfast the General and staff mounted and went to visit the defensive works. . . . The Negro soldiers are working at the parapets which are incomplete, not a heavy gun

12. Sterling Price, a Confederate general in the Western theatre during the war.

mounted yet, although the pieces are lying on the ground and the carriages ready. The Negroes worked very stupidly and as if they were disgusted with the subject. We rode out of town through the camps and out beyond the picket line. The Grand Guard was just returning in a straggling and most slovenly manner. In fact, the whole appearance of things was most unmilitary and unpromising. . . . A reconnoissance towards Port Hudson came upon the enemy's pickets eight miles out.

MARCH 10, TUESDAY.—Today we take the field. It presently commenced drizzling and from looks of things I don't think there will be any movement today. A thick fog covers the surface of the river and this will prevent Farragut's coming in time, so we must wait. The troops are very green and not in very good condition. Some drunken white soldiers assaulted the Negro soldiers and there was a brickbat fight in which the Negroes were worsted. . . . The introduction of the Negro soldier only complicates the confusion and inefficiency of our army composed of green troops. The white soldiers won't do anything now except make the Negroes work for them. They are more exacting and brutal than the masters were originally. A vulgar fellow unaccustomed to be waited on is always so with servants. . . . News that Farragut is on his way.

MARCH 12, THURSDAY.—. . . Went to review with the General and staff accompanied by Admiral Farragut and all the fleet captains. The sailors were roughly mounted on improvised horses and the scene was more lively than usual. The display was very fine and the ditch-jumping caused great excitement. I expected to see some of the Navy men fall into the ditch but they all got over safely. Captain [Charles] Sargent of our staff fell in and his horse over him, leaving only the horse's heels sticking out. My mare performed beautifully as usual. Scheffler had borrowed the General's horse, Shenandoah, and was run away with during the parade, and only escaped being thrown by running into a regiment of infantry. After dinner the General asked me my opinion of matters and I urged him strongly to march directly on Port Hudson. He said if he had ten thousand more men he would attack. . . . It has been reported in New Orleans that Stonewall Jackson was on his way to attack and recapture that place during our absence. General Sherman[13] writes that he has not faith in the report now, showing that he did credit it at first.

13. Thomas W. Sherman (1813-79), USMA '36, occupied Port Royal, South Carolina, in 1861. Shortly before Banks's arrival, Sherman commanded all Union troops above the city of New Orleans; at Port Hudson he led a division. An iron-clad disciplinarian, he alienated volunteers and thereby lost political support.

MARCH 13, FRIDAY.—A company of the Negro guard was formed on the levee. A fine-looking set of men and doubtless capable of being made good soldiers. [John A.] Nelson, their colonel, is very anxious that they should be tried and offers to storm any battery indicated. I introduced myself and asked him particularly about his regiment. He repeated what I had heard before, that he had the greatest confidence in them as fighting men although they had had no fair trial yet. They will drill with any white regiment, are vigilant on picket duty, are good night owls, are very docile, and obey orders without thinking or questioning. They are good workers and built all the works at Baton Rouge. This regiment is officered with white men altogether; the noncommissioned officers alone are blacks. Nelson sees no especial advantage that mulattoes possess over blacks. . . . About five o'clock the fleet started, a steamboat towing the bomb ketches, the twenty-seven-gun *Hartford* followed and then the twenty-four-gun *Richmond*, etc. The gallant fleet steamed out of sight behind the bend just as the sun went down. Just after dark we saw signal rockets from the enemy thrown up to the northwestward. By breakfast time tomorrow the question will be settled with them. . . .

MARCH 14, SATURDAY.—. . . We took breakfast and got off at seven. The ride was along a road encumbered with moving troops, trains, and artillery. As the General and staff passed, the regiments divided on each side of the road and cheered loudly. This caused some rapid and tiresome riding. The road was good all the way with a good deal of open cotton plantation ground with very inferior houses and improvements. The people are inferior to the sugar-growing population, being more local and secluded. . . . Colonel Clark seemed possessed with fidgetness and could not sit still, saying he was bound to do something and could not sit idle. He mounted and started to the outpost about a mile toward Port Hudson on our left. About half past three a cavalryman without a hat, covered with mud himself, his horse blind with mud, rode furiously up and reported that they had been attacked and that Colonel Clark was killed. Two other fellows followed in scarce better plight, one leading a wounded horse. These reported that their cavalry captain was also killed. This produced some stir and there was a general tightening of girths. A cross examination proved that Colonel Clark had been reconnoitering beyond our pickets with a half a dozen cavalry when they were fired upon by an ambushing party. The Colonel, who was a tall, showy figure, fell and the cavalry captain also. General Banks presently came in and afterward

Dr. Alexander, who told us that they were bringing Clark in, that the large bone of his left leg was broken three inches below the knee. The wound was severe but not dangerous.

The chief of artillery, Captain [Richard] Arnold was spoken to make a reconnoissance on the same road to Port Hudson until he discovered and unmasked the guns. [William S.] Abert was asked to accompany the force to make a sketch of the road. Abert replied he could not sketch and knew nobody present who could, except Strother. I stood forward and General Andrews asked me if I would go. I replied that I would, certainly. We were to take a regiment of infantry and a squadron of cavalry and to view the road to Slaughter's Landing until we could go no farther. This seemed a desperate duty, but it was one which could not be refused for that reason. I therefore took out my notebook and sketchbook and gave them to Frank, charging him to take care of them, as I was not willing they should fall into the hands of the enemy in case I was shot. I did not expect to be captured. As we took the road Captain Arnold seemed to have taken gloomier views of our service even than I had. But *allons,* it was late and the order must be accompanied. We put our horses at full speed to overtake our escort which was at an outpost a mile and a half distant. As we rode, we met a squad of men carrying Colonel Clark in a litter made of fence rails and blankets. His face was very livid and contracted, very different from the usual amiable and complaisant expression. I shouted as we passed, "Long life to you, Colonel. I'm glad it's no worse." The soldiers hurrahed and we dashed on at full speed.

The excitement had entirely dispelled all gloom and nervousness. We were full of eagerness and excitement and a countermand of our order would have brought disappointment. Skirmishers were thrown out. Within the next half mile we passed two dead horses, victims of the recent ambuscade. Within the next hundred yards our skirmishers opened. A dozen shots were fired and a Confederate scout killed, pierced by two balls. I took rapid notes by the way, until we arrived at a school house and crossroads where fires were still burning in a recently deserted picket post. Here Grover turned back, recommending us if attacked to fight stubbornly with the regiment and send for reinforcements. We were three and one-half miles from our starting point and night was approaching rapidly. In the next mile we saw ahead some ten or a dozen scouts in the road. Our skirmishers stopped and swore they saw a thousand men in the woods and also earth works. I expected a volley of cannon shot in our faces, but on using the glass discovered that the skirmishers had lively imaginations. The earthworks proved to be only some sheds where the picket guard rested.

It had now got so dark that we could not discern objects at a distance. The regiment halted and Captain Arnold came to consult me about going farther. I told him when we could no longer see it was useless to reconnoiter and that considering the character of the regiment I did not think we could push much further. It was a Massachusetts regiment, perfectly green, never having seen any service. He said the reconnoissance was of vast importance, or so considered at headquarters. So we pushed the troops on four hundred yards farther. They moved with reluctance and the woods were so dark that they huddled up together and stopped of their own accord. A dozen horse attacking them would have thrown the whole body into confusion. We reluctantly determined to go no farther. I rode alone several hundred yards beyond the troops, examining the ground and the distance with a glass, saw some horsemen in a cotton field but nothing more. I returned to the troops, ordered them to be countermarched, and was soon back within our picket lines. . . .

At half past eleven I was awakened to hear and see the bombardments by the mortar boats and the fleet running the batteries at Port Hudson. The noise and pyrotechnics were sublime, like the flashes and reverberations of a grand thunder storm. We could see the shells slowly circling from the boats to the town. The flash and the noise were forty counts apart. Through a glass you could see the bombs like red moons in the air. After watching this for half an hour I retired again and slept until three. I was then awakened again. This time I could see a light in the direction of the river which illumined the clouds above. This light had been slowly drifting southward down stream and was accompanied by flashes followed by the heavy booming of guns and rolling explosions. This was supposed to be one of our vessels on fire and drifting down the stream, the guns and shells on her decks exploding as the fire reached them. As the Admiral's flagship led the fleet we sorrowfully concluded that it must be her. [Lieutenant Charles A.] Hartwell, an aide-de-camp, was dispatched to ascertain the facts. The General paced to and fro in great perturbation. He believed the attempt at passage was a total failure and seeing the certainty that one of our first class ships was burning, he concluded the others had been sunk and the fleet beaten. He said the Admiral had been rash and headstrong and that the whole matter was at his door. The order was given to strike tents and load baggage for Baton Rouge. The theory that the burning vessel was a Rebel fire ship was started and eagerly accepted. Why did she not blow up if a warship? Just then the whole western horizon was lit by a red flame, vast and widespreading. In thirty seconds the breathless silence was broken by a roar, pealing and long continued, which made the earth tremble. Then utter darkness followed. There was the ship's magazine. Good-bye, *Hartford*.

MARCH 15, SUNDAY.—Hartwell's report confirmed the fire raft theory. He had seen the vessel pass the signal station, and she was pronounced a fire raft without masts. This was encouraging. The fleet had passed up scot-free and the Rebel pyrotechnic had hurt nothing. So day filled and the order to move was countermanded. Just then an orderly brought a dispatch to [Richard B.] Irwin, Assistant Adjutant General. He read it, then started hastily to the General's tent. The dispatch from the signal station read as follows: "The *Hartford* and *Albatross* have passed the batteries and are now above Port Hudson. The *Mississippi* got aground opposite the town, was abandoned by her crew, set fire to, and after drifting down the current for several miles, blew up and perished. Her loss in men is heavy. The *Richmond* got a shot through her steam drum and drifted back below. The *Monongahela* broke her machinery and fell back also. The gun boats, four of them, and the *Essex* lay back to protect the bomb ketches." This was in brief the history of the naval battle of Port Hudson.

The General told me he thought of retiring behind the Bayou Montecino. I advised him to remain to develop Port Hudson better. He hesitated, but on consultation with his division generals the move was ordered and commenced. The soldiers plundered without restraint, keeping up a skirmishing fire all around on pigs, poultry, and cattle. The whole land was covered with blood, guts, horns, hair, and feathers. The discipline was very bad, mules and horses were taken everywhere, and some houses wantonly robbed. The man near whose house we encamped told me that I had gone the evening before within one and one-half miles of Port Hudson and perhaps half a mile of the works. Our ride back to Baton Rouge was without incident. I took lunch with the General, who seemed pleased with the manner we had escaped from what he now thought was a rash and unwise movement. . . . Presently a violent thunder storm came up and flooded the whole ground and all the tents; mine only escaped because of a mound. The five cavalry men who stampeded when Colonel Clark was shot were brought in under guard and put to work ditching the tents in the rain. Thus endeth the first campaign of the Army of the Gulf.

VIII

The Campaign on the Teche

March 16, 1863—May 9, 1863

The return of Banks's army to New Orleans in late March, 1863, was far from joyous. Washington protested against inactivity in the Department of the Gulf, the troops were demoralized, and the city clamored against a regime welcomed three months before. Banks needed a victory. Since the navy now commanded the mouth of the Red River, the General undertook a connecting movement by the Atchafalaya River to the west of the Mississippi. The Teche Campaign began early in April.

The Nineteenth Corps was opposed by the smaller force of General Richard Taylor, entrenched near Franklin. While Banks's major force crossed Berwick Bay on April 9, Grover's division was transported by steamer to a position in Taylor's rear. Although the effort to trap the Confederates failed, the Union army was successful in driving the outnumbered Rebels out of the Teche and in opening communication with Grant at Vicksburg. The Union capture of Port Hudson now became merely a matter of time. Washington had its victory, and Banks had the pleasure of pursuing a Confederate army.

At the conclusion of the Teche Campaign, Strother resigned from Banks's staff in order to return to the Eastern theatre of the war. The campaigning in Louisiana had seemed strangely remote from his abilities and interests; furthermore, his knowledge of Virginia topography was of no value there. He sailed to New York by way of Havana, festive with Rebel blockade-runners under the walls of the Morro Castle, and arrived home in time to hear that Hooker had just been cut to pieces at Chancellorsville.

MARCH 16, MONDAY.—. . . Commander [Melancton] Smith of the *Mississippi* came in to report to the General. He says the vessel reached the point opposite Port Hudson and got aground. She was stuck fast, receiving the fire of two batteries and lost about fifteen men killed and twenty-five wounded. He set fire to her and, putting the men in the boats, abandoned her and floated down the river under a heavy fire. The Commanders threw all the arms overboard to prevent their falling into the enemy's hands. To burn the vessel he had a fire built in the gun room, but a shell of the enemy entered, exploded, and put the fire out. He kindled another fire and waited to see it well caught before he left. The Commander cannot tell what damage we did to the enemy. . . .

The General had a conference with the Admiral before they started up the river. A bottle of champagne was opened and after a glass or two, old Farragut opened. "General," said he, "We have more men and more resources than these traitors and five times as much money. We must beat them in the end, but we must do it by poking them, butting them whenever we see them. By God, shall a United States ship of war hesitate to go in and destroy a dozen of these wretched Mississippi steamers? I am sick of hearing my officers talk of cotton-clad boats and impregnable rams. They should pitch in and destroy them. What matters it, General, whether you and I are killed or not. We came here to die. It is our business and must happen sooner or later. We must fight this thing out until there is no more than one man left and that man must be a Union man. Here's to his health." The Admiral is low in stature, about five-feet-five, a very handsome, gentlemanly face, soft in manner and speech, and womanly quiet except when aroused. He is a fine representative of the glory of the Old Navy. Commander Smith looks as if he feared reprimanded for abandoning and destroying his ship. He says the crew of the *Richmond* manned her starboard battery and were preparing a broadside for Port Hudson, when her steam drum was struck. She turned so suddenly that her loaded broadside bore upon the *Mississippi,* and the crew fired four guns into her before they discovered they were turned about. . . . At quarters I found the General at tea and was invited to join him. We took a walk and had a long talk foreshadowing great and important movements and indicating to me that the General is developing his latent[1] power as he becomes more confident in the field.

MARCH 17, TUESDAY.—. . . A bottle was found in the river at Donaldsonville with a note from Admiral Farragut above Port Hudson

1. Some time later "latent" was scratched out and replaced by "blatant" in Strother's handwriting.

saying they were all safe, having sustained no damage and lost but six men, one marine killed, and five sailors wounded. . . .

MARCH 19, THURSDAY.—Was aroused by uncommon noises and puffing of the steamers. On going on deck saw a wild scene around us. We were aground on the levee in the midst of a vast crevasse through which the swelled river was pouring over the bordering country, drowning plantations with all their improvements, dwellings, Negro cabins, and sugar houses. Our boat, the *Empire Parish*, had drifted into the current and was hard aground on the outer levee. The *Morning Light*, a smaller boat, also crowded with troops, had been sucked into the midst of a cotton field two hundred yards or more distant. Our situation was prospectively dangerous. The mist concealed the woods and buildings from which a fire might be opened with field artillery by the Rebels, to which we could make no response. [Colonel Nathan] Dudley wanted to hang the pilots, suspecting them of treachery. Meanwhile the steamer *St. Maurice* came alongside of us and, attaching a hawser, attempted to draw us off. The hawser broke at the first try. Our regiment of troops and all our horses and mules were transferred to the *St. Maurice* and, thus lightened, we were pulled off the bar after several attempts. We left the *Morning Light* to her fate as she seemed beyond help. . . . A captured Rebel captain wanted to be parolled that he might go into the cotton speculation business. He said the city of New Orleans in Federal hands furnishes more aid and comfort to the Confederacy than it did before the capture. Outside speculators flood the South with gold for cotton and with medicines and material of living and of war. . . . Arrived at Baton Rouge at eight o'clock. . . .

MARCH 20, FRIDAY.—. . . Went aboard the *Empire Parish* and started down the river. Had a long talk with the Confederate captain. He admired the audacity of the Navy and said their fire was most appalling, although too high generally. He said there was a reserve between Port Hudson and Vicksburg ready to strengthen either place when necessary. This man was a Tennesseean and not an impracticable Secessionist, but representing a class who would easily return to allegiance.

MARCH 26, THURSDAY.—At breakfast an article in the paper turned the conversation on H. L. Scott,[2] son-in-law of General Winfield Scott. This officer aide-de-camp of the General and author of the *Military Dictionary* has since the beginning of this war disappeared from the

2. Henry L. Scott, USMA '33, was appointed Inspector General of the army in May, 1861, retired in October, 1861, and resigned in October, 1862.

country and is living in France. During the time that McClellan was associated in command with General Scott, the plans of the war councils were betrayed to the enemy. After the failure of Munson's Hill, McClellan called a council of war: the President, General Scott, Cameron, and himself. He laid his card upon the table and stated his case thus: "Mr. President and Gentlemen, our plans, which have never been confided to anyone outside this circle, are continually betrayed to the enemy. At the last meeting I drew two topographical plans and gave one to Mr. Lincoln and the other to General Scott. No copy of this plan was made and none other existed except those made by my hands. Yet the enemy has received a copy of this plan. Who is the traitor?" Mr. Lincoln and General Scott both betrayed great emotion, wept, they say, the President fearing the treason would be found chargeable to his wife. General Scott spoke up, "The plan I carried home in my pocket and it was in my bedroom. No one could have had access to it but my son-in-law, Colonel Scott. He has betrayed the plan to the enemy as I believe he has done in other cases. In one week he shall leave the country." It was so arranged, and as further stated, H. L. Scott lives in France, retired on the pay of a lieutenant colonel of cavalry. Tucker[3] vouches for this story, which is doubtless founded on facts. . . .

MARCH 27, FRIDAY.—. . . With the coming spring the air is gay with gorgeous butterflies and gigantic moths and the hedges wriggling with lizards. Goats (not pigs) have the freedom of the city and at every turn one meets them with their kids grazing in the public squares and along the side drains. . . . [A. A.] Atocha having had some experiences in the Sequestration Committee apologizes today for having stated that the officers of that commission did nothing. He knows the reason now.

Our Bayou Teche expedition is resolved on, I believe. I hope it may be speedily put in execution. General Sherman is the most efficient and manly officer in this department. Cool, decisive, and soldierly. Pope is the nearest man to a soldier I have yet seen. Decisive, a good topographer, pugnacious, reckless, and unscrupulous.

MARCH 30, MONDAY.—. . . Tucker says he was present at a political debate between Abraham Lincoln and Stephen A. Douglas during their congressional canvass. At the village where Lincoln spent his youth he addressed the crowd, pointing out the rude cottage where he

3. Tucker, who specialized in anecdotes about the great and near-great, was Banks's private secretary. Since Strother first referred to him as "Mr. Tucker," he may have been a civilian aide.

had lived, the fields where he had labored, the wood where he had split rails, and in the audience old friends and fellow laborers. When Douglas replied, he alluded to these touching reminiscences and said the orator had forgotten to point out one spot where he had conspicuously figured in his former intercourse with the citizens of the community. He pointed to the doggery where Lincoln had formerly sold bad whisky to his fellow citizens and to the graveyard where many of them had prematurely gone from the effects of this noxious liquor. In his rejoinder Lincoln said he remembered well the modest tenement where he had once sold bad whiskey. It was closed and remained now as he left it. He had not mentioned it out of consideration for his honorable opponent, for if anyone should go into it now he would see long scores chalked upon the walls against Stephen A. Douglas, who was always his most liberal customer in drinking and treating but who never paid cash and whose scores remained unsettled to the present day. The orators told the truth of each other without malice or exaggeration. . . .

MARCH 31, TUESDAY.—The expedition against Opelousas is to be undertaken on a grand scale, and our means of sustenance, offense, and defense were summed up this morning. Called on Mrs. Penn and was introduced to a Miss Penn, who lives in Richmond. Miss Penn informed me that I was the first and only United States officer she had ever spoken to or who had ever crossed her threshold. I suppose their invitation to stay arose from feminine curiosity to see something of the gentle Yahoo. . . .

In our conversation of the morning I signified my intention of leaving the service to the General. He made no objection and I feel now assured he will make none when I propose the matter to him in form. I have lost everything in this war and have preserved nothing but my self-respect. I must be content with that and retire. There is no chance of any recognition of my sacrifice and services by the present Government. Let them go for what they are worth.

APRIL 4, SATURDAY.—We are informed that the Mississippi is not to be opened until the Pennsylvania Central and the New York Railroad and the Illinois Central (which are having a good business in transportation) shall be satisfied. That the aims and objects of the war, its conduct and its conductors, are matters of traffic and have been so since the commencement there can be no doubt. Thus is faithful valor bought and sold. . . .

APRIL 6, MONDAY.—. . . Tucker tells me we take to the field tomorrow at Brashear City. Weitzel thinks Sibley intends to attack him, not knowing that Emory and Grover are behind him.[4] I do not myself think that Sibley is such a fool, but rather imagine that he is making a demonstration to cover his retreat and gain time, or to attract attention from some other proposed movement of the enemy. . . . Rode out with the General in his carriage. Several miles out on the shell road the horses took fright and ran away violently. The General started to jump out but I prevented him. We ran upon a carriage filled with ladies and I supposed we would run into them. We however escaped them by a collision of the wheels only. This checked the speed of our animals. The driver and orderly were thrown violently for some distance. The General jumped out safely. As the carriage was getting under way again, I jumped out and was thrown forward on my hands, cutting my left one and jarring my shoulders considerably. . . .

APRIL 7, TUESDAY.—. . . Got a letter from my wife. Conney Carey with her bridal trousseau has been arrested on her way South. She is about to be married to Fitzhugh Lee and slipped north to get her bridal robes. This is of a piece with arresting women and children for singing "The Bonnie Blue Flag" and carrying Confederate handkerchiefs. We are a small people and delight in small things. The General has very just views on these subjects, but the littleness goes on here all the same. The General received from Boston houses a number of financial claims against persons here, with a request that he should collect them. He is expected to use his military authority to do so and is authorized on the Boston parties for the amount. He is additionally informed that the Presidency is before him and this is one of the means to obtain it. . . .

APRIL 8, WEDNESDAY.—. . . Started in the cars for Berwick's Bay. There a site was chosen for our encampment and the men detailed to pitch the tents, but the tents were not forthcoming. Luce and I sat on a stump, both of us out of humor. He says when they were reconnoitering above Baton Rouge, [Rev. George] Hepworth saw a poor fellow digging a trench and levee to keep out the water. They arrested him, accusing him of digging a rifle pit. He explained to them but they would not listen to him. On this, they returned to camp with a story that the whole rural population was engaged in digging rifle pits. I remember ridiculing the story at the time. . . .

APRIL 9, THURSDAY.—. . . At breakfast the General said he would

4. The Confederate troops, estimated at four or five thousand men, were commanded by General Richard Taylor, not by Henry H. Sibley.

make this campaign and then go home. He wanted rest and I added it was time to retire from the excitement and smoke of actual war, to take a cool and comprehensive survey of the field. The attempt to conquer the Rebellion in its present condition is simply absurd. We cannot exterminate eight millions of people and occupy a territory one half larger than the whole loyal states. There must be a radical change of policy that will affect the Southern people themselves and by enabling them to return to the United States as free citizens. At present the Government offers them nothing but subjugation, ruin, and death whether they yield or fight us to the bitter end. We cannot beat them but the nation will perish in the struggle. . . .

Yesterday as we were talking together, a private soldier addressed the General and wanted to know if the 4th Massachusetts was gone yet. The General didn't know but thought it was. Presently the soldier came back and interrupted our conversation a second time by asking if the regiment was gone would the General furnish him transportation on another train. The General said he would. . . .

General Grover called in to see me. He is going to embark his division and, taking a circuit by the lake, land opposite Franklin and marching on that place will cut off the enemy's retreat. Meanwhile another division will advance and amuse the enemy by menacing the fortified lines near Pattersonville. Grover thinks the plan will succeed and is full of delight at the idea of catching Sibley. Sibley, he says, used to run against him in the old army. There was a sort of rivalry between them and now for Grover to catch him would be too rich. . . . Heard that the soldiers were robbing houses and had broken open the trunks of some officers' wives and gutted them, stealing a package of silver from one, which was very probably stolen by the officer himself from some unlucky widow or Secessionist. What would an officer's wife be doing here with a package of silver? . . .

APRIL 11, SATURDAY.—The tantara of drums and bugles sounded agreeably to me this morning. War is a business as natural to man as hunting squirrels or tilling the soil. Oh, seraphine philosophers, preachers, and poetic politicians, how vain are your theories and futile efforts, how they evaporate before the great fire of human nature as the dew and mists of morning dry up in the face of the sun. How long are we to permit ourselves to be deceived by ideologists and babblers! Man the peace lover is simply a poltroon and coward. Roll your drums, flaunt your banners, and advance to the battlefield. War is a joy and glory of our race. . . . We embarked men and horses in the steamer *Laurel Hill* and, steaming across the bay, landed at the village and planted our headquarters flag at a private residence at the landing. Grover leaves tomorrow at two in the morning. This is the second procrastination of this important move. . . .

APRIL 12, SUNDAY.—. . . I had a talk with the doctor's wife of the plantation. They arrested her husband for holding his hand to his jaw when he had a toothache, supposing he was making signals to the enemy. Her brother-in-law stayed with her to protect her and he was arrested because he didn't hold his jaw. . . . The General saw personally to everything, exposing himself and suite without regard to consequences. The shot flew hot and thick until sundown. We occupied a deserted plantation house on the banks of the Teche. We have no news of Grover yet.

APRIL 13, MONDAY.—. . . Luce climbed a tree this morning and noticed a retrograde movement of the enemy's troops. They have smoked Grover's movement and will probably retire without a heavy fight. Grover's movements indicate hesitation and more prudence than was expected from that quarter. . . . The staff as usual were under fire all day. The troops throughout have behaved with firmness and spirit. There were very few skulkers and everything looked encouraging. As we rode we saw a stout young fellow in an ambulance railing and laughing at some comrades by the roadside. The General asked him if he was hurt. "Nothing," said he, "but a leg broke." "I'm sorry for you," said the General. "I'll soon be well," replied the youth, "and ready to be at them again." I never saw better troops for pluck and spirit. Four months ago the majority of these troops

NO SKULKING

came out with us as raw and unpromising as was possible. Now, having fought for two days with success, they were ready for anything. . . .

APRIL 14, TUESDAY.—. . . Our whole force, horse, foot, and artillery were started in rapid pursuit. Thus we rode over the enemy's earthwork, now deserted. Some demijohns emptied of sugar rum, some rags, cannon ammunition, and some dead bodies and a few graves was all that was left of Governor Mouton's occupation. . . . Advancing a mile or two we came upon large camps enough to accommodate five thousand men. These were deserted as they stood with arms, ammunition, quartermaster stores, clothes, pans, and cooking utensils. The General ordered a guard to protect these tents and property. As we passed here a troop of the wildest looking Negroes I had yet seen came rushing out from the cabins of a plantation. They saluted us with guns and grotesquely joyful gesticulations. They had been told they could plunder the camp, but the guard was in before them, so they only got some old pots and pans which I said they might have. . . .

Riding still to the front, I stopped at a house where I saw a number of women and children on the porch. The man came down to receive me with great urbanity, proclaiming himself a Secessionist but offering social hospitality. The man's name was Washington of Kentucky and the family of Westmoreland, Virginia. A man rode up like an officer and asked which way the army of Rebels had gone. Washington said he could not give him any information on that subject. The fellow rudely answered, "Do you want to get your house burned?" I asked him fiercely if he meant that as a threat. He wanted to know if this expedition was got up to protect Rebel property. I told him the expedition was got up to beat the Rebel Army in front of us and not to abuse women, children, and mannered persons. A soldier cried out, "That's the way I like to hear a man talk," and the sneak rode off. The man thanked me for my kindness, gave me his hand, and said he recognized a gentleman. We exchanged names and I departed, the firing in front commencing. . . .

We entered Franklin, a town of three thousand inhabitants and many rurally beautiful residences. A stern-wheeler filled with Confederate wounded was our only capture. The people were evidently appalled and were utterly astounded that their troops had been beaten. Headquarters was established at the house of Mr. Pierret, the family having fled to escape the impending battle. After we were in full occupation they returned. They were content to let the house remain in possession of headquarters and went off to stay with some relatives. . . . The General is much chagrined at the failure to capture the army of Taylor and Sibley, but will march rapidly on New Iberia tomorrow. We have clearly thrashed these people and the Battles of the Teche will tell well in the history of the war. . . .

APRIL 15, WEDNESDAY.—. . . Started early and rode rapidly for several miles to a small bayou where the bridges had been destroyed. They were being reconstructed for the heavy artillery. We presently met three Texans on horseback, prisoners. They were fine, desperate-looking fellows. In a mile or so we came to a vast prairie with fine, short grass and level as a parlor carpet. Our column was marching through in grand show. Hundreds of ponies, cattle, and mules were grazing around the distance. We first saw Camp Hunter, a camp of instruction for recruits of the Confederates. A lovelier spot could not be found in the world. A hundred thousand men could be formed and marched here in turf as smooth as a billiard table. This beautiful common was in Indian Bend, some three miles from the entrance to Indian Village. I rode aside to visit the reservation of the aboriginal race. They had a poor village of cabins and about a hundred inhabitants. They said they had nothing to do with the war and had not been impressed, although they were threatened with imprisonment. They seemed glad we had come, for they could now go to the lake to fish. Heretofore the Confederates had prevented them. . . .

We stopped two miles from Jeanerette at the house of an old Frenchman named Say. The old man spoke no English but gave us to understand that the neighboring house of his married daughter had been sacked even to the destruction of his granddaughter's toys. A guard was promised and set but the whole plantation rang for the rest of the evening with the cackling of chickens and geese, the squealing of pigs, and the lowering of cattle. The plundering went on under our noses while an order was being composed to forbid it. The men arrested amounted to about a hundred. The General asked what he should do with these fellows. I suggested he should lecture the crowd and send them to their regiments. He took me at my word and had them mustered up. As he spoke to them, every fellow commenced with a rigamarole apology, one breaking in after another until the whole band were in full blast like an orchestra. He silenced them, recalled their offense, its evil consequences, and dismissed them with an admonition. Three cheers for the General and promises to lick the

Rebels followed and they scattered like a group of excused schoolboys. The General was in high spirits. We were to start early march on New Iberia. If the enemy makes a stand there, pitch in without a minute's delay. That is my idea of making war. . . .

APRIL 16, THURSDAY.—. . . I mentioned that I would like to show some civility to my cousins, Mrs. Weeks and Miss Fanny Hunter, who lived about Jeanerette. I mounted and rode to the front to General Weitzel, whom I overtook just as he got opposite the place. He gave me a corporal's guard, and I rode down to the bridge but it was open and the draw chains broken. I called to a stupid Negro on the opposite pier who told me the family was at home. I dismissed the guard and started up the opposite side of the bayou with two orderlies through a half swampy forest with thick undergrowth suggesting guerilla ambuscades. Presently my dragoon cocked his carbine and exclaimed, "There's Secesh in the woods." About fifty yards distant I saw gray caps in the thickets which disappeared as my men handled their arms. I told the dragoon not to fire and called to the men to come out. Five soldiers came out unarmed and surrendered themselves. They were conscripts of the 18th Louisiana and all spoke French. . . . The bridgekeeper then came up and told me that Captain Kerr, a Confederate officer, would surrender to any U. S. officer at hand. I told him to tell the Captain to report to Mr. Weeks' house.

I then rode up to the gate of the plantation, and as I appeared I noticed some women disappearing behind the house. I wrote my name on a leaf of my notebook with the following, "I have called to see you and to offer a guard for the protection of your property. Directed to Alfred Weeks or any of the family." I sent this up with the orderly. Presently I saw and recognized Fanny Hunter on the porch with another young lady. I did not move, however, until the orderly came back and reported that they would see me. Fanny Hunter stood upon the porch as erect and white as a marble statue. Beside her stood a beautiful young girl as mute and sad as a tomb. I could scarcely recognize in her the child who six years ago had been my daughter's playmate and had wept upon her neck at the parting on the banks of the bayou. Fanny addressed me as Colonel Strother and presented the young lady as Mary Weeks. I frankly cousined them both, took Fanny's hand which accepted mine mechanically. It was as cold and lifeless as a dead hand. I have never seen as strong a picture of concentrated pride, anger, and distress. Fanny told me that her sister, Mrs. Weeks, had been brought to bed with a child two days before.

Otherwise they would not have been there, and as for herself, no circumstances could have induced her to accept any protection from the United States flag. Death would be preferable, but on account of the helpless condition of her sister and the eight children, she had concluded to accept my offer. Mary put in, "If we can accept it without oaths, promises, or conditions." I smiled and told her I knew the blood from whence she sprung too well to have an idea of proposing compromising conditions.

They then inquired the fate of Captain Semmes of the gunboat *Diana*.[5] The inquiry was made with an earnestness that fixed my eyes on the flushed cheek of the young lady. I told her that Semmes was a prisoner. He was among friends who had formerly known him, who respected his valor, and would treat him as a brave man merited. Bright eyes sparkled and all the ice was gone. Fanny's face relaxed and her voice warbled with the kindly music of a former day. The other children, boys, and girls, were presented, and I took the youngest on my knee and he began to play with my buttons. Inquiries were made for father and mother. Both dead. Other friends dead or estranged, then some talk of former days. Tears gushed to my eyes, and I covered my face with my hands and sobbed. Those proud, generous, fiery, and loving hearts had been of my dearest and earliest friends. Mary drew near, thanked me for the news of Captain Semmes and said, "I too can admire a brave and generous enemy." I was then invited to see Nancy Weeks. She wept aloud and grasped my hand convulsively. I soothed her to quiet and sat down beside her. "Thank God," she exclaimed, "he was born day before yesterday while the Confederate flag still floated here.". . . I took leave, carrying a letter to Captain Semmes from the family. Mrs. Weeks told me of the engagement between the gallant officer and Mary. . . . How beautiful an instrument is the human heart. All the hot pride and bitter discord stilled and turned to ancient friendship by touching gently the proper chords.

I rode to Kerr's and found him on crutches. He was a cripple from rheumatism and very polished in his manners. He had once been private secretary of Henry Clay and was an old line conservative Whig. I accepted his surrender but declined taking his sword and exchanged written papers with him amounting to a parole of honor. This proceeding, although unlawful, I was compelled to adopt from feelings

5. Captain O. J. Semmes of the Confederate artillery was assigned to the captured gunboat *Diana*, which resisted the Federal advance in the Teche Campaign until it was captured by Weitzel.

of humanity, as he could not properly be moved. . . . At two o'clock I overtook the staff in New Iberia. The General was in a high gale, swore he would hold the country and push on to Alexandria. I urged it strongly. Grant was pushing a column on Alexandria from the north. We could meet at Bayou Black or Black River, then combine and take Port Hudson.

APRIL 17, FRIDAY. Colonel Seward, son of the Secretary of State, arrived with dispatches for the General. These were of a secret nature. They were read to me and destroyed. Five million for secret service. The General wrote letters to the President and Seward which he read to me, giving an account of our campaign. I think Louisiana is settled for the war. . . . The town of St. Martinsville is a lonesome-looking village, very few inhabitants appearing. There were more men than usual, evil-looking fellows whom I suspected were of the late army now turned into civilians. . . . We stopped at a deserted plantation in the midst of the plains. Our guard immediately went to work and the premises resounded with the outcries of pigs, sheep, and poultry. The General and myself went to the bayou to wash, but the water was so black and filthy that we contented ourselves with a very partial ablution. This refreshed us wonderfully and the Major General ran and rampaged up and down the green banks of the water in Adam's costume, jumping like a young colt. . . . Grover reported the enemy's rear guard with sharpshooters and artillery posted on the opposite side of a bayou ready apparently to contest the advance.

JUNE 18, SATURDAY.—. . . A Rebel mail was taken and its contents emptied on the front verandah. Innumerable letters were ruthlessly broken open and laughed over. Some contained valuable hints and information. Bobtailed journals printed on the reverse side of yellow and brown wall paper show the straits to which journalism is reduced in the Confederacy. We will probably be detained here another night by the burning of the bridges on our route. Walked with the General and talked over the campaign and its chances. He will go on to Alexandria. This accomplished, and a junction effected with Grant, the game of the Confederacy will be up in the Southwest. . .

APRIL 19, SUNDAY.—. . . It was pitiful to see in what a condition we would leave our French host and family. Not a fowl except a few motherless peeping chickens just hatched, not a fourfooted beast, fences all burnt, his blacksmith shop burnt, and his family left without a mouthful to eat. He walked to and fro like a ghost, silent and when spoken to about the waste would reply, sighing, *"c'est rien, c'est rien."*

We left him an order on the Quartermaster for fifteen days' provision to keep him from starving. . . . Rode to Lafayette or Vermillionville, a village of perhaps a thousand inhabitants. At every house hung a white flag and a sentinel was posted by the rear guard to prevent pillage. Beyond this village the campfires of the enemy's rear guard were seen burning. A Negress told me that Sibley was wounded, and she had seen him get into a carriage with his thigh bandaged. . . . The staff stopped at a cottage to examine some Frenchmen. One of these, an ex-soldier of Algeria, said the enemy's force had passed—four thousand strong of which were four hundred horse, all Texans but one company. The infantry was much jaded, hatless, and many unarmed. Many were riding in wagons and the arms of nearly all were carried in wagons. They are too far ahead, however, and will reach Alexandria before us. . . . At four o'clock we forded the Carrion Crow Bayou and stopped for the night at the house of a Confederate captain. Old Governor Mouton[6] was arrested at his residence near Vermillionville and was brought along under guard. . . .

APRIL 20, MONDAY.—. . . We at length came in sight of Opelousas, a steeple rising out of a grove. The cavalry formed and with drawn sabres charged through the place. The staff followed. We saw more people on the streets than usual, looking at us with curiosity but no ill-feeling manifested. Several ladies welcomed us with handkerchiefs waving to salute us. We rode to the opposite end of the town where a large Catholic church crosses the street. As we moved, a good-looking man spoke to me to know the commanding officer. I pointed out the General, and the Mayor (as the speaker was) formally surrendered the town and begged the protection of the Federal flag. It was granted and orders immediately sent to the division commanders to guard the place carefully. . . . A padre asked protection for the religious house of sisters opposite. We accorded it and placed the guard. I am not sure but some of the girls and young sisters would rather the men had been allowed to break in.

At my suggestion, [Major Harai] Robinson was ordered forward immediately to seize Washington with his cavalry. I rode back to the courthouse. We found posted on the door a number of stirring appeals to the militia of Louisiana to arise and defend their houses. These contained the important information that they expected reinforcements only from points where we knew they were not to be had.

6. Alexander Mouton (1804-85) had been a United States senator from 1837 to 1842 and governor of Louisiana from 1843 to 1846. In 1861 he was president of the Louisiana secession convention.

The sheriff and county clerk came up and we examined the office, getting only some newspapers of late date. In this courthouse the Rebel Legislature held its meetings. Loafers came around curious and good-humored, desirous of gossiping with the strangers. The ladies on the verandahs looked smiling and curious, a new thing for us. . . . Thus far our advance had been an uninterrupted success. We will breathe here for a day and think what next. . . .

APRIL 21, TUESDAY.—. . . The General's best boots were taken at Brasher City, and last night two of our horses which we stole from the inhabitants on the route were stolen from us by a Negro. The Negro, being the weaker party, ought to be hanged. A man named Rogers came in from the country to complain that two Negroes had come to his house to buy chickens and eggs and had scared his wife into fits. I asked if the Negroes had committed any outrage. He said no, but his wife was a nervous woman and was frightened. So this fool, because he had a silly nervous wife, runs into our lines to complain to the Major General and of course will remain inside our lines for several days, leaving his nervous wife to her own resources. . . . The General counseled with me in regard to future operations. The march on Alexandria will cost more than it would be worth. It was therefore concluded to send an expedition toward Holmesville for forage, cotton, and sugar. Another westward to sweep the plains of cattle, horses, etc. The Texans are playing the devil through the country as they retreat, and the people follow them with curses. Hundreds are willing to come in and take the oath of allegiance to the United States, but as we do not propose to remain here, the General is not in favor of administering. . . .

APRIL 22, WEDNESDAY.—. . . Official news of the capture of Butte à la Rose was at length received. This completes our expedition. We have nothing left to do but to clean out the country and return to New Orleans. . . . News has come that the attack on Charleston has failed, one monitor sunk and two disabled. I hope this will settle [General David] Hunter,[7] who is a fool and [Admiral Samuel F.] DuPont, who lacks enterprise. . . .

APRIL 23, THURSDAY.—. . . News came that five gun boats have passed Vicksburg and are now in the Red River. The presence of this co-operating fleet will probably induce us to push on to Alexandria, at least with a division. Our prospects, which seemed limited, are now opening. The General is in high spirits. We have full command

7. Hunter's name was scratched out, perhaps because of Strother's later service with that General in the Valley of Virginia, but the word is still faintly legible.

of all the labyrinthine navigation of this country which will make it impossible for the enemy to reoccupy any part of it with safety. . . . Robinson has had one of his men court-martialed on charges as follows—when the cavalry entered Washington, the citizens were peaceful and cooked rations for them. One woman saluted them with welcome. That night this trooper robbed the same women of a gold watch and committed other outrages on her property. The court sentenced him to be shot and Robinson fears the General will pardon him, which he certainly will do. . . .

APRIL 24, FRIDAY.—. . . The General returns to New Orleans on the *Laurel Hill*, when she comes up, and has asked me to accompany him. This I hope will close my campaigning in this country. . . .

APRIL 25, SATURDAY.—. . . We have captured and examined the contents of several Rebel mails, thereby obtaining important information of the conditions and prospects of the enemy. All sigh for peace and private distress is universal. A poor Virginian from Amelia County writes to a friend in Opelousas to know if he can buy a quiet little farm, so that he may be out of the hearing of the war and Yankees. Those who have fled to Shreveport write to advise their friends to seek some other retreat. Love letters in abundance. My knowledge of French has been a trump in this campaign. . . . It is doubtful whether our military operations will be carried further at present. When the blood cools, indecision begins and it requires some strong motive power to start again. . . . A long moonlight drive took us to Barra's Landing, where the *Laurel Hill* lay. Army stores were piled on the bank and Negroes were rolling cotton aboard by the light of fires on the shore.

APRIL 26, SUNDAY.—. . . After the course of an hour or two we entered the Atchafalaya, a wider stream than the Bayou with a stronger current and very crooked. About midday arrived at Butte à la Rose. There was no hill here as I expected, but a miserable triangular earthwork revetted with boards and the footways paved with brick. The whole work was surrounded by water and the trees were cut down for some distance around to open a range for the guns. Altogether the scene was most forlorn. . . . We again started on our way about two P.M., promising ourselves that we would reach Brasher City at seven this evening. All day we have been passing the most miserable of human habitations standing in the woods and water. Some are deserted, some inhabited, teeming with children who all flock to the porches to stare at our boat. Fowls sit about on logs and sunken cypress fences looking as forlorn as the scene. The whole region seems to be under water, and a more hopeless scene of desolation I cannot imagine. As we progress, huge alligators flop into the water from every stump and log, and the amusement of the day has been firing at them. . . . We discovered that we had lost our way. In fact, in this labyrinth of streams all alike it is very easy to do so. Waking up from a nap I found we had turned back and were retracing our course to Butte à la Rose, which we reached at eight P.M. We tied up for the night. The soldiers of the 8th Infantry are on board. I overheard one of them on the lower deck giving his penitentiary experiences to an admiring circle. He had been imprisoned for two years, I don't know what for.

APRIL 27, MONDAY.—. . . Got to Berwick Station at eleven o'clock and found things as usual. Ashore was a seething mass of soldiers, Negroes, and dirty people. These processions crossed each other. The water's edge was lined with Negroes and soldiers fishing, tents, cooking booths, pie shops, sutler's stores, dancing, loading, and rolling in the dirt, drumming, jabbering, swearing, and drinking. Chickens and pigs were extinct. . . . Tucker showed me orders he had received to carry dispatches immediately to Grant via New York. This will be a long route and it seems to me a shorter one might be found.

APRIL 28, TUESDAY. . . . At headquarters I spoke to General Banks and received permission to return North. Officially speaking, I was relieved from duty in this Department at my own request. Commander [H. W.] Morris read a letter from Admiral Farragut, who knows of our move on the Teche. He wants coal sent to him by that route and will with [General Alfred W.] Fleet clean out the Red River. He says the enemy are pinched already and are on half rations at Port Hudson. He says the ships following him at Port Hudson fired too much and thus lost themselves in the smoke and got aground. To which unnecessary accidents he attributes the loss and not to the strength of the batteries. . . . Had a talk with Colonel Beckwith. After the steam tug sent by Sherman to the mouth of the River deserted to the enemy and ran into Mobile, all the wives of the men aboard came for rations. The Colonel told them to go to Mobile. Then when the levee on the Fourche was cut for the purpose of inundating our railroad communications, the Colonel was informed that 250 families over there were starving. He replied, "Let them fast until they find out who cut the levee."

APRIL 29, WEDNESDAY. Met [Captain William W.] Rowley and
went with him to headquarters where we got our orders officially
relieving us of duty here. Went to the office of the steamship *Morning Star* and purchased tickets for New York. We will stop twenty-
four hours in Havana. All other business, civil and military, that I can
think of is fully closed. . . . We had tea with the General and he
started soon after for Opelousas. On taking leave I asked him always
to remember me in council. "Yes," he answered with vivacity, "I will."
And, turning to the others, he said, "The Colonel has always voted
for pitching in. At all times and under all circumstances." I then sat
down with Beckwith and we had a long talk. We feared that Emory
and others surrounding the General would check his career of victory
by timid counsels. We had advised him to go to Alexandria and
thence to Shreveport, lick Kirby Smith if he showed himself, and clean
out the whole country on the Red River.

APRIL 30, THURSDAY.—. . . The trip down the river was rapid and
without incident. After we were out of sight of land, we passed the
distinct line between the muddy water discharged by the Mississippi
and the green shoal water of the Gulf. I walked the deck until half
past ten, alone in the moonlight. I enjoyed a sense of freedom from
Army restraint and responsibility, and yet there are feelings of regret
mingled with pleasure. I think, however, that I have fought my last
battle.

MAY 2, SATURDAY.—Rose early cheered with the expectation of being in Havana today and one day nearer my loved ones. . . . Saw a
vessel dimly through the rain which looked like an armed steamer
but a cloud covered her and she disappeared. I presently saw our fat
captain seize his glass and look earnestly in the direction of the vessel.
The cloud passed over and she reappeared near to us. I took a look
through Rowley's glass. She was evidently an armed vessel and bearing
down on us rapidly. She showed no colors or we could not make them
out at the distance. I had determined if we were pursued by one of the
enemy's cruisers to make the captain of our vessel run for it to the last
extremity. The interest on board was increased by seeing a cloud
of white smoke puff from the side of the stranger, a signal for us to
lay to and show our colors. Things began to look serious. Another
volume of smoke rolled out from the black hull of the pursuing vessel.
The second blank gun, the next one would be a shot. The captain
stopped our vessel and hoisted the United States flag. I went to him
and demanded firmly why he stopped. He replied, "She can run

us down in an hour. We have no chance." Tucker packed his dispatches with a weight ready to throw overboard.

Men were dividing their money with the women and children and devising ways and means to save themselves from robbery and captivity. I went to the wheelhouse apart with the Captain, who after looking through his glass, said, "Colonel, get your dispatches ready to throw overboard." I replied they were ready. The stranger was now within a quarter mile of us and yet we could see no colors. Prevailing opinion on board was that we had fallen into the hands of a Confederate cruiser. Some Secession refugee women were in ecstasy. I retired to my stateroom to man myself against the coming misfortune. Tucker was in the hall, pale and with his dispatch packet in his hand. I told him not to throw them over yet, but to wait until I warned him. There was nothing in my baggage that I cared to destroy except my notebooks, and I thought they might take their chances.

It seemed hard after so many campaigns and escaping so many dangers to fall thus, a helpless prisoner without firing a shot in the way of defense. The shame and mortification of marching a prisoner to Richmond—even if I should be well treated—to accept courtesy from my personal enemies was a trial worse than death, but there was no help for it. I reproached myself that I had not forced the Captain pistol in hand to put on all steam and try our speed. It was too late now, so I determined to put on my uniform and go on deck to meet my fate as a United States officer. On deck I found the tremor at its height. The strange ship was almost within hailing distance. Her colors which flew from her mizzen staff were behind the smoke and rigging so that we could not make them out. I took the glass and examined attentively. "They are," I said, "United States colors." The Captain looked, "They are the stars and stripes," he said with radiant face. "Look, they are hauling them down." This everyone supposed was to lower the flag and hoist the Confederate colors, but they dipped them three times. This was our national salute. The next moment we recognized the uniforms and gold bands of our Navy officers on her crowded decks. . . . It was the vessel *Huntsville*.

I went below and told Tucker to unpack his dispatches. In all this war I have not had a more terrible trial than the hour between the opening and the denouement of this drama. When the wine at dinner loosened all tongues, I found that I was not alone in the impression it made. . . . At half-past four land was seen in front of us which proved to be the shores of Cuba. An hour later we saw Havana and the white villas along the shore. No vessel is admitted to the harbor after nightfall, so we will lay out all night. . . .

MAY 3, SUNDAY.—With the morning light the boat commenced moving. The sun was just rising and the Morro Castle rose before us in all its romantic and picturesque beauty. I have rarely seen anything more striking in its way than this lone fort with its embrasures, turrents, towers, and gateways, and cannon crowning the sea-washed cliff. Among the shipping were several sharp, low, lead-colored vessels said to be blockade-runners. Landed at the crowded quay and walked along it some distance, then entered the city by a gateway and passed through the public square on which the governor's palace stands.

Our volante was one of the worst of its kind, narrow, dirty, swinging on its poles like a milk cart. Our horse was a bony, white-speckled hack with tail cued tightly and tied to the harness around his left hip, a huge cracked leather saddle mounted by a scruffy Negro with a segar in his mouth and his bare sprawling feet dangling on either side heeled with brass spurs. With this ridiculous turnout we made the tour of several narrow streets, stopping at some fashionable saloon to refresh ourselves with a glass of sherbert or almond water. . . . At the hotel saw a tall fellow at a neighboring table whose cravat was all blazoned with Secession colors and wearing a Secession badge on his coat. This, I judged, was a captain of one of the blockade-runners. . . . The Paseo is a fine double road about a mile in length shaded with double rows of trees. At each end is a statue of some historic Cuban dignitary. The carriages drive in line, turning at these statues, and keep on the round until dark or until they are tired. Sentinels of the horseguard are posted at intervals and everything has a royal Old World air. . . . Our beds were nothing more than sacking and what with the heat and mosquitoes we slept but little. Near morning I got out on the cool marble floor and got a little rest in that way.

MAY 4, MONDAY.—. . . At midday, according to programme, we were at sea again. Before sunset had faded land had disappeared and thus we bid adieu to the Queen of the Antilles. I was altogether much charmed with my visit. The picturesque wealth of the country surpassed my expectations. That the Spanish class should dislike the Anglo-American is quite natural, arrogant and unmannered filibuster that he is.

MAY 6, WEDNESDAY.—Our sails were set and with wind, gulf stream, and steam we were making good speed. Blow breeze, blow, and waft me still more swiftly to the home of those I love, for this is the anniversary of my wedding day. . . . Tucker gives a humorous account of Kirkland on the Paseo. They had a miserable rope harness and barefoot Negro turnout, which Kirkland was always endeavoring to urge to greater speed, having filled his pockets with stones to throw at the conductor mounted on the distant animal which moved the volante. *"Hombre vamos, hombre vamos,"* Kirkland would shout (all the Spanish he knew), the Negro would turn and gesticulate with two fingers, Kirkland would answer with three, then the fellow would whip and spur the miserable beast into a trot. On getting into a line on the Paseo the elegant turnout of some Cuban hidalgo was in his way, so he pitched in cursing the coachman and lackey until they made way for him; then as they passed along the line, he pointed right and left in true American style, indicating this lady or that vehicle with vociferous expression of praise or contempt. Tucker's description was truly humorous and characteristic and I only wonder at the well-bred patience of the public and police. . . .

MAY 9, SATURDAY. Arrived at the pier, foot of Beach Street, at about one o'clock in the morning. At six went on deck and heard the first news that Hooker had been thrashed on the Rappahannock. All this I had been apprehending as we sailed and consequently was not so furiously anxious to get to land as some of our passengers were. Telegraphed Mrs. Strother to meet me in Washington. Called at Harpers and was warmly solicited to write an account of the campaign in Louisiana. Took the matter into consideration and will answer finally when I settle my affairs in Washington. Met Leutze today. He is just going to Europe to return again in September. Tucker called and made me a present of a very handsome pair of sleeve buttons, with a grace and warmth not at all savoring of the Yankee. I then left for Washington at 7:30 P.M.

IX

Behind the Lines at Gettysburg

May 10, 1863—August 6, 1863

*On May 10 Strother reached Washington. With neither command
nor commander, he received a sixty-day leave and awaited assignment
by the War Department. In the middle of June the news came that the
Confederate army was moving through the Valley of Virginia. The
Gettysburg Campaign had begun, and for the next three weeks the nation anxiously awaited the engagement north of the Potomac.*

*Strother's record of the campaign reflects something of the helpless
waiting in beleaguered Washington. When news came through the
wires that Lee had been turned back, Strother knew that the Confederacy had lost its last chance. Only a war of attrition remained.*

*Although commissioned colonel of the 3rd West Virginia Cavalry
on July 18, Strother continued to serve as a staff officer. After an interview with the Secretary of War, he was assigned to the Department
of West Virginia, a large military district including most of the state
that had come into being only a few weeks before. It was a wise
choice, since he was familiar with the topography of the region and
would be in a position to assist his family and friends through the
rigors of never-ending border warfare. Early in August he left for
New Creek, West Virginia, to report to his new commander, General
Benjamin F. Kelley.*

MAY 10, SUNDAY.—After a disagreeable night I arrived at Washington in the morning at seven. . . . At the hotel a servant called and
informed me that a lady wished to see me in the reception room.
"What sort of lady?" The servant said, "She's your wife." This
was a most unexpected pleasure. She had got my first telegram from
New York and had started that night. . . .

MAY 11, MONDAY.—Visited General Halleck's office and delivered
my dispatches. Saw General Halleck for a few minutes and talked

about General Banks' matters. Called on the assistant Secretary of War, who gave me an order for a leave of sixty days. . . .

MAY 13, WEDNESDAY.—. . . Took a carriage and with Mrs. Strother drove to the Capitol to see Leutze's picture, "Westward the Course of Empire Takes Its Way." It is a fresco and a very strong work, powerfully characteristic and real. The statuary and other art about the place is painfully feeble. With its preposterous dome swelling over the humble base of the building, the Capitol itself is an architectural nightmare. The Goddess of Liberty in bronze has a flamboyant air and the colors of a coppersnake. I don't think she will ever mount that dome. . . .

MAY 16, SATURDAY.—Took the cars for Harpers Ferry, and arrived there at 12:30. A voice called my name from another car. I turned and saw young Tom Buchanan among a squad of Confederate prisoners. I went in and shook hands with him. He was a lieutenant in my cadet company and I paid a drill sergeant to teach him to drill. When the war broke out he and a number of others joined the Confederacy. He looked sunburned and dirty. . . . Was told that Mosby had made a raid into Charles Town and had captured our troops. This, of course, changed my plans, and I determined to remain at the Ferry until the next train of cars going west. . . .

MAY 17, SUNDAY.—. . . We went to see General Morris,[1] son of Morris the editor and poet. The General is a stout, easy-mannered man of thirty or thirty-five, not much of a soldier in appearance. He seemed to get all his orders from General [Robert C.] Schenck and declined doing anything on his own responsibility. He expressed great apprehension about the safety of the place, and about midday a train arrived from the west with a regiment aboard to reinforce Harpers Ferry. At dinner came news that the Confederate raiders into Charles Town had been attacked by Union cavalry and beaten with the loss of spoils, prisoners, and a number of their own men killed and wounded. . . . Took a walk around the hills with Mrs. Strother. We remained out until sunset, and I never saw more beautiful natural pictures than those we enjoyed, looking up and down the two rivers.

1. William H. Morris (1827-1900), USMA '51, was the son of George P. Morris, a poet best known for his "Woodman, Spare That Tree." After service on the Peninsula, Morris was assigned to command Maryland Heights until July, 1863. In 1864 his brigade of the Sixth Corps fought through the Wilderness Campaign. He was mustered out of the army in August, 1864, and in later years became a militia general in New York.

MAY 18, MONDAY.—. . . The captured troops are all returned to Charles Town and are in a great glee at the result of the affair. We took forty-six prisoners, horses, and accouterments, so that the raid has terminated greatly in our favor. . . . Took the cars and passed Duffields, Martinsburg, and on to Sir John's without seeing anyone that I knew. There were soldiers at every station, and the land seemed to be possessed by strangers. At Sir John's called on the commander of the post and was advised not to go to Bath, as it was outside of our lines and the country not free from guerillas. . . .

MAY 19, TUESDAY.—Got a guard of twelve men from the post and walked over with my wife to Berkeley Springs. The guard had marched ahead up the road and, as we approached, formed line and gave us a salute, then four men took the advance and the main body with the sergeant followed us. Thus we entered Bath and, posting sentinels on the roads, went down in the valley to see our friends. The village and grounds looked silent and dilapidated but the budding forests and green grass made it pleasant withal. No living soul was to be seen. Presently we saw Em Randolph on the porch.[2] Then Emmy, my daughter, and the children. James Randolph was absent in the fields dropping corn. Things looked natural and pleasant. The great changes which had taken place since I last looked upon Berkeley as my home, produced no emotion or sadness. The great events in which I had been acting a part for the two years past seemed to have strengthened my nature. I was happy in the friends I saw and had about me, and the past was nothing but bygone dream. Some of the old pictures were in the house in their places. My father's portrait hung in the back parlor. I looked at it a moment and went away to prevent my heart from stirring. I hastily passed the closed door of his office. It will not do to dwell on those things. . . . At five o'clock the guard was mustered and returned in state to Sir John's. . . .

JUNE 1, MONDAY [Martinsburg].—. . . Adam, my former servant and banjo player, called to pay his respects. He is following the army as an assistant sutler. He was at Harpers Ferry and escaped the surrender by going out with the cavalry and was present when they captured Longstreet's wagons near Williamsport. Went on to Harpers Ferry. . . .

JUNE 2, TUESDAY.—Rose early and walked in the air. On returning

2. Emily Strother Randolph was Strother's sister. She was the wife of James L. Randolph, the chief engineer of the Baltimore and Ohio Railroad after the war.

to our room I found a lady in my bed, Mrs. Von Hagen, the wife of a German officer. In this house they let the beds by relays; as soon as one gets up, another takes possession. I called on General Kelley.[3] He is physically in better condition than when I saw him before, and the good opinion I had of his courage and practical good sense was confirmed by the conversation. He has had successful experience in restoring the districts to allegiance over which he has been placed. He believes in a discriminating conciliatory policy and has proved the efficiency of it by success. . . . Mrs. Strother and myself took the train for Baltimore and arrived at the Eutaw House in due time.

JUNE 4, THURSDAY.—. . . At the Eutaw House I met my old friend, General Hatch. He thought I ought to accept a position on General Schenck's staff and offered to have me transferred. Hatch said that Banks would fail as a leader because he never served his friends in any way. He would do nothing to sustain Hatch, when Pope relieved him of command last summer.

JUNE 8, MONDAY.—. . . Mr. Clarke, Andrew Hunter's brother-in-law, called. He was in Clarke County, Virginia, when Joe Johnston's troops left Winchester to join Beauregard at Manassas. He says they passed the house at four o'clock in the afternoon. The advance passed and the others were passing all night. There were many stragglers; especially the 2nd Virginia went unwillingly. The officers and men lagged behind, some men deserted and the officers discussed the subject of refusing to go. News of some great victory manufactured for the occasion was then read to them. The men cheered and were double-quicked for some distance. Thus they were deluded from point to point until they were fully embarked in the war. The company from Martinsburg were especially unwilling victims. . . .

JUNE 10, WEDNESDAY.—. . . The military news is cheering. Vicksburg and Port Hudson will presently fall and the enemy is powerless to prevent it. Nelson's Negro troops fought well at Port Hudson, Stafford's also. This will give a stimulus to the enlistment of Negro soldiers, and their assistance in putting down the Rebellion will be great. They should be officered by whites and the best officers given them that can be found. They will not volunteer at first, but will have to be conscripted. From long habit their will is too inert to enable

3. Benjamin F. Kelley (1807-91) had been active in saving Western Virginia for the Union in 1861 and had recruited the first regiment of loyal troops south of the Mason and Dixon. Throughout the war Kelley commanded in the Department of West Virginia.

them to act for themselves. No acts of emancipation, no fanciful appeals of liberty, virtue, and independence will have any effect on them. To be made available he must be taken hold of, controlled, and ordered. The Negro is not a colored white man, but has a separate character of his own. He is intelligent enough but his intelligence is like the white man's, under control of his natural instincts. Thus he is lazy, and has a large animal passion. He is fond of show and of praise. Fine clothes and hope of distinction are not alone sufficient to make him a soldier. He is too ease-loving. Absolute power is necessary, so he must be drafted. . . .

JUNE 13, SATURDAY.—In the Valley of Virginia an old woman came to the commissary's office with butter and eggs to sell. She declared, however, that she would take no United States money. In the corner lay some seventy or eighty thousand dollars in Confederate notes which had been recently captured. "What money would you take?" asked the officer. "Give me the eggs," and, pointing to the pile of printed promises, the commissary told her to help herself. The old woman looked aghast at the pile of wealth, tens, twenties, fifties, and one hundreds lay in gorgeous profusion like the sweepings of a printing office. "Good Lord, Mister," cried the Dame, "I don't want all this, but couldn't you give me a dollar and a half in Maryland money?"

JUNE 15, MONDAY.—This morning the news is that the enemy have attacked our forces in the Valley. This looks like a solid movement on their part but Milroy and Kelley will give them trouble. . . . We left for Washington at 10 o'clock and took rooms with Mrs. Codwise at 284 G Street. There we learned that Hooker had broken up his depot at Acquia Creek and was moving on the route toward Centerville and Leesburg, it being supposed that Lee's whole army was on its way northward by the Valley. . . . Clarke says that Butler's conduct toward foreign consuls was the cause of his removal, precisely the same remark I made to General Banks shortly after landing in New Orleans. His atrocious conduct toward the people of New Orleans and outrageous tyranny have only made him very popular at the North and are not among the charges against him here. What every outrage against common honesty and decency could not produce, was brought about by the cringing cowardice of our government toward foreign nations. . . .

JUNE 16, TUESDAY. . . . I walked to Willard's. I have concluded that the movement of the enemy is nothing more than a cavalry raid into Pennsylvania, Ewell being sent up into the Valley in order to back them up. Meanwhile Lee is watching with his main body until Hooker gets into some false position, when he will attack him.

JUNE 17, WEDNESDAY.—. . . On the street met the old cook of the Excelsior mess of Pope's campaign, Stuttering Joe. Joe says I should join Hooker and enlighten him in regard to the country in Virginia. He knows nothing about it. Joe is decidedly a partisan of Pope. As the force in Pennsylvania is a small one, only two thousand cavalry under [Albert G.] Jenkins, it is probable that they will not push on to Harrisburg. That appearing, the people are flocking to Harrisburg to defend it, and all other places not menaced are valiantly in arms. . . .

JUNE 18, THURSDAY.—The raid seems to have stopped at Chambersburg for the present at least. The conduct of our troops in the Valley has been most miserable. Milroy has lost all his stores and artillery and has valiantly escaped from a body of troops scarcely superior to his in numbers. The newspaper accounts of the Rebel raid are so confused and contradictory that I can make nothing of them. There is an impression that this raid covers a retrograde movement to reinforce Vicksburg. There is a decided pressure upon the executive to induce the restoration of McClellan to command. He is certainly the best tactician we have and the most popular man in the army. Your tactician, however, is but half a soldier. The great, brave, moral leader has not yet appeared. In the interim we can't do better than restore McClellan, although I do not consider him by any means a first-class man. The Western leaders seem to do better in making the troops fight. Yet I don't think we have any leaders who can handle one hundred thousand men. . . .

JUNE 22, MONDAY.—. . . Pleasonton heads our cavalry, [General George] Stoneman having left on account of some disgust with Hooker, it is said. Have finished Emil Schalk's book on the art of war.[4] It is clear, scientific, and contains useful ideas. The leading strategic idea is that of concentrating superior forces upon weak points and inferior forces of the enemy. A very good system for martinets and probably all that can be taught on the subject. That military genius whose fiery soul incites me to superhuman efforts and makes one man do the work of three, who stultifies all military rule by celerity and audacity, he inherits a gift of nature. Jackson was a man of that sort.

4. Emil Schalk wrote *Summary of the Art of War: Written Expressly for and Dedicated to the U.S. Volunteer Army* (1862).

June 23, Tuesday.—Saw a major of the artillery just in from the Army of the Potomac. He says Pleasonton's reconnoissance towards Ashby's Gap shows that Lee is not in the Loudoun Valley. Query: Where is he? . . .

June 25, Thursday.—. . . It is now clear that Lee's whole army is in the Valley of Virginia and the continuation of that same Valley in Maryland and Pennsylvania. Their object is to forage and enrich themselves from these fat regions and, when pressed, retire with their spoils. Should they defeat us in a decisive battle, they will march on Washington and Baltimore. Saw the engineers and trains moving through the city. Met Colonel Alexander, who told me that Hooker was moving and crossing into Maryland at Poolesville and Edwards Ferry. He had taken most of the troops from about Washington and these with others will enable him to put in the field 130,000 men. This looks like a great battle and I felt stirred up. . . .

June 26, Friday.—. . . Remained in the house the great part of the day on account of the bad weather. After tea walked down to Willard's and found folks in a state of stampede; all the staff officers in the city had been ordered to report to headquarters and the provost guard ordered out on picket duty. Talked with Duane on the subject of the battle of Antietam. The talk corroborated all my previous ideas and gave me no new ones. If Burnside had attacked when ordered, he would have marched into Sharpsburg with ease and thus crushed the enemy early. Meade's corps, which should have been 15,000 strong, reported next morning only 2,000 for duty, the rest having straggled. The condition of this corps from which he expected assistance, is one of McClellan's apologies for not attacking next morning. . . .

June 27, Saturday.—. . . No news in the wind about Hooker's army. Everyone thinks the government and army leaders are as much in the dark as the public. . . . Walked to Jackson Square in the afternoon to hear the music. Walked on to the circle to see the statue of Washington. An English critic insists the attitude is that of a man very drunk. An Englishman should be a judge of the position. My wife says the figure reminds her of Captain Jim Hurst, who could ride when so drunk that he could not walk. There is an ambitious flaunting of the mane and tail that reminds me of Bernini. These ingenious attempts to find fault with and misunderstand the artist are, after all, but one ungracious manner of showing one's refined discrimination. The statues have merit and are pleasing, much better than most equestrian statues, ancient and modern. Let us therefore appreciate them kindly and enjoy them.

JUNE 28, SUNDAY.—. . . In the afternoon walked out with Mrs. Strother. Coming back, the city appeared to be in a state of unusual excitement. The streets were full of people, groups talking together earnestly. Horsemen galloping up and down. The news is stirring the people. Hooker has been relieved of command and [George G.] Meade has been appointed. This has been done, it is said, at the instance of the officers of the Army of the Potomac. Rebel cavalry has attacked and captured commissary trains between Tenallytown and Rockville capturing 150 wagons and 900 mules. This force 2,000 strong is said to be Fitzhugh Lee's command. York, on the Pennsylvania Railroad, is in the hands of the Rebels. This is forty miles from Baltimore. The streets of Baltimore are barricaded and the town will be destroyed before it will be surrendered. This is the grand budget for today. Who knows what tomorrow may bring.

JUNE 30, TUESDAY.—. . . Things look confused today and nobody knows anything. The newspapers are equally unsatisfactory. Rumors are rife that Butler is Secretary of War and McClellan commander-in-chief of the army. This would only be a compromise with blackguardism. . . . Walked in the Smithsonian grounds with Mrs. Strother and saw there the monument to A. J. Downing,[5] the author of cottage architecture, etc. The monument was suggestive of the superior usefulness of art and literature to human society, and I joined heartily in the tribute thus paid to Downing's artistic taste and talents. What more noble act than that of building and beautifying our dwellings and cities? The sight of this monument awakened strongly my love of art and literature so long dimmed by war's excitements.

JULY 1, WEDNESDAY.—. . . The hope that McClellan will be restored seems to be universal. The Rebel advance in Pennsylvania has been checked by the closing in of Meade's army on Lee's rear. A few days will decide the fate of the Rebellion. I cannot imagine what has induced Lee to make so decisive and desperate a move, unless it is true that the Confederacy is on its last legs at home and this is the last effort of a desperate cause. Or it may be that he feels such absolute confidence in his troops that he can risk the movement with almost a certainty of winning if driven to a battle. . . .

5. A. J. Downing (1815-52), a landscape gardener and architect, probably exerted more influence upon public taste in the United States during the middle decades of the nineteenth century than any other single person. Strother refers to his book, *Cottage Residences* (1842).

JULY 2, THURSDAY.—The great armies are closing in Pennsylvania. News of a battle at Gettysburg between Longstreet's and Hill's corps and two of our army corps. General [John F.] Reynolds killed. I stayed down street hoping to get some further news. They talked rather despondingly and said we had been worsted in the fight yesterday. Of the great battle supposed to be going on today, we can hear nothing. . . .

JULY 3, FRIDAY.—Details of the Gettysburg fight are favorable, although no positive success was achieved. Yet our troops fought well, even the Dutch Corps, and, if our troops fight fairly, we must beat the enemy by force of superior numbers. There was a battle going on yesterday of which the government must have had information, yet at twelve o'clock today, the public have no information whatever on the subject. Nor is any allusion made to it in the evening papers. This creates great uneasiness in my mind. . . .

JULY 4, SATURDAY.—News this morning conflicting. The enemy has attacked and been repulsed at all points. The McClellan democrats give unfavorable versions of the battles. Meade has determination to fight to the last, and, if he is properly reinforced by the troops at Baltimore and Washington, he must win. If Lee does not defeat our army decisively, his army must inevitably be forced to fall back and will consequently be destroyed. The events of today will be decisive of the war if favorable to us. . . . Walked into the grounds of the President's house where I found a great crowd of people in holiday attire. They were collected here to hear the Declaration of Independence read and an oration by an Honorable Mr. Walbridge.[6] There was a canopy of board where the orators and the marine band sat. Someone was reading the Declaration of Independence and then read the names of the signers by states. At each state there was a faint round of applause, at some names such as Franklin, Carroll of Carrollton, etc., there was general applause. As the Southern seceded states were read out, Virginia, North Carolina, South Carolina, and Georgia, there was dead silence. I had been trained from youth to a great veneration of our national history and all these national Dii Majorum Gentium. What a mockery seemed their celebration, how painful the recapitulation of these honored names and themes. The star-spangled banner seemed a funeral dirge, the national flag a pall, each venerated name a burning curse on the page of history. I left

6. Probably Hiram Walbridge, who had been a congressman from New York in 1853 but who failed to be elected for 1863.

the ground. How awful did the Rebellion appear to me then and how deep the damnation they have brought upon us.

As I approached the street I met Hall, our fellow boarder, who told me the news of the defeat of Lee. I hastened to the office of the *Herald* agent where I found the statement recapitulated. I hurried to the house, and, seeing Mrs. Randolph in great tribulation, I told her the news. She was in such excitement that she wept. Mrs. Wade came in and joined the chorus. I ran upstairs and told my wife, who looked as if she would presently cry. I went down and got an extra *Star*. All Lee's attacks were repulsed with great slaughter, and failure to beat us must destroy him. Now let us throw every man, horse, and gun upon them and the war is ended with a blow. . . . At 8:30 went to the grounds back of the President's house to see the fireworks. There was a great crowd, a bonfire, some men setting up the scaffolds, and nothing more. We waited an hour beyond the appointed time when it began drizzling and we retired. . . .

JULY 5, SUNDAY.—. . . There is quiet today and the tenor of the good news confirmed. Doubtless powerful reinforcements are on their way to the Army of the Potomac. General [Daniel E.] Sickles has just been brought in minus a leg. Duane says Stuart's men acknowledged they were handled by Buford's cavalry. . . . Dr. Bellows[7] has written a pamphlet to show that all religion in New England has been lost by running to individualism. It is easy to see how the baleful dogmas of Democracy teaching a preference of localism and engendering individualism in politics have destroyed our nationality. The spirit is nearly as bad in the United States as in the seceded states and if not quashed must eventually lead to the ruin of all government.

JULY 7, TUESDAY.—. . . Official news has been received that Vicksburg surrendered on the fourth of July. I heard it told at Willard's Bar and hurried to the War Department. There I heard the workmen, clerks, and citizens shouting and cheering. At night a large procession of citizens with a band of music marched to call on the President to felicitate on the fall of Vicksburg, etc. We gathered under the portico of the White House and the band played some national airs. Presently the President, who had been at the War Office, slipped through the crowds and entering the front door appeared at an upper window. He was greeted by three cheers. Then Grant,

7. Henry W. Bellows (1814-82) was a popular Unitarian writer of New York. He is now better known for his organization of the Sanitary Commission during the Civil War.

Meade, and the Union were cheered. The President made a speech, short and appropriate. His manner was somewhat of the buffoon and his appearance ungainly and indicative of long-continued anxiety. Yet his manner impressed you with his honesty and sincerity. I felt warmed towards Old Abe and for the first time felt a sentiment of personal loyalty to a man who under so many disadvantages, through much vituperation, through weakness, indecision, blunders, and ignorance had yet sustained the war with unbending firmness and tenacity. He deserves well of his country and of history.

Returning from this scene met General Hooker at Willard's. I spoke to him and had some conversation. He asked with interest about Banks. Hooker looked red and dissipated. He has been drinking hard lately and it shows on him, but has not broken his strength. He was a dashing and brave leader of any army corps. His organization and discipline of the Army of the Potomac told at Gettysburg. He failed to command the army successfully because it was perhaps over his strength. He has lost caste with the people because he did not succeed and with the army because he was treacherous with McClellan.

JULY 12, SUNDAY.—Saw General Hunter[8] at Willard's and had a long and pleasant talk with him. I gave him my reasons for desiring the division of the state of Virginia. First, by making a state which the United States in any settlement could not abandon and which the Confederacy could not yield, any peace upon a basis of division would be virtually impossible. Second, the people of West Virginia were ready and willing to abolish slavery immediately. This done, the question of slavery in the Border States would be definitely and speedily settled because with a free state so situated, Maryland, Kentucky, and Lower Virginia would be obliged to get rid of the institution. Third, by thus organizing the people of this region into a separate state, they were preserved more surely from a relapse into secessionism. . . . My wife's father, David Hunter, was at West Point with the General. He was called "Big Dave" Hunter and the General, "Little Dave."

JULY 13, MONDAY.—Heard of the death of William Luce, killed by a musket ball before Port Hudson. Luce was my old comrade in the

8. David Hunter (1802-86), USMA '22, had been in charge of Lincoln's White House guard in 1861. In 1862 he commanded the Department of the South, and was proclaimed a felon by the Confederacy for his freeing of the slaves in his department. In May, 1864, he superseded Sigel in the Department of West Virginia, captured Staunton, and was repulsed from Lynchburg. After his retreat to the Kanawha Valley, Hunter was replaced by Sheridan.

topographical corps at the beginning of the war, simple in manners and character as a child, he was full of talents. He was captured at Berryville on the day of the battle of Kernstown and was taken to Richmond and afterwards to Salisbury, North Carolina. At the end of five months he was exchanged, but having no lies to tell about his sufferings and the cruelty of the Rebels, he was not lionized or promoted, but quietly returned to the same position he had left. His fall at Port Hudson has deprived me of one of my most valued friends. . . .

Visited Governor Pierpont at the Metropolitan, and we had there a talk on the administration of the government of eastern Virginia. The Governor and myself agreed well in our views both general and detailed. He will insist on the abolition of slavery and desired to know what would be done with them. I proposed as follows. Get as many out of the state northward as possible. Let the Government use what it can as soldiers. Afford suitable facilities to slave owners for going South and West. Emancipate the remainder directly and then institute a system of disciplined peonage, which will bring the Negro to labor and order his normal condition while the buying and selling and other objectionable features of slavery will be abolished. The present population and society of the Old Dominion must go under. Confiscation and political disenfranchisement will reduce them to poverty and drive them to banishment, while the state will be occupied by a new people. This seems to be a hard decision, but I believe it essential. This will answer for the present. Saw General Hunter and we had a two-hour talk. We talked of Negro troops. He spoke well of them and asked why Banks had not raised more of them. We concluded that they would hereafter be extensively used.

JULY 15, WEDNESDAY.—The particulars of Lee's escape are confirmed. We got a brigade of infantry and two cannon of the rear guard. This is about the meanest and most humiliating incident of the war. Hooker would have done better and no one could have done worse. Meade is proved—a plain soldier fit to lead a corps but without power or ambition and utterly incompetent at the head of a hundred thousand men. . . . Walked in the Smithsonian groups and went down to Willard's where I talked with Colonel Alexander until ten o'clock. He says he will look out for a place for me. In the early part of the war, [Salmon P.] Chase consulted with Alexander about marching a column to East Tennessee and to Chattanooga. Alexander asked for thirty thousand men. Chase thought that four regiments would be enough, so the plan fell through. Chattanooga has been all along the vital spot of the Rebellion.

JULY 18, SATURDAY.—Called at Mr. Stanton's office. When Mr. Stanton came in, I introduced myself and was invited into the sanctuary. The room was filled with business papers, maps of the seat of war, etc. The Secretary asked me after my health, but before we could join conversation he was interrupted by so many calls of business that he asked me to call again at eight o'clock. I returned at this hour, but he was not in, so I registered my name and hour of calling. Colonel [James A.] Hardie says the Secretary is a reader of character and likes a prompt, quick-talking man. Your hesitating, slow speaker, he soon disposes of. This coincides with what I saw in a former visit. Stanton was a Democrat formerly, and like many Democrats who have gone against the Rebellion is truculently zealous. This accords with my temper as well as my judgment. . . .

JULY 21, TUESDAY.—. . . In the evening started to see Mr. Stanton. Registered my name and hour of calling. Sent in my card and waited in the afternoon. Presently was invited in with another man. This person was an officer of some staff and was boring the Secretary for a pass to get his wife and daughter to Mt. Vernon. The Secretary declined his request and gave a good reason for it. When this *important* conference ended the Secretary turned to me and asked what he could do for me? As I had expected from his sending for me that he had some proposition to make to me, I was totally unprepared for this question and, having nothing to ask for, felt flat. He said then he would assign me to duty on any staff that I preferred. As I had made up my mind not to go into active service and knew no Generals except those that were in active service or entirely retired, I was driven to think of Kelley in Western Virginia and named him. Stanton then told me to communicate with Kelley and if he desired it, he would assign me to his staff. The only advantage I can expect from this is that it will take me to Western Virginia where by seeing the Governor I may secure some suitable service. I rose to go and Mr. Stanton said he would accompany me.

As we passed out of the door, he spoke of Meade's failure to destroy Lee as the greatest mortification of the war and the more he thought of it, the worse it seemed. I suggested by way of consolation that it would not alter but only prolong the decisive result. This he agreed to as certain, but it brought on us these New York riots. On the door steps he spoke to me kindly of the pleasure my writings had given him, taking me familiarly by the arm and asking many questions about the personages of my work. I have felt disappointed in the result of this interview, although perhaps I have no right to feel so.

JULY 23, THURSDAY.—. . . Mrs. Strother received a letter from my daughter Emily giving news from Berkeley Springs. All well. General [John D.] Imboden was there and asked my daughter where I was. She replied I was in the Federal Army. He said, "When you see him, tell him he should resign; if he thinks he is fighting for the Union, he is mistaken. He and all the Yankee Army are only fighting for the Negroes. . . .

JULY 25, SATURDAY.—. . . The idea that this war is caused by slavery is fallacious. Nothing could have worked more prosperously and more smoothly than the two systems together, each assisting the other. The spirit of party heated by ambitious demagogues was the cause of the war and Slavery and Anti-Slavery the watchwords used by crafty and ambitious men to fool the simple. . . .

JULY 26, SUNDAY.—. . . One of the great scourges of the earth is Philanthropy. Woe to that unhappy people upon whom the British or Anglo-American philanthropist fixes his attention. The East Indian, South Sea Islander, and American Indian have wilted and perished from the earth before their fiery zeal, and now the poor Negro, hitherto fat and prosperous, is likely to be the victim of the philanthropist. To save him from an occasional whipping, wholesome stimulant at times, an occasional change of ownership which he did not in the main take very hard, he is to be turned loose, naked and helpless, to struggle for his life with the remorseless Anglo-Saxon and to perish miserably amid the tortures of philanthropy. Alas, poor Negro. He must go under and make room for the white man, as the Indian has done before him, and it is right that it should be so. Where the interests of a great nation require that a portion of its inhabitants should be sacrificed, let them go under, that the nationality may live and prosper. . . .

AUGUST 1, SATURDAY. [in Baltimore].—. . . At the breakfast table [Eutaw House] saw General Milroy[9] and two officers which I supposed were of his staff. Milroy is a man of fifty, tall and well made, florid complexion with red beard, sharp features crowned with stiff, grey hair

9. Robert H. Milroy (1816-90) served in Western Virginia throughout most of the war. Commanding at Winchester during Lee's march to Pennsylvania, Milroy was routed and his losses were so heavy that they were subjected to an investigation. After the war he was a superintendent of Indian affairs in the Washington Territory.

which rose from his forehead like a porcupine's quills. The whole party had a jaded, dejected look. I could not but feel sorry for the unfortunate general. . . .

At Frederick the coach for Hagerstown was crowded. I got a seat on top. The heat was intense and the bouquet of dead horse was never out of our nostrils. Dead horses and mules marked the highway of war. The Middletown Valley looked charming and the crossing of South Mountain over the ground of last year's battle filled my mind with vivid reminiscences. We passed the house where McClellan spent the night after the battle. The yard was then full of wounded and I slept upon the stair landing. At the foot of the mountain we met a train of seven ambulances filled with Confederate convalescents taken at Gettysburg. These fellows looked well cared for and cheerful, as if they were glad to be where they were.

Arrived at Hagerstown after sunset. The Washington House closed and used as a hospital. The landlord was civil and gave us the best room in his house. Arranged with a man to furnish us a hack in the morning to drive me to Hancock for $15. The price is heavy but anything rather than endure this place for twenty-four hours longer. . . .

AUGUST 2, SUNDAY.—. . . The cook, Aunt Maria, an old Berkeley servant, called on us and testified extreme pleasure at meeting us. These meetings with old servants are the most agreeable social rencontres I have nowadays. The drive to Clear Spring was pleasant. Just before arriving there, we passed two soldiers on foot, one of whom in a peremptory manner ordered our coachman to stop. The Negro (an old cripple) reined up and the man told him he wanted to ride. I told the soldier the carriage was privately hired for the convenience of my family and that we could take no more passengers. He then asked if we could take his knapsack, which was in Clear Spring. I replied I would see about it when we got there, but the horses were already overloaded and I was not sure if it would be done. He said he belonged to the 137th Ohio Volunteers. He had been captured at Winchester with Milroy and was on his way to Ohio to join the camp of paroled prisoners. The speaker was a stout, fine-looking man, and had blue cavalry pants, a grey shirt, a rolled blanket, and a horseman's pistol. The other man hung back and said nothing. I ordered my Negro to drive on, and after we had gone half a mile, the soldiers following up the road, my acquaintance started at a dogtrot and presently overtook us with the drawn pistol in his hand. He called loudly to our coachman to stop, menacing him with the pistol. The man stopped. Then with oaths and loud voice, he swore he would ride at hazards. I then spoke from the window, told him that I was an officer of the 3rd Virginia Cavalry, seizing my sword at the same time, and told him that he should not ride. He insolently asked why he could not ride, as he was a tired soldier. I told him he should not ride because I said so. I then ordered the man to drive on. The fellow walked along with pistol in hand as if not entirely satisfied to abandon his determination, but at length fell back to his comrade who had taken no part in the matter. As soon as we stopped at the hotel in Clear Spring, I inquired for the office of the provost guard and laid in my complaint. The captain promptly ordered three men to take their arms and arrest the soldiers as they came into town. . . .

In Hancock we stopped at Barton's Tavern. Imboden's men occupied the town for a week. They stole horses, store goods, and jewelry. They carried off hoop skirts, laces, silks, either to sell or as presents for their sweethearts. A party entered the premises of a Pennsylvania farmer led by a man whom they thought they recognized. The guide turned out to be a Baptist minister who had formerly preached in the vicinity and lived at this house, praying morning and evening with the family and saying grace over many a hearty meal. . . .

AUGUST 3, MONDAY.—. . . There had been a flood in Bath and the hotel and public grounds looked dreadfully dilapidated. The condition of the county is very bad. There is no law of any kind. In town, idle, half-grown boys and silly women are continually in mischief and keep up a continual irritation. Men too cowardly to settle their private quarrels face to face are continually informing on each other and fomenting bitterness. Most of the ruin in the public square has been wrought by idle citizens. A provost guard with a military law is the only government we can have here for some time to come. . . . Em Randolph had a time with Milroy's retreating troops. They were famished and ran into the kitchen snatching the bread out of her hands. She ordered them out and finally seized a cup of hot lard and threatened to scald them. With a coffee pot in one hand and the molten lard in the other, she finally cleared the kitchen. . . . A guard of fifteen infantry got up late in the afternoon and sentinels were posted on the different roads around the village.

AUGUST 6, THURSDAY.—Wife packed my carpet bag for my intended trip to join Kelley's headquarters. I talked a long while with my daughter, who is grown up in body and mind and shows traces of good training. No man could be more blessed than I am in my domestic relations, and it seems hard that inexorable fate will not yet let me be in quiet enjoyment of them. I start on this journey much against my will. . . . At Cumberland the train laid over. Stopped at the Revere House.

X

In the Department of West Virginia

August 7, 1863—March 13, 1864

Strother's account of his service in the Department of West Virginia during the fall and winter of 1863-64 deals with no significant military activity, but rather with routine headquarters existence during the interlude between Gettysburg and the Virginia campaigns of 1864. Kelley was responsible for guarding a mountainous and inaccessible line several hundred miles in length from the sudden attacks by Rebel partisans. On one September night a band of guerillas swept in and out of Berkeley Springs, nearly catching the prize they had coveted since the early days of the war—David Strother himself.

In February the tempo accelerated as preparations for the spring campaigns began. Political expediency required that the capable Kelley relinquish command of the Department to General Franz Sigel. The German constituents were pleased by the transfer, but the demoralization of the army, including the staff, commenced. And Colonel Strother sensed disaster ahead for the army commanded by Sigel.

AUGUST 7, FRIDAY.—. . . Started for New Creek by 6:30. Found General Kelley's quarters in a railroad shanty. He received me pleasantly. From incidental accounts of the undisciplined condition of the regiment and from the dirt, loutishness, and confusion I see around me, I am almost inclined to resign without looking further. Kelley said he would be glad to have me on his staff, but my rank was too high. I told him there would be no difficulty in procuring a special order, as the Secretary of War had promised to assign me to any staff I desired. He then asked me if I would accompany him down to Cumberland. I was glad of the move as it relieved me on the score of lodging. I was not sure I could find a place to sleep at New Creek. Dirt and dilapidation on all sides. In the wooden depot buildings are army stores, officers' quarters, and offices. A dirty tavern, sutler's stores, and country stores occupy the other half of the dismantled wooden building. Dead horses and soldiers' shallow graves perfume the air. Dirty camps and dirtier camping grounds occupy the flat country adjacent. The platforms swarm with dirty soldiers of all arms, Negroes, loafers, convalescents, teamsters, and camp followers crowding about the trains as they arrive and depart. Smoking, swearing, and hastening to and fro. Country girls of uncouth deportment and gay-colored dresses thread the crowd to visit the stores or to take leave of friends going on trains. The soft verdure of meadows and mountains, the romantic cliffs, the crystal river, and winding creek are all too lovely and a precious setting for this dirty and confused picture. . . .

AUGUST 8, SATURDAY.—Took the cars for Wheeling at 6:30. Some egg vendors came on at Grafton and sold boiled eggs to a neighbor of mine who as he picked them open found them rotten and loudly proclaimed this fact. Gangs of idle, dirty, and insolent boys infested the cars while the passengers were at dinner. They wanted to drink the water from the cooler but were prevented by a man, whom they insulted. I then ordered them all out. They cursed me and went.

At Wheeling stopped at the McClure House and a more dirty and forlorn establishment would be difficult to imagine. Governor Boreman[1] boarded at the place and was pointed out at a neighboring table. I introduced myself and he promptly invited me to his room. Here we had a long and animated talk, interrupted twice by officer seekers. The impression received of the Governor's personal character is very pleasing. He has good sense, is modest, and evidently inexperienced in public affairs, which his modesty proves. He is highly spoken of by all who know him and seems to be radical in regard to his treatment of Rebels. He sustains strong measures and thinks Kelley is too timid and mild. . . .

AUGUST 9, SUNDAY.—. . . The landlord seemed anxious to hunt up some society for me, but I declined, wishing to enjoy a luxury he knows nothing of, that is, a day of solitude and leisure. Walked down to the river, the town quiet as a village. At dinner there was a show with a huge bill of fare, French dishes misspelled and misunderstood. Things generally in this country are pretty rough. . . .

AUGUST 11, TUESDAY.—. . . The most wretched hole I have yet seen is Clarksburg on first acquaintance. I called at the best tavern I could

1. Arthur J. Boreman (1823-96), the first governor of West Virginia, had presided over the Wheeling Convention of 1861, which had established a "loyal" Virginia government.

HALT AT CLARKSBURG

find and asked for a room and breakfast. A pot-bellied, red-faced, grey-headed landlord received me, and a dirty, clay-colored Negro showed me to the dirtiest room it has yet been my misfortune to occupy. The walls were of grey plaster without picture frame or looking glass. Three beds that were positively and undisguisably filthy. They looked as if they stunk. A washbowl with a gap in it, an empty pitcher with the mouth broken off, and a glass tumbler with one side broken and half full of dead flies. The whole face of the country here looks dingy, and neither the grass nor the foliage looks as fresh as that east of the mountains. The dwellings and settlements look mean and the people rough and uncouth. They remind me of villages in the remote southwest of Virginia. I lay on the floor and slept with my head pillowed on an upturned chair. . . . About four o'clock I called up to General Kelley's quarters. He has a private car and engine, which took us to Grafton, where we followed the night train eastward.

[Strother is granted an indefinite leave of absence on August 13, and he returns to his family at Berkeley Springs.]

AUGUST 28, FRIDAY.—Walked to Sir John's, wife accompanying me part of the way. At the Martinsburg landing saw a young lady. This proved to be Belle Boyd, who saluted me respectfully and held out her hand, which I took kindly. She told me she was going to the Old Capitol Prison. She has been arrested for breaking her parole, having been sent across the lines formerly and forbidden to return. . . . Saw the railroad gunboats, ironclad cars, armed with howitzers and loopholed for musketry.

AUGUST 31, MONDAY.—Berkeley Springs. The country outside our lines is full of guerillas and horse thieves. The staid people in the country wish them to the devil, although their own friends and relatives are among the plunderers. They fear the consequences of the crimes will be visited on their heads. This seems hard at first view, but who started these fellows out with blessings and equipment to make war on their country and their government? Who but these very parents and friends. And now that these very boys turn to them, lousy, itchy, drunken, and demoralized highwaymen, plundering friend and foe in their reckless folly, these parents fear to see them and beg them to come near them no more. . . . Talked with Henry, a Negro porter, who agrees that the Northern people do not treat the blacks as kindly as their old masters do. He hopes always to live in Virginia.

SEPTEMBER 1, TUESDAY.—. . . Morris came in from Winchester. He had heard strangers in Winchester extolling my father's courage when a prisoner there. Winchester is dead and rotten. No business, nothing to eat. Houses deserted, population leaving going north and south. You may look on the Main Street at midday and not see half a dozen persons. The banks are closed, there is no money that will pass. Country people will not bring marketing to town because they have no confidence in the currency. They wish an army there because they would have protection and something to live on. Morris wisely counsels that no army should be permitted to occupy the place, that they may suffer the evils that they have brought on themselves. . . .

SEPTEMBER 3, THURSDAY.—. . . I talked with Allen, the sheriff, who says that every man in the county would vote against Secession now. With my wife, walked to the old race ground, where I recalled a picnic with Captain [Arnold] Elzey and others before the war. He is now a general in the Confederate service. . . .

SEPTEMBER 7, MONDAY.—This morning at half past two I was awakened by cries and shouts in the direction of the cavalry camp. I at first supposed that there was a fire and went to the windows to see. The yells and shouts were followed by loud vociferations and furious swearing. I could distinguish no particulars. This continued for some moments, then there was a pistol shot followed by several scattering shots which presently thickened into a sharp fusillade. Then the sound of horses' feet rapidly moving toward the courthouse and the mountain road to Sir John's. I said to my wife, "There is a fight going on, and I must be on the alert." I groped for my clothes and found my pantaloons and pistol which I put on. I then got my shoes and military overcoat and hat. Meanwhile the fight continued sharply. Tom the Negro came to my door to awaken me. I went downstairs and found Randolph and wife up. I went to the front door with Randolph and, looking around, saw nobody. In a few moments Morris Hopewell knocked at the front door. I stood on my guard, but soon saw it was a friend. The fight was over at the camp and dead silence ensued there, but horses' hoofs were heard going in the direction of the Winchester road.

I had looked each moment for an advance upon our house, but as yet no horsemen had appeared on the street. This puzzled me, for I felt sure if they were an attacking party of Rebels they would have paid their respects to me. Then the trampling of horses advancing rapidly toward town on the grade was heard. I went out the back door and retreated to the head of the grove. These two horsemen that rode back proved to be two of our pickets on the Winchester road who had been surprised in the rear by the attacking Rebels. I then went to the top of the mountain, keeping away from the beaten road, and arriving there I heard the snorting of horses on the Sir John's road and presently saw a body of cavalry amounting to one company approaching. At the distance at which they passed I could not tell whether they were our troops or not, the moon being in her last quarter and the light very dim. I conjectured, however, that they were our troops and started down the hill. As I walked, the cocks in the village began to crow and, by the time I reached the house, day was fairly dawning. The newly arrived cavalry had hesitated to enter the town, but young Bechtol had informed them that our troops still held the camp. On this information the troop rode to the camp.

As it grew lighter, citizens began to gather in the streets, and after a while I ascertained that an attack had been made by a gang of Rebels forty or fifty in number. They were resisted and had gone off, carrying with them some forty-five horses and twenty prisoners. As I stood talking, Captain Hummel and five or six others came riding up the street with drawn sabres, threatening destruction to all of us. The exhibition was so farcical that I lost all confidence in the courage and efficiency of the actors. Lieutenant [George D.] Stroud with his company from Hancock got up and with prancing started up the road in pursuit of the enemy. Tom says he heard one voice inquire loudly if Dave Strother was not here. This question was repeated and no one answered. The widow of Ed Hunter said she heard them say, "Let us go down there," but one whose voice she knew as George Hunter's replied, "No, we have not time. Follow me." When I went to my room I found my wife unpacking my notebooks and money which with admirable presence of mind she had concealed about her person. She had also noted the hour the attack was made and had concealed my watch and sabre. She showed throughout the affair the coolness and presence of mind of an uncommon character. . . .

Captain [Christian B.] Hebble in the upper camp had answered the summons to surrender with an oath and pistol shot wounding the Rebel leader in the hand. The party had come in the Winchester road and caught the picket guard asleep perhaps. One man escaping gave the alarm. Major [James M.] Comly ran to town, a quarter of a mile distant, to arouse Captain Blackburn. While he was gone the attack commenced, and neither of them appeared until all was over. The men of Captain Hebble stood their ground and saved their camp and horses. The better men from the other camp ran into Hebble's ranks and stood there. On the part of the Rebels the act was most audacious and well conducted. They escaped all pursuit. The force from here having spent too much valor in their exhibition in the streets soon gave up the chase. . . .

SEPTEMBER 9, WEDNESDAY.— . . . Met in the old bar room and organized the court of inquiry of which I was presiding officer. We spent the whole day examining officers, noncommissioned officers, and privates. The result of our examination was to show that about forty Rebels had attacked the Federal camp containing about eighty men and had driven them all away and had retired, taking with them about forty horses and twenty men. All the officers and about sixty men had run away without making any respectable resistance. Captain Hebble had behaved well in the fight. Major Comly and Lieutenant Eaches had behaved feebly but not cowardly. Captain Hummel had shown himself an arrant coward and jackass, and Lieutenant Babb was in the same box. The Captain had run away at the first fire, followed by two men. He made the men throw away their sabres for fear the rattling would betray them to the enemy. He ran to the picket on the Martinsburg road, a mile and a half distant, and there demanded the fastest horse to be had, on the ground that he was a captain. Arriving near Alpine, he fell off his horse twice riding through the bushes and then was afraid to approach the encampment of Stroud's command lest it should be in possession of the enemy. A sergeant went forward and got assurance that all was right. Hummel then advanced and conjured the men to arise and avenge their slaughtered comrades whom he had seen fall one after another by his side. The command being mounted, Captain Hummel rode into Bath at the head of it, charging furiously with drawn sabre on a crowd of gossiping citizens and making himself generally ridiculous. In the pursuit started from here he assumed command for several miles and then as signs of overtaking the enemy appeared, he fell back to a less prominent position in the column. Lieutenant Babb in the beginning of the attack tore off his shoulder straps and threw them away, escaping in the bushes. After a while he started for Hancock and ran the whole way on foot, arriving in great terror and exhaustion. In all this firing and scuffling, not one of the Federals was wounded, and we are not sure that more than one of the Rebels was hurt. On the part of the Rebels the attack was most boldly and skillfully executed. This and the fact that they were all uniformed shows that they were a detachment of organized cavalry and not bushwhackers. The finding of the court was that Captain Hebble be released from arrest and commended, that Major Comly and Lieutenant Eaches be released from arrest, and that Captain Hummel and Lieutenant Babb be tried by a court-martial for grave misconduct in face of the enemy. . . .

[On September 10, Strother rejoins the staff of General Kelley.]

SEPTEMBER 11, FRIDAY.—. . . Lieutenant Meigs[2] says the Southern and Northern students lived apart at West Point in different wings of the buildings and were also socially separated. The same arrogant and quarrelsome presumption characterized the Southern men there as about the seat of government. . . .

SEPTEMBER 13, SUNDAY.—General Kelley came in and we talked all morning, more or less. We concluded that in the management

2. John R. Meigs (1842-64), the son of General Montgomery Meigs, had graduated first in his West Point class of 1863. He served under Sigel, Hunter, and Sheridan in the Valley of Virginia until killed by a bushwhacker near Harrisonburg in October, 1864.

of this great war, the President has shown honesty, firmness, and great ability. That his early measures failed and his comprehension did not at first grasp the subject is true. But whose fancy ever conceived the magnitude of the work which fell upon the President? Shall we condemn the engineer because his work could not resist the earthquake? Although failing at first, the President has gathered up his strength and has met the crisis. It looks now as if he had conquered. Kelley thinks well of Stanton. He is not a politician or party man and stoutly labors for the one great end. An effort was lately made to have General Kelley displaced from the Department of West Virginia and Fremont put in command. A paper signed by forty-some-odd-members of the Legislature was presented to the President, who, on looking at it, replied—"Gentlemen, no complaints of General Kelley have reached me through the War Department. This seems a political move. I therefore decline considering it." The ground of discontent with the General is his liberal policy toward the disaffected people of the country. The motive power in bringing this discontent into action is the restiveness of certain speculators. . . . After talking with General Kelley I commend the superiority of practical good sense over book learning. I have almost come to the conclusion that in some departments books are a decided disadvantage. . . . Talked with Lieutenant Meigs and sustained that the moderns are equal to the ancients in all respects and that ancient history is half fable. We went to the fine arts and decided that nature, animate and inanimate, is the great arbiter of taste and that modern art excels ancient in all things.

SEPTEMBER 16, WEDNESDAY.—. . . The rule has been that our troops have showed courage and efficiency in proportion as they have been used in large numbers, while their conduct in inferior detachments has for the most part been cowardly and mean. The philosophy of this is perhaps that our people are communists, acting powerfully in masses, but wanting in self-reliance and individuality. The Southern troops have been more successful in small affairs, owing perhaps to their superior individuality of character, although their knowledge of the field of operations and facilities for getting information are to be taken into account. [George A.] Custer, my old chum of the topographicals on McClellan's staff, now a general of cavalry, made a charge at Culpeper and took three guns and fifty prisoners. . . . Meade is on the Rapidan. There must be a breakup somewhere very soon. If Lee falls back from Virginia, the Rebels are politically ruined.

SEPTEMBER 20, SUNDAY. Passed the morning reading the report of Congressional Committee on the Conduct of the War, Patterson's Campaign. A Colonel Price testifies that "Porte Crayon was one of the parties who gave them information that Johnson had forty thousand men in Winchester, he having been there when Johnson left with thirty-five thousand men for Manassas." The truth is that I was at that time with General Patterson's staff, serving as assistant in the engineer corps and had not been near Winchester since the beginning of the war. I moreover took all the pains in my power to discourage the belief in the silly cock and bull story about forty thousand men in Winchester, being fully assured that Johnson's force did not approach half that number. There is proof in this report of what I always believed, that Patterson wanted to go forward but was prevented by Colonel Fitz-John Porter, his adjutant general. Porter persuaded him to retain the order for an advance from Bunker Hill which he was about to issue, until he could call a council, and then as usual all the old army officers opposed an advance.

No general who is influenced by a council of war is fit to command an army. Men may read medical books until they are afraid to eat or breathe, lest they should contract disease. The real apology for Patterson on that occasion was in the unreliable quality of his troops. They were not howling for a fight until they felt assured there was to be none. Then they went home forsaken because they couldn't have a fight. Johnson's troops were no better than Patterson's, and I have always thought the chances were with the United States Army on being better equipped and armed. . . .

SEPTEMBER 26, SATURDAY [In Wheeling].—. . . Went to Benwood. Saw the pontoon bridge which was in process of construction.[3] It was building from each shore. Three large coal barges with decks on the Virginia side and two on the Ohio side. The center was filled with thirteen army pontoon boats. The whole made a good crossing of eight or nine hundred feet. The stream was low and there was little current, so the undertaking was not difficult. . . .

SEPTEMBER 27, SUNDAY.—. . . About midday the soldiers arrived

3. On September 25, after hearing of Rosecran's defeat at Chickamauga, the Government transferred the Eleventh (Howard's) and the Twelfth (Slocum's) Corps from the Army of the Potomac to Tennessee for service under Hooker. The speed of this transfer was in itself a major victory for the Engineering and the Quartermaster departments.

and six regiments crossed to Bellaire. They bivouacked and lunched on the river shore. There were several men desperately drunk, some dead drunk, some fighting drunk, and the efforts of the guard to get them along produced great merriment. The troops were of the Army of the Potomac and wore a crescent as their distinctive mark. A captain told me they were the Eleventh Army Corps, late Sigel's, now [General Oliver O.] Howard's. . . . Arrived at Wheeling after dark.

SEPTEMBER 28, MONDAY.—. . . Mankind is much given to fetish worship. The poor African makes himself a hideous image of mud, sticks, and beads and falls down and worships it, hoping thereby to get the image's assistance in some scheme for cheating his friends or revenging against his enemies. If the result disappoints him, he flings his god into the fire and makes himself another. What are all our popular great men but fetishes compounded of mud, sticks, and feathers, furnished by our passion-led fancies, worshipped for the nonce, and when the furor which created them is over, cast into the fire and trampled under foot with the ashes of the past. . . .

SEPTEMBER 29, TUESDAY.—Joe Hooker passed over this morning. Two Army Corps, Eleventh and Twelfth are on their way to Rosecrans. Things are in a jumble. Gold at forty, Russian fleet at New York, siege of Charleston at a standstill. What next? My health is improving, whether from the cool weather or from four months' repose I cannot tell. But I now feel well assured that my physique will not stand the active duties of a cavalry officer in the field. . . . A meeting was held by the discontented members of the legislature to make a formal demand on the national Government to remove Kelley. He is charged with military inefficiency and with being under the influence of Copperheads and returned Rebels. The Governor told them they had had Rosecrans and they had complained of him. They had Fremont, Milroy, and what not, all of whom had been equally distasteful and that on speaking to Mr. Stanton about a change, he had threatened them with worse. They had better put up with what they have or they may fare worse. . . .

SEPTEMBER 30, WEDNESDAY.—. . . Captain [Tredwell] Moore of the U. S. Army called for me in a buggy and drove me by a pleasant road to Bellaire, crossing the suspension bridge and going down the Ohio side. Moore is a West Pointer and has lived fourteen years in the West and California and speaks enthusiastically of that country. He has served during the war chiefly in New Mexico and Arizona. He has a turn for driving fast horses. Moore thinks it would be a good plan to sell all the Negroes to Cuba and Brazil and thus get rid of the trouble and pay the expenses of the war. . . .

OCTOBER 13, TUESDAY [In Clarksburg].—Read the diary of an English officer who was in the Pennsylvania Campaign and at the Battle of Gettysburg.[4] He was evidently penetrated with Southern views on that occasion but his account of the battle is graphic and interesting. He scorns the idea of the Southern power being broken by that battle, but his account in that differs from what I hear in Virginia at Martinsburg. . . .

OCTOBER 14, WEDNESDAY.—. . . Visited the Old Academy and found Dr. [Socrates] Sherman installed there. We had a long talk about the war. We are making history which will make the nineteenth century memorable. It will one day be considered a great privilege to have lived in these days, to have played a part in the greatest war that has shaken the earth for many a year, to have been acquainted with the actors, leaders, and localities of so famous a drama—the crushing out of the last traces of feudalism in the United States. . . .

OCTOBER 16, FRIDAY.—. . . Talked to the mustering officer of this department. My regiment must be full in numbers and complete in companies before I can be legally mustered as colonel. Received the appointment of chief of cavalry for this department. Startling news that Lee was across the Rappahannock and that a general engagement was going on at the Old Bull Run battleground, and that Dan Sickles was at the head of the Army. This sounds bogus. A telegram from Martinsburg that two divisions of Longstreet's Corps were marching up Back Creek Valley to burn the railroad bridge. Some of [Harry] Gilmor's men were really engaged in such an enterprise and thirty-nine of them were captured.

OCTOBER 18, SUNDAY.—. . . A squad of prisoners passed through yesterday, about twenty in number. Our own teamsters arrested for plundering their own wagons, stealing public property therefrom. The teamsters, as a rule, are the worst men we have about the army. . . . The movements look as if Lee was about to repeat his first Maryland Campaign. Kelley evidently thinks so and, contemplating the investment of Harpers Ferry, telegraphed Sullivan[5] to hold it at all

4. This was Arthur J. L. Fremantle's *Three Months in the Southern States, April-June, 1863* (1863).

5. Jeremiah C. Sullivan had commanded a brigade under Shields in the Valley of Virginia during 1862. Transferred to the West, he fought at Iuka, Corinth, and Vicksburg before returning to Virginia to lead the First Infantry Brigade under Sigel and Hunter.

hazards, even if Lee's whole army came against it. General Halleck seconds the order saying "Any officer who would abandon it or surrender it deserves to be hung." This is the proper spirit. . . .

OCTOBER 19, MONDAY.—. . . Read a sketch of General Kelley's life, prepared by Major [John B.] Frothingham, formerly of his staff. He was born in New Hampshire, removed to Wheeling, married Mary King who died of cholera in 1833, the first year after her marriage. Afterwards he went into business with a merchant of that place and married a daughter in due time, who was the mother of his living children, three boys and two girls. His second wife died insane of erysipelas in the head. Kelley was at one time freight agent for the B & O Railroad, but at the opening of the war was merchandizing in Philadelphia. He was offered the command of the 1st Virginia regiment and led the attack at Philippi where Porterfield's Rebs were so signally defeated. Here he was gravely wounded, supposedly mortally, but recovered and licked McDonald at Romney where I saw him for the first time during the winter of 1861-62. He afterwards thrashed a force of Jackson's posted at Blue's Gap and thus relieved Lander who was defending Hancock. The General improves on closer acquaintance and is, I think, a valuable man in this place. General Averell and staff arrived this evening. He is much heartier than when I saw him last. Colonel [John H.] Oley says Averell is the most particular man for detail, and takes personally a rigid account of everything pertaining to his command, even to the horseshoe nails. The routine and discipline of his camp is most rigid and exact. This accounts for the complaints I have heard against him. . . .

OCTOBER 20, TUESDAY.—. . . Had a talk with General Averell[6] in the reception room of General Kelley. He gave a most graphic and poetic description of scenery in the Rocky Mountains. He wishes me to visit Beverly to see the cavalry and stay a few days. . . . The condition of our armies from present appearances seems to be most critical and the whole situation most humiliating to the Government. Are we actually weaker than the enemy on both essential points or are we afraid to cope with him? The elections are immensely in favor of the Government, yet gold and the enemy advancing at a fearful rate, unchecked.

6. William Woods Averell (1832-1900), USMA '54, led the movement in March, 1862, upon Manassas. He joined McClellan on the Peninsula, served in the Virginia Campaign, and in 1863 was transferred to the Department of West Virginia. After the war Averell engaged in engineering and manufacturing and was Strother's closest friend of general rank.

OCTOBER 21, WEDNESDAY. Got leave to go to Beverly with Averell. The day, the road, and the company were agreeable. The valleys along the road cleared and in grass. Arrived at Buckhannon, twenty-eight miles, about seven P.M. and took supper at the hotel. There was a major there who speaks well of the companies of the 3rd Virginia, but they lack discipline and respect for officers, a very common failing among U. S. Volunteer troops. . . .

OCTOBER 22, THURSDAY.—Buckhannon a pleasanter-looking town than Clarksburg. Went out to the review and received the honors as chief of cavalry. There were six companies in the battalion, all nearly full, which made a good show. The men looked neat and the horses looked well. . . . We started on horseback for Beverly at ten o'clock. At Rich Mountain was the ground where McClellan and Rosecrans encamped before the battle.[7] We started again and presently came upon the field works that the Rebel Pegram had made covering the road just at the foot of the mountain. The Federal generals had a road cut to the right and flanked them so that they fell back, taking position on a high place and thence to the top of the ridge. The ascent is long and winding. On nearing the summit the General's quick eye perceived a man like a scout riding rapidly from us. This excited some comment, and as we approached the summit we found we were waylaid, but not by an enemy. A number of officers of the command at Beverly had ridden to meet the General, and they all rode ceremoniously to welcome us. The effect was very agreeable and a general felicitation took place with an uncorking of flasks. On the spot where we met, the forces of McClellan and Pegram had met two and half years ago in the Battle of Rich Mountain. Under the trees where our officers were then halted were the graves of the soldiers who fell in that affair. . . . There is a fine view from this summit of Tygart's Valley, changing as the road winds down the mountainside deeper and deeper into an abyss of shadow. General Averell introduced me to Colonel Moor,[8] the father-in-law of General Weitzel, which afforded me an opportunity of speaking handsomely of Weitzel as he deserved. An odor of dead horses indicated the neighboring

7. The Battle of Rich Mountain (July 11, 1861) had two important results: it saved Western Virginia for the Union, and it made McClellan the man of the hour and brought him to Washington as head of the Army of the Potomac.

8. Augustus Moor had commanded the 28th Ohio under Fremont in West Virginia earlier in the war. At South Mountain he led a brigade of the Kanawha Division. After being captured and paroled, Moor returned to the Department of West Virginia and commanded a brigade under Sigel and Hunter in the Valley of Virginia campaigns of 1864.

cavalry force. Crossing a bridge about 250 feet over the river, we entered Beverly, an insignificant war-wasted village and stopped in front of a long, low, dirty tavern in the center of town. A cheerful fire, of wood and coal mixed, welcomed us in the General's room which was office and bedchamber for the commander and staff. The evening passed off with music and pleasant talk. . . .

OCTOBER 23, FRIDAY.—. . . This village situated in the midst of a fine valley is the most miserable and dilapidated I have yet seen. To the eastward is Cheat Mountain, a high and rugged range. I took a walk about the town. The troops have no tents but have built themselves shelters of boards, tarpaulins, and boughs of trees which present a very curious and picturesque appearance. . . . The General was anxious that I should accompany him on another raid which he will make presently. I feel very much like going in and will think it over. Rosecrans is relieved and Grant put into command of the Army of Tennessee. Lee is falling back and Meade is following him. Lee's intention is developed, I think. He is going to abandon Virginia and concentrate against Grant in East Tennessee. Banks has occupied Point Isabel in Texas. This is for the future. The question decided in Tennessee, Texas will be the last point where the Rebellion will exist and the French imbroglio in Mexico will make that frontier the center of interest about the time of the next Presidential election, and Banks is to be the hero.

OCTOBER 27, TUESDAY.—There is a literary and artistic atmosphere about these headquarters that I have not seen since the days of Abert's topographical camp. Averell was with McClellan in front of Richmond during the Seven Days' Battle. He proposed that after Gaines Mill they should turn and take Richmond, leaving the enemy where they then were, north of the Chickahominy River. Prince de Joinville also urged this move. McClellan said, "No. Upon the Army of the Potomac depends the safety of the nation. If we take Richmond, they will immediately march upon Washington." I cannot see the force of this objection, however, for by the retreat to Turkey Bend, Washington was entirely uncovered and the Army of the Potomac as powerless to protect it as if that Army had been in Richmond. . . . There was a review of Averell's whole force this morning. The line of troops was formed on the plain east of the village and was three-quarters of a mile in length, a magnificent display. General Averell commanded the brigade and I received the review. The riding around the line was quite a journey. The infantry was in superb condition. I have seen no neater, better-drilled, nor more serviceable regiment. The cavalry was also highly to be commended. The mounted infantry was a wild and dangerous-looking force. Averell says they are capital fighters. . . .

[Strother's journal covering the period from November 1, 1863, through January 31, 1864, has been lost. However, during this time he continued to serve as chief of cavalry in the Department and he did no active campaigning.]

FEBRUARY 4, THURSDAY.—It seems that General Scammon,[9] two aides, and about forty privates were captured by about twenty guerillas without making any resistance. I think if the circumstances of the capture are true as stated, it would be as well to let them go. General Kelley tells me that he expected to get General Crook[10] at Kanawha in place of Scammon, which is very well, as I think Crook is a fine officer. The General thinks he will have a rough time in the spring and that the Rebels will make extraordinary efforts to retake Western Virginia. This I doubt. . . .

FEBRUARY 7, SUNDAY.—. . . The West Virginia Senate passed a resolution, denouncing General Kelley because of the capture of Scammon and requiring the Government to change commanders, appointing Sigel or Milroy. The Senate could not have made a more ridiculous exhibition of itself. . . .

FEBRUARY 11, THURSDAY. Was introduced to a Judge Sherman of New York. He says McClellan didn't desire to destroy the Rebellion but wished to prolong the war indefinitely until some compromise could be made and the Democratic party reinstated in power. McClellan's conduct since his retirement gives the impression that he might have been in the hands of some political schemers who used him, but I am not willing to believe that he was in any way false. . . . I see by the papers that Toombs has been arrested in Savannah for spouting treason against the Confederacy. He says he owes no

9. Eliakim P. Scammon (1816-94), USMA '37, had been dismissed from the army in 1856 for disobedience of orders. From 1862 to 1864 he was in command of the District of Kanawha. After his release by the Confederacy in August, 1864, Scammon was assigned the District of Florida for the remainder of the war.

10. George Crook (1829-90), USMA '52, a veteran of the Antietam and Chickamauga campaigns, was transferred to the District of Kanawha after Scammon's capture. Ordered to interrupt communication between Lynchburg and East Tennessee, Crook defeated the Confederate forces at Cloyd's Mountain and destroyed the New River bridge. With Hunter he engaged in the Lynchburg Campaign and with Sheridan he fought at Winchester and Cedar Creek. As an Indian fighter after the war, Crook had an even more distinguished career.

allegiance to any government but that of Georgia. Thus, as I have always believed, will the Confederacy perish by its own fire. Its absurd and impracticable doctrines of States Rights will destroy it before we can conquer its armies.

FEBRUARY 16, TUESDAY. . . . At night I dreamed that I was in Richmond with the Federal forces, having approached that city from the west. Our force was small and our mission to destroy all public stores, mills, factories, and railways. Met some friendly people there and some indifferent ones, all poor and ruined. I rode among the manufactories and was anxious for the burning to begin, but waked up before it began.

FEBRUARY 18, THURSDAY. General Kelley sent for me before tea. He thinks he will be superseded in his command, not from the action of the West Virginia legislature, but from outside political influences. There are fourteen major generals out of service drawing pay from the government. These will be dropped unless employed and it is important to find a place for them. The Department of West Virginia is commanded by a brigadier. The place fits a major general; hence political influences are brought to bear on the President, who easily yields. . . .

FEBRUARY 28, SUNDAY.—. . . Walked down with Mrs. Strother to call upon General Kelley and met him on the street with his daughter, Belle. There is no doubt of Sigel's appointment to the command of this department. Halleck they say is indignant, but the Dutch vote must be secured at all hazards for the Government and the sacrifice of West Virginia is a small matter. . . .

MARCH 12, SATURDAY.—. . . Last night was aroused by cannon, which announced the arrival of Sigel. General Kelley met him at the train which got in about eleven P.M. Received notice that General Kelley desired to present his staff officers to General Sigel at ten A.M. this morning. Donned full uniform and went to the office where I found the General. Went on to the Revere House and entered the parlor. We paraded on one side of the room. Presently General Sigel entered. His hair and beard are tawny, his jaws and cheek bones square and angular, his eyes light blue, forehead narrow, and too small for his face. Small in stature and ungraceful. He had on a plain slouch hat and a major general's uniform. General Kelley introduced General Sigel, who spoke English with more difficulty than I had supposed. He seemed also awkward and different. Sigel with some hesitation commenced an unpretending address in broken English, saying that he received us fellow soldiers and hoped we would assist him in the arduous duties which had been assigned to him. He entered upon them with great self-distrust and feared his ability to manage them properly, therefore hoped we would do our best to sustain him more as a brother officer than as a commander.

He then went off with General Kelley to the office to learn somewhat the extent and nature of his duties, while the staff went home admired by boys and niggers. Sigel was not reassured when he heard that he had a frontier of six hundred miles to defend, nor had he any idea of the number of troops he had to manage. He says he had nothing to do with his appointment to this department. . . . General Kelley has a leave of absence for thirty days and has mentioned to General Sigel that when he returns to duty he will want me to accompany him. He thinks Sigel desires to have Milroy on duty in this department. I do not think it at all certain that General Kelley will be put on duty again at the end of his leave unless in a subordinate position in the department, because he has no political significance at all, and that seems to be the chief object of all appointments now, to bring strength to the party in favor. . . .

MARCH 13, SUNDAY.—. . . Retired with Averell to his room and talked over public affairs. I think General Kelley's chance for a position other than a division in this department is very small. Averell thinks our horizon is not as bright as it was a month ago, but he has been to Washington and that always discourages one. He thinks the enlisting and killing off of the Negroes will help to solve the question of the African in America. . . . Party spirit is rampant now and everything succumbs to it. All this will pass away some day and with peace the empire of reason will again return. When that will be, God knows.

XI

With Sigel at New Market

March 15, 1864—May 23, 1864

When Grant launched his spring campaign in 1864, Sigel was charged with two objectives—to destroy the New River bridge of the Virginia and Tennessee Railroad near Dublin and to divert the Confederacy from the attack by menacing the Virginia Central Railroad at Staunton. In accordance with this plan, Generals Crook and Averell moved from the Kanawha early in May while Sigel started up the Valley of Virginia from Martinsburg. Although Crook defeated the Confederates at Cloyd's Mountain and burned the New River bridge, Sigel was routed on New Market on May 15 and was replaced by Hunter four days later.

For the South the victory at New Market possessed greater psychological than military significance, for the Confederates lost Staunton less than a month later, after Hunter's defeat of Jones at Piedmont. Sigel had no business engaging the enemy at New Market in the first place. On the day of the battle his forces were strung out along the Valley turnpike for eighteen miles, and his total force on the field of battle was far less than the total number he commanded. That the retreat of his army did not become a rout was largely the result of a wet day, the fatigue of the Confederates, and the mismanagement of Imboden's cavalry. A harrowing night march back to Woodstock by a disorganized mob was the only fruit of Sigel's Valley Campaign.

Before the army left Martinsburg, Strother, fearing disaster ahead, left his journal behind and relied upon his memory to fill in the details of the Campaign. He felt that the Union army had never been so badly commanded, and in his journal is an adequate summary of the operation: "We can afford to lose such a battle as New Market to get rid of such a mistake as Major General Sigel."

MARCH 15, TUESDAY.—. . . General Sigel sent for me after tea. At his room I met Captain [G. G.] Lyon, a clerical attaché, I think.

He was with Sigel when I first met him. Sigel says West Virginia is loyal and has been badly treated and has not been properly protected. This he gets from the Wheeling clique. I would like to see anyone attempt to protect more territory with the troops on hand, unless a forward movement is made by the Army of the Potomac. His business with me is to get an idea of the number of available men in the department and where posted—wanted immediately. . . .

MARCH 16, WEDNESDAY.—. . . I will be relieved of the duties of chief of cavalry, and Averell is to have charge of all cavalry east of the Allegheny Mountains. I now understood what Averell meant when he asked me how old my commission as colonel was. If I had been a ranking colonel, he wished to put me in command of a portion of his troops. . . . Lieutenant General Grant is at the head of the Army in Washington. That will kill his usefulness I fear. General Lew Wallace is assigned the command in Baltimore to supersede Lockwood. Politics.

MARCH 19, SATURDAY.—Was sent for by General Sigel. He wanted a diagram made of his command by divisions, brigades, regiments, etc. He showed me several which he had made of former commands, very neat and soldierly. He then told me that he wished me to remain with him and asked me what I wished to do, saying that if I liked, he would retain me in my present position and appoint an assistant to do the active duties. I told him of my general duties with General Banks, etc., that I was a native of the country, knew the people and topography, and that in accepting the colonelcy of the 3rd Virginia Cavalry I had been requested by the Governor to remain at headquarters and do staff duty. The General then repeated the request that I would remain with him, as he had many things to do in which I could assist him. I promised to do so. . . .

MARCH 22, TUESDAY.—. . . The General commanding called Wilson the reporter to account for having written against him in the *Herald*. He said, "You have injured me much. You publish everything bad. You must not do dat. You must ah-ah-ah (he agonized for an expression). You must, puff—." The General has not sufficient knowledge of English to gloss his ideas and what other generals would have expressed in subtle phrases and circumlocutions, with glasses of whiskey and invitations to dinner, he says in that single, dry, uncouth word, "Puff—."

MARCH 23, WEDNESDAY.—It seems that Robbins the speculator has been going the rounds talking and tampering with the quartermaster clerks and assistants, promising to have that one retained in place and that one dismissed. Captain [Augustus V.] Barringer hearing him called on General Sigel and made complaint, asking if such conduct was authorized. Sigel told him that Robbins was a friend of his and that he (Barringer) would be displaced as he was supposed to be a Kelley man. . . . .

MARCH 25, FRIDAY.—. . . In the General's room I saw a little fellow, rather insignificant, looking for all the world like a traveling clerk in dress and figure. General Sigel introduced him to me as Major General Stahel.[1] Stahel says he remembered meeting me at Charlestown during the Brown Raid and he went out with me to the house of Andrew Hunter. . . . Moray Randolph says that Harry Hunter[2] was at Moorefield with Early's raid and said to Randolph's wife, "Give my regards to Strother and say I shall be glad to see him on this side." I can't get at his meaning. . . .

MARCH 27, SUNDAY.—Made a sketch of the Martinsburg railroad bridge ruin for the Baltimore Sanitary Fair.[3] It does not please me and I have no time to make another. My literary sketch also gives me much trouble. General Stahel joined us. He is a Hungarian and talked of the grapes and wines of Hungary. He is no wine drinker, however. He must have been one of the Kossuth refugees. . . . Came home to my room, read "The Raven" of Poe, and felt intolerably lonesome. . . .

MARCH 28, MONDAY.—. . . General [Frank] Wheaton came in and we all went up to Colonel [William C.] Starr's room. It there came out that Grant was concentrating all the power of the nation on the Rappahannock, twenty-five thousand Western troops having gone eastward within a week or ten days past. He will have very soon an army of from 150,000 to 200,000 men on hand. This will sweep all before it behind the James and onward. The train came in and I saw General Crook on his way eastward, confirming the report that he had been ordered to report to General Grant. I wish I could get into the Army of the Potomac myself, as I begin to scorn my present position. . . . Met General Stahel who today relieves me of the duties

1. Julius Stahel (1825-1912), a Kossuth revolutionary, came to New York in 1856 and became a journalist. A favorite of Sigel, Stahel was a likable but undistinguished officer. His cavalry charge at New Market was routed.

2. Harry Hunter, the son of Andrew Hunter, was in the Confederate Army. He doubtless intended a personal threat to Strother.

3. John Pendleton Kennedy requested a sketch and essay from Strother for publication in *Autograph Leaves of Our Country's Authors* (1864), an anthology being prepared for the Sanitary Fair at Baltimore. Strother's pieces arrived too late to be included in the book.

of chief of cavalry in this department. He desires to see me at my office that the business may be turned over to him. . . .

Talked politics and philosophy all morning with George. Henry Lee, the elder brother of Robert Lee, led a most disreputable life. Having ruined his wife's sister, spent the fortune of both wife and sister, seeing both these unfortunate ladies buried and himself a social outlaw, he obtained the appointment of consul to Algiers. During the bombardment of that place by the French, several wealthy citizens deposited their treasure with him as American consul. After the city was taken, he carried away the whole of the plunder to France and spent the rest of his life in Paris enjoying his ill-gotten wealth. The only good thing he did was to collect and publish the correspondence of Tom Jefferson, which exhibited him [Jefferson] in the light of a hypocritical and false man and base political intriguer. Light Horse Harry Lee, the father, was a fine soldier and a polished gentleman, a Federalist, and friend of Washington. After the Revolution he became an extensive Jeremy Diddler and lived by borrowing money on false pretenses and selling farms he did not own. He was one of the sufferers from the mob who destroyed the office of the *Federalist* in Baltimore in 1812, having been dreadfully beaten and disfigured. When Jackson was spoken of for the presidency, Lee was sent to drill him in manners, it being feared that the old hero was something of a Yahoo. In those days such things were deemed important, but times have changed. Smith Lee is a naval officer and Carter Lee is living in Richmond, a sort of *bon vivant* and easy buffoon. Neither of them are men of any talent or much repute.

MARCH 31, THURSDAY.—. . . Received an order from General Sigel in his own handwriting as follows:

Colonel. It is my desire that you immediately begin a journal of all military events in this department with the necessary statistical notes and maps and copies of all orders, letters, and telegrams pertaining to this important subject. The details I will communicate to you as soon as you find it convenient to see me.

Very respectfully your obed. ser.
F. Sigel
Major General

I called on the General and he further explained the order, saying he wished it as a confidential record for himself and the Secretary of War. He also wished me to have an office nearer to him, and we went upstairs to see if there was a better room. Yet, he said, you will be hot in the third story. This showed thoughtfulness. . . . Saw handbills that R. Stockett Matthews[4] would address the public this evening. I went up and seeing him on the stage shook hands with him. He recognized me directly. His audience was composed of not very flattering material. I have sometimes thought myself of speaking to the people. A man cannot thoroughly realize his contempt for the masses until he accustoms himself to face the greasy thousands and hear them applaud his twaddle and balderdash. . . .

APRIL 1, FRIDAY.—. . . The General wanted to know the strength of regiments, and I telegraphed and received a satisfactory reply at night. This looks toward activity. At headquarters a man came in desiring to see General Sigel. The General had just left orders to deny him to all except staff officers. His application was therefore denied. He looked knowingly at the secretary. "My name is Burns," said he, "I am a member of the West Virginia legislature. I was the first man that signed a paper to git General Sigel this place. I just wanted to see him, to let him know who I was, the first man that started the move to git rid of that Copperhead, Kelley." The secretary didn't see the importance of the individual and sent him away. When the door was closed, a laugh of derision and contempt followed him. . . .

APRIL 8, FRIDAY.—. . . A Negro regiment was stationed in Winchester to recruit and conscript all the Negroes about there. Returning to Martinsburg they were attacked by bushwhackers and resisted with spirit. At length they met with a scout of the 1st New York Cavalry and, their blood being up, they opened on it. The New Yorkers tried to convince them that they were friends, but being unable to stop the fire they returned it, killing and wounding some of the Negroes. During the fight, all the conscripts obtained at Winchester ran away. In Martinsburg the Negroes then went around searching houses to find Negro men for recruits, taking them by force. Ed Pendleton hid his man and armed himself to resist the search of his house. . . . I hear that Hunter Boyd[5] was very pompous and absurd in his opinions expressed at Aunt Hoge's. She got so excited she rose and left the room. He never talked in that manner before me. These preachers are very valiant before women. . . .

4. Stockett Matthews was a noted religious speaker of the age.
5. Hunter Boyd, a pre-war friend of Strother, was a Martinsburg minister who was an outspoken Southern sympathizer.

APRIL 10, SUNDAY.—Yesterday evening on returning from my walk I heard the salute of fifteen guns fired. Hurrying up the street I was informed that the Vice-President of the United States had arrived. A person of less significance could not have been named. I had forgotten that he existed, as I have not heard his name since the election. . . . Received General Sigel's special order requiring all staff officers to appear every morning at headquarters to receive orders between ten and eleven o'clock.

APRIL 18, MONDAY.—. . . Old Magruder talked to me about General Sigel's order to disarm the border population. He thought it very injudicious and I agreed with him. The execution of the order will disarm the loyal population and will not get a pop gun from the disloyal. . . .

APRIL 19, TUESDAY.—I was called upon by Major [W. Watron] Anderson, now inspector general on Stahel's staff. Anderson was in the Pope Campaign and on one occasion brought a message from the colonel of his regiment to General Pope. He delivered the message. Pope replied, "Tell your colonel that he is a damned coward. Tell him John Pope commanding the Army of Virginia says so. Be off, damn you and deliver my message." Anderson stood astonished and mortified and asked, "Is this General Pope, and am I to deliver that message?" He replied, "Yes, by God, I am General Pope and I order you to report that message. Be off, damn you, immediately. . . ."

APRIL 22, FRIDAY.—I am told that [General E. O. C.] Ord was relieved from command in this department at his own request. He is much broken and sighs for rest, which is the old story. He curses the department as given up to politicians, spies, speculators, and quartermasters. I begin to think that Ben Butler is the only man in public life fit to be President, as he alone has shown nerve enough to punish crime.

The Gettysburgers laugh at the idea of building a monument over "Sweet Jenny Wade," a girl who was accidentally killed in the great battle. She did nothing to entitle her to credit, was nothing particular in character, and was a Copperhead. Never was a people more besotted with fetish worship than the American. They have built monuments over the old greasy thief John Brown, and now this silly mawkish sentimentality over Jenny Wade. Truly it reminds me of my childhood when I used to grow sentimental over corn cobs. . . .

APRIL 30, SATURDAY.—Martinsburg. Had news from headquarters that the messing arrangements made with Major Lyon of Sigel's staff cannot be carried out, and we are recommended to provide ourselves with messing fixtures, etc. This leaves us in the lurch completely, as we have relied on the arrangements to mess together and have neither servants nor fixtures of any kind. No servants can be got. Adam after some difficulty procured me a mulatto boy, Tom, a raw cornfield boy who admits himself uninstructed in all duties and accomplishments except that of stealing chickens. [Captain Thayer] Melvin, [Captain Philip G.] Bier, and myself mounted and started for headquarters at Bunker Hill. Things look gloomy and uncomfortable. Fearing some disaster in this campaign, I left this book of notes with my wife and commenced journalizing in a small book, which has since been lost at Harpers Ferry, I think. I have therefore written up the date April 30th until the date of my next volume [May 16th] from memory.

MAY 1, SUNDAY.—On going out was informed by the sergeant that Bier and myself must give up the horses we had ridden as they were originally intended for General Sigel's private orders and the quartermaster had no right to transfer them. I told the sergeant that I would not give up the horse unless General Sigel's request was conveyed by a commissioned officer. Presently Lyon came and claimed the horses for the General. I yielded with us much grace as possible. Bier was furious and declared he would resign. I told him there was a campaign ahead and we must now go on, if we had to go afoot. I now found myself fairly embarked on the campaign without messing utensils, nothing to eat, and on foot. The prospect was gloomy enough, especially as I found General Sigel was surrounded by a set of low scouts, spies, detectives, and speculators. These fellows were next to him while his staff officers were outside. . . .

About 12 o'clock Sigel started. I accepted an invitation to ride in a carriage with Major Lyon. It cleared off and the day became warm and clear. As we were about starting, a crowd of country people gathered to see Sigel. He remarked them and asked fretfully who they were. On being answered, he threatened to have them all arrested if they did not immediately disperse. On the road to Winchester I recognized the destruction of campaigning armies. The country was a picture of desolation, although its sterner features were relieved by the tender green and the fresh budding of spring. On all sides were seen graves, bones, and dead animals.

Winchester looked gloomy and forbidding. Entering the town with the column I saw only groups of Negroes on the streets, well dressed and grinning. On the portico of the Taylor House I recognized Nan Burns. When I called up to see her, she at first began to reproach me for being in the United States service, but I told her she was a humbug and would be Union herself if only she had independence enough. She afterwards confessed it and said she had taken the oath of allegiance and hoped we would clear out the Rebels forever. She said I was a subject of great vituperation among the Rebel women of Winchester, especially of my kindred and that it required a great deal of moral courage for anyone to speak in my favor. Headquarters was established at the Stone mill about two miles south of Winchester. I slept on a sofa where I found but little comfort and soon discovered it had been previously used by the Rebels, it being lousy. Milroy had fought a battle around this house and near it was the spot where Shields was wounded the evening previous to the battle of Winchester. . . .

MAY 2, MONDAY. Went into Winchester. . . . Called on Aunt Sarah Strange to get her assistance in hiring a cook, but the Negroes were all afraid to go with us, the reverses of the Federal troops having made them timid. The more enterprising among them have gone off long ago. I was unable to find anyone after all my searching. . . . I made several attempts to get a horse from the A.Q.M. at Martinsburg but was not able to do so. Meanwhile I had the satisfaction of seeing my black colt taken possession of by Major Lyon and afterward ridden by [Lt. Col. William L.] Graham, a sort of penitentiary bird attached to Sigel's service. . . . I saw that Mason's house had been utterly destroyed and the grounds laid waste.

Lyon told me that Sigel was a Prussian and had studied at a military school and then at the university and was a professor at one of them. He was engaged in the last revolutionary attempt there and fled the country when it failed. He afterward went to Italy and had some command there. Thence he retired to London and came over here to offer his services at the breaking out of this revolution. Sullivan stated that in some conversation with him, Sigel had alluded to his sojourn in London and spoke of playing the piano in some lager beer saloon. Sigel has the air to me of a military pedagogue, given to technical shams and trifles of military art, but narrow minded and totally wanting in practical capacity. He has a low set about him, and between him and his staff there was no social adoptation and no confidential relations. He has retained us at the suggestion of higher authority or rather of public opinion and the result was disagreeable

to both parties. I thought at one time or, rather, hoped that Sigel
was honest and patriotic, but I have since been led to believe that he
was a mere adventurer and connived at the dishonest practices of his
set. This of itself fully accounted for the suspicious temper and want
of confidence showed toward his staff.

Major General Stahel was a Hungarian exile, a very young man of
mild and polite manners. He was said to be a scion of Hungarian
nobility, which his very unpretending manner indicated. He was
also said to have been teaching a dancing school in New York when
the War broke out. He got his commission when the fury for foreign-
ers was at its height and when the German influence was high in
Washington. Stahel is a very good fancy cavalry officer who has never
done anything in the field and never will do anything. He is entirely
too mild and amiable for any such position. For the rest, he is a sen-
sible man, and honorable and in no way mixed up in politics or speculations.

The day after we entered Winchester some houses on Main Street
were burned by our troops, wherefore I do not know. One day as I
stopped in the street a graceful girl passing dropped her veil on the
crossing. My impulse was to dismount and hand it to her, but I
remembered that three years ago on a similar occasion in this same street
an American officer who handed a lady a dropped veil had been treated
with scorn and insult, she refusing to touch an article which had
been contaminated by the touch of a Yankee. My gallant impulse was
therefore stifled. But a sergeant whose memory did not go back so
far picked up the veil and followed her, respectfully handing it to
her. The attention was most graciously thanked. The feeling against
Yankees is much modified in Winchester since Banks' first entry in
1862.

MAY [includes time up to May 11].—Tents struck and the army
moved southward toward Strasburg. Graves and dead animals in all
stages of decomposition marked the way. We took headquarters at the
house of Isaac Hite on Cedar Creek between Middletown and Strasburg, the same house where Fremont had his headquarters when he
was relieved of command in 1862. The old house of cut limestone is
of baronial size and was built many years ago in the style of the old
Viriginia mansions of the colonies. Hite was one of those who
squatted on Lord Fairfax's manor, and in the garret were found barrels of old papers illuminating the history of the family, neighborhood
and times of Lord Fairfax. There were some autograph papers, re-

ceipts, and business letters of Thomas Jefferson and George Washington, besides many other names famous in their day. As the house was only occupied by a poor family of tenants, our officers helped themselves to these literary mementos. The ample oak floors of the dwelling afforded us bedroom and office room, while a semicircle of tents was pitched in the front lawn under an immense lilac hedge in full bloom. A most beautiful and fragrant shade. Here we remained for several days. . . .

MAY 11 [includes also the time up to May 15].—We moved on Woodstock, I riding a small sorrel pony lent me by Captain [Richard G.] Prendergast. The rains have been almost continuous since we came out from Martinsburg and all side roads were very muddy and the streams swollen. . . . Colonel [William H.] Boyd with a battalion on a scout about this time, moving up the Luray Valley, entered Luray and crossed the ridge to the New Market turnpike. There he fell upon the whole Confederate force under Imboden and was cut to pieces. He lost about 100 men and nearly all their horses. Boyd escaped with about 150 men, most of them on foot, having been forced to abandon their horses and take to the mountains.[6] Sigel it seems wished to take possession of New Market to secure the roads leading over the mountains east and west of that place. This was the reason he gave me for pushing so far forward. At the same time this did not excuse him for sending detachments of his force so far from the main body as to be destroyed in detail and to court destruction as in the case of Moor's brigade which was at this time twenty miles in advance of the main army.[7]

MAY 15, SUNDAY [Woodstock].—Rose early and tents were struck. While the troops were moving and everyone about packing up, General Sigel came out of the house at a full run towards the camp of teamsters and Negro servants. His high boots were hanging down and altogether he cut a very absurd figure as he ran, exclaiming at every jump, "By Got, I vill catch dot dam tief." It seems that in moving he had lost a favorite brandy flask and was accusing everyone he met of stealing it. Our hostess Madame Cheney appearing at the

6. This reconnoissance by Boyd with three hundred cavalry was complemented by another by Colonel Jacob Higgins with five hundred in the direction of Wardensville. Both forces were severely routed.

7. Colonel Augustus Moor had been sent forward on May 13 with three regiments of infantry and nine hundred cavalry. On the following day he made contact with Breckinridge at New Market. Although the rest of Sigel's force was scattered along the turnpike as far back as Woodstock, Sigel attempted to push his army to New Market on the morning of May 15.

time was flatly accused of stealing it. She was horrified and indignant. She got Captain [Thomas G.] Putnam aside in a room
and, after stating her wrongs, lifted her hands to heaven exclaiming,
"May the vengeance of the Almighty follow that man. He has
wounded my feelings too deeply for healing or apology."

We at length got off in the mud and rain as gruff and uncomfortable as we could well be. In the village of Edinburg we found the
shops and houses full of unarmed stragglers from Boyd's command.
The sound of cannon in front was heard at intervals growing more
distinct as we advanced, showing that the enemy had made a stand
somewhere and was no longer retiring. With alternate rain and sunshine we rode on to Mount Jackson where the staff halted for some
time. A Negro here told us that Breckinridge was up at New Market
with four thousand men to reinforce Imboden. This was doubtful or,
if true, the aggregate of the force did not equal ours which was seven
or eight thousand or perhaps counting the cavalry nine thousand in
all. Major [Theodore F.] Lang once lay sick in this place and was
kindly nursed by a woman and her daughters. As we tarried he called
to see them and was cheerfully met and asked to stay and eat a meal.
He replied he had not time then. The girl laughingly said, "You
can call then as you come back and take supper, if you have the time
to stop, which I doubt."

The cannonading beginning to grow more lively, we started forward again, crossing the Shenandoah by the bridge, which was in
good condition. I felt uneasy when I observed this, as the river was
raging and the enemy might have very easily stopped our advance by
burning the bridge if such had been their policy. Having a well-built
bridge for us to cross looked as if they were ready for us and confident. After we crossed and occupied Rude's Hill, the General halted
again on the top of the hill from whence we could see the cannon
firing between Moor and the enemy. I had given General Sigel a
drink of my sherry by the way for which he gave me some lunch of
bread and meat. This was the last drink I got of my wine that day,
as the cook came out and I lost the whole of it.

My sorrel pony went heavily, having traveled fifty miles the day
before on a scout. Pushing forward from this point we presently
reached Colonel Moor's position on a hill at the right of Dr. Rice's
house at the northern extremity of New Market. Stahel was on the
right with a portion of his cavalry, while a battery on the hill was
exchanging shots with the enemy's artillery posted on an opposing hill

at the other end of town. Having communicated with Moor, Sigel left his staff near Rice's house and rode forward to reconnoiter. While he was absent, a number of shells whistled over our heads. This was about midday.

Meanwhile our cavalry skirmishers stretched along to the village were briskly occupied and the whole Rebel artillery opened up, showing a dozen or sixteen pieces. Sending messengers back along the route Sigel gave the order to fall back to the second position. This was about half a mile in rear of the first and to my judgment not so good a position as the first for defense. His object in falling back, however, may have been to meet the forces which were slow in coming up. At this point about twenty guns were placed in position. Two batteries on our extreme right on an eminence. Von Kleiser's battery of brass ten pounders on the center too far advanced I think for the support of the main line.[8] The infantry which had got up, six regiments about three thousand men in all, were drawn up in two lines, one hundred yards apart, supporting these batteries. The line of battle thus formed reached from the heights to the turnpike road. On the left of the turnpike Stahel's Cavalry, about three thousand strong, was posted with a section of Ewing's horse battery.

Sigel seemed in a state of excitement and rode here and there with Stahel and Moor, all jabbering in German. In his excitement he seemed to forget his English entirely, and the purely American portion of his staff were totally useless to him. I followed him up and down until I got tired, and, finding a group of his staff officers together near a battery, I stopped and got a drink of whiskey and a cracker which an artillery man gave me. These officers said the General had ordered them to remain there, but seeing him riding rapidly to the artillery position on our right, we started to join him. Just then the enemy appeared, advancing in two lines of battle extending unbroken along our whole front, while along the front of the cavalry a line of skirmishers was seen pushing forward. Our artillery immediately opened, all the guns firing with great rapidity. The enemy's artillery played chiefly on our cavalry which after making a few futile movements was totally withdrawn to the rear. The Rebel infantry continued to move in advance; in spite of our furious artillery fire their lines were steady and clean, no officers either mounted or on foot appearing among them. When within three hundred yards they began to yell

8. The cadets of the Virginia Military Institute proved Strother's fears were valid ones when they attacked Captain Albert Von Kleiser's battery and captured one of the guns.

as usual, and the musketry from both lines opened with great fury. Our men began to break immediately, running to the rear by ones, twos, and finally by streams.

Seeing this demoralization beginning, I drew my sword and attempted to rally the fugitives. The example was followed by many other officers of the staff. Lieutenant Meigs was especially excited, and I saw him cut down a straggler with his sabre. Our position was becoming very hot. Our lines were falling back and were rapidly disintegrating and becoming a rout. As they retired, the Rebel yells approached rapidly and their fire both of musketry and artillery now concentrated on the crumbling lines. The staff officers gradually retreated, exposed to a hail of balls and shells. As I was about to sabre a fugitive, he fell struck by a ball in the side and cried to his comrades to carry him away. Colonel Starr's horse received a severe wound from a shell which he died of that night. While we stood together trying to form a line of the rallied men, a cannon shot ploughed the ground just at our horses' feet, not twelve inches from their hoofs. A moment later a spent musket ball struck me plump in the breast and bounded off without hurting me. Seeing that our attempts to rally the infantry were futile and that the artillery were retiring as fast as possible, I also retired, hoping to be able to rally the men on Rude's Hill when we could get out of range of the Rebel fire.

I rode back and presently overtook Sullivan riding alone toward the rear. When we neared the turnpike which was crowded with artillery, ambulances, and fugitive troops, I asked Sullivan if there were no reserves. He replied, "None whatever." I then told him it would be judicious to post the batteries on the hill before us where they could cover the retreat and afford a cover to rally the troops. He told me to give the order, but I replied his rank would have more weight with the officers, and he accordingly posted the guns.[9] Arriving on this hill I found Sigel and Stahel already there and two solid regiments of infantry with some cavalry already posted behind the crest to sustain the batteries. As the enemy advanced, a very rapid cannonade was opened on them. They replied with all their power and we stood for half an hour, our batteries exposed to the return fire. Sigel, as the shells flew over and burst, snapped his fingers at them and whistled an imitation of them, thus to show his contempt of the danger. One of

9. This was probably the battery of Captain H. A. DuPont, which slowed down the Confederate advance and allowed the Union forces to retreat from the field.

these shells flew over and burst between two cavalry men and killed both men and horses.

After checking the enemy decidedly at this point, we fell back half a mile nearer to the brow of Rude's Hill and, leaving the fresh regiments to support a battery, we retired to Mount Jackson, arriving there about four o'clock. Here a line of battle was posted behind the river should the enemy attempt to advance. By six in the afternoon all our troops were withdrawn from the south side of the river and the enemy appeared in small force on Rude's Hill, delivering some shots from their batteries which fell short generally but one of which struck the bridge. I was wet and fatigued to extremity, and a cheerless supper at the house of Major Lang's landlady did not much toward restoring me.

About dark a movement was made northward, the trains and ambulances retiring toward Strasburg. I looked in vain for my pony and could not find him. In the rain and mud and I was desperate at losing my only means of locomotion and also at losing a horse that I had borrowed. Just as I was starting I found Prendergast's sergeant who had taken the pony to feed him, and he restored the animal to me somewhat improved. I mounted and overtook the staff. The night was alternate rain and moonlight. A few miles from Mount Jackson the main road runs along the bank of the Shenandoah. The enemy by coming down on the opposite side might have prevented our using the road without their having to cross the river. Trains and stragglers poured along it, however, without interruption. At Edinburg I lost the General entirely. . . . Concluded to ride to Woodstock and as there were no troops near us we were not free from apprehension of Rebel cavalry. At Narrow Passage we overtook the wagons again which at least afforded us company. My horse was so nearly exhausted that I looked for the animal to fall down with me at any moment. Sympathy with him increased my fatigue, which was extreme. Arrived at length at Woodstock and aroused the landlord of the hotel there. He had neither beds nor food nor drink nor provender for our horses. Yet there was stable room and house room. So tied our horses to the empty mangers and then returned to the house. Our host turned us into a parlor and brought us half a dozen quilts and blankets. I had already sunk upon a sofa, booted, belted, and spurred, stiff with mud and soaked with rain. The landlord covered me over and I slept profoundly.

MAY 16, MONDAY.—I awoke refreshed. Cannon, wagons, and

stragglers were still training through the town. I got a wretched meal in the house. In the barroom on one side I found a long pine box containing the body of a dead soldier, stiff in his bloody garments. On another cot lay a soldier with the death rattle in his throat. On a third lay one mortally wounded in the bowels awaiting a slower death. A fourth had just been carried out and buried. These were the victims of bushwhackers at Fisher's Hill a few days before. The General and staff stayed at Edinburg. . . . Sigel got news that Averell and Crook had been successful in their raid upon the Tennessee Railroad, having beaten the enemy with a loss of nine hundred wounded to him, wounded, killed, and missing.[10] To one who told me of this news I replied, "We are doing a good business in this department. Averell is tearing up the Virginia and Tennessee Railroad while Sigel is tearing down the Valley turnpike." This took and spread like wildfire and was repeated all over the department.[11] At Cheney's house Mrs. Cheney called to Starr and inquired about the news. When she heard of Sigel's defeat she thanked God fervently, declaring that her prayers were always answered and that she never cursed anyone in life who did not presently come to grief. . . .

The campaign was conducted miserably by Sigel. In the first place he sent a brigade under Moor with some cavalry some twenty miles ahead of his main body, so far as to be entirely out of supporting distance. When he went forward at length to support this force he joined battle with his troops strung out along the road for fourteen miles. He chose a weak position to receive Breckinridge's attack when he might have fallen back to Rude's Hill, which he could have held with artillery alone until his troops were all up and rested. During the battle he was talking German and fiddling with the artillery instead of looking to the general position of the army, and the infantry is after all the decisive arm. I came to the conclusion that Sigel is merely a book soldier acquainted with the techniques of the art of war but having no capacity to fight with troops in the field. For the rest he is given to detail and littleness and without comprehensiveness and is entirely below the commission which he bears. I had hoped when he first came into the department that he was at least honest and enthusiastic for an idea, but I think now he was an

10. On May 8 Crook's force had defeated those of Jenkins and Jones at Cloyd's Mountain. Although Averell had been turned back from Saltville, he destroyed part of the Virginia and Tennessee Railroad near Christianburg.

11. Strother's remark was, as he says, widely circulated; moreover, it was published in Charles Halpine's *Baked Meats of the Funeral* (1866) with further elaboration.

adventurer and speculator, venal and intriguing. We can afford to lose such a battle as New Market to get rid of such a mistake as Major General Sigel.[12]

MAY 17, TUESDAY.—Headquarters at Hite's stone house near Middletown. There are rumors that Grant has fallen back to Acquia Creek. I wonder that officers would repeat such things invented by desperate Rebels or Baltimore [patriots]. Some of the guns we lost at New Market are said to have been taken by three hundred cadets from the Lexington institute. The commanders of the batteries tell me their guns were lost by the killing of the horses by sharpshooters to prevent getting them off. No guns were taken by assault or a charge. Sigel says we had fifty-five hundred men in the action. . . .

MAY 18, WEDNESDAY.—We had a fine serenade from the band of the 34th Massachusetts. Massachusetts is certainly the most civilized state in the world. . . . Lieutenant [Josiah H. V.] Field arrived today as chief of ordnance. He is just from West Point and raw in the field. He is a tall, lank, hatchet-faced youth, amiable, boyish, and green. News that J. E. B. Stuart is dead, killed in a cavalry skirmish near Richmond. . . .

MAY 19, THURSDAY.—. . . A soldier arrived today from Martinsburg with a grand budget of news from the army and also brings the report that General Kelley was under arrest for disloyalty. He desires a position as scout, and gives this as a specimen of his capacity for lying. . . .

MAY 21, SATURDAY.—The papers are filled with critical sneers on Sigel's management. Captain Putnam seemed annoyed with the criticisms of the General and spoke to me about writing something to support him. I felt little inclined to do so but was thinking all day about asking leave to retire to Martinsburg, as I was still without a horse and as it appeared to me I was playing a very insignificant part, following in the train of this feeble and corrupt adventure. I had made up my mind to ask leave and on mentioning the matter to [Major T. A.] Meysenburg he said it would have been accorded with great pleasure. In fact I think Sigel would have been glad to get rid of me at that time, as he had heard the anecdote about "tearing down the turnpike." I was thoroughly disgusted with my present position and yearning for the quiet and peaceful companionship of my family.

It was near sunset when as I was standing on the front portico of

12. Strother's evaluation of Sigel compares with Halleck's remark to Grant on May 17: "He is already in full retreat on Strasburg. If you expect anything from him you will be mistaken. He will do nothing but run. He never did anything else."

the Hite House we saw a cavalcade approaching from the direction of Middletown. As the horsemen drew nearer I perceived that it was something uncommon. The escort turned into a wood while half a dozen distinguished-looking cavaliers came on toward the house. The first idea that presented itself was that it was a committee of Congress. At the front gate they dismounted, and I saw the triple buttons of a major general among them. "What does this mean?" asked Putnam with a look of blank dismay. "It means that our Captain is relieved," said I (with a very different feeling from the Captain's). By this time I had recognized my kinsman, Major General David Hunter, and walked down the steps to meet him. He received me cordially and immediately took me aside and we walked arm in arm to a secluded spot where he said, "I have come to relieve General Sigel. You know it is customary with a general who has been unfortunate to relieve him whether he has committed a fault or not." He then asked me to remain with him and to talk to him like a man and kinsman and give him my views freely. In a few words I described the campaign from which we had just returned and, in giving my views of the situation, advised an immediate move up the Valley to Staunton, there to meet Crook and Averell, and with the combined force to occupy Charlottesville. We then scarcely thought of venturing so far as Lynchburg, although I proposed it as one of the

LIVING ON THE COUNTRY

possibilities. The General immediately telegraphed Crook to advance without delay on Staunton and to ensure the message, asked me to procure two trusty scouts who would ride through the country with the message. This I arranged with Captain [John] McEntee. Hunter's assistant adjutant general, Major Charles G. Halpine, and his nephew and aide-de-camp, Major Samuel Stockton, were next introduced. Halpine was the original "Miles O'Reilley," an Irishman, a clever writer and humorist. Stockton was a son of Mary Hunter of Princeton, a cousin of my mother who once visited us and was called Jersey Mary. We are to advance without baggage and to cut loose entirely from our base of operations and live on the country. The value of a secondary movement up this Valley seems at length to be recognized at headquarters. This doubtless comes from Grant. I have always thought it most important.

MAY 22, SUNDAY.—Called on General Sigel and gave him my journal completed to date of yesterday with a full description of the battle. The tears were standing in his eyes and his lips were quivering. He said it were better to have died on that battlefield than to have suffered this disgrace. I felt touched by his appearance. He is a stranger who has come over here to fight for a sentiment and he seems utterly cast down by his failure. . . . After dinner selected a poor roan horse from the quartermaster's, the best I could find. I got an old captured saddle from Colonel Starr and am at length in a way to have a riding outfit. The order cutting down our baggage to a minimum is issued. We take with us only coffee, sugar, salt, and hard bread for some days, depending upon the country for everything else. Our army will start for Staunton tomorrow perhaps. The prospect of hardship and suffering is not attractive to me, with the wearing of my physical strength my zeal and hopefulness have also declined. The plan proposed to be carried out is a bold and almost desperate one, especially as its success must be based on the certainty that Breckinridge has retired from the Valley. In the late campaign we lost a thousand men and have been reinforced only by Colonel [Robert S.] Rodgers' Eastern Shore regiment and the 160th Ohio, one-hundred-day men and I fear very green and unreliable troops. Lieutenant Meigs is decidedly averse to the advance, although he is usually so zealous. If our spirits are affected by the recent defeat, how much more must the men be demoralized? General Hunter discoursed on the inefficiency of the cavalry commander and is determined to be rid of him. He offered me the command of a brigade of cavalry which I declined on the ground that I was not sufficiently prepared to accept it immediately. The risk to the public service and to my own reputation is more than I care to assume under present circumstances. . . .

MAY 23, MONDAY.—There is a general sending off of superfluous baggage. Sigel is quite sick with overexcitement and mortification. He is of fragile body and excitable temperament. An enthusiast and bookman, not a practical soldier. Captain [H. A.] DuPont is to be chief of artillery. . . . I mentioned to General Hunter the idea that Breckinridge has been reinforced. He said he had got a telegram from Halleck saying that we would be well employed if we could hold these troops to watch us. It looks therefore as if we could do no more than demonstrations. We cannot go safely beyond Mt. Jackson. . . . The train to Martinsburg at length started. Sigel, Meysenburg, and Putnam with some scouts and orderlies also left. The General seems entirely brokenhearted and refused to be comforted. I spoke to him kindly about the journal and he only groaned in reply. . . . General Hunter is charmed with the aspect of the country. I had a long talk with Halpine. He has been deeply engaged in the newspaper literature of New York, having written for the *Herald, Tribune, Times,* and others. Captain McEntee is of the secret service of Grant's army, having been attached here for the purpose of furthering the acquisition of complete information respecting the enemy's forces. He represents Lee's army as not over seventy thousand strong and has a list of all the regiments and organizations. . . .

XII

The Hunter Raid

May 24, 1864—June 30, 1864

Not only is Strother's account of the Hunter Raid the most interesting portion of his military journals but also it is the most valuable, since it treats a campaign of the Civil War that has too often been overlooked by military historians, whose interests lie primarily with the campaigns east of the Blue Ridge. The objectives of Hunter were nearly the same as those of Sigel—to march up the Valley to a position where he could threaten Charlottesville and Lynchburg, to effect a junction with the armies of Crook and Averell, and to compel Lee to detach a force from his depleted army in front of Richmond. But where Sigel had failed, Hunter succeeded. The flag of the United States flew in the streets of Staunton for the first time in three years, a Union army won a decisive victory over the Confederates in the Valley, and Lexington was taken.

Crossing the Blue Ridge, Hunter reached the outskirts of Lynchburg before being turned back by Jubal Early, who had been sent by Lee to defend that railroad center. While Hunter retreated across the Alleghenies to his supply depot at Charleston, Early began the northward march that would take him to the outer fortifications of Washington and that would cause the third panic in the North in as many years. Meanwhile Hunter prepared to move his army by boat and by train to Harpers Ferry to engage Early again.

As chief of staff for General Hunter, Strother held the position of highest authority he ever attained in the Civil War. Unfortunately he was often unjustly blamed for the singular destruction that followed the movement of the Federal army. While he was an active maker of policy and strategy during the campaign, he was nowhere responsible for depredations to civilians or their property. He held firmly to his conviction that all military installations and appurtenances must be destroyed—including the Virginia Military Institute—but he inter-

*vened countless times to spare the property of the innocent. By a
curious turn of fate, Strother was the man most responsible for the
burning of the Virginia Military Institute, yet in 1865 as adjutant
general of Virginia he was the one most active in pressing for its
restoration.*

MAY 24, TUESDAY.—. . . Crook and Averell are in fine condition
and are advancing with sixteen thousand men as directed. Averell
was wounded in the late action near New River, hit by a spent
ball or buckshot in the forehead, inflicting a slight bruise. Drank hock
and dined with General Hunter. A wagon train guard was fired on at
Newtown and a sergeant wounded. The houses of three Secessionists
were burned there by order today. . . . I am published today as chief
of staff. The General has news from Halleck that Breckinridge has
joined Lee. An order is issued threatening destruction of property
and reprisals for the attacks of guerillas and bushwhackers. In case
a train or a man is fired on by anyone behind our lines, houses of
Secessionists and their property are to be burned without mercy. . . .

MAY 25, WEDNESDAY.—General Hunter is requested by the President
to retain the Dutch in some position if possible. General Sigel is
therefore assigned to command the railroad reserves including Kelley at
Cumberland and Max Weber at Harpers Ferry. . . .

A committee of citizens from Newtown sent in a communication
desiring an interview with General Hunter. The General asked me to
ride and meet them at the outer picket. Below Middletown I found
four men composing the committee. They informed me that among the
houses burnt by Major [Timothy] Quinn was one of the Reverend
J. Wolff, the parson. He is a sentimental Secessionist but otherwise a
worthy, upright man. It was in front of his house and from his yard
that the guerillas fired upon our guard. The next was a house belonging to one White, a rich Secessionist residing in Lexington. This
house was occupied by a tenant who was esteemed loyal and had taken
the oath. The third was the house of one Harman, a bushwhacker,
and the house was used as a rendezvous for guerillas. I gave to each
of these men a copy of General Hunter's order and told them that
vengeance would surely fall upon the country if these robberies and
murders continued and that the only way to protect themselves and
their innocent neighbors was to indicate to us the guilty persons. This
they promised to do, and commenced by informing me that Captain
Glenn was at the head of one of these parties which was chiefly composed of young men from Maryland. A Captain Sheerer of Winchester

was also of notoriety among them. They also reported the house of a Mrs. Wilson in Newtown as being a rendezvous for the guerillas. . . .

I also spoke to some citizens of Middletown as I gave them copies of the "retaliation order." They replied sensibly and promised to give all the information in their power. On my return to General Hunter he forthwith ordered the arrest of Mrs. Wilson, intending to deport her South. The Widow Wilson was brought in a prisoner, charged with feeding and harboring guerillas. Finding that she lived in a hired house, the officer arresting her commenced carrying her traps and furniture into the street. Thinking that the house was to be burnt, she and her daughters assisted in the removal with great alacrity, thanking the officer for his consideration. Her astonishment and grief was great when the heap of furniture instead of the house was set fire to and consumed. The woman herself was then arrested and trudged six miles to Starr's guard tent. Rough are the wages of war.

Another woman was brought in having been arrested trying to pass the pickets outward. When she found she would be detained for a day or two, she broke into loud lamentations, wringing her hands and tearing her hair. She had left a baby at home six weeks old and it would certainly perish with hunger as there was no one on the place. Starr felt her breasts, which were entirely flat and showed no signs of milking. He told her that from all appearances she would be of little use to the baby and so she must be content to stay. She abused Starr and then laughed, and when I saw her she was sitting quietly under a tree smoking a short clay pipe and chatting in a friendly manner with the guard. . . .

MAY 26, THURSDAY.—Started about 8:30 the road muddy and the world gloomy. Beyond Cedar Creek met a guard with two refugees and was directed by the General to examine them. They were conscripts who had been detailed to work at the iron furnaces in the Fort Valley and, hearing they were to be ordered to join the Rebel army, were fleeing to Pennsylvania. . . . At the four-mile house beyond Strasburg the army halted to rest. Looking back we saw a volume of black smoke rising from the house of Boyden, a farmer. This house was burnt by Colonel [George D.] Wells because it was said to be a rendezvous for bushwhackers and hard by at Fisher's Hill five men of ours were lately murdered. Two and a half miles north of Woodstock we selected a camp ground on the banks of Pugle's Run. When Major Lang rode up to Cheney's house, the Madame asked if that wretched Dutchman was with us yet. On being informed, she thanked God fervently and said again that she had never prayed for vengeance against anyone that her prayer had not been granted. . . .

MAY 27, FRIDAY.—I have received congratulations from all quarters on my appointment as chief of staff by general, field, and subaltern officers. There seems to be a general sense of relief at the change of commanders. The General asked me to go into Woodstock to ascertain who the parties were that attempted to confuse our scouts yesterday as he wished to burn a few houses. Stopped at Sullivan's quarters and had some music on the piano. Advised Sullivan to conduct himself as to secure the blessing of Mrs. Cheney, as her prayers seemed to be efficacious. In Woodstock stopped to talk with a man who was sitting before his door with his wife and two daughters. The girls were dressed in flaming red and were evidently parading to attract attention from officers and soldiers. The man's name was Chipley. He was a fiery Secessionist and took occasion to express his high scorn of Yankees and especially of renegade Virginians. I told the girls they both would marry Yankees, the first good-looking fellow who asked them. They were not near so much horrified as I expected, although they got up some scornful airs. Yet they blushed, giggled, and finally simperingly acknowledged that if we drove the Rebels out of the Valley they would make us a Union flag. The old man then took me aside and told me he had a son in the Rebel army and bespoke kind treatment for him if perchance he should fall into our hands. I promised sincerely to look to the matter, should I see or hear of him. . . .

The whole town was squalling with women, children, chickens, and geese. The feathers were flying like a cloud. The whole place seemed in such an excitement about chickens that I conclude they must have had easy times heretofore. As I rode down street I saw Meigs and Fields, two greenhorns, talking with two sharp girls at a window. They were evidently of a better style than the Chipleys and got the better of the officers in the way of wit. They twitted them politely about New Market and said that General Hunter's burning order was uncivilized and unmilitary, as the attacking of trains and cutting off of escorts were legitimate acts of war. Finding that the lieutenants were getting behind in the argument, I rode off.

I also determined to have no more social intercourse with the people of the country as it interferes with my military duties too much and brought me continually in view of outrage and distresses which awaken my sympathies but which I could not prevent. On the route to headquarters met a cavalryman who gave me a letter from my old schoolmate, Reverend John Wolff of Newtown, asking me to meet him at the pickets. It was written simply and no doubt truthfully and I am sorry I did not see him before the Army moved, but I could not have helped him in any case.

Met Dr. [Thomas B.] Reed, medical director, just from Martinsburg who brings me congratulations from all the staff there on my promotion. It is flattering to perceive that my luck has given such general satisfaction. Captain [George M.] Ellicott was sent out to burn the house of a bushwhacker but came back and reported that he had found there a woman with three little children and they had nowhere to go, so his heart failed him and he came away without executing the order. The General reprimanded him, and in reply he said the house was such a mean affair and had so little in it that it was not worth burning. The General laughed and excused him. . . . Old Painter, our host, came to see me about his horse which the cavalry had taken. He said she was over twenty years old, blind, spavined, split-hoofed, and threatened with the botts and could not possibly be of any use to us and might communicate disease to our stock. He finally got her back and she seemed to be quite a respectable, sleek, well-made animal. As the old man led her back, he greeted me with the first smile I had seen on his face since we arrived. . . .

MAY 28, SATURDAY.—An officer came back from the front with news from Moor of Mt. Jackson that Imboden has fallen back six miles beyond New Market and is pressing transportation and supplies for a move. I repeated this to the General, who told me he had received orders from Halleck to destroy the railroad at Charlottesville, cutting the communication with Lynchburg. . . . Meigs went out scouting and burned the house of a man who had assisted in killing and capturing stragglers during Sigel's retreat. Certain women are said to have armed themselves and to have assisted in the capture. . . .

MAY 29, SUNDAY.—Rose at four and started on the march at sunrise. Passing through the town of Woodstock, the General halted and had the jail searched but found no one in it. He was evidently seeking an apology to burn something and proposed to set fire to the Hollingsworth Hotel, but I told him that our wounded had lain there and had been well cared for while the place was occupied by the enemy. At Narrow Passage Creek found the bridge had been destroyed by our own troops on the retreat. The chasm through which the stream passed was deep and difficult so that the bridge had to be rebuilt before the wagons could get over. . . .

We rode through Mt. Jackson without stopping, it being reported that the enemy had appeared on Rude's Hill. On reaching the foot of it, the General sent me to Rude's House to see if it would answer for headquarters. The enemy has doubtless fallen back to Harrisonburg. . . . The General with some mystery invited me to go up into his room where he opened a pint bottle of champagne, the greater part of it I drank and in my exhausted state found it delicious. . . . A late *Rockingham Register* of the 27th instant informs us from Staunton that there has been no communication with Richmond for five days. General Hunter expects co-operation from Sheridan in that direction, and he has doubtless got possession of the Virginia Central Railroad.

MAY 30, MONDAY.—. . . Rode toward New Market, passing over the late battlefield. I found difficulty in recognizing the ground, but on going forward to the first position held by our troops I easily traced the movement of our troops and the different points of the action. The dead horses I observed had been carefully skinned and their shoes taken off. Our dead soldiers had been hastily buried and parts of their bodies were exposed. A working party was engaged in reburying them and reported not more than sixty bodies. In the church yard at New Market we found thirty-three labeled graves and eight not labeled, all of the Rebel dead. Among them were four of the Lexington cadets. . . .

Ellicott having been out on a scout toward North Mountain came in reporting that he had lost two men captured. In return he had gobbled up some two dozen tanned fox skins, of which he presented me with one. Not long after, the captured men came in bringing with them six prisoners, some horses, and several old flintlock hunting pieces. One of the prisoners had a furlough in his pocket from a Rebel officer. He had tried to get into our lines to recover some lost horses. The General wanted to hang him. Stockton was much troubled at this and engaged me to use my influence in saving him. I was sent out to examine the prisoners. They were all of the Home Guard, late conscripts over forty-five years of age, poor devils who had been raked up under the late conscription act of the Rebel Congress, and had been sent home to assist in conscripting their neighbors. They had returned home as ordered and were taking it easy, ploughing, attending to their farms, or sitting about with their families. I recommended they should be paroled and prepared a rough oath for them to take. This was approved by the General, who ordered it to be administered to them. The men were to be set at liberty. . . .

MAY 31, TUESDAY.—. . . In the kitchen of Rude's House lived a woman of the mountain breed with a large family and one or more married daughters. Last night two of these women had babies. The General had rebuked Provost Marshal Starr for permitting Rebels to come within our lines, and he was sore on the subject. Seeing Starr drinking punch in the tent, I approached him with an alarmed look. "Colonel," I said, "two Rebel citizens came into camp last night without papers and are now about headquarters kicking up a row." The Colonel, alarmed and indignant, called hastily to the guard to arrest them. He wanted to know who had seen them. I referred him to Dr. [R. S.] Hayes and the joke came out.

At midday it was intensely hot and everybody slept. We are not to move until we hear from Crook. A regiment under Major [Joseph K.] Stearns has been sent to burn Newtown in revenge for the loss of our train there. It seems this train was taken in the streets of the town by Harry Gilmor. A captain of the guard was killed and some prisoners taken, and by wine, drunk, no doubt.

JUNE 1, WEDNESDAY.—La Rouchefoucauld says the way men bring themselves to face danger is by turning their thoughts aside from it and occupying their thoughts with something else. I yesterday overheard a freckled-faced boy discoursing with a comrade in this wise, "Some men when they go in think they are going to be killed. That's not a good way. I try not to think about it at all." It seemed singular to me to hear the maxim of a philosopher, scholar, and wit repeated so exactly by a raw boy who never thought much and perhaps never read anything. Thus it is that the wisdom of the sage renowned in history goes no further and teaches no more than the practical experience of the people. . . . We move tomorrow. Fired and reloaded my pistol.

JUNE 2, THURSDAY.—My fine bay horse disappeared this morning, stolen probably. . . . The ground along the road from New Market to Spartapolis lies just as it does at New Market, a series of similar military positions. We were stopped near Big Spring by a Rebel picket which skirmished with our cavalry. While halted here to reconnoiter, news came that our rear was attacked. This produced some excitement and tremor, more than was agreeable to see. The attack was nothing more than a bushwhacking of a wagon guard which had tarried behind for forage. Nobody was hurt. We stopped in sight of Harrisonburg on the hills north of town. Our advanced cavalry skirmished sharply with the enemy, driving him out of the town. . . .

After locating the troops we took the house of a Mr. Grey for headquarters, a fine brick house on a hill above the town and where taste and comfort were visible at every turn. In his library I found John P. Kennedy's *Swallow Barn* with my illustrations and also *Harper's Magazine* with the "Porte Crayon" series. The office of the *Rockingham Register* was gutted, the press broken up, and the débris burned in the street, the rain falling on the heap of ashes. . . .

JUNE 3, FRIDAY.—. . . The enemy is reported to be at Mt. Crawford in a strong position with the River in front. They are fortifying and intend to fight us there, and their force including Bradley Johnson's command and militia is about twenty-five hundred. The sound of distant cannon has been heard by several persons, some report from the direction of Buffalo Gap and others say from the gunboats below Richmond. This is an immense distance to hear guns, but they are one- and two-hundred-pounders and the citizens say they are frequently heard here. . . .

I advised the General to move by way of Port Republic, cross the river there, and take Waynesboro with his cavalry, thereby cutting off stores and railroad stock at Staunton. He would also cut off the enemy that way, which would demoralize him greatly. This he determined to do, moving in the morning. . . . The requisition on the town for meat and flour has created great consternation and disgust. It seems hard but it is necessary as the army must feed. The soldiers in addition are plundering dreadfully from all accounts. This is not necessary and should not be permitted, especially as there are some wounded Union soldiers here who have been well treated by the citizens.

Major Stearns who was sent back to burn Newtown got in today. The people he said were in no wise guilty and had made a general submission to the Government, taking the oath of allegiance. He therefore had used his discretion and not burned the place. The General was angry and ordered him to make a written report. I complimented Stearns and told him the chief's anger would blow over. I took an opportunity to speak on the subject and satisfied the General that Stearns was right. After nightfall a number of rockets were sent up from the top of the house to warn Crook of our position. There was no response that we could see.

JUNE 4, SATURDAY.—Rose early and left Harrisonburg by the Port Republic road. Passed the spot where Ashby fell and the Cross Keys battleground. At the urgent request of Meigs and myself a regiment of cavalry was sent to demonstrate against Mt. Crawford, Meigs conducting the troops himself. Our advance drove off a picket of the enemy who escaped toward Mt. Crawford. The enemy evidently did not expect us to move by this route and so far have had no information of our line of march. This picket will carry the news by the time we have crossed the river. . . . At the river in front of Port Republic we stopped and getting up the pontoon train started to throw the bridge. It was awkwardly done and so slow that it was evident that we would lose all the benefit of our early march. There seemed to be no one of the engineers who understood how to put up the canvas pontoons, and Meigs was absent with the cavalry demonstration. In an orchard under an apple tree I found General Stahel who gave me a Rebel newspaper to read. There was in it a letter from a Sanitary Commission agent thanking persons for contributions. It was ludicrous and yet painful to read, as indicating the dreadful poverty of the country. The articles detailed were—a bundle of rags from J——B——, three eggs from Mrs. A——M——, four chickens from X——, a dozen red peppers and two onions from Q——E——, etc., a long list.

Thirteen wagons carrying forage to the enemy were captured at Port Republic by our cavalry and scouts. Ellicott says they should have captured a hundred, but the cavalry was cowardly. While we were talking, a cavalry trumpeter attempted to cross the river and was washed from his horse and drowned. Half a dozen men stripped and went in to save him, but were not able to do this or to find his body. At the same time the woolen factory on the opposite side was in flames. We were not able to cross the pontoon bridge until six P.M. The troops were bivouacked in line of battle a mile south of the town. The hill in which Weyer's Cave is found was in full view two miles distant. By the delay in crossing the river and this untimely halt we lost the opportunity of making a dash to Waynesboro.

JUNE 5, SUNDAY.—I was awaked this morning by General Hunter himself. We felt certain that this would be a day of battle, and after advancing a few miles the cavalry began skirmishing and the first New York battalion led by Major Stearns made a fine charge, driving the enemy pell mell and capturing over seventy prisoners. Among our prisoners was Captain Imboden, brother of the general, and a Captain Phillips from the James River near Brandon. I was ordered to examine these men and got from the first batch but little of importance. Captain Imboden was a handsome fellow, gay and excited from the recent "Echaufferie." I gave him a drink from my bottle and went to the front again. . . .

The whole army was drawn up in order of battle. Behind us a large mill at Mt. Meridian was ascending in volumed flame. The 13th Connecticut which disgraced itself at New Market was drawn up to hear an address from the General. His address was not oratorical but direct and soldierly. He told them the enemy was before them and they would presently have a chance of retrieving their reputation. They didn't seem much elated with the prospect and scarcely got up a decent cheer in response.

As the enemy did not advance, our troops were put in motion and the cavalry continued to drive the enemy back upon their main position. Forward was the word to horse, foot, and artillery. We were advancing over some hills and slopes, the enemy was posted on the rising ground around the village of Piedmont [New Hope] concealed in the woods as usual. Already the shells and shot began to whistle around our ears. Our artillery I thought all this time was too distant, and I persuaded the General to have it all brought up. He consented and ordered DuPont to place two batteries in positions on a spur on the left. . . . About 11:30 the enemy's artillery seemed to be silenced by our heavier fire and he seemed to be retiring at all points. There was doubt whether the enemy's silence was not a deceitful calm covering some important movement. The General and staff rode forward for some distance in front of the batteries to reconnoiter.

The enemy's position was strong and well chosen. It was on a conclave of wooded hills commanding an open valley between and open, gentle slopes in front. On our right in advance of the village of Piedmont was a line of log and rail defenses very advantageously located in the edge of a forest and just behind the rise of a smooth, open hill so that troops moving over this hill could be mowed down by musketry from the works at short range and to prevent artillery being used against them. The left flank of this palisade rested on a steep and impracticable bluff sixty feet high and washed at its base by the Shenandoah. Just behind this work was the village itself, a single street of wooden houses, and nearly a mile in the rear was another line of rail defenses also located in the border of a wood crossing the valley and terminating with the twenty-pounder battery on the ridge to their extreme right. This was the view of the field from the bluff whence we made the reconnoissance.

No sooner had the staff appeared on the open, rising ground than the whole of the enemy's heretofore silent guns opened on it. After a satisfactory view the General retired into an adjoining wood where the vengeful shell pursued him until the prompt and well-delivered return from our two batteries directed by Captain DuPont in person silenced them. While we were in this position Sullivan advanced to attack the palisades in his front. The advance was gallantly made and the roar of musketry continuous. This was about one P.M. But in a few moments we had the mortification to see the lines break and retire in confusion, while the enemy followed, advancing from their works with yells of triumph mingled with the derisive cries of "New Market, New Market." The staff withdrew to a house in the center of the valley to watch the movements. The escort was ordered to dismount behind the house so as not to attract fatal fire. We found here some skulkers plundering and two women crying bitterly. The soldiers were kicked and driven out and the women reassured. The General asked for the owner of the house and was informed that he was down in the cellar with the little children. The General had him brought out and reviled him for his cowardice. He said he was a Dunkard preacher and a Union man and begged we would not let our horses bark his apple trees. This request at a time when a bloody battle was going on with death around and the fate of an army uncertain disgusted us all. [Major Daniel H.] Harkins cursed the fellow and ordered him into the cellar again with his whimpering boys. . . .

It became evident that the enemy was massing his whole power in front of Sullivan for a decisive attack. The troops could be seen moving from behind the more distant works around the village and into the wood. Colonel Starr was ordered to ride with full speed to Colonel Thoburn[1] and order him to move his brigade across the valley and assail the enemy's open flank. The critical point of the day had arrived as the yells of the combatants increased. At length Thoburn's columns appeared moving in gallant array across the open field. He crossed the meadow and was rising the opposite slope before the enemy seemed to notice his movement. Even then only a few shots from the distant battery struck his lines. The shells struck and burst, and the line closed up without confusion or appearance of trepidation. As this gallant infantry moved in line and column to its destination, news came that General Stahel had been wounded and also

1. Colonel Joseph Thoburn originally commanded the 1st West Virginia Regiment, but in the Valley Campaign of 1864 led the 2nd Brigade in Sullivan's division. He was killed at Cedar Creek in October, 1864.

that a train of supply wagons convoyed by five hundred cavalry instead of following us to Port Republic had taken the direct road to Staunton. . . .

I rode back to see Stahel, who had been wounded in the arm by a piece of shell. He said it pained his arm too much to ride but he started on foot to the front. I rode back then at a full trot, the earth shook with the roar of guns and musketry, and the fresh, hearty cheers rose with the smoke and sounded like victory. Back rolled the cheers from the front. Stretcher men, ambulance drivers, wounded men, butchers, bummers, and all took up the shout and back upon the hill crests. Negroes, teamsters, and camp followers re-echoed the joyful shout. I saw streams of greybacks and butternuts passing from the woods at a double-quick guarded by cavalry men with drawn sabres. The cheers redoubled as the squads of captives continued to stream across the open ground to our rear. . . .

While we stood there I saw some Rebel officers talking with their guard and gesturing toward our group. Presently an orderly approached and said that two officers wished to see the General. Two spry-looking officers advanced, and one addressing the General introduced himself as Captain [Boyd] Faulkner of Martinsburg and claimed kindred. The General was curt and hardly civil and presently ordered the sergeant to take them to the rear. I said nothing but Lang asked Faulkner if he did not know Colonel Strother. I had so far said nothing but upon this introduction I bowed. The Captain exclaimed, "What, Colonel Strother, are you here too?" He came up and shook hands, introducing his companion whose name I forget. He said he could have escaped but that he preferred to be taken rallying his men.

At three P.M. the enemy were routed and in full retreat. The cavalry came in with the report that the Rebel General Jones was killed and brought some papers and small articles taken from the body to prove the statement. The General desired me to go down and verify it beyond a doubt. I found a crowd around a body coarsely clothed in a dirty grey suit without any military trappings or insignia about it. He had on a pair of fine military boots well worn and fine woolen underclothes perfectly clean and new. His hands were small and white, and his features, high white forehead, brown beard, and long hair indicated the gentleman and man of the upper class. I concluded that this was truly the body of the General. Just then four Rebel prisoners came up with a stretcher to carry the body to burial under the orders of the provost marshal. I asked each of these men if they recognized the body. They said, "Yes, that is the body of our commander, General William E. Jones." Meanwhile Lang visited his pockets and got some curious papers from it. One contained a memorandum in figures giving a summation of his forces at seven thousand men and sixteen guns. The other was a letter to General Jones from General Imboden. . . .

The cavalry followed the enemy about a mile and then got a round of grape and canister in their faces which drove them back. I was very anxious to follow up vigorously, but to my mortification the General ordered the troops to go into camp on the battlefield, we taking headquarters in a small cottage in the village of Piedmont. The worthlessness of our cavalry was probably what induced the General to content himself with the affair as it stood. We had a good supper and a triumphant evening. The bands played and the men sang and shouted. The army was intoxicated with joy. Verily they had wiped out the disgrace of New Market. Sullivan had three horses shot under him and won laurels for gallantry today. The General wrote him a very complimentary letter. . . .

JUNE 6, MONDAY.—Started for Staunton. . . . A goose story. A soldier baited a hook with a piece of bread and set his line to catch something. A fighting gander belonged to an old woman and swallowed the bait. The soldier, having the other end of the line tied to his leg, walked off, the goose following and flapping his wings in a vain struggle to escape. The old lady went to the door and, seeing her, the soldier began to run, the gander now flapping vehemently. "Oh, don't run, sir," she cried, "He won't hurt you. Don't run. He is not dangerous at all." But the soldier kept on until out of sight and the gander was bagged.

At the junction of the Waynesboro and Staunton road we halted. I would have preferred to see our column take the Waynesboro road to finish Imboden, but the General kept on the Staunton. The people along our route were either much frightened or very glad to see us. They greeted us pleasantly, waved their handkerchiefs, such as had them, and brought buckets of water or milk to quench our thirsts. As we neared the town a dozen or more girls in their Sunday dresses stood by the roadside in front of a cottage and presented us with bouquets. Whether this compliment was sincere and loyal or meant as a propitiation of the demons I could not tell.

Sam Stockton and several others who with a squad of cavalry

had been sent forward to occupy the town sent back to report that they had been fired on by several men from the hills adjoining. I got two bands with a large American flag to accompany the staff as we entered the town. We made a tour of the principal streets playing "Hail Columbia" and "Yankee Doodle" and other such airs as we thought might be useful and pleasing to the inhabitants. A few skinny, sallow women peeped from between the half-closed window blinds, but generally the houses were closed and the town looked frightened. The staff dismounted at the American Hotel kept by [John X.] Nadenbousche (late Colonel) of Martinsburg. Had a good dinner and afterward took a room with Halpine and slept.

I was awakened by a messenger from the General, who, having been waited on by the mayor and town council and leading citizens, desired me to receive and talk to them. The Honorable Alexander Stuart[2] was the spokesman and introduced me to the mayor, the chief of the insane asylum, principal of a female seminary, and some others. He opened the conversation with some civil allusions to my literary fame and then turned in upon the present condition of the town. I told them that we were warring according to the rules of civilized nations, that all warlike stores, manufactures, and buildings which appertained to the Confederacy would be destroyed but that private property and noncombatants would be respected. The schools and charitable institutions would be carefully protected. I warned them that disorders might take place such as were to be expected among an ill-disciplined soldiery, but that no pains would be spared to keep peace and order in the town and I hoped these efforts would be successful. This discourse seemed to give satisfaction and allayed the evident "tremor" which our coming had produced. . . .

Colonel Starr called the General's attention to the prison. He went there and released all its inmates, thieves, spies, forgers, deserters, Irishmen, Union men, Yankee soldiers, Confederate officers, murderers, and rioters generally. Irons were knocked off and there was a general rejoicing and jail delivery. One fellow got up tears for the occasion. A Confederate officer who was in for shooting a soldier refused to leave. The General ordered the jailor's family to move out their furniture immediately, as he intended to have the building burnt. He also threatened to iron the jailor with the same fetters he had taken from a so-called Union soldier. It was a wet and cloudy after-

2. Alexander H. H. Stuart (1809-91) had been a United States congressman and Secretary of the Interior under Fillmore. After the war he became the man most responsible for the restoration of home rule in Virginia.

noon. I wandered about until dark and stumbled upon Sullivan's quarters. I was hospitably received here and got supper and stayed the night.

JUNE 7, TUESDAY.—. . . In the morning I rode into town and found everything in shocking confusion. They were burning the railroad property and public stores and work shops. A mixed mob of Federal soldiers, Negroes, Secessionists, mulatto women, children, Jews, and camp followers and the riff raff of the town were engaged in plundering the stores and depots. Quantities of army goods were found, blankets, clothes, a thousand saddles, shoes, tobacco, etc., without end. These stores were distributed among our people *ad libitum* and plundered as freely by Negroes, Confederate bummers, and citizens. At the Virginia Hotel Hospital, the provost guard were knocking the heads out of numerous barrels of apple brandy. The precious stream was running over the curbstones in cascades and rushing down the gutters with floating chips, paper, horse dung, and dead rats. This luscious mixture was greedily drunk by dozens of soldiers and vagabonds on their hands and knees and their mouths in the gutter while the more nice were setting their canteens to catch it as it flowed over the curbs.

Columns of cavalry were moving toward Waynesboro. The General it seems has determined to move directly on Charlottesville. The staff and other officers are opposed to the move, and several have asked me to use my influence to dissuade him from it. I was not opposed to the move but thought it a good one. Yet perhaps it might be better not to move until we hear from Crook and Averell. I saw the General and told him I had seen some Negroes who said they had seen Averell's force near Buffalo Gap. On hearing this report the General suddenly determined to move on the Gap, hoping to take McCausland in the rear.

I met Alexander Stuart again and had some agreeable talk with him. He is high-toned and conservative, and had my position permitted I would have gladly had more intercourse with him. He had come to headquarters to ask that a certain carriage factory should not be burned, as it would endanger much private property. He proposed that it should be left to the citizens to destroy and guaranteed that it should be totally destroyed by them under his orders. This Lieutenant Meigs, who was charged with the destruction of the building, readily accorded upon my representations. Presently the work was done most thoroughly without the dangerous use of fire. At the request of Nadenbousche I also procured respite of a warehouse adjoining the hotel. From all other buildings and public storehouses the devouring flames were rolling upward. Nadenbousche was heartily sick of Secession and desired to return home. He asked me to assist him and I promised to do so. . . .

An old Irishman whom we liberated from the prison yesterday came up to shake hands with me with many grateful benedictions. His hands looked swelled and scabby and I looked hard at them. Then he remarked, "That looks pretty bad, Sir, don't it?" "Yes," I said. "What is it?" "They say, Sir, it's the calf itch." "The calf itch! And you dare to shake hands with me, you d——d scoundrel!" I threatened to have him ducked and rode off washing my hands with applejack. In passing out of town the General saw the carriage factory which had just been the subject of arrangement between myself and Stuart. In spite of my explanations and remonstrances he ordered it to be burned forthwith, and before we got out of town the flames were ascending. No accidents occurred, however, as we afterward learned, our soldiers working zealously to save the adjoining houses.

After advancing with the whole army for five or six miles, we met a scouting party whose advance had passed Buffalo Gap and found it vacant. But what was singular and vexatious, they brought us no news of the enemy or of Crook. The command was halted to await further news. We sent out some scouting parties who returned with confirmed reports of the enemy to the southward of us. This was no doubt [John] McCausland or [William L.] Jackson passing around us from the Gap toward Waynesboro. Perceiving that we were marching away from the enemy, we faced about and returned to our encampment near Staunton the same day. During our absence some adventurous guerillas had entered the town and had captured some of our stragglers. . . . The two scouts sent out from Cedar Creek to communicate with Crook arrived and reported they had left Crook advancing only ten miles distant. He had struck the Central Railroad at Goshen and was marching along the line burning and destroying the track effectively in his advance. Crook joins us tomorrow with twelve regiments of infantry, two batteries, and cavalry.

The General asked me to give my views on the future campaign. I proposed to follow up the Valley via Lexington and Buchanan and thence by the Peaks of Otter road to Liberty and Lynchburg, thus threatening the enemy's great depot of supplies and the whole central railroad communicating with the Confederacy. From this point too unless Lee could detach a predominating force to drive us out, we had all Western North Carolina at our mercy. In fact, we would have our grip upon the vitals of the Confederacy. . . .

JUNE 8, WEDNESDAY.—As I lay awake just about dawn I was disturbed with the crowd of prisoners and refugees we had with us, when the idea struck me suddenly that we should send them back to our lines by way of Buffalo Gap and Beverly. This solution of the difficulty was so facile and so great a relief that I spoke to the General, whose pallet was next to mine. He was also awake and I proposed the plan. He jumped at it and was hardly content to wait until he got up before giving the orders. Colonel Moor of the 28th Ohio, whose time of service had expired wanted to return home, and he with his veteran regiment would be detailed to convey the train and prisoners. . . . Crook is within one mile of us and Averell is in Staunton. I wrote a report of the campaign from Cedar Creek to Staunton for the adjutant general of the U. S. Army to be forwarded by Colonel Moor. . . . Averell called and proposed much the same plan of compaign as mine. The only drawback is that ammunition is scarce and we must send back for a supply (and here I may mention that this accounts for our delays here and at Lexington).

JUNE 9, THURSDAY.—I was aroused in the night by the arrival of a Negro from near Waynesboro. He says Imboden and his men were badly frightened by the reconnoissance yesterday, and that many are deserting. He has been joined by McCausland and Jackson, and is expecting further reinforcements from Richmond. . . . Called to see General Crook and got his views. He was drier and less sanguine than either Averell or myself. He asked what we proposed by moving on Lynchburg. I told him we hoped thereby to drive Lee out of Richmond by seizing and threatening all his Southern and Western communications and sources of supply. He asked if we thought we could accomplish it with our present force. I replied that we could easily beat all the force that the enemy had in the Valley and in West Virginia combined, that we hoped Lee would not be able to reinforce the Valley, being too closely pressed by Grant, that in the event of his detailing a division or two it would be cut off by Sheridan who was moving with his cavalry toward Gordonsville and would cooperate with us. Crook said we might take Lynchburg but, depend upon it, Lee would not permit us to hold it long, nor could we do so for want of supplies. If we expected to take Lynchburg at all we must move upon it immediately and rapidly. I agreed with

him that such be our proper and safe course but mentioned our lack
of ammunition. Crook said he had plenty and if permitted would
march on Lynchburg with his division alone, saying that celerity
was more important than numbers or ammunition. This conversation I reported to the General, giving force to General Crook's views
in regard to the danger of delay. He heard me approvingly but replied that a good deal of delay was unavoidable. I wrote the orders of
march for the division commanders. We move tomorrow. . . .

Some small arms having been found concealed near the town,
A. K. Trout, mayor of Staunton, has been arrested and charged with
ordering their concealment. Alex Stuart and two others wrote to me
explaining the circumstances and asking his release. His wife with
nine children waited on the General, who referred the case to me, saying my decision should control the matter and so I ordered his release. . . .

JUNE 10, FRIDAY.—. . . Starr caught a fellow trying to steal his
horse and, collaring him, brought him down to the General's tent.
The General having abused him to the extent of his limited vocabulary
(he does not swear), cuffed and kicked him around the tent and let
him go. If the General's principles would have permitted him to have
cursed the fellow heartily, he would probably have avoided a rather
undignified scene. . . . In town I met Nadenbousche and by General
Hunter's direction gave him a permit to return home to live as a
loyal citizen and to claim the necessary protection from Federal and
military authorities. He seemed very grateful for the favor.

To sum up what was accomplished at Staunton, we took five hundred wounded and invalid prisoners and paroled them. We destroyed
one thousand stands of small arms and three guns, one thousand
cavalry saddles, horse equipment and shoes and leather, several woolen
factories and quantities of grey cloth and other stores, and some ammunition. The depot buildings and fifty miles of the Virginia Central
railroad were destroyed. Public stores were found in the asylum concealed. Stribling, the superintendent, was frightened sadly. In fact,
I remember now that he brought the information to me himself,
fearing they might be discovered and the asylum made accountable.
We were also told by some detectives that the banks had concealed
their treasure in the sewers of their establishment. This I did not
believe and advised the General frankly not to have a search as I
was sure the banks with their usual timidity and forethought had got
their cash boxes off by railway at the first alarm. The female schools

and every establishment of that kind was carefully respected and guarded.

The Army of the Shenandoah which had come with General Hunter was here with about eight thousand effectives. The Army of the Kanawha under Crook brought about twelve thousand. The Army of West Virginia (as I named it in general orders the day of the junction) moved from Staunton with twenty thousand men and thirty-six cannon. Our cavalry numbered about five thousand. We moved on four parallel roads with orders to concentrate at Lexington on the second day and to move toward any point where the sound of cannon indicated a serious engagement. Crook with his division of infantry took the main Valley road through Brownsburg. Averell with his cavalry division moved on the extreme right or western road. Sullivan's infantry division took the left hand Valley road through Greenville. General Duffié[3] with the Second cavalry division took the eastern road running along the Blue Ridge. . . . A courier from Martinsburg arrived bringing dispatches and late newspapers. A supply train of two hundred wagons is following us convoyed by two regiments of infantry and several squadrons of cavalry. The train contains some necessary supplies and some ammunition, all of which is acceptable and due to Sigel's promptness. The General is in high good humor.

JUNE 11, SATURDAY.—. . . The 2nd Maryland and an Ohio one-hundred-day regiment under Colonel [David] Putnam with the supply train have arrived safely. At Fairfield another mill was burnt. We heard guns on Crook's line and hurried our march accordingly. I stopped at a fine country house where I talked with some ladies, old and young. They were frightened but reassured when I spoke to them kindly. They said that our men had so far treated them better than their own soldiers. We found General Crook in front of Lexington about midday. The enemy had burned the bridge and were attempting a defense with artillery and sharpshooters. We rode forward to a hill for the purpose of reconnoitering. The river was deep, being used to feed a branch of the James River Canal. The opposite bank was a perpendicular cliff fifty or sixty feet in height and crowned by a thicket of cedars. In this thicket and in some buildings attached to the Virginia Military Institute, which stood near the cliff, the enemy had disposed his sharpshooters. The bridge, a

3. Alfred N. Duffié, a brigadier general of cavalry, was born in France. In 1863 he commanded a brigade under Pleasonton, and in 1864 scouted on the left flank of Hunter's army.

covered wooden structure, had burned and fallen into the river, still affording a crossing place for infantry on its charred boards and beams.

The skirmishing was sharp and so keenly did the balls whistle about us that we were obliged to dismount and hide our horses in the woods. Our artillery in force crowned the hill on this side which entirely commanded the town, but not being able to see the enemy only a few shots were fired. Averell with a brigade crossed by a ford above and flanked them to the right. Perceiving the movement in time, the enemy retired hastily toward Buchanan. The Cadets, about 250 strong under Professor Colonel [Francis H.] Smith, retired by the Balcony Falls road to Lynchburg. The General was dissatisfied with the movement of Averell's, believing that if it had been promptly and boldly executed, he might have caught the enemy and have captured or dispersed the greater part of his force. Our gunners put several shells through the Institute and one burst immediately in the cupola, one of the towers rather.

We entered the town from the west. The cavalry of Averell were coming in from the south, and numerous stragglers of our infantry crossing by the burnt bridge were peeping about for plunder. We rode directly to the Institute and found the sack already far advanced, soldiers, Negroes, and riffraff disputing over the plunder. The private trunks of the cadets seemed to be quite fat and remunerative, and I heard that one soldier got one hundred dollars in gold from one of them. The plunderers came out loaded with beds, carpets, cut velvet chairs, mathematical glasses and instruments, stuffed birds, charts, books, papers, arms, cadet uniforms, and hats in most ridiculous confusion. The General stopped at the house of Major [William] Gilham, a professor of the Institute, and told the lady to get out her furniture as he intended to burn the house in the morning. She was eminently ladylike and was troubled, but yet firm. The house was a state building and it was fair to destroy it, yet it was her only home and it was hard to lose it, but she was a soldier's wife and a soldier's daughter so she set us out some good applejack, apologizing she had nothing better, and then went to move out her furniture to the lawn.

I walked into the town with Stockton and, seeing a number of sweet-looking girls with some matrons on a porch, Stockton expressed a wish to know them saying he would give a great deal if he had the boldness to go up and make their acquaintance. I told him I would introduce him and walked up on the porch with the pretense of inquiring whether they had been disturbed by the soldiers, and whether they wanted a guard. They thanked me courteously and said they had a guard, which I knew, and that he had pestered them. They seemed cheerful and talkative, so I introduced Stockton and myself as members of the General's staff. This was the house of General [R. E.] Colston of the Institute. There was also there a Mrs. Bayard, who claimed kin with Stockton. We were invited to tea which I declined and then to come again. I took leave and left Stockton, who became an inmate of the house while we stayed in town and took good care of them. We took our headquarters at the house of Colonel Smith on the lawn of the Institute. It was an elegant establishment and we were served at a table by an old-fashioned Virginia house servant named Robinson. . . .

We saw a great deal of smoke in the mountains eastward and were told it came from the camps of the refugees who were hiding from us with their Negroes and cattle. Their campfires had fired the dry leaves and the air was misty with smoke. Our cavalry also burned some extensive iron works in that direction. The satisfaction of these people in regard to their Negroes is surprising. They seem to believe firmly that their Negroes are so much attached to them that they will not leave them on any terms. Thus when running off their cattle, horses, and the goods into the mountains, they take their Negroes with them. The Negroes take the first opportunity they find of running into our lines and giving information as to where their masters are hidden and conduct our foragers to their retreats. In this way our supply of cattle has been kept up. Negroes were continually running to us with information of all kinds and they are the only persons upon whose correct truth we can rely. Of course, we cannot always rely upon their reports for lack of judgment and means of obtaining military information. With that obsequiousness of spirit, born of slavery, they have too often a tendency to tell us what they think will be agreeable to us rather than what they know. Still there is no doubt of their good will to us.

Stores of arms and ordnance were found in the Institute. In the court of the main building were several pieces of light artillery with a number of limbers and carriages. In front are twelve pieces of bronze cannon of the old French pattern, and there is also a fine copy in bronze of Houdon's statue of Washington.

JUNE 12, SUNDAY.—. . . The General asked my opinion in regard to the destruction of the Institute. I told him I looked upon it as a most dangerous establishment where treason was systematically taught. That I believed the States Rights conspirators had with subtlety and forethought established and encouraged the school for the express purpose of educating the youth of the country into such opinions as would render them ready and efficient tools wherewith to overthrow the government of the country when the hour and opportunity arrived. Throughout the pamphlet literature of the school, addresses, speeches, and circulars, we saw one prominent and leading idea—that the Cadet in receiving this education from the sovereign state owed allegiance and military service to the state alone, and if he should be called to serve the Government of the United States he could only do so by the order and permission of the sovereign state of Virginia. The same infamous and treasonable doctrines were taught at the University of Virginia, and, while all the other educational institutions in the state had dwindled into insignificance, these two expressly used as schools of treason were fostered by the state authorities until they were prosperous and plethoric. To their joint influence might be traced the prevalence and fixedness of their monstrous doctrines among the educated men in the South. The catalogue of the Institute itself showed what a list of capable military officers had been there raised up against the government of the country. This was the great paramount reason for its destruction by fire.

There were military reasons besides. The professors and cadets had taken the field against government troops, as an organized corps. The buildings had been used as a Rebel arsenal and recently as a fortress. Professor Smith, who understood the liabilities incurred by this use of the building, protested against McCausland's appropriation of it for defensive purposes, hoping that otherwise it might be spared. Smith also protested against an attempted defense of the town, as useless and unmilitary. McCausland had fifteen hundred men and a battery while the Federals had twenty thousand men and thirty-six guns. The order was given to fire the building and all the houses and outbuildings.

As this order was executed, the plunderers came running out, their arms full of spoils. One fellow had a stuffed gannet from the museum of natural history; others had the high-topped hats of cadet officers, and most of them were loaded with the most useless and impracticable articles. Lieutenant Meigs came out with fine mathematical instruments, and Dr. Patton followed with a beautiful human skeleton.

Some of the officers brought out some beautifully illustrated volumes of natural history which they presented to me. I, however, felt averse to taking anything and left them at Professor Smith's. My only spoil was a new gilt button marked "V.M.I." and a pair of gilt epaulettes which some of the clerks had picked up and handed to me. The burning of the Institute made a grand picture, a vast volume of black smoke rolled above the flames and covered half the horizon.

While this was burning, an officer brought to General Hunter a proclamation issued by ex-Governor Letcher[4] inciting the people to arise and wage a guerilla warfare upon the vandal hordes of Yankee invaders. After issuing this foolish and abusive paper, the ex-Governor himself took to his heels. General Hunter ordered Captain [James F.?] Berry forthwith to burn the property, allowing his family ten minutes to get out of the house. The order was executed without delay. I walked with General Averell and Halpine to an opposite hill to view the scene which was grand, although the burning went on very slowly.

There seemed to be a very few people of the lower class and loose Negroes in this place. There was quite an excitement around the Letcher house lest the flames should communicate to adjoining houses belonging to his mother, an old woman who used to keep a boarding house. Our soldiers with some difficulty saved it. The Institute burnt out about two P.M. and the arsenal blew up with a smart explosion. The General seemed to enjoy this scene and turning to me expressed his great satisfaction at having me with him.

A trustee of Washington College called to explain that the soldiers were sacking the building and desired a guard to protect it. I ordered it immediately and explained to him why we were disposed to treat his college in a different manner from the Institute. He said, "I do not wish to discuss the matter, Sir." I pointed to the burning buildings and replied, "You perceive that we do not intend to discuss it either." The soldiers it seems have been sacking the Washington College and pelting the statue of the father of their country on the cupola, supposing it to represent Jefferson Davis.

I rode out around the town and, passing the cemetery, saw Stonewall Jackson's grave in the midst of an enclosure with a tall flag staff near it. A number of curious men and officers of our army were collected around it. I suggested to the General that the bronze statue of

4. John Letcher (1813-84), the "Watchdog of the Treasury," had been an ardent states' rights man in Congress before the war. Elected governor of Virginia in 1860, he served until 1864.

Washington in front of the Institute should be sent to Wheeling by the train as a trophy for West Virginia. Meigs, who undertook the boxing and moving of it, insisted that it should go to West Point, and as I was indifferent as to what was its destination I consented readily.[5] The fire had not injured the statue in the least, and as I looked at the dignified and noble countenance I felt indignant that this effigy should be left to adorn a country whose inhabitants were striving to destroy a government which he founded. The cottages occupied by Major Gilham and Colonel [Thomas] Williamson were burned. Mrs. Williamson had got her things off. Mrs. Gilham's were all piled on the parade ground and she sat in the midst, firm and ladylike. I asked Prendergast to let her have two wagons and some orderlies to move it. I also got a protection for her at the house she moved into to prevent soldiers from plundering her there.

Ellicott brought in a prisoner, a Major Bell, late an editor of some Winchester sheet. He was captured near Midway scouting from Imboden's command. I gave him a drink and his supper and he told me that Imboden was still at Waynesboro. Bell gave a great account of Lee's victory over Grant and supposed that Hunter should now supersede Grant as the latter had been so unlucky. He says the Rebels give me the credit for engineering this column up the Valley. I told him I was quite willing they should credit me with the move. . . .

Wrote an order to Averell to move at two A.M. tomorrow on Buchanan, to drive McCausland off and secure the bridge at that place if possible. This indicates that we are to take that route to Lynchburg. Averell detached two hundred picked men to cross the ridge and to ride around Lynchburg, cut the roads, and get news and rejoin us at Liberty or thereabouts.

JUNE 13, MONDAY.—. . . The General has decided to spare Colonel Smith's house. I suppose he feels that the roof which has sheltered us and the house where we have been entertained should be saved, whatever be its character otherwise. We received a dispatch from Duffie. He is on White's Gap holding both passes and has captured a number of horses. A dispatch from Averell says he is within four miles of Buchanan driving McCausland who has two thousand men and artillery. Went out to sketch the ruins of the Institute. . . .

Lieutenant Fields was ordered to burn the printing press and fixtures. The editor had concealed it in the woods—The *Rockbridge*

5. The statue of Washington ultimately made its way to Wheeling as a trophy for the state of West Virginia, but after the war Strother, then adjutant general of Virginia, had it returned to Lexington.

Gazette. He was arrested and showed his paper issued in 1861 to prove that he was a Union man. Crook's men got the canal boats with stores and found six pieces of cannon on board. The boats were burned and a heavy cannonade from the bursting of shells which they contained reminded me of a well-contested battle. Mrs. Gilham applied for rations, she being entirely without food for her family. A supply was issued to her. Negroes and white refugees coming in continually, desiring to go in our train.

Duffie at length reported in person, all sunburned and dusty. He crossed to Waynesboro and drove the pickets into the town, then turned southward and fought with Colonel Jackson's command who were trying to join Imboden by dodging around our column. He then crossed Tye River Gap, lit upon the Charlottesville and Lynchburg Railroad, destroyed it for five miles, capturing seventy prisoners, seven hundred horses, and three hundred waggons. Conversation with subalterns on the expedition have induced me to think this report exaggerated. They say not over fifty waggons were captured. In concluding his verbal report Duffie drew out a package containing several millions of Confederate money, saying, "Eh, bien, General. I gob all dis monnoie. I gob de waggon, by gar. I have gob de whole administration of Staunton."

Eighty prisoners of Duffie's gobbing being brought in, I examined some of them. Some said that Fitzhugh Lee had defeated a body of cavalry sent by Grant to open communication with us. Two fellows, hard youths apparently, told me that Ewell was advancing with a powerful column. They spoke earnestly and warningly. These men were West Virginians from Wheeling, and I did not credit what they said at the time, setting it down to ballying, but I now think they were thus frank, hoping to obtain leave to go home. Unfortunately, however, Duffie came in to be present at the examination and got to wrangling with the prisoners as to whether he "whipped" them or not. This interruption entirely broke up my plan of examination and prevented me from carefully weighing and comparing the evidence. Two officers should never examine prisoners at the same time. . . .

JUNE 14, TUESDAY.—Averell's courier brings us papers from Lynchburg and Richmond. These acknowledge that the siege of Richmond has regularly begun. Sheridan is on a raid toward Charlottesville. This is the information we have wanted for some days.[6] A long, dusty, but not unpleasant march brought us to Buchanan about sun-

6. Sheridan's force was intercepted by a detachment of Confederate cavalry and was not able to co-operate with Hunter as had been planned.

set. We took quarters in the Haynes Hotel. We passed within three miles of the Natural Bridge. Officers were much disappointed by not being able to see it. Lieutenant Meigs and some others did go by that road. . . .

Averell called after supper. He drove McCausland, pressing him as rapidly as possible but was unable to save the bridge [at Buchanan]. The people of the town begged McCausland not to set fire to it, as its burning would involve the destruction of a number of buildings adjoining. He disregarded their prayers and persisted, although its loss did not delay our crossing for any considerable time and half the village perished in the conflagration. Eleven houses were burned and the further progress of the fire was stopped by the friendly efforts of our troops. After he arrived here, a fellow appeared among his scouts who was recognized by someone at headquarters as one of McCausland's men. He had tried to deceive Averell by passing himself off for one of our scouts. On hearing this, General Hunter spoke up quickly, "Let him be hung forthwith." "Well, no," Averell answered coolly, "I had him shot yesterday." A Negro who was attached to his command attempted to rape a white woman and was seized and shot immediately.

In the vicinity of Buchanan several iron works were burnt, one a branch of the Tredegar works which employs five hundred hands. When we first approached, the inhabitants all ran away, but getting over their panic they came back and behaved themselves civilly. Tomorrow's march was arranged. Crook and Averell will move by the Otter Peaks road to Liberty [Bedford]. Sullivan and Duffie will wait until our train passes the river here and then will follow by the same road. The General has concluded not to send back the grand wagon train, but will retain it until it becomes troublesome. He will then destroy it and use the mules and horses for other purposes.

June 15, Wednesday.—Early this morning the General entered my room and said, "We have captured that old vagabond, Colonel Angus McDonald. He had the impudence to ask to see me, but I declined to see him." He then said he would turn the prisoner over to me that I might work my pleasure with him. I replied to the General, declining the charge, saying that I was not a fit judge in McDonald's case, that while he behaved in an insolent and inhuman manner toward my father, I did not care to use my position in the United States service to avenge a private quarrel or injury. I then went downstairs and saw McDonald sitting on the porch. He was thin and grey but looked healthy and was dressed in a grey military suit and cap. I stood in the door and looked at him. He recognized me immediately and saluted me civilly with a "Good morning, Sir." I made no reply but eyed him sternly. He seemed as if about to accost me again when I said, "Do you know me, Sir?" He replied, "Yes, I know you and you know me very well. And yet, Sir, you do not know me. No, you do not know me." This was said apologetically as if to open an opportunity to explain his treatment of my father. I could not listen to more, but said quietly but emphatically, "I think I do know you, Sir," and then turned on my heel and went away.

My blood boiled but I could not insult a prisoner, especially one with grey hair. Yet I remembered my father and bitter tears rolled down my cheeks. After three years the hour had at length come and this tyrannical old brute who had treated my aged father with such wanton indignity was himself a prisoner in my hands and I clothed with authority for life or death. That single look was vengeance enough for me. I could see remorse in his countenance when he recognized me and his aged appearance filled me with pity. If I had followed my impulses at the moment I should have liberated him. But the tongues of so many grievous wrongs cried out against him. Old and young of both parties accused him of so many acts of petty and vindictive tyranny that while my own wrong was forgotten, I considered that I had not right to interfere with the course of public justice, so I determined to leave him to his fate.

The General turned him over to the provost marshal to be held among the common prisoners and treated like the rest. His young sixteen-year-old son taken at the same time was also in the gang. Captain [Franklin G.] Martindale with a dozen men of the 1st New York Cavalry took McDonald near the Natural Bridge. It seems that he held the position of provost marshal or tax collector for the Confederacy in Rockbridge and was escaping into the woods with several wagons loaded with stores, with two or three white men and a half a dozen Negroes. When followed by our cavalry they fought desperately. The old man had twenty or thirty pieces, muskets, carbines, pistols, and double-barreled guns. These he used as rapidly as they could be loaded. The Negroes and his son assisted in the loading. When at length they closed on him, he used his sabre and only surrendered when he was in no condition for a further fight. Two of the white men were killed and McDonald himself was wounded in the head. Two or three of the New Yorkers were wounded and several of their horses were killed.

McDonald seemed much disgusted at his capture and said repeatedly that he ought to have died, but had yielded only because his son was with him. Major Quinn, to whom Martindale reported with the prisoner, was inclined to treat him with great courtesy on account of his age and thought of paroling him. This induced the old man to inquire no doubt that he might be paroled, and seeing me at headquarters no doubt attributed his different treatment to my influence, his conscience telling him that I owed him a generous debt. Major Harkins and Captain [William] Alexander tell me that McDonald denies that he was responsible for my father's treatment at Winchester. He endeavors to exculpate himself by explanations and desires to see me. I hardly expected this much of him, but declined seeing him. When the gang of prisoners started, the officer told McDonald he must walk. He protested and swore they would shoot him first. He said he was sorry they had not shot him when they captured him. . . .

When in sight of South Peak we recognized the signal officers there, and several of our staff officers including Lieutenant Meigs rode ahead to scale the Peak and when they got there found there was not a field glass in the party. They were delighted with their experiences but got no sight of the enemy. We halted at the Hotel between the Peaks and while there our cavalry escort plundered the smoke house, getting a hundred pieces of bacon. On the Hotel books they found the name of Major Harkins and written opposite, "He didn't pay his bill." This was bona fide and Harkins was considerably run on the subject.

A dispatch from Crook says he hears that Breckinridge is at Balcony Falls with ten thousand men and that some detachment from Lee's army is at Lynchburg. Averell occupies Liberty with a brigade. The detachment he sent from Lexington had cut the Charlottesville road near Amherst Court House and passing around Lynchburg by the southwest has rejoined the General at Liberty. This raid had been accomplished with a loss of a dozen or twenty men who straggled and were overtaken. We took headquarters in a house of one Kelso, an old-fashioned brick house handsomely located in a grove of oaks with a full view of the Peaks of Otter. . . .

I was given a horse of extraordinary ugliness but said to be swift and powerful. He has one eye milky like a huge opal, a hanging nether lip, a barrel like a rhinoceros, and prominent hip bones and a long, thin neck. I named him the Giraffe and think he may be useful to me as we are going into the jaws of the enemy, blind.

JUNE 16, THURSDAY.—Orders are sent to Duffie and Sullivan to advance as soon as possible. The town of Liberty which we entered this morning is much improved since I saw it last. Our troops I fear are plundering the town and misbehaving terribly as women and children are besieging the General's door for protection.... Averell told me he had seen a Confederate soldier's wife just from Lynchburg who gave him important intelligence. I called to see her and she told me she had left Lynchburg yesterday morning. The place is not strongly fortified and in this direction the only works were shallow rifle pits. All the sick and wounded had been organized to defend the place. As soon as I reported this news at headquarters, horse, foot, and artillery were started en route for Lynchburg. The day was very hot and the climate quite different from the Valley. Water was not plentiful, the land was poorer, and grazing not near so good or abundant.... Averell sends back word that he will encamp beyond the Great Otter River tonight. Crook is marching on the line of the Virginia and Tennessee Railroad, destroying as he moves. We see the smoke columns from burning bridges on the left....

When passing a very pretty country mansion, Brown called to me and said some ladies wanted to be introduced to me. I alighted and

LOCUST GROVE

was presented to two very handsome women. They had my book, *Virginia Illustrated*, and professed themselves admirers of my literature. While we were doing the amenities, the soldiers got into the house and commenced to plunder their trunks and bureaus. In the confusion which ensued, I mounted and escaped.

We halted for the night at a large deserted house, six miles from Liberty. It had been built on a stylish plan but had never been occupied and was said to be haunted. If its immaterial occupants were a more infernal set than those who occupied it that night, civil people do well to keep out of the way.... I feel a vague uneasiness as to the result of our move. Lee will certainly relieve Lynchburg if he can. If he cannot, the Confederacy is gone up. If he does succeed in detaching a force, our situation is most hazardous.

JUNE 17, FRIDAY.—Was aroused about two A.M. by the General. He showed me a dispatch from Averell stating that he had had a sharp fight at New London, about eight miles from here. The staff and escort were ordered to saddle and mount. I was directed to go to Sullivan and inform him of the situation and order him to move immediately on New London.... I had difficulty in getting two orderlies to go with me. I called on the sergeant of the escort who awakened an orderly and the fellow was mutinous and drew a pistol. I dismounted and went in sword in hand to quell him. I had to set off with one orderly. Was delayed two hours' time which might have been fatal under some circumstances. I may say here that I never saw such damnable ignorance and carelessness. The greater part of the sentries did not know where the headquarters of their regiments were. This want of system in this respect is common to our army and is the cause of great delay....

As we moved we found the bridge at Great Otter not ready. Neither the artillery nor the trains could get across. This further delay will prove fatal to us. [Captain Thomas K.] McCann reported that a man named Leftwich had told him some stories of our troops being badly defeated both East and West. This irritated the General so much that he had Leftwich arrested and ordered his house to be burnt. It was a very pretty country residence, and the man had a sweet daughter about sixteen and a nice family. The house was burnt and destroyed. Halpine, Stockton, and myself rode away saying nothing, but we did not wish to look upon the scene. One of our couriers had been fired upon from the yard of one Colonel Mosby (whether the guerilla or not I do not know).[7] The General doomed

7. The house in question did not belong to John S. Mosby, Rebel partisan.

this house to destruction, but after burning Leftwich's he seemed to relent and as we passed he said to me, "I don't think I'll burn it." I advised him to spare it and thus the matter ended. . . .

We came upon Averell's force at New London. The heat was intense. Some musketry skirmishing took place in our advance and here and there two or three cannon shot. The chiefs looked troubled. From 6:30 to 7 P.M. Crook's division engaged with musketry and artillery with great fury. During this engagement the General's staff arrived on the field, near enough to be under artillery fire and to witness the gallant conduct of Crook's troops driving the enemy in confusion from the field, capturing seventy prisoners and one gun. This handsome little affair took place at Quaker Church five miles from Lynchburg and cost us forty men killed and wounded. It concluded about dark and we were much disposed to follow on into the town, but the chiefs thought it more prudent to wait for the morning light. The staffs of all the Generals, Hunter, Crook, and Averell, took quarters at the house of one Major Hutter, formerly paymaster in the U. S. Army and an old acquaintance of General Hunter. A good supper and slept profoundly.

JUNE 18, SATURDAY.—When I went to the front I found our troops close up to the enemy's lines skirmishing continuously. The staff approached the toll gate on the Bedford road. We saw a strong redoubt on the left of the road and the enemy actively engaged in entrenching to their right. The appearance of the staff in the open ground was the signal for the opening of their batteries upon us. Ours replied and there was a rapid cannonade for twenty minutes. Duffie had been ordered to press vigorously on the Forestville line, and at 12:30 his guns were heard on our extreme left. The skirmishing fire was increasing and we heard the frequent report of telescopic rifles, an arm which had not before been brought to bear on us. The heavy balls came whistling back among the staff, one passing between the General and Stockton as they sat talking on horseback. The sound of these rifles suggested the presence of Richmond troops among the defenders.[8]

Passing through the recumbent lines I perceived that everybody was dismounted and lying down. I therefore dismounted myself and tied my horse to a swinging limb. At some distance to the front I saw

8. General Jubal Early had been sent from Richmond with the Second Corps for the relief of Lynchburg, but his entire command did not arrive until the afternoon of June 18. Arrangements were made to attack Hunter on the morning of the following day, but the Union army retired on the evening of the 18th.

Colonel Wells and another person behind some large oaks reconnoitering. I could hear the balls whistling and clipping among the trees, made my observations but saw nothing additional except that the works had progressed and were very full of men. I also saw the spires of Lynchburg in the distance. While we stood there, several rifle balls struck the tree and scattered bark upon us. I called on Sullivan who was with Colonel Thoburn lying on the ground on some boards. Sullivan said he had heard the railroad trains coming and going all night, also cheering and military music which indicated the arrival of troops in the town. Since morning the lines were very much strengthened and were pressing him hard. He was sustaining himself with difficulty. He said he was ready to attack if ordered but he felt assured it would end in disaster. Thoburn spoke in the same strain and in somewhat more decided language. I said I had begun to suspect they were right and that I would represent their views to the General. At the same time if an attack were ordered I wanted to know where he would advise attacking. He had no choice and would not suggest, so convinced was he that the enemy was strongly reinforced. I reported to General Hunter Sullivan's views as I heard them. He seemed dissatisfied and at the same time hesitated to order the advance.

Feeling badly jaded, I laid upon a board and slept soundly until I was awakened by an uproar of musketry and yells. This was at one P.M. The Rebel yell of attack sounded along our whole front. All sprang into saddle. The storm of yells and musketry rapidly approached and groups of fugitives began to appear through the woods. The General and staff drew their swords and rushed in, rallying these men with shouts and vituperation. Further on we met Sullivan's line retiring in good order but in haste. The General immediately faced them about and waving his sword led them back to their original position. This attack was violent and sudden and it overwhelmed us like a surprise, but owing to the lionlike bearing of the commander, things were reinstated in a few minutes and the storm of musketry shook the earth. For half an hour the battle raged when the cheers of our men indicated the enemy was checked. Then the attempt of the enemy to press the left flank of our lines. Crook's whole force hurried in to the left, regiment after regiment, and the fire was tremendous. We busied ourselves hurrying stragglers and presently great and continued cheering from the front told us the enemy had been routed and driven back into his works. The 116th Ohio followed them and entered the works, but being unsupported, fell back to its original position losing some prisoners. On their first attack the enemy drove three hundred sheep into our lines, all of which were butchered and issued for supper. This attack ended about two P.M.

Five prisoners brought in by Sullivan were questioned, which indicated beyond a doubt that Ewell's Corps commanded by General Early was in Lynchburg. These fellows were North Carolinians and said they had marched four days from Richmond to Charlottesville and had come thence by railroad last night. They represented the force in Lynchburg at thirty thousand men. The commanders acknowledged the position to be critical and all agreed that we must get out if possible. Crook was cool and matter of fact. Averell was excited and angry. He said to me, "I would give my head this night if we could have taken Lynchburg." I replied that the desire was past. We had but to make good our retreat. He said he was not afraid of them. I said neither was I and I be damned to them, nevertheless we should have to retreat. General Hunter immediately ordered the trains to move on the back track toward Buford's Gap.

The infantry was ordered to press the enemy with skirmishers, keeping up a bold front. The enemy then perceiving our flanks were so far extended, thought the center weakened and hoped by a sudden attack to cut our line in two. In this they failed signally; yet as there was still five hours of daylight, I had great apprehension that the attack would be renewed in the afternoon. I have since learned that Early had his troops in Lynchburg, but being sure of his game had determined to give his men rest until daylight the next morning. The rough handling they got in their attack no doubt made them cautious. The General and staff retired to Major Hutter's from where we had started in the morning.

About five o'clock news came from Duffie that the enemy were falling back into Lynchburg. This excited Averell who rode to the front to see about it. I did not give the slightest credit to the news and drank four more glasses of buttermilk. Our loss in this engagement did not amount to more than 500 men killed and wounded. The firing was kept up until dark and when it died, we started to Liberty. The troops were all withdrawn in silence and our picket line remained until midnight, when it also withdrew and overtook the main body in safety. We took off everything except about 150 wounded which Dr. Hayes had in a temporary hospital and left because he had no notice of the move. This withdrawal in the face of a superior force was well conducted and successful. We had a pleasant ride by moonlight and by two o'clock in the morning got back to our old quarters in the vacant house five miles from Liberty. Dissatisfied with Meigs, the General had Captain Martindale appointed chief engineer, and the promptness with which he built the bridge over the Big Otter to facilitate our return justified his selection.

June 19, Sunday.—. . . Officers of the rear guard report that the moving of trains and music of bands were heard in Lynchburg again last night, indicating the arrival of further reinforcements. We will probably be followed and continue our movement this morning. I wrote an order for Averell to move with his cavalry to Danville, to destroy the railroad there and release the Union prisoners. On receiving the paper he read it with a gesture of violent dissatisfaction. The Captain commanding the detachment sent by Averell to operate on the railroad below Lynchburg reports that he found all the points well guarded with cavalry, infantry, and artillery. He menaced them, but retired without accomplishing anything. Duffie is in safe. We moved through Liberty, Averell with the rear guard occupying that town. Duffie who had been sent ahead to seize Buford's Gap reports that there is an enemy in the Gap. He had ordered to clear them out at all hazards. At the same time a report came from Averell that the rear guard was attacked and ere long we could hear the rattle of a fight. Our lines were evidently being forced back.

Dinner was served but the firing was so rapid and approaching so near that the General left the table, ordered the staff to horse. . . . Averell was driven through the town, losing 100 men killed and wounded. The infantry and artillery were quickly disposed in order of battle, building fires and cooking their supper. At midnight we took the road again in the full moon shining gloriously. Some were in dread that we might fall into the hands of Rebel Raiders. At a railroad station we stopped and destroyed the telegraph wires, the General assisting personally.

June 20, Monday.—On the road all night and at dawn entered Buford's Gap, a rocky, muddy road with numerous defensible positions. We hear nothing more of the enemy either front or rear. Our cavalry looks very much used up and demoralized. We found headquarters established at Bonsack's Station a short distance ahead. It was a humble house and I found the General and Stockton lying on the floor. There is a rumor that John Morgan is in front of us with thirty-five thousand men. I suppose they mean thirty-five hundred. An Englishman told me of this and there seems to be such a report in the country. We don't fear that force. A courier from Averell reports the enemy at 2 P.M. advancing on our rear guard in force. At 2:30 Crook reported the enemy pressing him and threatening both flanks. Orders to saddle are given in haste to the cruel disappointment of many who had hoped for a night's rest. Averell says we must prepare to fight immediately and this is the crisis of our fate, as this battle will save or ruin us. The trains move toward Salem in charge of Duffie. . . .

We marched on the Salem road burning and destroying the railroad, stores, and station houses as we moved. The demonstration on our rear amounted to nothing. A Yankee straggler who was behind the enemy and escaped over the mountain told me they had not over a thousand men. We rode all night, stopping an hour to graze our horses in a clover field. Burning bridges and railroad stations lighted our way. . . . As soon as we entered Salem at sunrise, I threw myself upon a table in the barroom and slept soundly for an hour. Some one wakened me to come to breakfast. I was utterly disgusted, as sleep was then with me the one thing needful.

JUNE 21, TUESDAY.—. . . The report of cannon roused us again and the news came in that Crook was cut off. The train was hurried through the town on the Newcastle road accompanied by a disorganized rabble of mounted men, Negroes, skulkers, and fricoteurs. The General and staff rode to the front but the firing had ceased, and there seemed to have been no adequate cause for the excitement, only some cavalry appearing in our rear. . . .

At 10:30 we had news that our artillery en route with the train had been attacked and was all captured. Averell with his cavalry and Sullivan with infantry are ordered to advance rapidly. It seems as if we are getting into an ugly position, artillery gone and cavalry worthless. We can only get our infantry to depend on to get through. Two prisoners were brought in. They say two brigades of cavalry under Ransom are following us, one of four regiments under McCausland. Another prisoner says there are three brigades. They both report Ewell's Corps under Early is following on foot. Early's division is said to be twenty thousand strong and they have thirty days' rations and are determined to drive us out of Virginia. It was McCausland's men who cut in upon our line of retreat this morning. They lit upon the artillery, capturing and disabling two batteries, cutting up the carriages with axes, and carrying off the horses and some men prisoners, among them Captain Von Kleiser. He was said to have been murdered after surrendering, but we have no means of verifying the statement. . . .

The road was blocked with our disabled artillery, their carriages hacked to pieces, guns spiked, horses and harness gone. Captain DuPont was fitting some of them up and succeeded in restoring four pieces. We abandoned eight pieces, destroying them completely by burning the wood work of guns and caissons. This after all had only been a bushwhacking business as they could only carry off the horses. At 2 P.M. stopped and lunched with Averell. He seemed hopeful of getting out whole, but he is more sanguine than I. At 3:20 our troops and trains were crossing the mountain gap from whence we will have three roads to choose between. We ascended the mountain road with the cavalry column, a dusty and wearisome ride. The pass was of great height surmounted by a zigzag road. Averell with all the cavalry was sent forward to clear the road to Newcastle and to hold all the flanking roads until we came up. He was to fight if necessary to accomplish his purpose, and, if he failed, we could still retire by the Blacksburg road toward New River. . . . Finally Crook arrived and reported that he had safely reached the foot of Catawba Mountain (the mountain we had crossed) with the rear guard. The stupor of fatigue overcame the anxieties of our position, and taking possession of a rude sofa I slept profoundly.

JUNE 22, WEDNESDAY.—Our position will be a gloomy one if the reports we hear are confirmed. Worn out with fatigue, without supplies in a country producing little at best and already wasted by war, the troops are beginning to show symptoms of demoralization, and short of ammunition we will hardly save our army if the enemy is as far ahead as appears and occupies the positions reported. The General must have had an anxious time last night. Averell is seven miles from Newcastle. He crossed Craig's Mountain and has so far found nothing to oppose him. The army moves immediately to Newcastle. . . .

At starting we made two blunders. Crook's division took the wrong road and had to countermarch, which delayed us two hours. At one o'clock we struck Craig's Creek, a beautiful, amber-colored stream, the aspect of which was most refreshing after the heat and dust of the highway. Just before getting here I rode off the main route to a house to inquire the way. I found our men plundering everything.

The man of the house was one of the secret Union Leaguers and claimed my protection with various signs which I did not comprehend. The soldiers were going over the bee hives and devouring great chunks of honey with brutal greediness. The honey as they ate it was streaming down their clothes and clotting in their beards. The vengeful bees swarmed around their faces, biting and stinging. They scraped them off with their hands when they got too thick for comfort and went on eating like a herd of grizzly bears.

As this day's march was considered the crisis of our retreat, there was great anxiety among the officers of the staff, and when a dispatch came in either from front or rear it caused quite a flutter of speculation. . . . At five o'clock we reached Newcastle and found Averell there. It is an airy and picturesque locality but the village forlorn and insignificant. I found Averell as usual sparking some girls, one of them a buxom, dimpled beauty.

While we were reposing on the bluff, Ellicott brought in a rumor that a force of twenty thousand men had passed near Fincastle, via Covington, to intercept us. An officer of Duffie's division in reconnoitering near Fincastle observed the Covington road tracked and beaten as if by a movement of a heavy column. The enemy's silence all day may also be accepted as an evil omen. I do not believe the report at all, yet it is within the range of possibility and if true must be met with a bold dash somewhere. The General was about to move, but I threw doubts on the report, and he agreed to remain at Newcastle until further information. In case we are cut off by a superior force, Crook proposes to move southward to the line of the Virginia and Tennessee Railroad by a narrow and rough road, blockading the road in the rear as we go. Striking this line we would move westward into Tennessee, destroying as we move, including the Wythe lead mines and Smythe County salt works, using up John Morgan in our route.

I proposed another plan, which was this—to burn baggage and take the wagons to transport the sick and fatigued men. To kill our cattle and load every man with three days' rations. To dash to Fincastle and Buchanan and across the Valley and over the Blue Ridge at Irish or White's Gap. Then move northward to Charlottesville. This would bring us back to our base where we wanted to be, near Harpers Ferry, and would leave the enemy entangled and astounded at Covington if he were there, or at Salem if he had concentrated there. This plan seemed too rash and impracticable, Crook declared, for we would be caught.[9] His plan was preferred. Mine was full of adventure and pleased me well enough, and I was almost sorry to doubt that the enemy was at Covington so much was I pleased with the promises of this dangerous escape. We took lodgings in the house of a poor woman on the outskirts of town and a comfortable camp supper and a sound sleep.

JUNE 23, THURSDAY.—Averell sent word he is on the Sweet Springs road and covering the Covington road. He is ordered to hold that at all hazards. The scout to Fincastle reports that only one brigade of Rebel cavalry and two regiments of mounted infantry passed there, so we have concluded to go on toward Lewisburg, fighting anything that molests us. Marched by a narrow mountain road between the regiments of Crook and Sullivan. Crossing Barbour's Mountain, we arrived at the Widow Spotts at 9:30 A.M. From here taking the Sweet Springs road we crossed Middle Mountain, the heat being excessive. Many horses have been stolen from the staff officers by these dogs [the soldiers] so that one servant riding extra horses had to be marched under a guard to protect them. I have already lost two, one of them fully equipped. . . .

Descended to Potts Creek and found the troops cooking dinner. I found General Crook and staff at a wayside tavern and there got a glass of native wine. This fellow was said to have been a bushwhacker and a bad man. Fortunately the General did not hear this report until we had passed on. From hence we crossed the Warm Spring Mountain and arrived at the springs early in the afternoon. This place is the most elegantly improved watering place in Virginia. The soldiers were plundering generally or rather seeking plunder as there was little to be found here. Chairs, bedstands, mattresses, and crockery were all they found here except some spoiled sauces and some claret. The owner had run off and hid himself. Some Negro women gave us towels and water for a good wash, which we much needed. I found my way to the bath house but found the pool dirty with a green ooze and full of soldiers. In the ladies' pool, which was less crowded, I took a swim.

We here ascertained that the train we sent through from Liberty was attacked by guerillas under one Phil Thurman. The Lewisburg road was blockaded and the train consequently turned northward

9. Had it been adopted, Strother's plan would have proved the most dangerous, although certainly the most interesting. Since Early was now marching toward Washington, Hunter's army would have been following in the Confederate rear. This Union movement would perhaps have prevented Early from crossing the Potomac, although it might have proved disastrous for Hunter's army.

toward Beverly. The news irritated the General and he threatened to burn right and left. The hotel was made general headquarters and our officers and men helped themselves to mattresses, laying them in the halls and porches, and slept luxuriously. A Catholic priest came to ask a guard for his chapel and the sacred vessels. He had better not let our troops hear of the sacred vessels. . . .

JUNE 24, FRIDAY.—I was awakened this morning by an animated conversation between the General and a Mrs. Lewis, who called to have her house spared from being burned as had been threatened. Someone told the General that Oliver Byrne, the manager of the hotel, and Lewis had given advice to the guerillas in regard to the returning supply train and upon this he had determined to burn all their property. I did not believe this story myself and told the General so. It was not at all likely that men of their character would engage in such inglorious warfare. Mrs. Lewis' eloquence convinced him he was wrong and he countermanded the order. . . . .

It was understood here that we were not likely to be further disturbed by the enemy in force, I therefore urged the General that we should return to our base by way of Warm Springs, Franklin, and Moorefield, that valley affording forage, supplies, and practicable roads and running parallel with the Shenandoah Valley would bring us out at New Creek or in case we got ahead of the enemy, we could take the route by Winchester, thus being on hand to meet a counter-raid on Sigel's forces which I was sure would be made as soon as it appeared that our force was out of the way. Crook, who was more familiar with the Lewisburg and Kanawha country, was in favor of that route as by it the army would sooner reach supplies. There were a million of rations at Charleston and large supplies at Gauley and Meadow Bluff, this latter only three days' march distant. The Army was much disorganized by fatigue and the necessity of seeking supplies in a country already wasted and beset with enemies. The Franklin Valley, Averell said, was naked and we cannot risk being attacked in flank or headed off by the enemy. It should be our policy to avoid fighting in the present condition of our troops, and the sooner we could reach supplies the sooner the army would be brought into an effective condition to meet the enemy. Once arrived at Charleston we would have river and railroad transportation to the front, and we would reach there as soon and stronger than by any other route. Averell backed Crook in his views, but I still sustained that we could move by the Franklin Valley and that there was feed enough for us. The General accepted Crook's views and determined to march upon Kanawha. Averell changed his opinion later and advised the Franklin route. As the decision was made I was content, but I felt sure that a movement would be forthwith set on foot against Sigel, although I did not foresee that it would be on so formidable a scale. . . .

We started en route for the White Sulphur at two P.M. One mile from the Sweet is the Red Sweet, a pretty, rural place. The proprietor passes for a Union man and has some pretty daughters that are fond of Federal officers. The greater part of this road is through narrow gorges and dense forest well-fitted for bushwhacking. We arrived at the White Sulphur about sunset, and in spite of its handsome buildings and extensive improvements it has a desolate and forlorn appearance. The new mammoth hotel was entirely dismantled and has been for some time used as a hospital for the Confederates. There was a good deal of waste and decay visible. I went to the famous spring, but could not bring myself to quench my thirst with the mineral water. Yet there was none other to be found. I found the General at the house of one Geary and, going in, flung myself on a sofa to sleep. Troops and wagons were passing all night.

JUNE 25, SATURDAY.—Took breakfast with the General on the green near the great hotel. Starvation being the only enemy we had to contend with, the route to Charleston was taken, and a courier dispatched to hurry up the supplies as fast as possible. The road to Lewisburg showed signs of the recent guerilla operations. There were dead horses, burnt wagons, burnt bridges, and farmhouses. Provisions of all kinds were ruthlessly ravished by our hungry swarms. Lewisburg is a quite well-built village in the midst of great levels, a fair, open, rolling country. Further news of one train which had turned northward toward Beverly induced the General to send a regiment of cavalry to follow after and assist in its protection. . . .

The staff and escort pushed forward and we rode until dark. The family where we stopped consisted of a man, his wife, and two grown daughters. They were evidently Rebels and bitter ones. The old man I doubt not was a bushwhacker himself, and I had no doubt that any of the family would have betrayed us to Thurman if a chance occurred. Staff and escort did not number over forty men and, sleepy as we were, I thought it not unlikely that we might be attacked during the night. The shadow of this idea haunted the others as well. Our churlish hosts had nothing for us to eat. I had some hardtack and Tom got me two onions. Upon these I supped and taking a stiff nightcap of applejack threw myself on the floor for a sleep. About nine o'clock was relieved to see a detachment of cavalry arrive and dismount near us. . . .

JUNE 26, SUNDAY.—Crook who is up recommended that the General and staff ride on rapidly to Charleston and he engages to bring up the army. He wished to repeat the campaign in the fall and thinks the General and myself should go to Washington to urge the matter on the authorities there. . . . We crossed Meadow Bluff, little and big Sewell mountains, the scenes of the campaigns between Rosecrans, Wise, and Floyd. Most of the houses by the way have been burnt. All the bridges have been destroyed, and as the streams run in very deep beds the inconvenience is great. We have met several citizens but get no news from the United States. We have heard nothing for twenty days. At six P.M. stopped twenty miles from Gauley. Crook and his command is only eight miles behind.

JUNE 27, MONDAY.—Ho for Gauley. We passed the old positions of Rosecrans and the Rebels familiar to us from newspaper reports in the beginning of the war. We turned aside to see Hawk's Nest on the New River, a fine mountain view. On a bet of a bottle of wine with Starr I threw across the river, the only one present who did it. Here we met the trains with seventy thousand rations going out to meet our troops. We are now among our friends and in a friendly country where we may ride ahead of our escort with a sense of security which I have not felt for sixty days. . . . We got news from Grant up to the 22nd. He is investing Petersburg and will probably take it. Gold is 205. Vallandigham has returned to the country. . . .[10]

JUNE 28, TUESDAY.—Having arrived here ahead of the troops, I hope the General will push ahead to Martinsburg and to department headquarters where he may choose to locate. We wait here until our luggage is up. I feel a delicious sense of repose. The air is cool and misty and here sitting on the banks of the beautiful Kanawha, I long again for the enjoyment of peace, literature, and the arts. Commenced writing a report of the campaign by the General's order. . . .

JUNE 29, WEDNESDAY.—. . . All the way from Salem and especially from White Sulphur the stragglers have been ahead of the column. The danger being behind, they break for the front. The additional

10. Clement L. Vallandigham (1820-71) had been branded a Copperhead for his advocacy of freedom of speech and his policy of peace on any terms. Banished to the Confederacy, Vallandigham was recalled by the Peace Democrats of Ohio to run for governor. He exhorted against the Federal government and the conduct of the war until Appomattox.

inducement of rations ahead also hurried them on. For the last four or five days I have seen an old Negro hag about seventy-five years of age striding along on foot with wonderful endurance and zeal. She is walking for freedom I suppose.... Averell thinks our troops should all be back in the Valley to seize the ripening crops. If our troops are not there, the Rebels certainly will be.

JUNE 30, THURSDAY.—We moved back toward Charleston, the General in an ambulance, the rest of us on horseback. At Camp Platt we embarked for Charleston on the stern wheel steamer, *General Crook*. Ho for Charleston. The river is narrow and smooth and on its shores all along are the famous salt works. They are rude in appearance, inferior in size to those of Smythe County, and not picturesque. The Valley of the Kanawha is deep and narrow, a mere gutter and not very pleasing. The habitations along the banks have a dingy and decadent aspect. Ten miles to Charleston where we landed after dark. It was raining and we got into an ambulance crowded with officers and drove to a saloon. We here imbibed native wine and sherry cobblers until we all got on a spree. Re-embarked in the ambulance and drove around for an hour jabbering and singing in search of our quarters.

Thus ends the Hunter Raid or the Lynchburg Campaign as we may choose to call it. Averell said of it, "Its greatness as a military achievement will be recognized by history." The thing is too close to us to be properly appreciated even by ourselves. Viewing the difficulties overcome and the results accomplished with inadequate means, its savage hardihood and audacity has not its parallel in the history of this bold and unexampled war.

XIII

The Colonel Leaves the Army

July 1, 1864—August 9, 1864

From Charleston the Army of West Virginia was rushed to Harpers Ferry to meet Early's thrust at Washington. While Early's demonstration was a bluff, it succeeded in creating a panic which compelled Grant to reinforce the city from Petersburg. While the Federal armies in Maryland maneuvered into strong defensive positions, Early sent McCausland to burn Chambersburg in retaliation for Hunter's destruction of the Valley. Finally, on August 7, General Philip Sheridan took command of the recreated Army of the Shenandoah, forcing the resignation of Hunter and his chief of staff, Colonel Strother.

After three years the Civil War seemed to be a drama consisting of a single act rehearsed again and again. In the spring the Federal armies advanced up the Valley of Virginia, in the summer they were driven out, and in the fall the Confederates harvested the crops. The North seemed as far from victory in 1864 as in 1861. Then, too, a wanton brutality had somewhere intruded in the war. Strother could not approve the unmilitary destruction of private homes, many of them owned by former friends, that was carried out by Union cavalry with barely a shrug of disapproval. The time had come for Colonel Strother to leave the army.

Until Appomattox, Strother lived with his wife and daughter in Baltimore, following the course of the war but no longer participating in it. After Lee had surrendered, they returned to Berkeley Springs. In August, David Strother received a commission making him brigadier general by brevet for meritorious service in the war. The battles were over; it was now time to resume his career as Porte Crayon.

JULY 1, FRIDAY.—. . . Charleston is awfully dirty, filthy, dingy, and dilapidated. News that Rebels are demonstrating in the Valley toward Martinsburg. This can be nothing more than cavalry. General news not clear. The provost marshal, a young officer, stated he had permitted McDonald to stay at the house of a friend. The General looked black and, I afterwards learned, ordered him to jail. . . .

JULY 3, SUNDAY.—Packed and got aboard the steamer *Powell* bound for Parkersburg. McDonald is on the boiler deck of the boat. . . . Passed into the Ohio at Point Pleasant and went up the river. As the river is very low, it is doubtful if we can get up to Parkersburg. Grant says Early is returned from Lynchburg and is in front of him.

JULY 4, MONDAY.—Awoke at five this morning to find the boat struggling up a rapid. After an hour's strife we got up. The shore was full of troops landed from other boats and I fear the whole steamboat move will fail. We have passed Ravenswood and Buffington shallows, after landing and walking some miles to lighten the boat. Arrived at Parkersburg about six P.M. and took quarters at the Spencer House. News that Sigel has been driven out of Martinsburg by a large force of the enemy under Ewell. He has been driven out and has retreated on Harpers Ferry. . . . I doubt whether this is more than a cavalry raid by the force that followed us from Lynchburg.

JULY 6, WEDNESDAY.—Sullivan left this morning with his division. Sigel telegraphs that the enemy is in front of him at Harpers Ferry, small squads going in and out of the town. He reports Rebel cavalry stealing horses at Boonsboro. Stahel with our cavalry occupying Pleasant Valley. The whole affair is one of the most miserable that can be imagined, and I hope it will finish the Dutch element in this department. . . . At tea a telegram arrived from Secretary Stanton urging that General Hunter move eastward with his whole force as fast as possible. Another from Sigel says the enemy have been crossing at Antietam ford for forty hours. This indicates either a big scare or there is a big thing on hand, the third invasion of Maryland by the Rebels.

JULY 7, THURSDAY.—. . . Sigel telegrams that General Stahel with his cavalry has operated against the enemy at Berlin (Stahel with at least two thousand men and the enemy with one hundred at least) and prevented his crossing at that place. We leave for Cumberland at 6:30 P.M. . . .

General Hunter says that Jeff Davis was the only Secretary of War who ignored politics and political appointments. His management of the Southern armies has shown the value of these principles, while the United States Government has nearly destroyed the vast resources of the people. Thousands and thousands of lives and millions and millions of property have been sacrificed to the filthy demon of politics. A fellow named Wharton, editor of the *Parkersburg Gazette*, published an editorial traducing the General and the expedition from which we have just returned. He was immediately arrested and cast into prison and his paper destroyed and his office closed. . . .

JULY 8, FRIDAY.—Slept in the engineer car in a bunk opposite the General. About two o'clock was awakened by the explosion of musketry. The General jumped up, Stockton came in and cried, "Bushwhackers!" There was general consternation and the lights were put out. The firing continued sharply. I thought our men were firing from the cars in return. I expected every moment the train to run off the track. I put on my boots, got my pistol ready, and stood on the defense. Everyone else was lying on the floor and the General looking out of the window. The firing ceased and the train kept on rapidly, yet I felt gloomy at this exhibition of insolent hostility and thinking it might be repeated at any moment. Presently the conductor came through and informed us that the firing was from our post guard at Clarksburg and was intended as a salute. Arrived at Cumberland at ten o'clock and stopped at the St. Nicolas Hotel. . . .

JULY 9, SATURDAY.—Various telegrams today all indicating that the enemy is moving through Frederick City, Urbana, and into Virginia. This looks like a mere cavalry raid making Jeb Stuart's circuit. . . . Wrote Governor Boreman by direction of General Hunter turning over the statue of Washington captured at Lexington to the State of West Virginia. Cregan, the old Hampshire cottager who was robbed and persecuted by McDonald, saw the prisoner yesterday and insulted him to his heart's relief. From reports of McDonald's conduct to Union men, the General has ordered him to be put in jail in irons with balls and chains. I met him face to face going to the jail, and he uttered a groan like a suffering wild beast when he saw me. Mrs. Strother arrived from Bath at five P.M. She showed me a letter from Edward McDonald, son of Angus, to her charging me with having been the cause of his father's detention in the guardhouse and threatening me with the vengeance of nine sons if any evil resulted to his father from it. This brutal and cowardly attempt to frighten a woman did not succeed, for Madame did not appear to be scared much.[1]

JULY 10, SUNDAY.—. . . Rebels have occupied Frederick. General Lew Wallace confronts them at Monocacy. All sorts of rumors about a co-operating column coming by way of Edwards Ferry. . . .

1. This letter to Mrs. Strother promised that if Angus McDonald died, nine of his sons were pledged to take Strother's life, no matter how long the war lasted or wherever he should be found. McDonald did die in 1865, shortly after his release from prison, but nothing ever came of the threat.

JULY 11, MONDAY.—. . . Sigel is relieved by General [Albion P.] Howe, late chief of artillery at Washington. He is ordered to report to General Hunter, who ordered him to report to the adjutant general at Washington. Thus ends this political speculation of the President, in disgust, mortification, and injury to all concerned. . . . Rebels advancing on Baltimore and Lew Wallace falling back before them. General Halleck orders Howe to join with Hunter and move on Washington as the enemy will probably attack that place or Baltimore. The military aspect is serious. This movement of the enemy is truly the energy of despair but what may be the result who can tell. The great financial crash which is rapidly approaching and the despairing fury of the Rebel armies may yet accomplish our ruin, and there is no great man to take the helm and guide us through.

JULY 13, WEDNESDAY.—. . . News that the Rebel forces are in Montgomery County and threatening Washington. Also that forty thousand men under Longstreet are moving from Gordonsville to support him. However, it looks to me as if the Rebels are rather retreating from their raid and returning into Virginia. . . . General Duffie and troops arrived. We start for Harpers Ferry tomorrow.

JULY 14, THURSDAY.—Got off in the train at nine A.M. with the staff. Martinsburg looking awfully desolate. Breckinridge's and Gordon's divisions passed through here, twenty-four thousand strong. They took headquarters at Aunt Martha's. Started for Harpers Ferry on horseback at five P.M., the dust horrible. General Duffie with a brigade of cavalry and some wagons accompanied us. Arrived here at one A.M. and slept at headquarters on the floor, supperless.

JULY 15, FRIDAY.—Harpers Ferry gutted and desolate. . . . The enemy retreating southward across the Potomac as we calculated, with all their spoils. This is the most disgraceful affair of the war for us. . . . General Hunter received a telegram from Halleck directing him to put his troops under command of Crook and send them to join [General Horatio G.] Wright or to join Wright personally and serve under his orders, Wright being at Poolesville and the enemy gone. The General asks to be relieved of command, considering himself insulted by the proposition. His letter to Secretary Stanton to this effect is written and gone. The enemy has made his raid and is gone scot-free without a fight. The damage he has done is small, but the disgrace unspeakable. . . .

JULY 16, SATURDAY.—Halpine is gone to Washington and New York. I have never felt so entirely discouraged and disgusted with the condition of public affairs as at present. Folly, faction, and feebleness seem to be more in the ascendant than ever. . . . Heard that Imboden and Rosser were in Winchester preparing to assail the railroad and annoy our forces with the intention of avenging Hunter's Raid and of gathering the crops. I told this to the General who determined that Averell should attack them as soon as he arrived at Martinsburg. . . .

JULY 17, SUNDAY.—. . . The General showed me a telegram sent by himself to the President asking to be relieved from command in this department, giving as reason that General Halleck's order of yesterday (placing Wright in command) is calculated to impair his usefulness and he will not be made the scapegoat for other people's blunders. At dinner General Hunter showed me a dispatch from President Lincoln apologizing for the order, transferring his troops to Wright, saying no offence was meant and it was only temporary and insisting that he remain in the department. This I seconded with my counsel and the General expressed himself satisfied.

Received a telegram from General Halleck informing General Hunter that the veteran troops under Wright would return to Washington after following the enemy a short distance. Hunter's forces were to follow them to Charlottesville if practicable and then to fall back if forced, toward Washington. He was to devastate the valleys south of the railroad as far as possible so that the crows flying over would have to carry knapsacks. This need not involve the burning of houses, dwellings. I have begged off Charles Town from being burnt for the third time. . . .

JULY 18, MONDAY.—. . . The house of Andrew Hunter was burned yesterday by Martindale.[2] I am sorry to see this warfare begun and would be glad to stop it, but I don't pity the individuals at all. A war of mutual devastation will depopulate the border counties which contain all my kindred on both sides of the question. I would fain save some of them but fear that all will go under alike in the end. . . . Martindale returned and reports that he burned Hunter's house and made prisoner of Hunter himself, who was concealed in the house. He snapped his fingers and told Martindale he would not care that for the burning if he were ten years younger. . . .

JULY 19, TUESDAY.—Orders given to burn the houses of E. J. Lee and Alex Boteler.[3] Martindale went forward to execute it. His descrip-

2. It is clear from this that Strother had no knowledge of the order to burn his uncle's house. The destruction of Andrew Hunter's house has often been cited as evidence of General Hunter's brutality, since David and Andrew Hunter were cousins.

3. Alexander P. Boteler (1815-92), a Confederate congressman and the designer of the Confederate seal, had been one of Strother's closest friends before the war. It

tion of the women and the scene is heart-rending. Saw Mrs. General Hunter at dinner. A rumor passed over the wires that Atlanta has fallen. . . .

JULY 20, WEDNESDAY.—. . . Harkins just from New York says the Money Gods have the following information in regard to the military situation. Sherman is in front of Atlanta 150,000 strong, his army well disciplined and supplied. They expect daily to hear of the occupation of that place. Grant has wasted his strength in bloody and fruitless assaults and can do nothing more than hold his own. They look for Sherman to terminate the war. Since our movement on Lynchburg I have had no confidence in Grant's operations and am glad to feel secure about Sherman.

JULY 21, THURSDAY.—. . . Crook arrived, which dashed all hopes of success against the enemy. Early is gone South leaving troops in the Valley probably in front of Averell. Early lay at Berryville apparently confident and ready to fight on the 18th. Crook pushed across and engaged him, but Wright lay in view of the battle and did not assist. Crook fell back, losing four hundred men. Rumor says Early received a courier from Richmond urging him to fall back to that place with all speed. He started southward in haste apparently in obedience to that order. Wright immediately fell back on Washington, leaving Crook in command in the Valley. The President's call for five hundred thousand troops and the order to devastate the Valley look like desperate measures and confirm the failure of Grant at Richmond, if confirmation was wanted.

The greatest cause of cowardice is the imagination. Men will coolly face a visible danger, who will stampede and disgrace themselves on some false report or fancied terror. A lively imagination is therefore a disadvantage in war and the greatest courage is that which is proof against imaginary terror. Characteristic incredulity and a contempt for the enemy has always been my safeguard against stampede. I am always sanguine of success and astonished and disgusted when we fail. I think we have nearly always failed from want of pluck and have retired before fancied dangers instead of real ones. Hence my anger and disgust. I think also our army has suffered from being overfed, and petted by friends of humanity, demagogues, and sanitary commissions.

---

is a tribute to their friendship to find that Boteler always denied that Strother had anything to do with the burning of his house, "Fountain Rock." Edmund Jennings Lee, a cousin of Robert E. Lee, had been another of Strother's friends before the war. In both cases the order was given by General Hunter and his chief of staff was powerless to stop it.

JULY 23, SATURDAY.—. . . Dr. Reed arrived from the front. He says I am blamed for all the severity and burnings of property in the Valley. . . . An order has notified Rebel sympathizers to move South within forty-eight hours.

JULY 24, SUNDAY.—Further reports that Longstreet's Corps is coming up the Valley. This last I doubt, although not impossible. We should put at least fifty thousand men in the Valley. The General showed me a telegram from Halleck with Grant's opinion. He desires the line of the Potomac to be held with a view to protection of Washington in case of necessity. I advised the line of Winchester, Berryville, Snicker's Gap, and Aldie. The General approved the idea and telegraphed Crook to hold Winchester and also to Averell to report to Crook. . . .

JULY 25, MONDAY.—It commenced raining hard in the night. Telegrams came in every half an hour all night, indicating the arrival at Martinsburg of numbers of fugitives from Crook, all reporting that he had been outflanked and beaten. About two A.M. a dispatch from Crook himself arrived. He had been attacked near Winchester and obliged to fall back. He halted for the night at Bunker Hill. Whether Early is reinforced from below does not appear. Martinsburg is in wild stampede, everything being sent off and the trains on the B & O stopped running. Crook is ordered to fall back across the river. I suggested Shepherdstown and thence by the Maryland side to Maryland Heights. Stores are being rapidly sent off by rail. . . .

JULY 26, TUESDAY.—Had my things packed and slept on the floor. Dispatches from Crook and others arrived in the night. Gangs of fugitives were pouring into Williamsport and Hagerstown reporting defeat and disaster. Crook's trains are safe across the river and everything out of Martinsburg. News from Washington that Wright is moving by Rockville to reinforce us. The result for the staff is that Frederick instead of Maryland Heights will be our next destination, as I suggested in the morning. Prendergast got back from last night's ride. As he rode by our picket posts, he found them deserted, the rascals fleeing at his approach. . . . At five P.M. Crook and Roberts of his staff came in. Roberts thinks their force twenty thousand men and no more and that they are simply covering their harvest and drove Crook out because he was inconveniently near their operations. . . .

JULY 27, WEDNESDAY—All quiet. We don't move today. About this date in 1861 the remnant of Patterson's army abandoned the

Valley. Annually since that date we have been driven out. Here we are in 1864 in the same position. It is essential that our Government take the upper hand in this Valley. Yet it is evident that they want men and don't know how to get them. The Great Democratic Whale has been so stuffed with compromise, bribes, in the shape of unheard of bounties that now he is unmanageable. General Kelley patroled the railroad to within a few miles of Martinsburg and found it intact and no enemy. . . .

Crook's army has been marching all day to encamp at Pleasant Valley, and in view of a certain defensive policy indicated at Washington I have recommended that they encamp on the Catoctin in the Middletown Valley, but the policy I despise. I think we should concentrate and attack Early, driving him from the Valley and at least concentrating our positions in front of the B & O Railroad. To remain on the defensive on the line of the Potomac is suggestive of continual excitement and disasters without cessation. Halpine has resigned. . . .

JULY 28, THURSDAY.—. . . Reports from Averell that the enemy are moving westward toward Cumberland. This is alarming, as it is a movement which might be made with great damage to us. We can only prevent it by falling immediately upon the enemy in full force. The General is making numerous peremptory dismissals of officers for various misdemeanors and misconduct. Colonel [Lewis B.] Pierce still persists in asking for orders and twaddling about headquarters and is included in this list. At length the blessed order for advance comes from the War Department. Crook moves to Halltown and Wright follows. The troops passing through of Wright's seem in fine order, hardly war-worn veterans. The bands discourse spirited and stirring music. Took a bath in the Potomac. Drank a glass of sparkling Moselle on the invitation of General Max Weber.[4] He was wounded at the Battle of Antietam and helped make the drama at Bloody Lane. There he won his star. When under an intolerable fire, instead of retreating he charged with the bayonet. A civil and amiable fellow. The General desires an order complimenting Crook's troops on their readiness to march again so soon after their recent fatigue.

JULY 29, FRIDAY.—Duffie's cavalry passed through this morning, a disorganized, broken-down body. They will not assist much in the

---

4. Max Weber (1824-1901) had served under Sigel in Germany. After immigrating to America, he ran a hotel for German refugees in New York. He commanded the garrison at Harpers Ferry during the Early raid.

coming fight. . . . Wrote the endorsement for Halpine's resignation. Happy man. Wrote the congratulatory order to the Army. The General concluded not to issue it at present, as he wished to blame a portion of the troops and praise others. . . . Wrote telegram to President Lincoln asking him not to commute or reverse sentence of summary dismissal of officers lately dismissed for inefficiency, cowardice, and drunkenness. Wright's Corps have been passing all day. The troops seem jaded and are straggling fearfully. . . .

Dust seen in the vicinity of Martinsburg indicated that the Rebels are moving out of that place. News came in later that the Rebels were crossing at Williamsport with all arms and driving Averell back on Chambersburg. So much the better, let them drive. Also news that they were crossing at Conrad's Ferry. Let them cross.

JULY 30, SATURDAY.—Intensely hot. Many of the regiments had led cows after them, and these cows with the oxen driven by the commissary had baggage loaded on the horns. . . . Sudden news from Washington that the enemy have entered Chambersburg[5] and wishing to know where we are that they may send Emory to reinforce. The order was given to Wright and Crook to move immediately back from Halltown to the Middletown Valley in Maryland. About one P.M. the wires of the telegraph were cut east, probably near Point of Rocks. Rode over the river in the most deadly heat I have ever felt. I never felt so disgusted. We permit our army of thirty thousand men to be stampeded by the silliest rumors and are now marching away from the enemy to take position to save Washington which is not menaced and to be reinforced against an enemy which has no existence. Stopped at a poor cottage near Knoxville. Slept on the floor.

JULY 31, SUNDAY.—. . . Felt badly and out of humor all morning at our movements. This feeling was not improved by seeing the men drop dead from sunstroke, two at a time. We lost several hundred men this way and will have more sick than if we had fought a battle. Got into Frederick about ten o'clock. Took rooms at the City Hotel. No ice—no bar. . . . News that Averell has driven the enemy out of Chambersburg where he was not more than two thousand strong. Saw Dr. Burkhart refugeeing. He says that I am blamed for the burning in Virginia and that Edward McDonald has declared his intention to burn the Berkeley Springs property. Thus while I am bound up with a large army in a cowardly retrograde protecting Washington against its own cowardice, a few thousand scoundrels are burning my

5. General John McCausland, under orders from Early, burned Chambersburg, Pennsylvania, in retaliation for Hunter's destruction in the Valley of Virginia.

property and insulting my family.[6]. . . . Several chief citizens called to see the General this evening. One told him a column of the enemy was at Littlestown near Gettysburg. I think the story absurd and wonder that the General should credit it for a moment. He is, however, taking steps to meet them which will permit the enemy to go scot-free in the West. . . .

AUGUST 1, MONDAY.—. . . News that Averell drove the enemy out of Chambersburg after they had burnt the place. News from Atlanta indicates that we have been roughly handled by Hood. News from Grant is that his assault [at the Crater] has failed with severe loss. This looks rough for the Union cause. . . . The mayor of Gettysburg telegraphs that no Rebels are known of in that neighborhood. A body of demoralized Union cavalry are there and no doubt gave rise to the report. Martindale left on a scout toward Martinsburg. I think the movement from Harpers Ferry to Frederick the most beastly of the war.

AUGUST 2, TUESDAY.—The General received a telegram that the enemy were moving in large force on Washington by way of Rockville. Everything was immediately ordered to horse. I was utterly disgusted for I didn't believe a word of it. After all the troops were ordered to move it was ascertained that a squad of cavalry caused the stampede. The General then said we would ride out and take headquarters at Monocacy. I received a telegram from J. W. Kennedy saying the Rebel force under Early was at Bunker Hill and never crossed the river. . . . Drank champagne with Generals Emory, Wright, and Kenley. Talked of the Teche Campaign and Fanny Hunter. She visited Emory's headquarters one day and was invited to dine with them. She declined. The General pressed his invitation and said he had some fine mutton. "Yes," said Fanny, "I've no doubt it's fine, and have no doubt it is my sheep." We took headquarters at the house of a Mr. Thomas, the center of the battleground of Monocacy. The trees, hedges, shrubbery all bear marks of battle more decidedly than any place I have seen. . . .

AUGUST 3, WEDNESDAY.—. . . Received a letter from Ed Pendleton on the subject of Andrew Hunter's arrest. I presented it to the General who said he would release him. This I advised him to do the other day. . . .

AUGUST 4, THURSDAY. News from Kelley that the enemy have attacked New Creek and that Averell is at Bath. Some thousands of

6. Strother's hotel property in Berkeley Springs survived the war but perished by fire in the 1890's, long after it had been sold to a hotel corporation.

enemy have crossed at Shepherdstown. I conclude that this means retreat rather than attack. . . .

AUGUST 5, FRIDAY.—No news from Harpers Ferry. Emory's whole force is there. . . . General Halleck reports some of Sheridan's cavalry arrived and are on their way to us. I spoke to the General concerning my intention of leaving the service and find there will be no difficulty on his part. I will get ready and tender my resignation immediately. News from Washington that General Grant will visit General Hunter's headquarters this afternoon at five o'clock. . . . At seven P.M. staff and escort mounted to receive General Grant at the station. He arrived in a special car with his aides, Colonels [Cyrus B.] Comstock, [Orville E.] Babcock, and others. Grant is a medium-sized, plain-looking and plain-mannered man, a reddish beard and florid skin. Care-worn and smoking a segar. The Generals talked and consulted together and at length it was whispered around that we would move forward to Harpers Ferry tomorrow.

AUGUST 6, SATURDAY.—Went to the Monocacy Depot in an ambulance with General Grant. His manner of speech is Western and Yankee. His face indicates firmness and his manner is quiet and cool. His general appearance is most unsoldierly. General Ricketts was here getting off his division and met his wife. She is not a beauty by daylight. She is taller than he. The Commanding General went with General Grant on his car, to return by passenger train. The staff took another train for Harpers Ferry, arriving there about midday. We have thrown away a week doing worse than nothing. At dinner sat opposite Major General Sheridan.[7] The General wished he had a drink. I went upstairs and got a bottle and carried it down to him. Troops are pouring through the town. Sheridan is put in command of all forces in the field and General Hunter remains in command of the department. Hunter says he feels relieved greatly for the responsibility of a command which was muddled with at Washington. Sheridan is short, broad-shouldered, and of an iron frame. Very short legs and small feet and naturally cannot be a good horseman. Neither is Grant. I ascertain that Sheridan is in supreme command of all the troops in the departments of Susquehanna, West Virginia, and Washington. This leaves the department commanders in the positions of simple provost marshals.

7. Philip H. Sheridan (1831-88), USMA '53, had been a successful brigade commander in the West and had commanded the Twentieth Corps at Chickamauga. In August, 1864, he was placed in command of the Army of the Shenandoah with instructions to destroy all supplies in the Valley of Virginia. He successfully defeated Early at Cedar Creek and ended serious opposition in the Valley.

AUGUST 7, SUNDAY.—. . . . Early says of our sending an editor south into his lines that if he has offended our laws, we should try him and punish him. That this sending of people south untried is contemptible and cowardly and shows weakness in our Government. He is right. It shows a lack both of power and principle. Crook reported a deserter returned to his command as a substitute. The General ordered a drumhead court. "Have him shot," said he, "it is too troublesome to hang men. We have not time to spare."

I have twenty days' leave of absence. General Hunter writes to the President insisting on being relieved on the ground of the President countermanding his order sending Marylanders south. I think he is right. He says I may prepare and send in my resignation to take effect at the end of my leave, and he will endorse it favorably so that his successor will understand it.

AUGUST 8, MONDAY. . . . Left Harpers Ferry at 1:30 P.M. and arrived at Baltimore at about 5:00. Stayed at the Eutaw House. . . .

AUGUST 9, TUESDAY.—. . . Got paid for six months at lieutenant colonel's pay, $1101.40. Went to a saloon and drank lager beer—four glasses—abominable. I find the feeling in favor of recalling McClellan is very strong, and I would not be surprised if it prevailed at length. This great nation of thirty millions cannot be governed by a faction of extremists. At the Eutaw House saw General Stahel just from Harpers Ferry. He says General Hunter has returned to Washington on twenty days' leave which probably will close his connection with the Department of West Virginia. He left Stahel in command and Sheridan immediately ordered Stahel to Baltimore and put Crook in command of the department.

[Here ends Strother's role in the Civil War.]

Index

Abert, James W., identified, 6n; mentioned, 6, 15, 19, 40, 53, 55, 211
Abert, William S., 156
Alexander, Barton S., 101-2, 187, 192
Alexander, William, 261
Alexandria, Virginia, 126
Anderson, W. Watron, 220
Andrews, George L., 153, 156
Antietam, battle of, 109-12, 119-20, 123-24, 187
Arnold, Richard, 156, 157
Ashby, Turner, commands rear guard, 16, 17, 24, 26, 30, 63; death of, 57, 60, 62; mentioned, 35, 38, 41, 47, 53, 242
Atocha, A. A., 163
Augur, Christopher C., identified, 146n; mentioned, 146, 151
Averell, William W., identified, 209n; a disciplinarian, 209, 211-12, 259; urges advance into Lynchburg, 266; commands rear guard, 267, 268; praises Hunter raid, 275; mentioned, 210, 216, 229, 231, 235, 248-73 passim, 283, 284, 285

Babcock, Orville E., 286
Baltimore, Maryland, 129-30, 184, 287
Banks, Nathaniel P., identified, 4n; lacks decisiveness, 6, 7, 11, 12, 23, 27, 31, 58, 153, 158, 161n; fairness of, 18, 22, 65, 145; attitude toward Negro, 32, 148, 149; courage of, 39, 40; plans reunionization of Louisiana, 134-35; growing disillusionment of, 143, 144, 147, 157-58, 166; lacks discipline, 166, 169-70, 174; mentioned, 4, 15, 21, 24, 28, 36, 38, 44, 53, 60, 63, 70, 73, 77, 88, 102, 127-45 passim, 150, 165, 167, 172, 175, 177, 184, 211

Barringer, Augustus V., 217
Baton Rouge, Louisiana, 146-47, 153-54
Beckwith, Edward G., identified, 4n; mentioned, 4, 23, 63, 66, 67, 81, 133, 135, 137, 148, 176, 177
Bellows, Henry W., 190
Benjamin, Samuel N., 115
Benwood, West Virginia, 206
Berkeley Springs, West Virginia, guerrilla raid at, 201-4; mentioned, 183, 196, 201
Berry, James F., 256
Berwick Station, Louisiana, 176
Best, Clermont L., 30
Beverly, West Virginia, 211
Bier, Philip G., 221
Birney, David H., 35
Boonsboro, Maryland, 108
Boreman, Arthur J., identified 199n; mentioned, 199, 207, 278
Boteler, Alexander P., identified, 280n; mentioned, 280
Boyd, Belle, identified, 37n; mentioned, 37, 201
Boyd, Hunter, 219
Boyd, William H., 224, 225
Briscoe, Fred, 7
Brodhead, Thornton F., death of, 100, 103-4; mentioned, 12, 15, 16, 22, 41
Brown, John, 220
Bryan, Tim, 76
Buchanan, Franklin, 146
Buchanan, Thomas M., 140, 145, 146
Buchanan, Virginia, 258-59
Buckhannon, West Virginia, 210
Buford, John, 73, 80, 100
Bull Run, Second battle of, 90-99
Burnside, Ambrose E., 105, 106, 110, 111, 112, 115, 127, 139, 187

Butler, Andrew J., 141
Butler, Benjamin F., identified, 135n; mentioned, 135-41 *passim*, 145, 185, 188, 220
Butler, Speed, 86
Byrne, Oliver, 272

Catlett's Station, Stuart's raid at, 87-88
Cedar Mountain, battle of, 76-78
Centerville, Virginia, 92, 98
Chambersburg, Pennsylvania, 186, 284
Charleston, West Virginia, 275, 276
Charles Town, West Virginia, under Federal occupation, 5-11; reconnoissance to, 47-48, 122-23; mentioned, 18, 56
Chase, Salmon P., 192-93
Clark, John S., identified, 4n; mentioned, 4, 11, 30, 36, 45, 46, 47, 85, 88, 102, 145, 148, 155
Clarksburg, West Virginia, 199-200
Clary, Robert E., 88
Colburn, A. V., 115
Coldston, R. E., 254
Collis, H. T., 35, 41
Comly, James M., 203, 204
Comstock, Cyrus B., 286
Copeland, R. Morris, 11, 30, 63
Cox, Jacob, 119
Craighill, William P., 8, 68
Crane, Joe, 9, 48
Crawford, Samuel W., identified, 38n; mentioned, 38, 42, 62, 75, 79, 108
Crook, George, identified, 212n; discourages Lynchburg expedition, 250-1; attacks Lexington, 252; destroys Virginia and Tennessee Railroad, 262; fights at Quaker Church, 264; at Lynchburg, 265-66; advises retreat to Kanawha, 272-73; defeated at Winchester, 283; mentioned, 212, 217, 229-35 *passim*, 240, 247, 259, 261, 268-74 *passim*, 281, 287
Culpeper, Virginia, 75
Curtin, Andrew G., 113
Custer, George A., 205

Dana, Napoleon, 111
Dandridge, Mrs. Phil, 21
Davis, Jefferson, 13, 28, 256, 277
De Forest, Othneil, 56
De Joinville, Prince, 4, 115, 211
Douglas, Stephen A., 163-64
Dudley, Nathan, 162
Duffié, Alfred N., identified, 252n; mentioned, 252, 257-64 *passim*

DuPont, Henry A., 233, 243, 244, 269
DuPont, Samuel F., 174
Duryee, Abram, 94
Dutton, W. B., 5
Dwight, Wilder, 55

Early, Jubal, 87n, 264n, 266, 277, 281, 285, 287
Edinburg, Virginia, 24-26
Ellicot, George M., 238, 239, 242, 257, 270
Elzey, Arnold, 201
Emory, William, identified, 151n; mentioned, 151, 165, 177, 284, 285, 286
Ewell, Richard, 62, 90, 185, 258, 268

Farragut, David G., identified, 136n; runs batteries at Port Hudson, 157-58; mentioned, 134-43 *passim*, 148, 153, 154, 161, 176
Faulkner, Boyd, 245
Fields, Josiah, 230, 237, 257
Fleet, Alfred W., 176
Foster, Robert S., 32
Franklin, Louisiana, 168
Franklin, William B., identified, 97n; mentioned, 97, 99, 104, 107, 108, 109, 112, 114, 120
Frederick, Maryland, 105-6, 284
Fremantle, Arthur J. L., 208
Fremont, John, identified, 81n; leaves the army, 63; mentioned, 23, 27, 45, 55, 61, 64, 65
Front Royal, Virginia, 36-37

Gardner, George H., 53
Garrett, John W., 102
Gettysburg, battle of, 189-90
Gibbon, John, 107
Gilham, William, 253, 257
Gilmor, Harry, 208, 240
Gordon, George H., identified, 20n; mentioned, 20, 44, 58, 79, 108
Gorman, Willis A., 108
Graham, William L., 222
Graham, William M., 111
Grant, Ulysses S., interview with, 286; mentioned, 137, 172, 176, 216, 230, 232, 250, 274
Greene, George S., 37
Grover, Cuvier, identified, 90n; mentioned, 90, 153, 156, 165, 166, 167, 172
Groveton, battle of, 91
Guernsey, Alfred H., 129

Hagerstown, Maryland, 195
Haight, Edward, 77, 88
Hall, Norman J., identified, 123n; mentioned, 123-24
Halleck, Henry W., identified, 69n; mentioned, 69, 121, 128, 181-82, 209, 213, 230n, 233, 238, 279-86 passim
Haller, Granville O., 120
Halpine, Charles G., 232, 247, 256, 263, 279, 283-84
Hamilton, Charles S., identified, 7n; mentioned, 7, 12, 46, 48, 51
Hancock, Maryland, 196
Hancock, Winfield S., 122, 123
Hardie, James A., 193
Harkins, Daniel H., 244, 261, 281
Harper, Fletcher, 129
Harpers Ferry, West Virginia, Jackson threatens, 50-54; surrender of, 109, 120-21, 128; mentioned, 4, 44, 122, 182, 184, 279
Harrisonburg, Virginia, 31, 32, 241
Hartsuff, George L., 111
Hartwell, Charles A., 157
Haskell, Leonidas, 63
Hatch, John P., identified, 33n; mentioned, 33, 43, 58, 60, 61, 70, 184
Havana, Cuba, 179
Hayes, R. S., 240, 266
Hebble, Christian, 203, 204
Heintzelman, Samuel P., identified, 89n; mentioned, 89, 91, 95
Hepworth, George, 165
Hill, A. P., 137
Holabird, Samuel B., 63, 150
Holliday, Jonas P., 26
Hooker, Joseph, identified, 89n; mentioned, 89, 90, 91, 107, 109, 110, 180, 185, 186
Hooper, W. Sturgis, 148-49
Hopewell, Morris, 202
Howe, Albion P., 279
Hunter, Andrew, identified, 122n; mentioned, 122, 217, 280, 285
Hunter, David, identified, 191n; favors Negro troops, 192; replaces Sigel, 231-32; attitude toward Southerners, 235, 236, 237, 238, 239, 240, 241, 247, 253, 256, 257, 259, 260, 263, 264, 271, 272, 280; commands at Piedmont, 242-46; burns V.M.I., 255-56; commands at Lynchburg, 265-66; arrival at Charleston, 275; admires Jefferson Davis, 277; threatens to resign, 279, 280, 287; replaced by Sheridan, 286-87
Hunter, George, 203

Imboden, John D., 194, 225, 238, 250, 257
Irwin, Richard B., 158

Jackson, Thomas J., retreat from Berkeley Springs, 14; attacks Banks, 39-41; arrival in Winchester, 49-50; threatens Harpers Ferry, 50-54, 61; escapes from Union armies, 55; rumored march to New Orleans, 154; military genius of, 186; mentioned, 13, 26, 27, 30, 31, 57, 64, 75, 91n, 107
Jackson, William L., 249, 250
James, Charles T., 70
Jenkins, Albert G., 186
Jenkins, Thornton A., 148, 153
Johnston, Joseph E., 13, 27
Jones, William E., 245, 246
Jones, Yancey, 20

Kearny, Philip, 91, 93, 99
Keedysville, Maryland, 108, 111
Kelley, Benjamin F., identified, 184n; conciliatory measures of, 184, 199, 204-5, 207, 212, 219; sketch of, 209; relieved by Sigel, 213-14; mentioned, 185, 193, 198, 200, 208, 213, 230, 283, 285
Kemble, William, 131
Kenley, John R., identified, 38n; mentioned, 38, 39, 47, 285
Kennedy, John P., identified, 130n; mentioned, 130, 217n, 241
Kernstown, battle of, 19-20
King, James, 21, 22, 31, 44
King, Rufus, identified, 80n; mentioned, 80, 86, 91n
Knipe, Joseph F., 76

Lafayette, Louisiana, 173
Lamon, Ward, 121
Lang, Theodore F., 225, 236, 245, 246
Lea, Edward, 143
Lee, Robert E., replaces Johnston, 28; invades Maryland, 106, 119; invades Pennsylvania, 187-90; mentioned, 112, 186, 192, 208, 218, 254, 263
Letcher, John, 256
Leutze, Emanuel, identified, 127n; mentioned, 127, 180, 182

Lexington, Virginia, occupation of, 252-58
Liberty, Virginia, 262
Lincoln, Abraham, unpopularity of his emancipation decree, 115-16, 147; distrusted by the army, 117, 118-19, 145, 163, 213; visits Antietam, 120, 121-22, 148; debate with Douglas, 163-64; as a speaker, 191; integrity of, 205; mentioned, 280, 284
Lovettsville, Virginia, 125
Luce, William, 150-51, 153, 165, 167, 191
Lynchburg, Virginia, battle of, 264-67; mentioned, 231, 249, 250, 251, 257, 261, 263
Lyon, G. G., 215, 220, 221, 222

McCann, Thomas K., 263
McCausland, John, 248, 249, 250, 255, 257, 259, 268, 284n
McClellan, George B., personal attractiveness of, 4, 103; lack of initiative of, 27, 115, 117, 138, 187, 211; popularity of, 100, 105, 108, 128; nature of his staff, 104, 129; at Antietam, 109-13; views on Harpers Ferry, 120-21, 128; replaced by Burnside, 127, 130; courtship of, 137; fears betrayal, 163; rumors of restoration to command, 186, 188, 287
McDonald, Angus, 60, 259-60, 277, 278
McDonald, Edward, 284
McDowell, Irvin, identified, 65n; rumors of treachery, 36, 100; mildness of, 65, 72, 80; mentioned, 27, 45, 70, 78, 79, 84, 90, 91, 95
McEntee, John, 232, 233
McGuire, Mrs. Hugh, 21-22
Macomb, John, 70
Manassas Junction, Virginia, 70-71, 91
Mansfield, Joseph K., identified 108n; mentioned, 108, 110, 112
Marcy, Randolph B., identified, 104n; mentioned, 104-8 passim, 115, 119, 130, 137
Martindale, Franklin G., 260, 261, 267, 280, 285
Martinsburg, West Virginia, retreat to, 43-44; Unionism in, 55, 121
Mason, James M., identified, 12n; mentioned, 12, 35, 222
Mason, John S., 16
Matthews, Stockett, 219
Maulsby, P. M. B., 9, 32

Meade, George G., 119, 187, 188, 189, 192, 193
Meagher, Thomas F., 109, 113
Meigs, John R., identified, 204n; mentioned, 204, 205, 227, 232-42 passim, 248, 255, 257, 259, 261, 267
Meigs, Montgomery C., 58
Meline, James F., 66, 71, 75, 77, 102
Melvin, Thayer, 221
Meysenburg, T. A., 230, 233
Middletown, Maryland, 106-7
Miles, Dixon S., identified, 46n; mentioned, 46, 51, 105, 106, 107, 109
Milroy, Robert H., identified, 194n; mentioned, 31, 64, 87, 185, 194-95, 212, 213, 222
Mitchel, Ormsby M., 68
Moor, Augustus, identified, 210n; mentioned, 210, 224, 225, 226, 229, 238, 250
Moore, Thomas O., 140
Moore, Tredwell, 207-8
Morgan, John, 267, 270
Morris, H. W., 176
Morris, William H., 182
Mosby, John S., 182, 263
Mt. Jackson, Virginia, 29, 225
Mouton, Alexander, 173

Nadenbousche, John, 247, 248, 251
Nelson, John A., 155, 184
Newcastle, Virginia, 270
New Creek, West Virginia, 198-99
New Hope, battle of. See Piedmont, battle of
New Iberia, Louisiana, 172
New Market, Virginia, battle of, 225-28; mentioned, 30, 239
New Orleans, Louisiana, 135-65 passim
Newtown, Virginia, 17, 40-41, 235
Nokes, Thomas, 119

Oley, John H., 209
Opelousas, Louisiana, 164, 173, 174
Ord, E. O. C., 220

Paris, Virginia, 125
Parkersburg, West Virginia, 277
Pendleton, Edmund, 54, 219, 295
Pendleton, John S., 81
Perkins, Delevan D., 21, 23, 60, 61
Piat, John H., 88
Piedmont, battle of, 243-46
Pierce, Lewis B., 283

Pierpont, Francis H., identified, 57n; mentioned, 57, 75, 192

Pinkerton, Allen, 148

Pleasonton, Alfred, identified, 110n; mentioned, 108, 110, 115, 116, 120, 121, 186

Poe, Edgar Allan, 217

Pope, John, identified, 64n; commands in the East, 63; personality of, 64, 72, 74-75, 90, 92, 95, 96, 99, 124-25, 163, 220; plans his campaign, 65-70 *passim*; at Cedar Mountain, 76-80; at Bull Run; 89-97; outcry against, 100; compared with McClellan, 103; mentioned, 73, 75, 84

Port Hudson, Louisiana, expedition to, 155-59; mentioned, 154, 161, 162, 172, 176, 184

Port Republic, Virginia, 242

Porter, Fitz-John, identified, 91n; mentioned, 91, 95, 99, 110, 115, 116, 119, 126, 129, 206

Prendergast, Richard G., 224, 282

Price, Sterling, 153

Prince, Henry, 66, 73

Putnam, David, 252

Putnam, Thomas G., 225, 230, 231, 233

Quinn, Timothy, 235, 261

Radowitz, Paul, 4

Randolph, Emily Strother, 183, 196, 202

Randolph, James L., 183, 202

Ransom, James, 29

Reed, Thomas B., 238, 282

Reno, Jesse L., identified, 82n; mentioned, 82, 93, 96, 106, 107

Renshaw, W. B., 143

Reynolds, John, 93, 189

Richardson, Israel B., 109, 111

Ricketts, James B., identified, 94n; mentioned, 92, 94, 286

Riddle, Horace, 5, 10, 15, 19, 122

Robinson, Harai, 173, 175

Rockville, Maryland, 102

Rodgers, Robert S., 232

Rowley, William W., 77, 177

Ruger, Thomas H., 5, 42

Ruggles, George D., 70, 77, 88, 91, 100, 124

Russel, Charles H., 107

St. Martinsville, Louisiana, 172

Salem, Virginia, 268

Sandy Hook, Maryland, 4, 52

Sargent, Charles, 154

Saxton, Rufus, identified, 46n; mentioned, 46, 50, 52

Scammon, Eliakim, 212

Schalk, Emil, 186

Scheffler, William, 23, 32, 43, 44, 46, 73, 154

Schenck, Robert C., 87, 182

Schurz, Carl, 74

Scott, Henry L., 162-63

Scott, Winfield, interview with, 131; mentioned, 13, 28, 163

Sedgwick, John, identified, 5n; mentioned, 5, 12, 111

Semmes, O. J., 171

Sharpsburg, Maryland, 46-47, 113

Shepherdstown, West Virginia, 46-47, 114

Shepley, C. F., 138

Sheridan, Philip, identified 286n; mentioned, 239, 250, 258, 286, 287

Sherman, Socrates, 208

Sherman, Thomas W., identified, 154n; mentioned, 154, 163, 176

Sherman, William T., 281

Shields, James, identified, 7n; quarrel with Jefferson Davis, 13, leads Union advance, 16-17; mentioned, 7-8, 19, 28, 37

Shriber, R. C., 23

Sibley, Henry, 165, 166, 169, 173

Sickles, Daniel E., 190, 208

Sigel, Franz, identified, 56n; at Bull Run, 93, 94, 95, 115; replaces Kelley, 213-14; reprimands journalist, 216; distrusted by his staff, 217, 220, 221, 222-23, 224-25, 226, 229-30, 230n, 233; at New Market, 224-28; personal bravery of, 227; replaced by Hunter, 231-32; commands reserves, 235, 252, 277; replaced by Howe, 279

Smalley, George W., 72

Smith, Francis H., 253, 254, 255, 257

Smith, Kirby, 177

Smith, Melancton, 160-61

Smith, T. C. H., 73

South Mountain, battle of, 106-8

Sperryville, Virginia, 74

Stafford, Spencer H., 151-52

Stahel, Julius, identified, 217n; mentioned, 217, 223, 225, 227, 242, 244, 245, 277, 287

Stanton, Edwin, interviews with, 58, 193-94; mentioned, 121

Starr, William C., 217, 227, 236, 240, 244, 247, 251, 274
Staub, Dick, 30-31
Staunton, Virginia, occupation of, 247-51; mentioned, 31
Stearns, Joseph K., 240, 241, 242
Stewart, James E., 37
Stockton, Samuel, 232, 239, 246, 253, 254, 263, 264, 278
Stone, Lincoln, 85
Stoneman, George, 186
Strasburg, Virginia, 32-35
Strother, David H., protects Southern property, 6, 7, 15, 47-48, 168, 170, 238, 240, 247, 248-49, 264, 272, 280; attitude toward the Negro, 10, 64, 69, 140, 148-49, 152, 154, 184-85, 194, 254; characteristic skepticism of, 11, 33, 39, 40, 46, 62, 165, 206, 212, 266, 270, 281, 285; resented by Secessionists, 12, 21, 122, 151, 194, 203, 217, 222, 282, 284; attitude toward Virginia, 21, 22, 28, 29, 35, 36, 87, 192; recommends advance of Union forces, 12, 23, 27, 65, 151, 158, 177, 283; disgust with Union retreats, 32, 35, 48, 58, 99, 281, 285; attitude toward government and democracy, 68, 104, 117, 119, 123, 133, 145, 164, 166, 190, 280; tactical decisions of, 50, 128, 227, 241, 249, 266; sentimentality of, 141-42, 171; personal integrity of, 148, 259, 260
Strother, Emily (daughter), 18, 31, 194, 197
Strother, John (father), 25, 60, 260
Strother, Mary Hunter (wife), 18, 36, 180, 181, 182, 184, 187-88, 190, 194, 202, 213, 278
Stroud, George D., 203
Stuart, Alexander H., identified, 247n; mentioned, 247, 248, 251
Stuart, Jeb, 80, 85, 86n, 123, 230
Sullivan, Jeremiah C., identified, 208n; at New Market, 227; at Piedmont, 244, 246; at Lynchburg, 263-66; mentioned, 208, 237, 262, 268, 271, 277
Sumner, Edwin V., identified, 97n; mentioned, 97, 99, 109-14 passim

Taylor, Richard, 169
Taylor, Zachary, 151

Thoburn, Joseph, 244, 265
Thoreau, Henry D., 66-67
Thorpe, Thomas B., 140, 141
Thrasher, Tad, 25
Thurman, Phil, 271
Tidball, Joe, 81
Trimble, Isaac R., 50
Trout, A. K., 251
Tucker, Nathaniel B., 150

Upperville, Virginia, 125
Urbana, Maryland, 105, 278

Vallandigham, Clement L., 274
Vicksburg, Mississippi, 162, 174, 184, 186, 190
Virginia Military Institute, 252-56 passim
Von Kleiser, Albert, 226, 269
Vought, Philip P., 39

Wade, Jenny, 220
Wainwright, J. M., 143
Walbridge, Hiram, 189
Wallace, Lew, 216, 278, 279
Warrenton, Virginia, 71-72
Washington, Fayette, 11
Washington, George, 20-21
Washington College, 256
Weber, Max, 235, 283
Weitzel, Godfrey, identified, 146n; mentioned, 145, 146, 151, 165, 170, 210
Wells, George D., 236, 265
Wheaton, Frank, 217
Wheeling, West Virginia, 199
White, Julius, 105, 106
White Sulphur Springs, West Virginia, 273
Williams, Alpheus S., identified, 12n; mentioned, 12, 15, 25, 58, 86, 108
Williams, Seth, 102
Williamson, Thomas, 257
Williamsport, Maryland, 45-46, 53, 55-56, 222-23
Winchester, Virginia, occupation of, 12-14, 55-56, 222-23; Secessionism of, 21, 42, 47, 61; battle of, 41-42
Winder, Charles S., 80
Wise, Henry Augustus, 67
Wolff, John, 238
Woodstock, Virginia, 24, 228, 237
Wright, Horatio G., 279-85 passim